동아출판이 만든 진짜 기출예상문제집

특급기출

중간고사

중학 영어 **3-2**

How to Study

이 책의 구성과 특징

Words 만점 노트
교과서 흐름대로 핵심 어휘와 표현을 학습합니다.

Words Plus 만점 노트
대표 어휘의 영어 뜻풀이 및 다의어, 반의어
등을 학습하며 어휘를 완벽히 이해합니다.

Words 연습 문제 &
Words Plus 연습 문제
다양한 유형의 연습 문제를 통해 어휘 실력을
다집니다.

Words 실전 TEST
학교 시험 유형의 어휘 문제를 풀며
실전에 대비합니다.

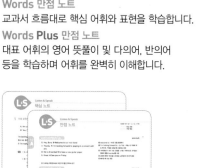

Listen & Speak 핵심 노트
교과서 속 핵심 의사소통 기능을
학습하고, 시험 포인트를 확인합니다.

Listen & Speak 만점 노트
교과서 속 모든 대화문의 심층 분석을
통해 대화문을 철저히 학습합니다.

Listen & Speak 연습 문제
빈칸 채우기와 대화 순서 배열하기를
통해 교과서 속 모든 대화문을 완벽히
이해합니다.

Listen & Speak 실전 TEST
학교 시험 유형의 Listen & Speak 문제를
풀며 실전에 대비합니다. 서술형 실전 문항으로
서술형 문제까지 대비합니다.

Grammar 핵심 노트
교과서 속 핵심 문법을 명쾌한 설명과
시험 포인트로 이해하고, Quick Check로
명확히 이해했는지 점검합니다.

Grammar 연습 문제
핵심 문법별로 연습 문제를 풀며
문법의 기본을 다집니다.

Grammar 실전 TEST
학교 시험 유형의 문법 문제를 풀며
실전에 대비합니다. 서술형 실전 문항으로
서술형 문제까지 대비합니다.

Reading 만점 노트
교과서 속 읽기 지문을
심층 분석하여 시험에
나올 내용을 완벽히
이해하도록 합니다.

Reading 연습 문제
빈칸 채우기, 바른 어휘·어법 고르기, 틀린 문장
고치기, 배열로 문장 완성하기 등 다양한 형태의
연습 문제를 풀며 읽기 지문을 완벽히 이해하고,
시험에 나올 내용에 완벽히 대비합니다.

Reading 실전 TEST
학교 시험 유형의 읽기 문제를
풀며 실전에 대비합니다. 서술형
실전 문항으로 서술형 문제까지
대비합니다.

**기타 지문 만점 노트 &
기타 지문 실전 TEST**
학교 시험에 나올 만한 각 영역의
기타 지문들을 학습하고 실전
문제를 풀며 시험에 빈틈없이
대비합니다.

STEP B 내신 만점을 위한 고득점 TEST 구간으로, 다양한 유형과 난이도의 학교 시험에 완벽히 대비합니다.

고득점을 위한 연습 문제
• Listen & Speak 영작하기
• Reading 영작하기
영작 완성 연습 문제를 통해, 대화문과
읽기 지문을 완벽히 암기합니다.

고득점 맞기 TEST
• Words 고득점 맞기   • Listen & Speak 고득점 맞기
• Grammar 고득점 맞기   • Reading 고득점 맞기
고난도 문제를 각 영역별로 풀며 실전에 대비합니다.
수준 높은 서술형 실전 문항으로 서술·논술형 문제까지
영역별로 완벽히 대비합니다.

서술형 100% TEST
다양한 유형의 서술형 문제를
통해 학교 시험에서 비중이
확대되고 있는 서술형 평가에
철저히 대비합니다.

내신 적중 모의고사 학교 시험과 유사한 모의고사로 실전 감각을 기르며, 내신에 최종적으로 대비합니다.

[1~3회] 대표 기출로 내신 적중 모의고사
학교 시험에 자주 출제되는 대표적인 기출 유형의
모의고사를 풀며 실전에 최종적으로 대비합니다.

[4회] 고난도로 내신 적중 모의고사
학교 시험에서 변별력을 높이기 위해 출제되는
고난도 문제 유형의 모의고사를 풀며 실전에
최종적으로 대비합니다.

오답 공략
모의고사에서 틀린 문제를 표시한 후, 부족한
영역과 학습 내용을 점검하여 내신 대비를
완벽히 마무리합니다.

Contents 차례

Lesson 7   Feel the Wonder

정답 및 해설

The future belongs to those who believe in the beauty of their dreams.

- Eleanor Roosevelt -

Lesson 5

Believe in Yourself

Words

만점 노트

Listen & Speak

☐☐ actor	몡 배우	☐☐ mask	몡 마스크, 가면
☐☐ award	몡 상	☐☐ ocean	몡 바다, 대양
☐☐ cheer	동 응원하다	☐☐ parade	몡 퍼레이드, 행진
☐☐ contest	몡 대회, 시합	☐☐ performance	몡 공연, 연주회
☐☐ drone	몡 무인 항공기, 드론	☐☐ take care of	~을 돌보다
☐☐ gym	몡 체육, 운동, 체육관	☐☐ take part in☆	~에 참가하다 (= participate in)
☐☐ hurt☆	동 다치게 하다	☐☐ volunteer work	자원봉사 활동
☐☐ look forward to☆	~을 기대하다	☐☐ without☆	전 ~ 없이

Reading

☐☐ afford☆	동 ~을 할 형편이 되다	☐☐ mostly	부 대부분, 일반적으로
☐☐ be able to	~할 수 있다	☐☐ musical instrument☆	악기
☐☐ cheek	몡 볼, 뺨	☐☐ one another	서로
☐☐ educator	몡 교육자	☐☐ orchestra☆	몡 오케스트라, 관현악단
☐☐ environmental	형 환경의	☐☐ out of tune☆	음이 맞지 않는
☐☐ expect	동 기대하다, 예상하다	☐☐ patience☆	몡 인내심
☐☐ from then on	그때부터 (쭉)	☐☐ piece	몡 (미술·음악 등의) 작품
☐☐ gather	동 모이다	☐☐ put ~ into practice☆	~을 실행에 옮기다
☐☐ giant☆	형 거대한	☐☐ roll	동 구르다, 굴러가다
☐☐ give ~ a big hand	~에게 큰 박수를 보내다	☐☐ step by step	점차로
☐☐ give up	포기하다	☐☐ talented	형 재능 있는
☐☐ huge	형 거대한	☐☐ tear	몡 눈물
☐☐ journey	몡 여행, 여정	☐☐ thrilled☆	형 황홀해하는, 아주 신이 난
☐☐ joy	몡 기쁨	☐☐ trash	몡 쓰레기
☐☐ landfill☆	몡 쓰레기 매립지		

Language Use

☐☐ appear	동 나타나다 (↔ disappear 사라지다)	☐☐ speech	몡 연설
☐☐ get ready for	~을 준비하다	☐☐ stick	동 붙이다 (stick – stuck – stuck)
☐☐ million	몡 100만	☐☐ take out	꺼내다
☐☐ president	몡 대통령	☐☐ turn off	~을 끄다 (↔ turn on ~을 켜다)

Think and Write · Project

☐☐ admiral	몡 해군 대장, 해군 장성	☐☐ hero	몡 영웅
☐☐ amazing	형 놀라운	☐☐ respect☆	동 존경하다
☐☐ battle	몡 전투, 투쟁	☐☐ save	동 구하다
☐☐ decorate	동 장식하다	☐☐ situation	몡 상황

연습 문제

A 다음 단어의 우리말 뜻을 쓰시오.

01 expect _____

02 journey _____

03 educator _____

04 patience _____

05 gym _____

06 orchestra _____

07 huge _____

08 piece _____

09 actor _____

10 cheer _____

11 amazing _____

12 admiral _____

13 thrilled _____

14 award _____

15 roll _____

16 mostly _____

17 giant _____

18 landfill _____

19 afford _____

20 performance _____

B 다음 우리말에 해당하는 영어 단어를 쓰시오.

21 환경의 _____

22 쓰레기 _____

23 볼, 뺨 _____

24 모이다 _____

25 상황 _____

26 ~ 없이 _____

27 다치게 하다 _____

28 바다, 대양 _____

29 재능 있는 _____

30 나타나다 _____

31 대통령 _____

32 구하다 _____

33 눈물 _____

34 퍼레이드, 행진 _____

35 악기 _____

36 100만 _____

37 존경하다 _____

38 붙이다 _____

39 연설 _____

40 전투, 투쟁 _____

C 다음 영어 표현의 우리말 뜻을 쓰시오.

01 step by step _____

02 one another _____

03 from then on _____

04 give ~ a big hand _____

05 out of tune _____

06 be able to _____

07 put ~ into practice _____

08 take part in _____

Words Plus 만점 노트

영어 뜻풀이

☐☐	able	~할 수 있는	having the power, skill, money, etc., that is needed to do something
☐☐	afford	~을 할 형편이 되다	to be able to pay for something
☐☐	cheek	볼, 뺨	either side of the face below the eyes
☐☐	drone	무인 항공기	an aircraft without a pilot that is controlled by someone on the ground
☐☐	drum	드럼통	a large container usually used for storing liquids
☐☐	educator	교육자	a person whose job is to teach or educate people
☐☐	environmental	환경의	related to the natural conditions in which people, animals and plants live
☐☐	giant	거대한	very large
☐☐	journey	여행	an act of traveling from one place to another
☐☐	landfill	쓰레기 매립지	an area where waste is buried under the ground
☐☐	mostly	대부분, 일반적으로	mainly, generally
☐☐	musical instrument	악기	a device that is used to make music
☐☐	orchestra	오케스트라, 관현악단	a group of musicians playing many different kinds of musical instruments
☐☐	patience	인내심	the ability to stay calm and accept a delay or suffering without complaining
☐☐	practice	실행, 실천	action rather than ideas
☐☐	roll	구르다, 굴러가다	to move along a surface by turning over and over
☐☐	talented	재능 있는	able or skillful
☐☐	thrilled	황홀해하는, 아주 신이 난	very excited and happy
☐☐	tune	곡, 곡조, 선율	a series of musical notes that make a pleasing sound when played together
☐☐	violinist	바이올린 연주자	a person who plays the violin

단어의 의미 관계

● 유의어

huge = giant (거대한)
joy = pleasure (기쁨)

● 명사 – 형용사

joy (기쁨) – joyful (기쁜)
patience (인내심) – patient (인내심 있는)
education (교육) – educational (교육적인)
environment (환경) – environmental (환경의)

● 감정을 나타내는 형용사

boring (지루한) – bored (지루해하는)
exciting (신나는, 흥미진진한) – excited (신이 난, 흥분한)
surprising (놀라운) – surprised (놀란, 놀라는)
scared (무서워하는, 겁먹은)
thrilled (아주 신이 난, 황홀해하는)
worried (걱정하는, 걱정스러운)

다의어

● **piece** 1. 명 조각, 일부분 2. 명 (글, 미술, 음악 등의) 작품

1. Sally cut the cake into six **pieces**.
   Sally는 케이크를 여섯 조각으로 잘랐다.
2. The school orchestra will perform a **piece** by J. S. Bach.
   학교 오케스트라는 바흐의 곡을 연주할 것이다.

● **save** 1. 통 구하다 2. 통 절약하다 3. 통 저축하다

1. Sam fell in the river, but his friend **saved** him.
   Sam이 강에 빠졌는데 그의 친구가 그를 구했다.
2. You'll **save** a lot of time if you go by car.
   차로 가면 너는 시간을 많이 절약할 것이다.
3. They **saved** enough money to buy the house.
   그들은 그 집을 살 충분한 돈을 저축했다.

Words Plus
연습 문제

A 다음 뜻풀이에 알맞은 말을 [보기]에서 골라 쓴 후, 우리말 뜻을 쓰시오.

| [보기] | landfill | afford | patience | journey | thrilled | roll | musical instrument | educator |

1 _____ : to be able to pay for something : _____

2 _____ : very excited and happy : _____

3 _____ : an act of traveling from one place to another : _____

4 _____ : to move along a surface by turning over and over : _____

5 _____ : an area where waste is buried under the ground : _____

6 _____ : a device that is used to make music : _____

7 _____ : a person whose job is to teach or educate people : _____

8 _____ : the ability to stay calm and accept a delay or suffering without complaining : _____

B 다음 짝 지어진 두 단어의 관계가 같도록 빈칸에 알맞은 말을 쓰시오.

1 education : educational = environment : _____

2 joy : pleasure = giant : _____

3 surprising : surprised = boring : _____

C 다음 빈칸에 알맞은 말을 [보기]에서 골라 쓰시오.

| [보기] | respect | talented | journey | mostly | gather |

1 My family wished Kevin a safe and pleasant _____.

2 The photographer _____ takes pictures of beautiful nature.

3 I expect that thousands of people will _____ in the food festival.

4 People _____ Dr. Johns because he always helps sick people.

5 Clare is a really _____ violinist. Her technique is perfect.

D 다음 우리말과 같도록 빈칸에 알맞은 말을 쓰시오.

1 점차로, Chris는 독감에서 회복되었다. → _____ _____ _____, Chris recovered from the flu.

2 Sara의 멋진 연설에 큰 박수를 보내 주시기 바랍니다.

→ Please _____ Sara _____ _____ _____ for her wonderful speech.

3 우리 동아리는 그 계획을 실행에 옮기려고 노력했다.

→ Our club tried to _____ the plan _____ _____.

4 나는 다음 주 토요일에 댄스 오디션에 참가할 예정이다.

→ I'm going to _____ _____ _____ the dance audition next Saturday.

5 Olivia는 1999년에 고향을 떠났고 그때부터 쭉 그녀는 혼자 살았다.

→ Olivia left her hometown in 1999 and _____ _____ _____ she lived alone.

실전 TEST

01 다음 중 단어의 품사가 다른 하나는?

① joy   ② admiral   ③ journey

④ mostly   ⑤ educator

02 다음 영어 뜻풀이에 알맞은 단어는?

action rather than ideas

① tune   ② landfill   ③ drone

④ practice   ⑤ patience

03 다음 우리말과 같도록 할 때 빈칸에 들어갈 말로 알맞은 것은?

그들은 아이들을 위해 새 코트를 살 형편이 안 되었다.

→ They couldn't _____ to buy new coats for the children.

① roll   ② hurt   ③ afford

④ stick   ⑤ respect

04 다음 중 밑줄 친 부분의 우리말 뜻이 알맞지 <u>않은</u> 것은?

① The guitar was <u>out of tune</u>. (음이 정확한)

② It's time to <u>get ready for</u> winter. (~을 준비하다)

③ Mina's family and Alice greeted <u>one another</u>. (서로)

④ Please <u>take out</u> a pencil and begin the test. (꺼내다)

⑤ The company decided to <u>put</u> the new ideas <u>into practice</u>. (~을 실행에 옮기다)

05 다음 문장의 빈칸에 들어갈 알맞은 말을 [보기]에서 골라 쓰시오.

[보기]   bored   excited   scared   sad

(1) I saw something moving in the dark. I was so _____ that I couldn't sleep.

(2) I'm going to visit my best friend in Paris. I am so _____.

고_{단도} 신_{유형}

06 다음 빈칸에 들어갈 단어로 알맞지 <u>않은</u> 것은?

• This medicine can ___①___ thousands of lives each year.

• My friends and I stood and ___②___ our school soccer team.

• Mike is a ___③___ actor, and many people love him.

• Look! A rock is ___④___ down the hill.

• The ___⑤___ tree is almost 10 meters tall.

① save   ② cheered

③ talented   ④ gathering

⑤ giant

07 괄호 안의 우리말과 같도록 빈칸에 알맞은 말을 쓰시오.

Please _____ the band a _____ _____ for their amazing performance.

(밴드의 놀라운 공연에 큰 박수를 보내 주세요.)

핵심 노트

1 기대 표현하기

A: Are you going to travel to Jeju-do next week?

B: Yes, **I'm really looking forward to** riding a horse.

너는 다음 주에 제주도로 여행 갈 예정이니?

응, 나는 말을 타는 것이 정말 기대돼.

I'm looking forward to ~.는 '나는 ~하기를 기대한다.'라는 뜻으로, 기대를 나타낼 때 사용하는 표현이다. 이때 to는 전치사이기 때문에 뒤에 명사 또는 동명사(구)가 이어진다. 기대를 표현할 때 I can't wait to ~.로 말할 수도 있는데, 이때 to 뒤에는 동사원형이 온다. 간절히 고대하는 것은 I'm really looking forward to ~.로 표현한다.

e.g. • A: Are you going to learn to fly a drone?

너는 드론을 날리는 것을 배울 거니?

• B: Yes, **I'm looking forward to** flying a drone in the park.

응, 나는 공원에서 드론을 날리는 게 기대돼.

Yes, **I'm really looking forward to** flying a drone in the park.

응, 나는 공원에서 드론을 날리는 게 정말 기대돼.

Yes, **I can't wait to** fly a drone in the park.

응, 나는 어서 공원에서 드론을 날렸으면 좋겠어.

> **point**
> 시험 포인트
> look forward to의 to가 전치사이므로 뒤에 명사나 동명사가 온다는 점에 유의하세요.

2 거절하기

A: I'm going to ride my bike. Do you want to join me?

B: **I'd love to, but I can't**. I have to do my homework.

나는 자전거를 탈 거야. 나와 함께 탈래?

그러고 싶지만, 안 돼. 나는 숙제를 해야 해.

I'd love to, but I can't.는 '나는 그러고 싶지만, 할 수 없어.'라는 뜻으로 상대방의 제안이나 요청을 거절할 때 사용하는 표현이다. 뒤에 거절할 수밖에 없는 이유를 덧붙여 상대방의 양해를 구할 수 있다. I'm sorry, but I can't. 또는 I'm afraid I can't. 또한 상대방의 제안이나 요청을 거절할 때 사용할 수 있는 표현이다.

e.g. • A: I'm going to play soccer. Do you want to join me?

나는 축구를 할 거야. 나와 함께 할래?

• B: **I'd love to, but I can't**. I have to visit my grandparents.

그러고 싶지만, 안 돼. 나는 조부모님을 찾아뵈어야 해.

I'm sorry, but I can't. I have to take care of my little brother.

미안하지만, 안 되겠어. 나는 남동생을 돌봐야 해.

I'm afraid I can't. I have to do volunteer work.

안 될 것 같아. 나는 자원봉사 활동을 해야 해.

> **point**
> 시험 포인트
> 제시된 상황이 거절하는 상황인지 수락하는 상황인지 파악해서 알맞은 대답을 고르는 문제가 많이 출제돼요. 거절의 말 뒤에는 거절하는 이유를 덧붙여 말하는 경우가 많으므로 잘 살펴보도록 해요.

Listen and Speak 1-A

교과서 86쪽

B: Hey, Bora. ❶ Welcome to our rock band.

G: Thanks. ❷ I'm looking forward to playing in a concert with you.

B: We're ❸ excited ❹ to have a new guitar player.

G: Great. ❺ See you on Friday.

Q1 보라는 록 밴드에서 어떤 악기를 연주하나요?

❶ welcome to: ~에 온 것을 환영하다

❷ I'm looking forward to ~.는 '나는 ~하는 게 기대돼.'라는 뜻으로, 기대를 나타낼 때 사용하는 표현

❸ 주어(We)가 신이 나는 감정을 느끼는 주체이므로 과거분사 형태의 형용사 excited를 사용

❹ 감정의 원인(~해서)을 나타내는 to부정사의 부사적 용법

❺ 헤어질 때 쓰는 표현

Listen and Speak 1-B

교과서 86쪽

G: Jiho, ❶ what are you reading?

B: I'm reading a book about a baseball player ❷ named Jim Abbott.

G: Oh, the man ❸ who was born without a right hand?

B: That's right. He tried really hard and even won the MVP award.

G: Yeah. His story ❹ was made into a movie. ❺ I'm going to watch it this Saturday.

B: Really? What's the title?

G: *Our Hero*. ❻ I'm really looking forward to watching it.

B: ❼ Can I join you?

G: Sure. See you on Saturday.

Q2 ❻을 해석해 보세요.

❶ 의문사(what)가 포함된 현재진행형(be동사+동사원형-ing)의 의문문

❷ named는 과거분사로, named Jim Abbott이 앞의 명사구 a baseball player를 수식

❸ who는 주격 관계대명사로, who was born without a right hand가 앞의 명사 the man을 수식
was born: 태어났다 / without ⑳ ~ 없이

❹ be made into: ~로 만들어지다

❺ be going to+동사원형: ~할 예정이다

❻ I'm really looking forward to ~.는 간절히 고대하는 것을 나타내는 표현으로, to는 전치사이므로 뒤에 명사나 동명사가 온다.

❼ 함께 해도 되는지 상대방에게 허락을 구하는 표현

Listen and Speak 1-C

교과서 86쪽

A: You ❶ look happy today. ❷ What's going on?

B: I'm so excited. ❸ I'm going to travel ❹ to Jeju-do.

A: That sounds great!

B: Yes, I'm really looking forward to riding a horse.

Q3 Why is B so excited? → Because B _____.

❶ look+형용사(보어): ~해 보이다

❷ 무슨 일이 있는지 묻는 표현

❸ be going to+동사원형: ~할 예정이다

❹ '~에, ~로'라는 의미의 장소를 나타내는 전치사

Listen and Speak 2-A

교과서 87쪽

G: Minho, did you finish the math homework?

B: ❶ Not yet. Math is difficult.

G: Yes, but it's interesting, too.

B: ❷ Then can you help me with my math homework?

G: ❸ I'd love to, but I can't. I ❹ have to ❺ take care of my brother.

Q4 소녀가 소년의 수학 숙제를 도와줄 수 없는 이유는 무엇인가요?

❶ 아직 못 끝냈어.

❷ Can you help me with ~?: '(내가) ~(하는 것)을 도와줄 수 있니?'라는 뜻으로, 상대방에게 도움을 요청하는 표현

❸ '나는 그러고 싶지만, 할 수 없어.'라는 뜻으로, 상대방의 제안이나 요청을 거절하는 표현

❹ have to+동사원형: ~해야 한다

❺ take care of: ~을 돌보다

교과서 87쪽

Listen and Speak 2-B

G: Alex, I'm going to ❶ take part in a singing contest next Monday.

B: That's great, Sumin!

G: You know ❷ how to play the guitar, right?

B: Yes, ❸ I've played the guitar for 3 years.

G: Great. ❹ Can you play the guitar ❺ while I sing in the contest?

B: ❻ I'd love to, but I can't. I hurt my hand in gym class yesterday.

G: Oh! ❼ I'm sorry to hear that.

B: Thanks. But I'll be there to cheer for you.

Q5 Alex는 얼마 동안 기타를 쳤나요?

Q6 What happened to Alex yesterday?

❶ ~에 참가하다 (= participate in)
❷ how+to부정사: ~하는 (방)법, 어떻게 ~할지
(❷는 동사 know의 목적어 역할)
❸ have played는 계속을 나타내는 현재완료(have+과거분사)
❹ Can you ~?: '~해 줄 수 있니?'라는 뜻으로 상대방에게 요청할 때 사용하는 표현
❺ '~하는 동안'의 뜻을 나타내는 접속사로, 뒤에 「주어+동사 ~」를 갖춘 완전한 절이 이어진다.
❻ 상대방의 제안이나 요청을 거절하는 표현
❼ 유감을 나타내는 표현

교과서 87쪽

Listen and Speak 2-C

A: ❶ What are you going to do this afternoon?

B: I'm going to ride my bike. ❷ Do you want to join me?

A: I'd love to, but I can't. I have to do my homework.

B: ❸ Okay, then next time.

Q7 A는 오늘 오후에 무엇을 해야 하나요?

❶ What are you going to do ~?: '너는 무엇을 할 거니?'라는 뜻의 계획을 묻는 표현
❷ '나와 함께 하고 싶니?'라는 뜻으로 상대방에게 제안하는 표현
❸ 자신의 제안에 대한 거절의 말에 알겠다며 다음에 함께 할 것을 기약하는 표현

교과서 88쪽

Real Life Talk > Watch a Video

Linda: Hi, Tony! ❶ What are you going to do this weekend?

Tony: I'm going to watch ❷ the musical, *Billy Elliot*.

Linda: *Billy Elliot*? ❸ What is it about?

Tony: It's about a boy ❹ who became a famous dancer. ❺ I'm looking forward to watching it.

Linda: Sounds interesting. ❻ Who is the main actor?

Tony: Jason Kim. ❼ He's a great dancer.

Linda: He's my favorite actor. I watched his musical last year.

Tony: Oh, really? Do you want to join me?

Linda: ❽ I'd love to, but I can't. I have ❾ volunteer work this weekend.

Tony: Okay. Maybe next time!

Q8 What is the musical *Billy Elliot* about?

Q9 Linda는 왜 Tony와 함께 뮤지컬을 보러 갈 수 없나요?

❶ 너는 이번 주말에 무엇을 할 거니?
❷ the musical = *Billy Elliot*
❸ '그것은 무엇에 관한 거니?'라는 뜻으로 뮤지컬의 내용을 묻는 표현
❹ who는 주격 관계대명사로, who became a famous dancer가 앞의 명사 a boy를 수식
❺ I'm looking forward to ~.는 기대를 나타내는 표현
❻ '누구'라는 의미의 의문사
❼ = Jason Kim
❽ 상대방의 제안이나 요청을 거절하는 표현
❾ 자원봉사 활동

우리말과 일치하도록 대화의 빈칸에 알맞은 말을 쓰시오.

주요 표현

1 Listen and Speak 1-A

B: Hey, Bora. _____ _____ our rock band.

G: Thanks. _____ _____ _____ _____ playing in a concert with you.

B: _____ _____ to have a new guitar player.

G: Great. See you on Friday.

교과서 86쪽

B: 얘, 보라야. 우리 록 밴드에 온 걸 환영해.

G: 고마워. 나는 공연에서 너희들과 함께 연주하는 게 기대돼.

B: 우리는 새로운 기타 연주자가 생겨서 신이 나.

G: 잘됐다. 금요일에 봐.

2 Listen and Speak 1-B

G: Jiho, _____ _____ _____ _____?

B: I'm reading a book about a baseball player named Jim Abbott.

G: Oh, the man _____ _____ _____ without a right hand?

B: That's right. He tried really hard and even won the MVP award.

G: Yeah. His story _____ _____ into a movie. I'm going to watch it this Saturday.

B: Really? What's the title?

G: *Our Hero*. I'm really looking forward _____ _____ _____.

B: _____ _____ _____ _____?

G: Sure. See you on Saturday.

교과서 86쪽

G: 지호야, 너는 뭘 읽고 있니?

B: 나는 Jim Abbott이라는 이름의 야구 선수에 관한 책을 읽고 있어.

G: 아, 오른손이 없이 태어난 그 사람?

B: 맞아. 그는 정말 열심히 노력해서 최우수 선수 상까지 받았어.

G: 그래. 그의 이야기가 영화로 만들어졌어. 나는 이번 주 토요일에 그 영화를 볼 거야.

B: 정말? 제목이 뭐니?

G: "우리의 영웅"이야. 나는 그 영화를 보는 게 정말 기대돼.

B: 나도 너와 함께 해도 될까?

G: 물론이지. 토요일에 봐.

3 Listen and Speak 1-C

A: You _____ _____ _____. What's going on?

B: I'm so excited. _____ _____ _____ _____ _____ to Jeju-do.

A: That sounds great!

B: Yes, I'm really looking forward to _____ _____ _____.

교과서 86쪽

A: 너는 오늘 행복해 보여. 무슨 일이니?

B: 나는 매우 신이 나. 나는 제주도로 여행을 갈 거야.

A: 그거 좋겠다!

B: 응. 나는 말을 타는 게 정말 기대돼.

4 Listen and Speak 2-A

G: Minho, did you finish the math homework?

B: Not yet. _____ _____ _____.

G: Yes, but it's interesting, too.

B: Then _____ _____ _____ _____ with my math homework?

G: I'd love to, _____ _____ _____. I have to _____ _____ _____ my brother.

교과서 87쪽

G: 민호야, 너는 수학 숙제를 끝냈니?

B: 아직 못 끝냈어. 수학은 어려워.

G: 맞아, 그렇지만 재미있기도 해.

B: 그럼 네가 내 수학 숙제를 좀 도와줄래?

G: 그러고 싶지만, 안 되겠어. 나는 내 남동생을 돌봐야 해.

5 Listen and Speak 2-B

교과서 87쪽

G: Alex, I'm going to _____ _____ _____ a singing contest next Monday.

B: That's great, Sumin!

G: You know _____ _____ _____ _____ _____, right?

B: Yes, I've played the guitar for 3 years.

G: Great. Can you play the guitar while I sing in the contest?

B: _____ _____ _____, but I can't. I hurt my hand in gym class yesterday.

G: Oh! _____ _____ _____ _____ _____.

B: Thanks. But I'll be there _____ _____ for you.

G: Alex, 나는 다음 주 월요일에 노래 대회에 참가할 거야.

B: 대단하다, 수민아!

G: 너는 기타를 치는 법을 알지, 그렇지?

B: 응, 나는 3년 동안 기타를 쳤어.

G: 잘됐다. 내가 대회에서 노래하는 동안 기타를 쳐 줄 수 있니?

B: 그러고 싶지만, 안 돼. 나는 어제 체육 수업 중에 손을 다쳤어.

G: 오! 그 말을 들어 유감이야.

B: 고마워. 하지만 너를 응원하러 거기에 갈게.

6 Listen and Speak 2-C

교과서 87쪽

A: What are you going to do this afternoon?

B: I'm going _____ _____ _____ _____. Do you want to join me?

A: I'd love to, but I can't. I _____ _____ _____ _____ _____.

B: Okay, then _____ _____.

A: 너는 오늘 오후에 무엇을 할 거니?

B: 나는 자전거를 탈 거야. 나와 함께 탈래?

A: 그러고 싶지만, 안 돼. 나는 숙제를 해야 해.

B: 알겠어. 그럼 다음에 같이 타자.

7 Real Life Talk > Watch a Video

교과서 88쪽

Linda: Hi, Tony! What are you going to do this weekend?

Tony: I'm going to _____ _____ _____, *Billy Elliot*.

Linda: *Billy Elliot*? What is it about?

Tony: It's about a boy _____ _____ _____ _____ _____. I'm looking forward to watching it.

Linda: Sounds interesting. Who is the main actor?

Tony: Jason Kim. He's a great dancer.

Linda: He's _____ _____ _____. I watched his musical last year.

Tony: Oh, really? Do you _____ _____ _____ _____?

Linda: I'd love to, but I can't. I _____ _____ _____ this weekend.

Tony: Okay. Maybe next time!

Linda: 안녕, Tony! 너는 이번 주말에 무엇을 할 거니?

Tony: 나는 뮤지컬 "빌리 엘리어트"를 볼 거야.

Linda: "빌리 엘리어트"? 무슨 내용이니?

Tony: 그건 유명한 무용수가 된 한 소년에 관한 거야. 나는 그 뮤지컬을 보는 게 기대돼.

Linda: 재미있겠다. 주연 배우가 누구니?

Tony: Jason Kim이야. 그는 훌륭한 무용수야.

Linda: 그는 내가 가장 좋아하는 배우야. 나는 작년에 그의 뮤지컬을 봤어.

Tony: 오, 정말? 나와 함께 가고 싶니?

Linda: 그러고 싶지만, 안 돼. 나는 이번 주말에 자원봉사 활동이 있어.

Tony: 알겠어. 다음에 같이 가자!

Listen & Speak

대화 순서 배열하기

자연스러운 대화가 되도록 순서를 바르게 배열하시오.

1 Listen and Speak 1-A

교과서 86쪽

ⓐ Great. See you on Friday.
ⓑ We're excited to have a new guitar player.
ⓒ Hey, Bora. Welcome to our rock band.
ⓓ Thanks. I'm looking forward to playing in a concert with you.

(   ) – (   ) – (   ) – (   )

2 Listen and Speak 1-B

교과서 86쪽

ⓐ Jiho, what are you reading?
ⓑ Really? What's the title?
ⓒ Oh, the man who was born without a right hand?
ⓓ Can I join you?
ⓔ That's right. He tried really hard and even won the MVP award.
ⓕ I'm reading a book about a baseball player named Jim Abbott.
ⓖ Sure. See you on Saturday.
ⓗ *Our Hero*. I'm really looking forward to watching it.
ⓘ Yeah. His story was made into a movie. I'm going to watch it this Saturday.

(ⓐ) – (   ) – (   ) – (   ) – (ⓘ) – (   ) – (   ) – (   ) – (   )

3 Listen and Speak 1-C

교과서 86쪽

ⓐ That sounds great!
ⓑ You look happy today. What's going on?
ⓒ I'm so excited. I'm going to travel to Jeju-do.
ⓓ Yes, I'm really looking forward to riding a horse.

(   ) – (   ) – (   ) – (   )

4 Listen and Speak 2-A

교과서 87쪽

ⓐ Not yet. Math is difficult.
ⓑ I'd love to, but I can't. I have to take care of my brother.
ⓒ Yes, but it's interesting, too.
ⓓ Minho, did you finish the math homework?
ⓔ Then can you help me with my math homework?

(   ) – (   ) – (   ) – (   ) – (   )

5 Listen and Speak 2-B

교과서 87쪽

ⓐ Yes, I've played the guitar for 3 years.

ⓑ I'd love to, but I can't. I hurt my hand in gym class yesterday.

ⓒ Alex, I'm going to take part in a singing contest next Monday.

ⓓ That's great, Sumin!

ⓔ Thanks. But I'll be there to cheer for you.

ⓕ Great. Can you play the guitar while I sing in the contest?

ⓖ You know how to play the guitar, right?

ⓗ Oh! I'm sorry to hear that.

(ⓒ) – ( ) – ( ) – ( ) – (ⓕ) – ( ) – ( ) – ( )

6 Listen and Speak 2-C

교과서 87쪽

ⓐ What are you going to do this afternoon?

ⓑ Okay, then next time.

ⓒ I'd love to, but I can't. I have to do my homework.

ⓓ I'm going to ride my bike. Do you want to join me?

( ) – ( ) – ( ) – ( )

7 Real Life Talk > Watch a Video

교과서 88쪽

ⓐ Jason Kim. He's a great dancer.

ⓑ *Billy Elliot*? What is it about?

ⓒ Oh, really? Do you want to join me?

ⓓ Hi, Tony! What are you going to do this weekend?

ⓔ Sounds interesting. Who is the main actor?

ⓕ He's my favorite actor. I watched his musical last year.

ⓖ It's about a boy who became a famous dancer. I'm looking forward to watching it.

ⓗ Okay. Maybe next time!

ⓘ I'm going to watch the musical, *Billy Elliot*.

ⓙ I'd love to, but I can't. I have volunteer work this weekend.

(ⓓ) – ( ) – ( ) – ( ) – (ⓔ) – ( ) – ( ) – ( ) – ( )

STEP A

01 다음 대화의 밑줄 친 부분의 의도로 가장 알맞은 것은?

A: Are you going to travel to Jeju-do this weekend?

B: Yes, I'm really looking forward to riding a horse.

① 승인하기
② 충고하기
③ 위로하기
④ 기대 표현하기
⑤ 선호 표현하기

02 다음 대화의 빈칸에 들어갈 말로 알맞은 것은?

A: I'm going to play soccer after school. Do you want to join me?

B: _____ I have to take care of my little sister.

A: Okay, then next time.

① No problem.
② Not bad.
③ That's too bad.
④ Sounds interesting.
⑤ I'd love to, but I can't.

03 다음 중 짝 지어진 대화가 자연스럽지 않은 것은?

① A: Did you finish the math homework?
  B: Not yet. Math is difficult.

② A: I'm going to visit the museum. Do you want to join me?
  B: Yes, I'd love to.

③ A: You look happy today. What's going on?
  B: I'm so excited. I'm going to learn to fly a drone.

④ A: Can you help me with my math homework?
  B: Of course. I have to do volunteer work.

⑤ A: What are you going to do at the festival?
  B: I'm going to watch a parade. I'm really looking forward to watching it.

04 자연스러운 대화가 되도록 (A)~(D)를 순서대로 배열한 것은?

(A) Thanks. I'm looking forward to playing in a concert with you.

(B) Great. See you on Friday.

(C) Hey, Bora. Welcome to our rock band.

(D) We're excited to have a new guitar player.

① (A) – (C) – (D) – (B)
② (A) – (D) – (B) – (C)
③ (C) – (A) – (D) – (B)
④ (C) – (D) – (B) – (A)
⑤ (D) – (B) – (A) – (C)

신유형
05 다음 대화의 밑줄 친 우리말을 영어로 옮길 때 사용하지 않는 단어는?

A: I'm going to make a mask. 나는 그것을 만드는 게 정말 기대돼.

B: Sounds fun.

① to
② make
③ forward
④ looking
⑤ really

[06-07] 다음 대화를 읽고, 물음에 답하시오.

Ann: Jiho, what are you reading? (①)

Jiho: I'm reading a book about a baseball player named Jim Abbott.

Ann: Oh, the man who was born without a right hand? (②)

Jiho: That's right. He tried really hard and even won the MVP award.

Ann: Yeah. (③) I'm going to watch it this Saturday.

Jiho: Really? What's the title?

Ann: (④) *Our Hero*. I'm really looking forward to watching it.

Jiho: Can I join you?

Ann: Sure. (⑤) See you on Saturday.

06 위 대화의 ①~⑤ 중 주어진 문장이 들어갈 알맞은 곳은?

His story was made into a movie.

      ④ ⑤

07 위 대화의 내용과 일치하지 <u>않는</u> 것은?

① 지호는 책을 읽고 있다.
② Jim Abbott은 야구 선수이다.
③ Jim Abbott은 오른손 없이 태어났다.
④ Jim Abbott은 최우수 선수 상을 받은 적이 있다.
⑤ Ann은 이번 주 토요일에 혼자 영화를 볼 것이다.

[08-09] 다음 대화를 읽고, 물음에 답하시오.

Linda: Hi, Tony! What are you going to do this weekend?
Tony: I'm going to watch the musical, *Billy Elliot*.
Linda: *Billy Elliot*? What is it about?
Tony: It's about a boy ____ⓐ____ became a famous dancer. I'm looking forward to watching it.
Linda: Sounds interesting. ____ⓑ____ is the main actor?
Tony: Jason Kim. He's a great dancer.
Linda: He's my favorite actor. I watched his musical last year.
Tony: Oh, really? Do you want to join me?
Linda: I'd love to, but I can't. I have volunteer work this weekend.
Tony: Okay. Maybe next time!

08 위 대화의 빈칸 ⓐ와 ⓑ에 공통으로 들어갈 말로 알맞은 것은?

① how(How) ② who(Who) ③ whom(Whom)
④ what(What) ⑤ which(Which)

09 위 대화를 통해 알 수 <u>없는</u> 것은?

① Tony가 주말에 할 일 ② 뮤지컬 "빌리 엘리어트"의 내용
③ Jason Kim의 직업 ④ Tony가 가장 좋아하는 배우
⑤ Linda가 주말에 할 일

10 다음 괄호 안의 말을 바르게 배열하여 대화의 빈칸에 알맞은 말을 쓰시오.

A: What are you going to do tomorrow?
B: I'm going to go to the beach with my family.
A: That sounds great!
B: Yes, _____
_____. (really, to, I'm, swimming, forward, the, in, ocean, looking)

[11-12] 다음 대화를 읽고, 물음에 답하시오.

A: Alex, I'm going to take part in a singing contest next Monday.
B: That's great, Sumin!
A: (1) _____
B: Yes, I've played the guitar for 3 years.
A: Great. (2) _____
B: I'd love to, but I can't. I hurt my hand in gym class yesterday.
A: Oh! (3) _____
B: Thanks. But I'll be there to cheer for you.

11 위 대화의 빈칸에 알맞은 말을 [보기]에서 골라 쓰시오.

[보기]
• I'm sorry to hear that.
• You know how to play the guitar, right?
• Can you play the guitar while I sing in the contest?

(1) _____
(2) _____
(3) _____

12 다음 질문에 완전한 영어 문장으로 답하시오.

Q: How long has Alex played the guitar?
A: _____

G Grammar

핵심 노트

1 가정법 과거

- If I **were** a bird, I **would fly**.

  내가 새라면, 나는 날아오를 텐데.

- If she **had** a flying carpet, she **could travel** all over the world.

  그녀가 날아다니는 양탄자를 가지고 있다면, 그녀는 전 세계를 여행할 수 있을 텐데.

- If he **knew** my address, he **would send** me a letter.

  그가 내 주소를 안다면, 그는 내게 편지를 보낼 텐데.

(1) 쓰임: 현재 사실과 반대되거나 실제 일어날 가능성이 없는 것을 가정할 때 사용한다.

(2) 형태와 의미: 「If+주어+동사의 과거형 ~, 주어+조동사의 과거형(would/could 등)+동사원형 .....」의 형태로 쓰며, '만약 ~라면, …할 텐데.'로 해석한다.

- If he **had** enough time, he **would visit** us. 〈가정법 과거〉

  그가 충분한 시간이 있다면, 그는 우리를 방문할 텐데.

  → As he doesn't have enough time, he doesn't visit us. 〈직설법 현재〉

  그는 충분한 시간이 없어서 우리를 방문하지 않는다.

- If I **had** enough eggs, I **could bake** bread for my family. 〈가정법 과거〉

  내가 충분한 달걀을 가지고 있다면, 나는 가족을 위한 빵을 구울 수 있을 텐데.

  → As I don't have enough eggs, I can't bake bread for my family. 〈직설법 현재〉

  나는 충분한 달걀이 없어서 가족을 위한 빵을 구울 수 없다.

  비교 If가 조건문에 쓰이면 실제로 일어날 수 있는 일에 대한 조건을 나타낸다.

- If you leave early, you can catch the train. ← 일찍 떠나는 것이 가능함

  네가 일찍 떠난다면, 너는 기차를 탈 수 있다.

(3) if절에 be동사가 쓰일 때는 주어의 인칭과 수에 관계없이 주로 were를 쓴다.

- If I **were** you, I **would accept** his offer. 내가 너라면, 나는 그의 제안을 받아들일 텐데.

> **point**
> 시험 포인트
> 가정법 과거 문장을 정확하게 쓸 수 있도록 가정법 과거의 형태 「If+주어+동사의 과거형 ~, 주어+조동사의 과거형(would/could 등)+동사원형 .....」을 반드시 기억해야 해요.

> 접속사 if
> • If you like today's idols, you will love the original idol.
> 만약 네가 요즘의 아이돌을 좋아한다면, 너는 본래의 아이돌도 좋아할 것이다.
> [중2 3과]

QUICK CHECK

1 다음 괄호 안에서 알맞은 것을 고르시오.

(1) If John (were / is) here, he could do the work.

(2) If today were Saturday, I (will / would) go to the park.

(3) If I (am / were) tall enough, I could ride the roller coaster.

2 다음 문장의 밑줄 친 부분이 어법상 틀렸으면 바르게 고쳐 쓰시오.

(1) If she had more time, she will visit her parents. → _____

(2) If he knows your phone number, he would call you. → _____

(3) If Bob were not tired, he could finish his work. → _____

2 의문사+to부정사

- We didn't know **how to read** music.
- I told him **when to feed** the dog.
- Alex found out **where to buy** the book.

우리는 악보를 읽는 법을 알지 못했다.

나는 개에게 언제 먹이를 주는지 그에게 말했다.

Alex는 그 책을 어디에서 사야 할지 알아냈다.

(1) 형태와 쓰임: 「의문사+to+동사원형」의 형태로 쓴다. 문장에서 주어, 목적어, 보어의 역할을 할 수 있으며, ask, tell, know, show, decide 등과 같은 동사의 목적어로 자주 쓰인다.

- **When to leave** is up to you. 〈주어〉 언제 떠날지는 너에게 달려 있다.
- I don't know **where to go**. 〈목적어〉 나는 어디로 가야 할지 모르겠다.
- The problem is **what to do** now. 〈보어〉 문제는 이제 무엇을 할지이다.

point

시험 포인트

문맥에 맞게 「의문사+to부정사」의 형태가 쓰이고, 적절한 의문사가 사용되었는지를 묻는 문제가 자주 출제돼요. 또한 「의문사 +to부정사」가 문장에서 어떤 역할을 하는지 구별할 수 있어야 해요.

(2) 종류와 의미 주의! 의문사 why는 to부정사와 함께 쓰지 않아요.

how+to부정사	어떻게 ~할지, ~하는 방법
when+to부정사	언제 ~할지
where+to부정사	어디에서(어디로) ~할지
what+to부정사	무엇을 ~할지

- Can you show me **how to make** a kite?

  너는 내게 연을 만드는 법을 보여 줄 수 있니?

- I don't know **when to take** the medicine. 나는 약을 언제 먹어야 할지 모른다.
- Tell me **where to take** the book. 그 책을 어디로 가져갈지 나에게 말해 줘.
- I haven't decided **what to buy**. 나는 무엇을 살지 결정하지 못했다.

(3) 「의문사+to부정사」는 「의문사+주어+should+동사원형」으로 바꿔 쓸 수 있다.

- Let me know **what to bring**. 무엇을 가져와야 하는지 내게 알려 줘.

  = Let me know **what I should bring**.

QUICK CHECK

1 다음 괄호 안에서 알맞은 것을 고르시오.

(1) I didn't know (when to tell / when telling) the truth.

(2) He decided (where / what) to put his new computer.

(3) I have a lot of homework. I don't know (how / what) to do first.

2 자연스러운 문장이 되도록 괄호 안의 말을 바르게 배열하시오.

(1) I learned _____. (how, a, ride, to, bike)

(2) Angela didn't tell _____. (us, to, when, arrive)

(3) Tommy _____ the empty bottles. (to, knows, put, where)

STEP A

1 가정법 과거

A 다음 괄호 안에서 알맞은 것을 고르시오.

1   If I were you, I (would / will) not buy those pants.

2   If you (live / lived) here, I could see you every day.

3   If I (am / were) a bird, I would fly to the clouds.

4   If she (were / is) home, we could visit her.

5   If I had enough milk, I (could / could have) make some cookies for my little brother.

B 다음 가정법 과거 문장에서 어법상 **틀린** 부분을 찾아 바르게 고쳐 쓰시오.

1   If she has flying shoes, she could fly in the sky.   _____ → _____

2   If it were Sunday, we can go camping.   _____ → _____

3   If Robin were here, he could fixed the computer.   _____ → _____

4   If I have had a lot of money, I could buy the building.   _____ → _____

C 다음 우리말과 같도록 괄호 안의 말을 사용하여 문장을 완성하시오.

1   그녀가 학생이라면, 그녀는 할인을 받을 수 있을 텐데. (get a discount)
→ If she were a student, _____.

2   내게 100만 달러가 있다면, 나는 무인 자동차를 살 텐데. (a million dollars)
→ _____, I would buy a driverless car.

3   그가 내 주소를 안다면, 그는 내게 편지를 보낼 텐데. (send me a letter)
→ If he knew my address, _____.

D 다음 두 문장의 의미가 같도록 빈칸에 알맞은 말을 쓰시오.

1   As I am tired, I _____.
→ If I were not tired, I could go shopping with Emma.

2   As they don't have enough time, they won't go to Paris on vacation.
→ If they _____, they would go to Paris on vacation.

3   As she doesn't have a time machine, she can't go back in time.
→ If she had a time machine, she _____.

2 의문사 + to부정사

A 다음 괄호 안에서 알맞은 것을 고르시오.

1 I haven't decided where (go / to go) during the vacation.

2 He taught me (how / that) to cook tomato spaghetti.

3 I need to meet Laura. Do you know (what / where) to find her?

4 Excuse me. Can you tell me (when / what) to board the plane?

5 Let's talk about (what / where) to do for African children in need.

B 다음 두 문장의 의미가 같도록 빈칸에 알맞은 말을 쓰시오.

1 I want to know when I should ask her the question.

→ I want to know _____ _____ _____ her the question.

2 Please tell me where to put this table.

→ Please tell me _____ _____ _____ this table.

C 다음 우리말과 같도록 괄호 안의 말을 바르게 배열하여 문장을 완성하시오.

1 그는 이 도구를 사용하는 방법을 배웠다. (this, use, how, to, tool)

→ He learned _____.

2 나에게 사과를 어디에서 사야 하는지 말해 줘. (buy, to, where, apples)

→ Please tell me _____.

3 그녀는 점심으로 무엇을 먹을지 이미 결정했다. (what, to, for lunch, eat)

→ She has already decided _____.

4 나는 언제 생일 케이크를 안으로 가져와야 하는지 모른다. (to, bring, when, the birthday cake)

→ I don't know _____ in.

D 다음 우리말과 같도록 괄호 안의 말을 사용하여 문장을 완성하시오.

1 그녀는 Tom에게 그 문제를 푸는 방법을 물었다. (to, the problem)

→ She asked Tom _____.

2 그는 나에게 오늘 무엇을 해야 하는지 말해 주었다. (to, today)

→ He told me _____.

3 나에게 언제 우회전을 해야 할지 알려 줘. (to, turn)

→ Let me know _____.

4 너는 이번 여름에 어디에서 머물지 정했니? (to, stay)

→ Have you decided _____?

[01-02] 다음 빈칸에 들어갈 말로 알맞은 것을 고르시오.

01 _____ my uncle were with me now, I would be happy.

① As   ② So   ③ If
④ When   ⑤ Unless

02 _____, I would tell you.

① If I know the answer
② If I knows the answer
③ If I knew the answer
④ If I will know the answer
⑤ If I has known the answer

03 다음 빈칸에 공통으로 들어갈 말로 알맞은 것은?

• Can you tell me _____ to use this camera?
• Do you know _____ to get there?

① why   ② how   ③ what
④ which   ⑤ where

04 다음 빈칸에 들어갈 have의 형태로 알맞은 것은?

If you _____ a better camera, you could take better photos.

① have   ② has   ③ had
④ to have   ⑤ having

신
유형
05 다음 우리말을 영어로 옮길 때 여섯 번째로 오는 단어는?

너는 내게 어디로 가는지 말해 줄 수 있니?

① tell   ② me   ③ to
④ go   ⑤ where

06 다음 빈칸에 들어갈 말로 알맞지 <u>않은</u> 것을 <u>모두</u> 고르면?

If I were you, _____.

① I won't eat fast food
② I would tell the truth
③ I wouldn't lie to them
④ I will join the magic club
⑤ I would help the children in need

07 다음 빈칸에 들어갈 말로 알맞지 <u>않은</u> 것은?

I want to know _____.

① when to start
② how to play chess
③ why to do the project
④ what to buy for the party
⑤ where to go during the holidays

08 다음 우리말을 영어로 바르게 옮긴 것은?

만약 내가 아름다운 목소리를 가진다면, 나는 유명한 가수가 될 수 있을 텐데.

① If I have a beautiful voice, I could be a famous singer.
② If I had a beautiful voice, I can be a famous singer.
③ If I were a beautiful voice, I could be a famous singer.
④ If I had a beautiful voice, I am a famous singer.
⑤ If I had a beautiful voice, I could be a famous singer.

09 다음 두 문장의 의미가 같도록 어법상 **틀린** 부분을 찾아 바르게 고쳐 쓰시오.

As I am busy, I can't have lunch with you.
→ If I were not busy, I can have lunch with you.

_____ → _____

[10-11] 다음 대화의 빈칸에 들어갈 말로 알맞은 것을 고르시오.

10　A: Do you know _____ this machine?
　　B: Yes. First, press the red button.

① how to use　　　② what to use
③ where to use　　④ when to use
⑤ why to use

11　A: Tell me _____ at the grocery store.
　　B: You should buy some apples and onions.

① how to buy　　　② what to buy
③ where to buy　　④ when to buy
⑤ that to buy

12 다음 두 문장의 의미가 같도록 할 때 빈칸에 알맞은 말이 순서대로 짝 지어진 것은?

As Chris has the flu, he can't go to the museum.
→ If Chris _____ the flu, he _____ to the museum.

① had – couldn't go
② didn't have – can go
③ didn't have – could go
④ doesn't have – could go
⑤ doesn't have – couldn't go

13 다음 밑줄 친 부분 중 어법상 **틀린** 것은?

①If I were you, I ②will ③invite ④him ⑤to my birthday party.

①　　　②　　　③　　　④　　　⑤

신유형
14 다음 우리말을 영어로 옮길 때, 빈칸에 쓰이지 **않는** 것은?

Steve는 언제 피아노를 치기 시작해야 하는지 알고 있다.
→ Steve knows _____ _____ _____
_____ the piano.

① to　　　② when　　　③ start
④ playing　　⑤ should

15 다음 중 어법상 **틀린** 문장은?

① If you lived here, we would be happy.
② We haven't decided what to buy for Paul.
③ If Nicole had the key, she could open this box.
④ Can you tell me how to do the volunteer work?
⑤ If I were Superman, I will save people in danger.

고난도
16 다음 두 문장의 의미가 같도록 should를 사용하여 빈칸에 알맞은 말을 쓰시오.

She doesn't know when to take the medicine.
= She doesn't know _____ _____
_____ _____ the medicine.

17 다음 빈칸에 알맞은 말이 순서대로 짝 지어진 것은?

> I don't have much time. If I _____ enough time, I _____ hiking with you.

① have – went
② have – could go
③ had – went
④ had – could go
⑤ had – have gone

신유형

18 다음 단어들을 자연스러운 문장이 되도록 순서대로 배열할 때 네 번째로 오는 단어는?

> haven't, where, we, stay, decided, to

① to
② stay
③ where
④ decided
⑤ haven't

19 다음 빈칸에 were가 들어갈 수 없는 것은?

① If I _____ younger, I would go abroad.
② If I _____ rich, I would travel in space.
③ If you _____ busy now, I'll stop by later.
④ If she _____ not busy, she could visit my family.
⑤ If the computer _____ cheaper, I would buy it.

고난도 신유형

20 다음 중 어법상 옳은 문장의 개수는?

> • I want to know how to joining the singing club.
> • We asked the girl where to take the subway.
> • If I had more time, I would finish my homework.
> • If Peter were not tired, he will come to the meeting.

① 0개
② 1개
③ 2개
④ 3개
⑤ 4개

신유형

21 다음 문장에 대한 설명으로 옳은 것은?

> If I were an inventor, I would make a magic lamp.

① If절의 주어가 I이므로 동사 were를 쓸 수 없다.
② 현재 사실의 반대를 가정하는 문장이다.
③ would를 will로 고쳐야 한다.
④ I는 현재 발명가이다.
⑤ would를 생략할 수 있다.

22 다음 대화의 빈칸에 알맞은 말이 순서대로 짝 지어진 것은?

> A: Mom, I'll cook the eggs. Please tell me _____ them.
> B: Cook the eggs in the boiling water.
> A: Okay. Let me know _____ the eggs.
> B: Take out the eggs after 10 minutes.
> A: I see. Thank you, Mom.

① what to cook – what to take out
② what to cook – where to take out
③ how to cook – when to take out
④ how to cook – where to take out
⑤ when to cook – where to take out

고난도

23 다음 밑줄 친 부분을 어법상 바르게 고친 것 중 옳지 <u>않은</u> 것은?

① Aron couldn't decide where to <u>traveling</u>. (→ travel)
② Let me know what <u>pack</u> for the trip. (→ to pack)
③ If it <u>is</u> sunny, I would go fishing. (→ be)
④ If I had time, I <u>will</u> drop you off at school. (→ would)
⑤ If I <u>am</u> a king, I would make my country more beautiful. (→ were)

24 다음 괄호 안의 말을 바르게 배열하여 문장을 완성한 후, 우리말로 해석하시오.

(1) Do you know (fix, how, this machine, to)?

→ Do you know _____?

→ 해석: _____

(2) Let's decide (where, in, to, New Zealand, go).

→ Let's decide _____.

→ 해석: _____

(3) I asked (do, the teacher, what, to) next.

→ I asked _____ next.

→ 해석: _____

고
/난도
25 Ⓐ와 Ⓑ에서 알맞은 말을 하나씩 골라 [조건]에 맞게 한 문장으로 쓰시오.

Ⓐ • If I (be) a super hero,

• If it (snow) a lot,

• If I (understand) French,

Ⓑ • I (enjoy) the French movie.

• I (build) a big snowman.

• I (save) people and the world.

[조건] 1. Ⓐ와 Ⓑ의 말을 모두 한 번씩만 사용할 것
2. 가정법 과거의 문장으로 쓸 것
3. 괄호 안의 동사를 알맞은 형태로 고쳐 쓸 것

(1) _____

(2) _____

(3) _____

26 다음 [조건]에 맞게 우리말을 영작하시오.

[조건] 1. [보기]에서 알맞은 말을 골라 쓸 것
2. 중복해서 사용하지 말 것

[보기]   when   how   where   what   why
the boy   to   for   told   me   I
get off   get on   getting off   getting on

그 소년은 내게 언제 내려야 할지 말해 주었다.

→ _____

27 다음 두 문장의 의미가 같도록 빈칸에 알맞은 말을 쓰시오.

(1) As I don't have enough time, I can't eat breakfast.

→ If I _____,

I _____.

(2) As I am tired, I can't play tennis with my dad.

→ If _____,

I _____.

28 다음 우리말과 같도록 괄호 안의 말을 이용하여 문장을 쓰시오.

(1) 그는 기타 치는 법을 배웠다. (learn, to, play)

→ _____

(2) 내게 우주선이 있다면, 나는 화성으로 여행을 갈 텐데.
(if, a spaceship, travel, Mars)

→ _____

(3) 나는 이 상자를 어디에 놓아야 할지 모르겠다.
(know, to, put)

→ _____

STEP A

쓰레기를 음악으로

From Trash to Music

01 기쁨의 눈물이 내 볼에 흘러내리고 있다.

01 Tears of joy are rolling down my cheeks.
현재진행형: be동사의 현재형+동사원형-ing

02 나는 정말 기쁘고 황홀하다.

02 I'm so happy and thrilled.

03 내가 새라면, 나는 날아오를 텐데.

03 If I were a bird, I would fly.
가정법 과거: If+주어+동사의 과거형 ~, 주어+조동사의 과거형+동사원형 ....

04 나는 주위를 둘러본다.

04 I look around.

05 우리 오케스트라의 다른 단원들이 서로 껴안고 있다.

05 The other members in my orchestra are hugging one another.
수 일치

06 우리의 연주회가 이제 막 끝났고 모든 사람들이 일어서서 우리에게 큰 박수를 보내고 있다.

06 Our concert has just finished and everyone is standing and giving us a big hand.
has+과거분사: 현재완료 (완료)   수 일치   is standing과 giving이 등위접속사 and에 의해 병렬 연결

07 우리 중 아무도 이런 날이 올 거라고 예상하지 못했다.

07 None of us ever expected that this day would come.
® 아무도 ~ 않다   목적절을 이끄는 접속사

08 그것은 긴 여정이었다.

08 It has been a long journey.

09 내 이름은 Andrea이고 나는 Recycled Orchestra(재활용 오케스트라)의 바이올린 연주자이다.

09 My name is Andrea and I'm a violinist in the Recycled Orchestra.
® 바이올린 연주자 (접미사 -ist: 행위자를 나타냄)

10 오케스트라가 왜 재활용 오케스트라로 불리냐고?

10 Why is it called the Recycled Orchestra?
의문사+be동사+주어+과거분사 ~? (수동태 의문문)

11 그것은 우리의 악기들이 쓰레기 매립지에서 나온 물건들로 만들어져 있기 때문이다.

11 It's because our musical instruments are made of objects from a landfill.
It's because ~: 그것은 ~이기 때문이다   ® ~에서, ~로부터

12 그것이 오케스트라가 Landfill Harmonic Orchestra로도 알려진 이유이다.

12 That's why it's also known as the Landfill Harmonic Orchestra.
That's why ~: 그것이 ~한 이유이다   of 뒤의 us와 수 일치

13 오케스트라의 우리들 대부분은 파라과이의 작은 마을인 카테우라 출신이다.

13 Most of us in the orchestra are from Cateura, a small town in Paraguay.
주어 (most of+대명사)   복수 동사   동격

14 우리 마을에는 거대한 쓰레기 매립지가 있다.

14 There is a huge landfill in our town.
There is+단수 명사: ~이 있다   목적절을 이끄는 접속사

15 몇몇 사람들은 심지어 카테우라 자체가 거대한 쓰레기 매립지라고 말한다.

15 Some people even say that Cateura itself is a giant landfill.
® 심지어 (say 수식)   재귀대명사 (강조 용법 / Cateura를 지칭)

16 우리들 중 많은 이들이 가난하다.

16 Many of us are poor.

17 우리 마을에는 희망과 꿈이 많지 않았다.

17 There weren't many hopes and dreams in our town.
There were+복수 명사: ~이 있었다   그러나 (앞 문장과 상반되는 내용 제시)

18 그러나 우리가 Favio Chávez 선생님을 만났을 때 모든 것이 바뀌기 시작했다.

18 Everything began to change, however, when we met Favio Chávez.
begin은 목적어로 to부정사와 동명사 모두 사용 가능   ~할 때 (시간의 접속사)
(begin-began-begun)

19 Favio 선생님은 환경 교육가이자 음악가였다.

19 Favio was an environmental educator and a musician.
® 교육가 (접미사 -or, -ian: 행위자를 나타냄)

20 그는 우리에게 음악을 가르치고 싶어 했지만, 큰 문제가 있었다.

20 He wanted to teach us music, but there was a big problem.
동사 want는 목적어로 to부정사 사용

21 온 마을에 악기가 단지 몇 개뿐이었다.

21 There were only a few musical instruments in the whole town.
약간의, 몇 개의 (셀 수 있는 명사 앞에 사용)   ® 전체의

22 We couldn't afford to buy new ones.
앞의 musical instruments를 가리킴

22 우리는 새 악기를 살 형편이 안 되었다.

23 But Favio didn't give up.

23 그러나 Favio 선생님은 포기하지 않았다.

24 He said that we could make musical instruments with objects from the
목적절을 이끄는 접속사   make A with B: B로 A를 만들다

landfill.

24 그는 우리가 쓰레기 매립지에서 나온 물건들로 악기를 만들 수 있다고 말했다.

25 A talented man named Nicholas was able to put this idea into practice.
앞의 명사구 수식   be able to: ~할 수 있다   put ~ into practice: ~을 실행에 옮기다
'쓰레기 매립지에서 나온 물건들로 악기를 만드는 것'을 가리킴

25 재주가 뛰어난 Nicholas 아저씨가 이 생각을 실행에 옮길 수 있었다.

26 He made violins from oil drums.

26 그는 기름통으로 바이올린을 만들었다.

27 He turned water pipes into flutes.
turn A into B: A를 B로 바꾸다

27 그는 수도관을 플루트로 바꾸었다.

28 We had another problem.
(형) 다른

28 우리는 또 다른 문제가 있었다.

29 No one knew how to play musical instruments.
how+to부정사: ~하는 방법, 어떻게 ~하는지

29 아무도 악기를 연주하는 법을 몰랐다.

30 We didn't even know how to read music.
how+to부정사: ~하는 방법, 어떻게 ~하는지

30 우리는 심지어 악보를 읽는 법도 알지 못했다.

31 Favio taught us with great patience.

31 Favio 선생님은 엄청난 인내심을 가지고 우리를 가르쳤다.

32 Step by step, we began to make some sounds on our instruments.
make sounds: 소리를 내다

32 점차로, 우리는 악기로 어떤 소리를 만들어 내기 시작했다.

33 I still remember the first piece of music that we played.
(부) 아직도, 여전히   선행사   목적격 관계대명사절
(that: 목적격 관계대명사)
(부) 대부분, 주로, 일반적으로

33 나는 아직도 우리가 연주했던 첫 곡을 기억한다.

34 It was very short and mostly out of tune.
앞 문장의 the first piece of music that we played를 가리킴

34 그 곡은 매우 짧고 대부분은 음이 맞지 않았다.

35 But it was the most beautiful music to us.
형용사 beautiful의 최상급

35 하지만 그것은 우리에게는 가장 아름다운 곡이었다.

36 We felt a new hope in our hearts.
heart (명) 마음

36 우리는 마음속에 새로운 희망을 느꼈다.

37 From then on, we gathered to practice every day.
to부정사의 부사적 용법 (목적: ~하기 위해)

37 그때부터, 우리는 매일 연습을 하기 위해 모였다.

38 One day, Favio told us some great news.
tell+간접목적어(us)+직접목적어(some great news) 〈4형식〉
= tell+직접목적어+to+간접목적어 〈3형식〉

38 어느 날, Favio 선생님은 우리에게 엄청난 소식을 말해 주었다.

39 We were going to have a concert, a real concert!

39 우리는 공연을, 진짜 공연을 하게 될 것이었다!

40 And here we are now in front of hundreds of people.
수백의

40 그리고 우리는 지금 여기 수백 명의 사람들 앞에 있다.

41 They love our music.
앞 문장의 hundreds of people을 가리킴

41 그들은 우리의 음악을 사랑한다.

42 The world sends us trash, but we send back music!
send+간접목적어(us)+직접목적어(trash) 〈4형식〉
= send+직접목적어+to+간접목적어 〈3형식〉

42 세상은 우리에게 쓰레기를 보내지만, 우리는 음악을 돌려보낸다!

Reading
빈칸 채우기

우리말 뜻과 일치하도록 교과서 본문의 문장을 완성하시오.

중요 문장

01 Tears of joy _____ _____ _____ my cheeks.

01 기쁨의 눈물이 내 볼에 흘러내리고 있다.

02 I'm so _____ _____ _____.

02 나는 정말 기쁘고 황홀하다.

03 If _____ _____ a bird, I _____ _____.

03 내가 새라면, 나는 날아오를 텐데.

04 I _____ _____.

04 나는 주위를 둘러본다.

05 The other members in my orchestra are hugging _____ _____.

05 우리 오케스트라의 다른 단원들이 서로 껴안고 있다.

06 Our concert _____ _____ _____ and everyone is standing and giving us a big hand.

06 우리의 연주회가 이제 막 끝났고 모든 사람들이 일어서서 우리에게 큰 박수를 보내고 있다.

07 _____ _____ us ever expected that this day would come.

07 우리 중 아무도 이런 날이 올 거라고 예상하지 못했다.

08 It has been a _____ _____.

08 그것은 긴 여정이었다.

09 My name is Andrea and I'm _____ _____ in the Recycled Orchestra.

09 내 이름은 Andrea이고 나는 Recycled Orchestra(재활용 오케스트라)의 바이올린 연주자이다.

10 Why _____ _____ _____ the Recycled Orchestra?

10 오케스트라가 왜 재활용 오케스트라로 불리냐고?

11 It's because our musical instruments are made of objects _____ _____ _____.

11 그것은 우리의 악기들이 쓰레기 매립지에서 나온 물건들로 만들어져 있기 때문이다.

12 That's why it's also _____ _____ the Landfill Harmonic Orchestra.

12 그것이 오케스트라가 Landfill Harmonic Orchestra로도 알려진 이유이다.

13 _____ _____ _____ in the orchestra are from Cateura, a small town in Paraguay.

13 오케스트라의 우리들 대부분은 파라과이의 작은 마을인 카테우라 출신이다.

14 There is _____ _____ _____ in our town.

14 우리 마을에는 거대한 쓰레기 매립지가 있다.

15 Some people even say that Cateura itself is _____ _____ _____.

15 몇몇 사람들은 심지어 카테우라 자체가 거대한 쓰레기 매립지라고 말한다.

16 Many of us _____ _____.

16 우리들 중 많은 이들이 가난하다.

17 There weren't _____ _____ _____ _____ in our town.

17 우리 마을에는 희망과 꿈이 많지 않았다.

18 Everything began to change, however, _____ _____ _____ Favio Chávez.

18 그러나 우리가 Favio Chávez 선생님을 만났을 때 모든 것이 바뀌기 시작했다.

19 Favio was _____ _____ _____ and a musician.

19 Favio 선생님은 환경 교육가이자 음악가였다.

20 He wanted to _____ _____ _____ _____, but there was a big problem.

20 그는 우리에게 음악을 가르치고 싶어 했지만, 큰 문제가 있었다.

21 There were only _____ _____ _____ _____ in the whole town.

21 온 마을에 악기가 단지 몇 개뿐이었다.

22 We couldn't _____ _____ _____ new ones.

23 But Favio _____ _____ _____ .

24 He said that we could _____ _____ _____ with objects from the landfill.

25 A talented man named Nicholas was able to _____ _____ _____ _____ _____ .

26 He _____ _____ from oil drums.

27 He _____ water pipes _____ flutes.

28 We had _____ _____ .

29 No one knew _____ _____ _____ musical instruments.

30 We _____ _____ _____ how to read music.

31 Favio taught us _____ _____ _____ .

32 _____ _____ _____ , we began to make some sounds on our instruments.

33 I still remember the first piece of music _____ _____ _____ .

34 It was very short and _____ _____ _____ _____ .

35 But it was _____ _____ _____ _____ _____ to us.

36 We felt a new hope _____ _____ _____ .

37 From then on, we _____ _____ _____ every day.

38 _____ _____ , Favio told us some great news.

39 We were going to _____ _____ _____ , a real concert!

40 And here we are now _____ _____ _____ hundreds of people.

41 _____ _____ our music.

42 The world sends us trash, but we _____ _____ _____ !

22 우리는 새 악기를 살 형편이 안 되었다.

23 그러나 Favio 선생님은 포기하지 않았다.

24 그는 우리가 쓰레기 매립지에서 나온 물건들로 악기를 만들 수 있다고 말했다.

25 재주가 뛰어난 Nicholas 아저씨가 이 생각을 실행에 옮길 수 있었다.

26 그는 기름통으로 바이올린을 만들었다.

27 그는 수도관을 플루트로 바꾸었다.

28 우리는 또 다른 문제가 있었다.

29 아무도 악기를 연주하는 법을 몰랐다.

30 우리는 심지어 악보를 읽는 법도 알지 못했다.

31 Favio 선생님은 엄청난 인내심을 가지고 우리를 가르쳤다.

32 점차로, 우리는 악기로 어떤 소리를 만들어 내기 시작했다.

33 나는 아직도 우리가 연주했던 첫 곡을 기억한다.

34 그 곡은 매우 짧고 대부분은 음이 맞지 않았다.

35 하지만 그것은 우리에게는 가장 아름다운 곡이었다.

36 우리는 마음속에 새로운 희망을 느꼈다.

37 그때부터, 우리는 매일 연습을 하기 위해 모였다.

38 어느 날, Favio 선생님은 우리에게 엄청난 소식을 말해 주었다.

39 우리는 공연을, 진짜 공연을 하게 될 것이었다!

40 그리고 우리는 지금 여기 수백 명의 사람들 앞에 있다.

41 그들은 우리의 음악을 사랑한다.

42 세상은 우리에게 쓰레기를 보내지만, 우리는 음악을 돌려보낸다!

STEP A

글의 내용과 문장의 어법에 맞게 괄호 안에서 알맞은 어휘를 고르시오.

01 Tears of joy (is / are) rolling down my cheeks.

02 I'm so happy and (thrilling / thrilled).

03 If I (were / am) a bird, I would fly.

04 I (look / looks) around.

05 The other members in my orchestra (is / are) hugging one another.

06 Our concert has just finished and everyone is standing and (gave / giving) us a big hand.

07 None of us ever expected that this day would (come / came).

08 It (has been / were) a long journey.

09 My name is Andrea (and / but) I'm a violinist in the Recycled Orchestra.

10 Why is it (calling / called) the Recycled Orchestra?

11 It's (because of / because) our musical instruments are made of objects from a landfill.

12 That's why it's also (knew / known) as the Landfill Harmonic Orchestra.

13 Most of us in the orchestra (is / are) from Cateura, a small town in Paraguay.

14 There (is / are) a huge landfill in our town.

15 Some people even say that Cateura (itself / themselves) is a giant landfill.

16 (Many / Much) of us are poor.

17 There (were / weren't) many hopes and dreams in our town.

18 Everything began to change, however, (when / whom) we met Favio Chávez.

19 Favio was (an / a) environmental educator and a musician.

20 He wanted to teach (us music / music us), but there was a big problem.

21 There were only (a little / a few) musical instruments in the whole town.

22 We couldn't afford (buying / to buy) new ones.

23 But Favio (gave up / didn't give up).

24 He said that we could make musical instruments with objects (for / from) the landfill.

25 A talented man named Nicholas was able to put this idea (into / with) practice.

26 He (made / make) violins from oil drums.

27 He turned water pipes (from / into) flutes.

28 We had (other / another) problem.

29 No one knew (how to play / how playing) musical instruments.

30 We didn't even know (what / how) to read music.

31 Favio taught us with great (patience / patient).

32 Step by step, we began (to make / make) some sounds on our instruments.

33 I still remember the first piece of music (that / what) we played.

34 It was very short and (most / mostly) out of tune.

35 But it was the most beautiful music (to / of) us.

36 We felt a new hope in our (heart / hearts).

37 From then on, we gathered (practice / to practice) every day.

38 One day, Favio told (us some great news / some great news us).

39 We were going to (have / watch) a concert, a real concert!

40 And here we are now (in front of / behind) hundreds of people.

41 They (love / loves) our music.

42 The world sends us (trash / music), but we send back (trash / music)!

R Reading
틀린 문장 고치기

STEP A

밑줄 친 부분이 내용이나 어법상 바르면 ○, 어색하면 ✕에 표시하고 고쳐 쓰시오.

01 Tears of joy <u>are rolling up</u> my cheeks. ○ ✕

02 I'm so happy and <u>thrilling</u>. ○ ✕

03 <u>As</u> I were a bird, I would fly. ○ ✕

04 I <u>look around</u>. ○ ✕

05 The other members in my orchestra are hugging <u>one another</u>. ○ ✕

06 Our concert has just finished and everyone is standing and <u>giving a big hand us</u>. ○ ✕

07 <u>None of us</u> ever expected that this day would come. ○ ✕

08 It has been a <u>short</u> journey. ○ ✕

09 My name is Andrea <u>and</u> I'm a violinist in the Recycled Orchestra. ○ ✕

10 <u>How</u> is it called the Recycled Orchestra? ○ ✕

11 It's because our musical instruments <u>make of</u> objects from a landfill. ○ ✕

12 That's <u>what</u> it's also known as the Landfill Harmonic Orchestra. ○ ✕

13 Most of us in the orchestra are <u>from</u> Cateura, a small town in Paraguay. ○ ✕

14 <u>There are</u> a huge landfill in our town. ○ ✕

15 Some people even say that Cateura <u>it</u> is a giant landfill. ○ ✕

16 Many of us <u>is</u> poor. ○ ✕

17 There weren't <u>much</u> hopes and dreams in our town. ○ ✕

18 Everything <u>began to change</u>, however, when we met Favio Chávez. ○ ✕

19 Favio was an <u>environment</u> educator and a musician. ○ ✕

20 He <u>wanted teaching</u> us music, but there was a big problem. ○ ✕

21 <u>There was</u> only a few musical instruments in the whole town. ○ ✕

22	We could afford to buy new ones.	○	×
23	But Favio didn't give up.	○	×
24	He said that we could make musical instruments for objects from the landfill.	○	×
25	A talented man named Nicholas was able to put this idea into participation.	○	×
26	He made violins into oil drums.	○	×
27	He turned water pipes into flutes.	○	×
28	We had another problem.	○	×
29	No one knew how to playing musical instruments.	○	×
30	We didn't even know how reading music.	○	×
31	Favio taught us with great patience.	○	×
32	Step to step, we began to make some sounds on our instruments.	○	×
33	I still forget the first piece of music that we played.	○	×
34	It was very short and most out of tune.	○	×
35	But it was most beautiful music to us.	○	×
36	We felt a new hope in our hearts.	○	×
37	From then on, we gathered practice every day.	○	×
38	One day, Favio told some great news us.	○	×
39	We were going to have a concert, a real concert!	○	×
40	And here we are now in front of hundreds of people.	○	×
41	They don't love our music.	○	×
42	The world sends trash us, but we send back music!	○	×

R ▶ Reading
배열로 문장 완성하기

STEP
A

주어진 단어를 바르게 배열하여 문장을 쓰시오.

01 기쁨의 눈물이 내 볼에 흘러내리고 있다. (rolling down / my cheeks / tears / are / of / joy)
→

02 나는 정말 기쁘고 황홀하다. (happy / so / thrilled / and / I'm)
→

03 내가 새라면, 나는 날아오를 텐데. (would / I / a bird, / I / if / were / fly)
→

04 나는 주위를 둘러본다. (look / I / around)
→

05 우리 오케스트라의 다른 단원들이 서로 껴안고 있다. (in my orchestra / one another / are / the other members / hugging)
→

06 우리의 연주회가 이제 막 끝났고 모든 사람들이 일어서서 우리에게 큰 박수를 보내고 있다.
(and / everyone / a big hand / has just finished / and / our concert / is standing / giving / us)
→

07 우리 중 아무도 이런 날이 올 거라고 예상하지 못했다. (that / would come / ever expected / none of us / this day)
→

08 그것은 긴 여정이었다. (has been / it / a long journey)
→

09 내 이름은 Andrea이고 나는 Recycled Orchestra(재활용 오케스트라)의 바이올린 연주자이다.
(and / a violinist / my name / Andrea / in the Recycled Orchestra / I'm / is)
→

10 그것이 왜 재활용 오케스트라로 불리냐고? (it / called / is / why / the Recycled Orchestra)
→

11 그것은 우리의 악기들이 쓰레기 매립지에서 나온 물건들로 만들어져 있기 때문이다.
(of objects / from a landfill / it's / our musical instruments / are made / because)
→

12 그것이 오케스트라가 Landfill Harmonic Orchestra로도 알려진 이유이다.
(known / why / that's / it's / the Landfill Harmonic Orchestra / also / as)
→

13 오케스트라의 우리들 대부분은 파라과이의 작은 마을인 카테우라 출신이다.
(in Paraguay / from Cateura, / a small town / most of us / in the orchestra / are)
→

14 우리 마을에는 거대한 쓰레기 매립지가 있다. (in our town / a huge landfill / is / there)
→

15 몇몇 사람들은 심지어 카테우라 자체가 거대한 쓰레기 매립지라고 말한다.
(is / even / say / Cateura / some people / itself / a giant landfill / that)
→

16 우리들 중 많은 이들이 가난하다. (poor / many of us / are)
→

17 우리 마을에는 희망과 꿈이 많지 않았다. (dreams / and / weren't / hopes / there / in our town / many)
→

18 그러나 우리가 Favio Chávez 선생님을 만났을 때 모든 것이 바뀌기 시작했다.
(however, / began / when / we / everything / met / Favio Chávez / to change,)
→

19 Favio 선생님은 환경 교육가이자 음악가였다. (was / Favio / a musician / and / an environmental educator)
→

20 그는 우리에게 음악을 가르치고 싶어 했지만, 큰 문제가 있었다. (there was / but / us / to teach / he / music, / wanted / a big problem)
→

21 온 마을에 악기가 단지 몇 개뿐이었다. (only / there were / a few / in the whole town / musical instruments)
→

22 우리는 새 악기를 살 형편이 안 되었다. (new ones / afford / couldn't / we / to buy)
→

23 그러나 Favio 선생님은 포기하지 않았다. (didn't / but / give up / Favio)
→

24 그는 우리가 쓰레기 매립지에서 나온 물건들로 악기를 만들 수 있다고 말했다.
(he / that / said / musical instruments / from the landfill / make / we / could / with objects)
→

25 재주가 뛰어난 Nicholas 아저씨가 이 생각을 실행에 옮길 수 있었다.
(named Nicholas / this idea / a talented man / into practice / was able / to put)
→

26 그는 기름통으로 바이올린을 만들었다. (made / he / oil drums / violins / from)
→

27 그는 수도관을 플루트로 바꾸었다. (water pipes / into / he / turned / flutes)
→

28 우리는 또 다른 문제가 있었다. (had / we / problem / another)
→

29 아무도 악기를 연주하는 법을 몰랐다. (how / no one / musical instruments / knew / to play)
→

30 우리는 심지어 악보를 읽는 법도 알지 못했다. (even / know / didn't / how / we / music / to read)
→

31 Favio 선생님은 엄청난 인내심을 가지고 우리를 가르쳤다. (taught / great patience / Favio / us / with)
→

32 점차로, 우리는 악기로 어떤 소리를 만들어 내기 시작했다.
(began / some sounds / step by step, / we / on our instruments / to make)
→

33 나는 아직도 우리가 연주했던 첫 곡을 기억한다. (of music / I / played / the first piece / that / we / still remember)
→

34 그것은 매우 짧고 대부분은 음이 맞지 않았다. (very short / out of tune / and / was / it / mostly)
→

35 하지만 그것은 우리에게는 가장 아름다운 곡이었다. (it / most beautiful music / but / was / to / us / the)
→

36 우리는 마음속에 새로운 희망을 느꼈다. (we / in our hearts / a new hope / felt)
→

37 그때부터, 우리는 매일 연습을 하기 위해 모였다. (to practice / from then on, / gathered / every day / we)
→

38 어느 날, Favio 선생님은 우리에게 엄청난 소식을 말해 주었다. (us / one day, / told / some great news / Favio)
→

39 우리는 공연을, 진짜 공연을 하게 될 것이었다! (were going / we / a real concert / to have / a concert,)
→

40 그리고 우리는 지금 여기 수백 명의 사람들 앞에 있다. (people / in front of / and / here we are now / hundreds of)
→

41 그들은 우리의 음악을 사랑한다. (music / love / they / our)
→

42 세상은 우리에게 쓰레기를 보내지만, 우리는 음악을 돌려보낸다! (trash, / we / sends / the world / us / but / send back / music)
→

[01-03] 다음 글을 읽고, 물음에 답하시오.

Tears of joy are rolling down my cheeks. I'm so _____ⓐ_____ . If I (A) am / were a bird, I would fly. I look around. The other members in my orchestra are hugging one another. Our concert has just finished and everyone is standing and (B) give / giving us a big hand. None of us ever expected that ⓑthis day would come. It has been a long journey.

01 윗글의 빈칸 ⓐ에 들어갈 말로 알맞은 것은?

① tired and down   ② worried and angry
③ sad and scared   ④ happy and thrilled
⑤ bored and sleepy

02 윗글의 (A)와 (B)에서 알맞은 것을 골라 쓰시오.

(A) _____   (B) _____

03 윗글의 밑줄 친 ⓑthis day가 가리키는 내용으로 알맞은 것은?

① 긴 여행을 함께 가는 날
② 처음으로 연주회에 초청받은 날
③ 유명한 오케스트라의 연주회를 관람하는 날
④ 많은 어려움을 이겨내고 오케스트라를 결성한 날
⑤ 연주회를 마치고 사람들에게서 큰 박수를 받는 날

[04-06] 다음 글을 읽고, 물음에 답하시오.

My name is Andrea and I'm a violinist in ①the Recycled Orchestra. Why is ②it called the Recycled Orchestra? ③It's because our musical instruments ⓐmake of objects from a landfill. That's why ④it's also known as ⑤the Landfill Harmonic Orchestra.

04 윗글의 밑줄 친 ①~⑤ 중 가리키는 것이 다른 하나는?

①   ②   ③   ④   ⑤

05 윗글의 밑줄 친 ⓐmake의 형태로 알맞은 것은?

① make   ② are made   ③ are making
④ will make   ⑤ have made

06 다음 영어 뜻풀이에 해당하는 단어를 윗글에서 찾아 쓰시오.

| an area where waste is buried under the ground |

→ _____

[07-09] 다음 글을 읽고, 물음에 답하시오.

Most of us in the orchestra are from Cateura, a small town in Paraguay. There is a huge landfill in our town. Some people even say that Cateura ⓐitself is a giant landfill. Many of us are poor. There weren't many hopes and dreams in our town. Everything began to change, _____ⓑ_____, when we met Favio Chávez.

고 신
╱산도 ╱유형
07 윗글의 밑줄 친 ⓐitself와 같은 용법으로 쓰인 재귀대명사끼리 짝 지어진 것은?

ⓐ We saw ourselves in the mirror.
ⓑ My father made this pizza himself.
ⓒ I myself saw the ghost last night.
ⓓ She asked herself, "What should I do?"

① ⓐ, ⓒ   ② ⓐ, ⓑ, ⓓ   ③ ⓑ, ⓒ
④ ⓑ, ⓓ   ⑤ ⓒ, ⓓ

08 윗글의 빈칸 ⓑ에 들어갈 말로 알맞은 것은?

① in short ② however ③ unfortunately
④ unluckily ⑤ for example

09 윗글의 내용과 일치하지 <u>않는</u> 것은?

① 카테우라는 파라과이에 있다.
② 카테우라에는 쓰레기 매립지가 있다.
③ 카테우라의 많은 사람들이 가난하다.
④ 카테우라 마을 사람들은 가난하지만 항상 희망에 차 있었다.
⑤ Favio 선생님은 카테우라의 상황을 변화시켰다.

[10-14] 다음 글을 읽고, 물음에 답하시오.

Favio was an environmental educator and a musician. (①) He wanted to _____ⓐ_____, but there was a big problem. (②) There were only a few musical instruments in the whole town. We couldn't afford to buy new ⓑones. (③) He said that we could make musical instruments with objects from the landfill. (④) A talented man named Nicholas was able to put this idea ____ⓒ____ practice. (⑤) He made violins from oil drums. He turned water pipes ____ⓓ____ flutes.

10 윗글의 ①~⑤ 중 주어진 문장이 들어갈 알맞은 곳은?

> But Favio didn't give up.

① ② ③ ④ ⑤

11 윗글의 빈칸 ⓐ에 들어갈 말로 알맞은 것은?

① teach us music ② teach music us
③ teach us to music ④ teach music of us
⑤ teach to us music

12 윗글의 밑줄 친 ⓑones가 가리키는 것을 윗글에서 찾아 쓰시오.

→ _____

13 윗글의 빈칸 ⓒ와 ⓓ에 공통으로 들어갈 말로 알맞은 것은?

① of ② for ③ with
④ into ⑤ through

신유형
14 윗글을 읽고 바르게 이해하지 <u>못한</u> 사람은?

① 수지: Favio 선생님은 환경 교육가이자 음악가였구나.
② 태호: 마을에 악기는 많았는데 다 낡아서 쓸 수 없었구나.
③ 윤서: 마을 사람들은 새 악기를 살 형편이 안 되었구나.
④ 강민: 쓰레기 매립지의 물건들을 이용해서 악기를 만들 수도 있구나.
⑤ 준혁: Nicolas 아저씨는 기름통으로 바이올린을 만들 만큼 재주가 뛰어났구나.

[15-18] 다음 글을 읽고, 물음에 답하시오.

We had another problem. No one knew how to play musical instruments. We didn't even know how to read music.
(A) It was very short and mostly ①out of tune.
(B) Favio taught us ②with great patience.
(C) I still remember the first piece of music that we played.
(D) ③Step by step, we began to make some sounds on our instruments.
But it was the most beautiful music to us. We felt _____ⓐ_____ in our hearts. ④From then on, we gathered ⓑto practice every day. One day, Favio told us some great news. We were going to have a concert, a real concert!
And here we are now ⑤in front of hundreds of people. They love our music. The world sends us trash, but we send back music!

STEP
A

15 자연스러운 글이 되도록 윗글의 (A)~(D)를 바르게 배열한 것은?

① (A) – (B) – (C) – (D) ② (B) – (C) – (A) – (D)
③ (B) – (D) – (C) – (A) ④ (C) – (A) – (D) – (B)
⑤ (C) – (D) – (B) – (A)

16 윗글의 밑줄 친 ①~⑤의 우리말 뜻이 알맞지 않은 것은?

① 음이 맞지 않는   ② 엄청난 인내심을 가지고
③ 즉시   ④ 그때부터
⑤ ~ 앞에

17 윗글의 빈칸 ⓐ에 들어갈 말로 알맞은 것은?

① a new hope   ② a sudden pain
③ a deep sadness   ④ a sense of loss
⑤ a great disappointment

18 윗글의 밑줄 친 ⓑto practice와 쓰임이 같은 것은?

① They decided to leave early.
② Amy has no pen to write with.
③ His dream is to be a movie star.
④ I'm very happy to see you again.
⑤ Harry turned on the TV to watch the news.

[19-21] 다음 글을 읽고, 물음에 답하시오.

My name is Andrea and I'm a violinist in the Recycled Orchestra. Why is it (A) calling / called the Recycled Orchestra? It's because our musical instruments are made of ①objects from a landfill. That's why it's also ②known as the Landfill Harmonic Orchestra.

Most of us in the orchestra (B) is / are from Cateura, a small town in Paraguay. There (C) is / are a huge landfill in our town. Some people even say that Cateura itself is a ③giant landfill. Many of us are ④rich. There weren't many hopes and dreams in our town. Everything began to ⑤change, however, when we met Favio Chávez.

19 윗글의 (A)~(C)에서 어법상 알맞은 말이 바르게 짝 지어진 것은?

(A)   (B)   (C)
① called – is – is
② calling – are – is
③ called – are – is
④ calling – is – are
⑤ called – are – are

20 윗글의 밑줄 친 ①~⑤ 중 흐름상 어색한 것은?

①   ②   ③   ④   ⑤

21 윗글을 읽고 Andrea에 대해 알 수 있는 것을 모두 고르면?

① 연주하는 악기
② 장래 희망
③ 국적과 사는 마을
④ 악기를 연주한 기간
⑤ Favio Chávez 선생님을 만난 때

[22-23] 다음 글을 읽고, 물음에 답하시오.

Favio was an environmental educator and a musician. He wanted to teach us music, but there was ⓐa big problem. There were only a few musical instruments in the whole town. We couldn't afford to buy new ones. But Favio didn't give up. He said that we could make musical instruments with objects from the landfill. ⓑNicholas라는 이름의 재주가 뛰어난 남자가 이 생각을 실행에 옮길 수 있었다. He made violins from oil drums. He turned water pipes into flutes.

22 윗글의 밑줄 친 ⓐa big problem이 의미하는 것을 우리말로 쓰시오.

→ _____

23 윗글의 밑줄 친 ⓑ의 우리말과 같도록 [조건]에 맞게 쓰시오.

> [조건]　　1. 주어진 단어들을 바르게 배열할 것
> 　　　　　2. 대소문자를 구별하고 문장 부호를 정확히 쓸 것

> was, this idea, a talented man, practice, named, able, put, Nicholas, into, to

→ _____
_____

24 다음 글을 읽고, 주어진 질문에 완전한 영어 문장으로 답하시오.

> My name is Andrea and I'm a violinist in the Recycled Orchestra. Why is it called the Recycled Orchestra? It's because our musical instruments are made of objects from a landfill. That's why it's also known as the Landfill Harmonic Orchestra.

(1) Which instrument does Andrea play in the orchestra?
　→ _____
(2) What are their musical instruments made of?
　→ _____

[25-27] 다음 글을 읽고, 물음에 답하시오.

We had another problem. No one knew how to playing musical instruments. We didn't even know how to read music. Favio taught us with great patience. Step by step, we began to make some sounds on our instruments. I still remember the first piece of music that we played. ⓐIt was very short and mostly out of tune. But it was the most beautiful music to us. We felt a new hope in our hearts. From then on, we gathered to practice every day. One day, Favio told to us some great news. We were going to have a concert, a real concert!

25 윗글의 밑줄 친 ⓐIt이 가리키는 것을 윗글에서 찾아 8단어로 쓰시오.

　→ _____

고/난도
26 윗글에서 어법상 틀린 문장을 두 개 찾아 바르게 고쳐 쓰시오.

(1) _____
_____
(2) _____
_____

고/난도
27 윗글의 내용과 일치하도록 Favio 선생님과 아이들의 대화를 완성하시오.

> A(Favio): Hello, everyone! I have some great news to tell you.
> B: What is it?
> A: _____
> C: Really? I can't believe it!

만점 노트

After You Read_B

Reporter: Congratulations! ❶ How do you feel now?

Andrea: I feel ❷ thrilled. We just performed our first concert.

Reporter: ❸ Why is the orchestra called the Recycled Orchestra?

Andrea: ❹ That's because our musical instruments ❺ are made of objects from a landfill.

Reporter: That's amazing.

Andrea: Yeah. None of us knew ❻ how to play musical instruments, but Favio taught us ❼ with great patience.

Reporter: That is a wonderful story.

기자: 축하합니다! 지금 기분이 어때요?

Andrea: 황홀해요. 우리는 막 우리의 첫 연주회를 했어요.

기자: 왜 오케스트라가 재활용 오케스트라로 불리나요?

Andrea: 그건 우리의 악기가 쓰레기 매립지에서 나온 물건들로 만들어져 있기 때문이에요.

기자: 놀랍네요.

Andrea: 네. 우리 중 누구도 악기를 연주하는 법을 알지 못했지만, Favio 선생님께서 엄청난 인내심으로 우리를 가르치셨어요.

기자: 멋진 이야기네요.

❶ 기분이 어떤지 묻는 표현 ❷ 주어인 I가 감정을 느끼는 주체이므로 과거분사 형태의 형용사 thrilled가 사용됨

❸ 「의문사(Why)+be동사(is)+주어(the orchestra)+과거분사(called) ~?」 형태의 의문사와 수동태가 포함된 의문문

❹ That's because ~.: 그것은 ~이기 때문이다. (이유를 나타낼 때 사용) ❺ be made of: ~로 만들어지다

❻ how+to부정사: ~하는 방법, 어떻게 ~할지 ❼ 엄청난 인내심으로, 엄청난 인내심을 가지고

Think and Write_Step 2

Dear Admiral Yi Sun-sin,

I'm Sumin. I really respect you ❶ because you never ❷ gave up in difficult situations. You ❸ saved the country and the people. ❹ It was amazing that you won the battle with only 12 ships. ❺ If I had a time machine, I would go to meet you! ❻ I'd like to ❼ ask you how to make geobukseon. You're my hero. Thank you.

Sincerely yours,
Sumin

이순신 장군님께,

저는 수민이에요. 저는 장군님이 어려운 상황에서 결코 포기하지 않았기 때문에 장군님을 정말 존경해요. 장군님은 나라와 국민을 구했어요. 단지 12척의 배로 전투에서 이긴 것은 놀라웠어요. 제게 타임머신이 있다면, 저는 장군님을 만나러 갈 텐데요! 저는 장군님께 거북선을 어떻게 만드는지 묻고 싶어요. 장군님은 제 영웅이에요. 감사합니다.

존경을 담아,
수민이가

❶ ~이기 때문에 (이유를 나타내는 접속사) ❷ give up: 포기하다 ❸ save ⑧ 구하다

❹ It은 가주어, that이 이끄는 절(that you won the battle with only 12 ships)이 진주어

❺ 가정법 과거: 「If+주어(I)+동사의 과거형(had) ~, 주어(I)+조동사의 과거형(would)+동사원형(go) .....」

❻ I'd like to+동사원형 ~.: 나는 ~하고 싶다.

❼ 「ask+간접목적어+직접목적어」의 형태로, how to make geobukseon(how+to부정사)이 직접목적어로 쓰임

Project_Step 3

This is a bottle shaker. ❶ To make it, you need a bottle and buttons. ❷ Clean the bottle and put the buttons in the bottle. ❸ Close the bottle and decorate it. You can also put different things ❹ like rice or sand in it. Different items make different sounds. Listen to my group's bottle shaker.

이것은 병 셰이커야. 이것을 만들기 위해서는 병과 단추들이 필요해. 병을 깨끗이 하고 병 안에 단추들을 넣어. 병을 막고 장식해. 병 속에 쌀이나 모래처럼 다른 것들을 넣을 수도 있어. 다른 물건들은 다른 소리를 만들어. 우리 모둠의 병 셰이커 소리를 들어 봐.

❶ 목적(~하기 위해서)을 나타내는 to부정사의 부사적 용법 ❷, ❸ 동사원형으로 시작하는 명령문 ❹ 逊 ~처럼, ~ 같은

[01-03] 다음 글을 읽고, 물음에 답하시오.

Reporter: Congratulations! _____ⓐ_____
Andrea: I feel ①thrilled. We just performed our first concert.
Reporter: Why is the orchestra ②calls the Recycled Orchestra?
Andrea: That's ③why our musical instruments are made of objects from a landfill.
Reporter: That's ④amazing.
Andrea: Yeah. None of us knew ⑤how to play musical instruments, but Favio taught us with great patience.
Reporter: That is a wonderful story.

01 윗글의 빈칸 ⓐ에 들어갈 말로 알맞은 것은?

① Why do you like it?
② How have you been?
③ How do you feel now?
④ What can I do for you?
⑤ What do you want me to do?

02 윗글의 밑줄 친 ①~⑤ 중 틀린 것의 개수는?

① 1개　　　② 2개　　　③ 3개
④ 4개　　　⑤ 5개

03 윗글의 내용과 일치하지 않는 것은?

① Andrea는 첫 연주회 시작 전에 인터뷰를 하고 있다.
② Andrea의 오케스트라는 재활용 오케스트라로 불린다.
③ Andrea의 오케스트라가 사용하는 악기는 쓰레기 매립지에서 나온 물건들로 만들어졌다.
④ Andrea의 오케스트라 단원들은 악기 연주하는 법을 알지 못했다.
⑤ Favio 선생님은 오케스트라 단원들을 인내심을 가지고 가르쳤다.

[04-05] 다음 글을 읽고, 물음에 답하시오.

Dear Admiral Yi Sun-sin,
　I'm Sumin. I really respect you because you never gave up in difficult situations. You ⓐsaved the country and the people. ⓑThis was amazing that you won the battle with only 12 ships. (A)제게 타임머신이 있다면, 저는 당신을 만나러 갈 텐데요! I'd like to ask you ⓒhow to make geobukseon. You're my hero. Thank you.
　　　　　　　　　　Sincerely yours,
　　　　　　　　　　　　Sumin

04 윗글을 읽고 바르게 이해하지 못한 사람은?

① 소민: 이 글은 편지글 형식이야.
② 찬영: 수민이가 이순신 장군님을 존경하는 이유는 장군님이 어려운 상황에서 결코 포기하지 않아서구나.
③ 아인: ⓐ의 saved는 '절약했다'라는 의미로 쓰였어.
④ 소윤: that절이 진주어이므로 ⓑ는 가주어 It으로 고쳐야 해.
⑤ 보람: ⓒ는 '거북선을 만드는 방법'이라는 의미야.

서술형
05 윗글의 밑줄 친 (A)의 우리말을 영작하시오.

→ _____

06 다음 글의 주제로 알맞은 것은?

　　This is a bottle shaker. To make it, you need a bottle and buttons. Clean the bottle and put the buttons in the bottle. Close the bottle and decorate it. You can also put different things like rice or sand in it. Different items make different sounds. Listen to my group's bottle shaker.

① how to make a bottle shaker
② why we should recycle bottles
③ unique artworks using bottles
④ different kinds of bottle shakers
⑤ the ways to decorate a bottle shaker

Words
고득점 맞기

01 다음 짝 지어진 두 단어의 관계가 [보기]와 같은 것은?

[보기]　　　　　　　joy – pleasure

① most – mostly
② huge – giant
③ cheer – cheerful
④ patience – patient
⑤ surprised – surprising

02 다음 영어 뜻풀이의 빈칸에 들어갈 말로 알맞은 것은?

landfill: an area where _____ is buried under the ground

① soil　　　② waste　　　③ a town
④ a stick　　　⑤ treasure

03 다음 빈칸에 들어갈 말로 알맞은 것은?

Sumi doesn't like to stay at home on Sundays. She _____ goes out and plays on Sundays.

① hardly　　　② exactly　　　③ mostly
④ politely　　　⑤ friendly

[04-05] 다음 빈칸에 공통으로 들어갈 말을 한 단어로 쓰시오.

04
• We should _____ the animals in danger.
• You'll _____ about two hours if you go this way.
• I plan to _____ my allowance to buy a new smartphone.

→ _____

05
• This _____ of music has a powerful cello sound.
• I'm going to have another _____ of cake.

→ _____

06 고/난도 다음 중 밑줄 친 부분의 쓰임이 알맞지 <u>않은</u> 것은?

① Let's <u>give</u> this great scientist <u>a big hand</u>.
② Kevin <u>took care of</u> his sick brother after school.
③ <u>Turn off</u> the light when you leave the room.
④ <u>Step by step</u>, our band began to make some beautiful sound.
⑤ Luckily, Rachel <u>was afford</u> to attend the meeting on time.

07 괄호 안의 우리말과 같도록 빈칸에 알맞은 말을 쓰시오.

Monica is poor at singing. Her singing is always _____ _____ _____.
(Monica는 노래를 잘하지 못한다. 그녀의 노래는 항상 음이 맞지 않는다.)

08 고/난도 신/유형 다음 빈칸에 들어가지 <u>않는</u> 단어는?

• Anne Sullivan was a great _____.
• Our club members _____ Kelly as our club president.
• We used tapes to _____ the birthday balloons on the wall.
• My classmates _____ to clean the park last Sunday.

① stick　　　② educator　　　③ respect
④ gathered　　　⑤ expect

09 다음 단어의 영어 뜻풀이로 알맞지 <u>않은</u> 것은?

① afford: to be able to pay for something
② cheek: either side of the face below the eyes
③ drone: an aircraft without a pilot that is controlled by someone on the ground
④ practice: the ability to stay calm and accept a delay or suffering without complaining
⑤ environmental: related to the natural conditions in which people, animals and plants live

10 다음 대화의 빈칸에 들어갈 말로 알맞은 것은?

A: Brian was absent from school today. Do you know why?
B: Yes. He _____ his back while he was carrying a heavy box.
A: Oh, I'm sorry to hear that.

① hurt   ② cheered   ③ afforded
④ practiced   ⑤ appeared

11 다음 빈칸에 들어갈 말을 [보기]에서 골라 쓰시오.

[보기] bored   boring   excited   exciting
worried   surprised   surprising

(1) I was really _____ when someone knocked loudly on the door.
(2) His speech was so _____ that I almost fell asleep.
(3) I'm going to the amusement park this weekend. I'm going to ride on the new roller coaster, so I'm _____.
(4) My brother broke his arm, and I'm _____ about him.

12 다음 짝 지어진 두 단어의 관계가 같도록 빈칸에 알맞은 단어를 쓰시오.

(1) create : creator = educate : _____
(2) agree : agreement = perform : _____
(3) joy : joyful = environment : _____

13 다음 빈칸에 들어갈 말이 순서대로 짝 지어진 것은?

• I will help you put your plan _____ practice.
• Andy told a lie again. _____ then on, we haven't trusted him any more.
• More than 200 students will take part _____ the marathon.

① on – For – at
② on – From – in
③ on – For – in
④ into – From – at
⑤ into – From – in

고_{난도} 신_{유형}
14 다음 영어 뜻이에 해당하는 단어가 쓰인 문장은?

a group of musicians playing many different kinds of musical instruments

① Listen carefully to this piece of music.
② My sister plays the flute in the school orchestra.
③ Did you see the tears of joy when Giho scored the winning goal?
④ After the team won the gold medals, the city had a parade for them.
⑤ My club members go to a children's hospital for volunteer work every month.

Listen & Speak
영작하기

정답 보기 >> 14~15쪽

STEP
B

우리말과 일치하도록 대화를 바르게 영작하시오.

1 Listen and Speak 1-A

B: _____

G: _____

B: _____

G: _____

해석   교과서 86쪽

B: 얘, 보라야. 우리 록 밴드에 온 걸 환영해.

G: 고마워. 나는 공연에서 너희들과 함께 연주하는 게 기대돼.

B: 우리는 새로운 기타 연주자가 생겨서 신이 나.

G: 잘됐다. 금요일에 봐.

2 Listen and Speak 1-B

G: _____

B: _____

G: _____

B: _____

G: _____

B: _____

G: _____

B: _____

G: _____

교과서 86쪽

G: 지호야, 너는 뭘 읽고 있니?

B: 나는 Jim Abbott이라는 이름의 야구 선수에 관한 책을 읽고 있어.

G: 아, 오른손이 없이 태어난 그 사람?

B: 맞아. 그는 정말 열심히 노력해서 최우수 선수 상까지 받았어.

G: 그래. 그의 이야기가 영화로 만들어졌어. 나는 이번 주 토요일에 그 영화를 볼 거야.

B: 정말? 제목이 뭐니?

G: "우리의 영웅"이야. 나는 그 영화를 보는 게 정말 기대돼.

B: 나도 너와 함께 해도 될까?

G: 물론이지. 토요일에 봐.

3 Listen and Speak 1-C

A: _____

B: _____

A: _____

B: _____

교과서 86쪽

A: 너는 오늘 행복해 보여. 무슨 일이니?

B: 나는 매우 신이 나. 나는 제주도로 여행을 갈 거야.

A: 그거 좋겠다!

B: 응, 나는 말을 타는 게 정말 기대돼.

4 Listen and Speak 2-A

G: _____

B: _____

G: _____

B: _____

G: _____

교과서 87쪽

G: 민호야, 너는 수학 숙제를 끝냈니?

B: 아직 못 끝냈어. 수학은 어려워.

G: 맞아, 그렇지만 재미있기도 해.

B: 그럼 네가 내 수학 숙제를 좀 도와줄래?

G: 그러고 싶지만, 안 되겠어. 나는 내 남동생을 돌봐야 해.

5 Listen and Speak 2-B

G: _____
B: _____
G: _____
B: _____
G: _____
B: _____
G: _____
B: _____

교과서 87쪽

해석

G: Alex, 나는 다음 주 월요일에 노래 대회에 참가할 거야.
B: 대단하다, 수민아!
G: 너는 기타를 치는 법을 알지, 그렇지?
B: 응, 나는 3년 동안 기타를 쳤어.
G: 잘됐다. 내가 대회에서 노래하는 동안 기타를 쳐 줄 수 있니?
B: 그러고 싶지만, 안 돼. 나는 어제 체육 수업 중에 손을 다쳤어.
G: 오! 그 말을 들어 유감이야.
B: 고마워. 하지만 너를 응원하러 거기에 갈게.

6 Listen and Speak 2-C

A: _____
B: _____
A: _____
B: _____

교과서 87쪽

A: 너는 오늘 오후에 무엇을 할 거니?
B: 나는 자전거를 탈 거야. 나와 함께 탈래?
A: 그러고 싶지만, 안 돼. 나는 숙제를 해야 해.
B: 알겠어, 그럼 다음에 같이 타자.

7 Real Life Talk > Watch a Video

Linda: _____
Tony: _____
Linda: _____
Tony: _____
Linda: _____
Tony: _____
Linda: _____
Tony: _____
Linda: _____
Tony: _____

교과서 88쪽

Linda: 안녕, Tony! 너는 이번 주말에 무엇을 할 거니?
Tony: 나는 뮤지컬 "빌리 엘리어트"를 볼 거야.
Linda: "빌리 엘리어트"? 무슨 내용이니?
Tony: 그건 유명한 무용수가 된 한 소년에 관한 거야. 나는 그 뮤지컬을 보는 게 기대돼.
Linda: 재미있겠다. 주연 배우가 누구니?
Tony: Jason Kim이야. 그는 훌륭한 무용수야.
Linda: 그는 내가 가장 좋아하는 배우야. 나는 작년에 그의 뮤지컬을 봤어.
Tony: 오, 정말? 나와 함께 가고 싶니?
Linda: 그러고 싶지만, 안 돼. 나는 이번 주말에 자원봉사 활동이 있어.
Tony: 알겠어. 다음에 같이 가자!

01 다음 대화의 빈칸에 들어갈 말로 알맞은 것을 <u>모두</u> 고르면?

> A: I'm going to visit the museum after school.
> Do you want to join me?
> B: _____ I have to do my
> homework.

① Why not?　　　② I'm afraid I can't.

③ Of course.　　　④ That sounds great.

⑤ I'd love to, but I can't.

[02-03] 다음 대화를 읽고, 물음에 답하시오.

> A: Jiho, what are you reading?
> B: I'm reading a book about a baseball player named Jim Abbott.
> A: Oh, the man who was born without a right hand?
> B: That's right. He tried really hard and even won the MVP award.
> A: Yeah. His story ⓐ(make) into a movie. I'm going to watch it this Saturday.
> B: Really? What's the title?
> A: *Our Hero*. I'm really looking forward to ⓑ(watch) it.
> B: Can I join you, Ann?
> A: Sure. See you on Saturday.

고 신
난도 유형

02 짝 지어진 대화 중 위 대화의 내용과 일치하지 <u>않는</u> 것은?

① A: What is Jiho reading?

　B: He is reading a book about Jim Abbott.

② A: Is Jim Abbott a baseball player?

　B: Yes, he is.

③ A: Was Jim Abbott born without his right hand?

　B: No, he lost it because of an accident.

④ A: What is the title of the movie about Jim Abbott?

　B: It's *Our Hero*.

⑤ A: What is Jiho going to do this Saturday?

　B: He's going to watch a movie with Ann.

03 위 대화의 ⓐ와 ⓑ의 동사를 알맞은 형태로 각각 쓰시오.

ⓐ _____　　ⓑ _____

[04-06] 다음 대화를 읽고, 물음에 답하시오.

> A: Alex, I'm going to take part in a singing contest next Monday.
> B: ①That's great, Sumin!
> A: You know how to play the guitar, right?
> B: Yes, ②I've played the guitar for 3 years.
> A: Great. Can you play the guitar ___ⓐ___ I sing in the contest?
> B: ③I'd love to, but I can't. I hurt my hand in gym class yesterday.
> A: Oh! ④I'm happy to hear that.
> B: Thanks. ⑤But I'll be there to cheer for you.

04 위 대화의 밑줄 친 ①~⑤ 중 흐름상 <u>어색한</u> 것은?

①　　　②　　　③　　　④　　　⑤

05 위 대화의 빈칸 ⓐ에 들어갈 말로 가장 알맞은 것은?

① since　　　② while　　　③ unless

④ though　　　⑤ even if

06 위 대화의 내용과 일치하는 것을 <u>모두</u> 고르면?

① 수민이는 다음 주 월요일에 노래 대회에서 노래를 부를 것이다.

② Alex는 기타 치는 법을 모른다.

③ Alex는 어제 체육 시간에 다리를 다쳤다.

④ Alex는 수민이의 요청을 수락했다.

⑤ Alex는 수민이를 응원하러 갈 것이다.

07 다음 대화의 빈칸에 알맞은 말을 [보기]에서 골라 쓰시오.

A: Minho, did you finish the math homework?
B: (1) _____ Math is difficult.
A: Yes, but it's interesting, too.
B: Then can you help me with my math homework?
A: (2) _____ I have to take care of my brother.

[보기]
- Not yet.
- Sounds great.
- Don't worry.
- Yes, I'd love to.
- No, you can't.
- I'd love to, but I can't.
- Sure, I've already done it.

[08-09] 다음 대화를 읽고, 물음에 답하시오.

Linda: Hi, Tony! What are you going to do this weekend?
Tony: I'm going to watch the musical, *Billy Elliot*.
Linda: *Billy Elliot*? What is it about?
Tony: It's about a boy which became a famous dancer. I'm looking forward to watching it.
Linda: Sounds interesting. Who is the main actor?
Tony: Jason Kim. He's a great dancer.
Linda: He's my favorite actor. I watched his musical last year.
Tony: Oh, really? Do you want to join me?
Linda: I'd love to, but I can't. I have volunteer work this weekend.
Tony: Okay. Maybe next time!

08 위 대화에서 어법상 틀린 부분이 있는 문장을 찾아 문장을 바르게 고쳐 쓰시오.

→ _____

09 위 대화의 내용과 일치하도록 다음 글을 완성하시오.

Tony is going to watch the _____, *Billy Elliot*, _____. The main actor in *Billy Elliot* is Jason Kim. He is Linda's _____. Linda can't join Tony because she _____.

10 다음 대화의 밑줄 친 우리말과 같도록 괄호 안의 말을 사용하여 영작하시오.

A: Welcome to our rock band.
B: Thanks. I'm looking forward to playing in a concert with you.
A: 우리는 새로운 기타 연주자가 생겨서 신이 나.
B: Great. See you on Friday.

→ _____
(excited, have, player)

11 다음 표를 보고, 내용에 맞게 대화를 완성하시오.

	What to do	Time
James	play a water balloon game	10:30
Mina	have the longest hot dog	10:30

A: Wow! Look at the festival! What are you going to do first, James?
B: (1) _____ at 10:30. I'm really looking forward (2) _____.
A: Sounds fun.
B: Do you want to join me, Mina?
A: I'm afraid I can't. (3) _____ at that time.

Grammar
고득점 맞기

01 다음 대화의 빈칸에 들어갈 말로 알맞은 것은?

> A: Please tell me _____
>   the balloons for the party.
> B: Stick them on the door.

① what to do   ② when to buy

③ how to make   ④ why to blow up

⑤ where to stick

02 다음 대화의 빈칸에 공통으로 들어갈 말로 알맞은 것은?

> A: What _____ you do if you were a millionaire?
> B: I _____ build a hospital in Africa.

① do   ② did   ③ will

④ can   ⑤ would

03 다음 빈칸에 알맞은 말이 순서대로 짝 지어진 것은?

> • If she _____ the exam, her life will change a lot.
> • If I _____ a laptop, I would not go to the library.

① fail – had   ② fails – had

③ failed – had   ④ fails – have

⑤ failed – have

04 다음 문장의 밑줄 친 ①~⑤ 중 어법상 틀린 것은?

> ①I ②don't know ③what ④eating ⑤for lunch.

05 다음 우리말을 영어로 옮길 때, 빈칸에 들어갈 말이 알맞지 <u>않은</u> 것은?

> 그는 내게 음표를 읽는 방법을 설명해 주었다.
> → He explained ___①___ ___②___ ___③___
>   ___④___ ___⑤___ a note.

① to   ② me   ③ when

④ to   ⑤ read

06 다음 밑줄 친 부분을 어법상 바르게 고친 것 중 <u>틀린</u> 것은?

> • The driver asked me where ①<u>stop</u>.
> • If I ②<u>am</u> you, I would not throw away the empty bottles.
> • Could you show me ③<u>what</u> to use this app?
> • If she ④<u>know</u> my address, she would write me a letter.
> • If Austin were taller, he ⑤<u>can</u> reach the top shelf.

① to stop   ② were   ③ how

④ knows   ⑤ could

07 다음 우리말을 영어로 <u>잘못</u> 옮긴 것을 <u>모두</u> 고르면?

① 우리는 먼저 무엇을 해야 하는지 모른다.
  → We don't know what we should do first.

② 나는 그에게 언제 기계를 켤지 물었다.
  → I asked him when to turn on the machine.

③ Steve는 체스를 두는 방법을 알고 싶어 한다.
  → Steve wants to know how to play chess.

④ 너는 벼룩시장에서 무엇을 팔지 결정했니?
  → Have you decided what to sold at the flea market?

⑤ 너는 나에게 표를 어디서 사야 할지 말해 줄 수 있니?
  → Can you tell me where to buying the ticket?

08 다음 중 어법상 <u>틀린</u> 것끼리 짝 지어진 것은?

> ⓐ If someone knew your secret, you would be upset.
> ⓑ I'd like to tell you why to help people in need.
> ⓒ He didn't know what to say next.
> ⓓ If I had a time machine, I will go back in time and meet King Sejong.

① ⓐ, ⓑ   ② ⓑ, ⓒ   ③ ⓑ, ⓓ
④ ⓑ, ⓒ, ⓓ   ⑤ ⓒ, ⓓ

09 다음 문장을 가정법 과거 문장으로 바르게 바꾼 것은?

> As I don't have a flying carpet, I can't travel all over the world.

① If I have a flying carpet, I can't travel all over the world.

② If I had a flying carpet, I could travel all over the world.

③ I had a flying carpet, I could travel all over the world.

④ If I had a flying carpet, I couldn't travel all over the world.

⑤ Unless I have a flying carpet, I can travel all over the world.

10 다음 대화의 밑줄 친 ①~⑤ 중 어법상 <u>틀린</u> 것은?

> A: I'm hungry now.
> B: ①Me, too. I want ②to eat tomato spaghetti.
> A: Do you know ③how to cook tomato spaghetti?
> B: No, I don't. If I were a good cook, I ④can make delicious tomato spaghetti.
> A: We ⑤can find the recipe on the Internet.
> B: You're right. Let's find it on the Internet right now.

11 다음 대화의 빈칸 ⓐ~ⓒ에 알맞은 말이 순서대로 짝 지어진 것은?

> A: I haven't decided ____ⓐ____ for Mary's birthday. How about you?
> B: I'm going to buy her a smartphone case.
> A: That's a good idea.
> B: But I don't know ____ⓑ____ to buy one.
> A: There is a good shop in the Great Shopping Mall.
> B: Really? Can you tell me ____ⓒ____ there?
> A: Well, why don't we go together? I'd like to look around the mall as well.
> B: Okay.

① what to buy – when to go – how to get
② where to buy – when to go – what to get
③ what to buy – where to go – how to get
④ where to buy – when to go – what to get
⑤ what to buy – where to go – when to get

12 다음 각 문장에 대한 설명으로 알맞지 <u>않은</u> 것은?

① Please tell me when to book our flight.
> → when to book은 '언제 예약할지'라는 의미이다.

② If the story were true, people would be surprised.
> → if절에서 동사 were를 사용한 것은 올바르다.

③ I don't know where to put this coat.
> → where to put this coat가 don't know의 목적어로 쓰였다.

④ If you apologize to him first, he will forgive you.
> → 과거 사실과 반대되는 상황을 가정하여 말하는 가정법 과거 문장이다.

⑤ He hasn't decided what to wear for the party.
> → what to wear는 what he should wear로 바꿔 쓸 수 있다.

서술형

STEP B

13 다음 우리말과 같도록 괄호 안의 말을 바르게 배열하여 문장을 쓰시오.

(1) 그는 내게 언제 저녁을 먹을지 물었다.

(have, me, dinner, when, asked, he, to)

→ _____

(2) 나는 그 지도를 어디에서 찾아야 할지 알고 있다.

(where, find, I, to, the map, know)

→ _____

(3) 만약 그가 여기 있다면, 그가 컴퓨터를 고칠 수 있을 텐데.

(could, he, if, the computer, were, here, he, fix)

→ _____

고/난도

14 다음 상황을 읽고, [조건]에 맞게 문장을 완성하시오.

> [조건] 1. 자신이 Mary라고 가정하고 문장을 완성할 것
> 2. 어법에 맞게 쓸 것

Mary is worried these days. Her best friend, Daisy, doesn't talk to her. Daisy even doesn't greet her. Mary doesn't know what to do. What would you do if you were Mary?

→ If I were Mary, _____

_____ .

고/난도

15 다음 중 어법상 틀린 문장을 골라 기호를 쓴 후, 문장을 바르게 고쳐 쓰시오.

ⓐ The notice showed where to park my car.

ⓑ If my uncle were here, he will help me.

ⓒ If I had a lot of money, I wouldn't stay here.

ⓓ My friends and I talked about what we should do the next day.

( ) → _____

16 다음 문장을 가정법 과거 문장으로 바꿔 쓰시오.

(1) As I am not rich, I can't travel all around the world.

→ If _____,

_____ .

(2) As she doesn't help me, I can't make a robot.

→ If _____,

_____ .

(3) As he plays mobile games so much, he can't read more books.

→ If _____,

_____ .

17 다음 [조건]에 맞게 대화를 완성하시오.

> [조건] 1. 각 빈칸에 「의문사+to부정사」 형태를 반드시 사용할 것
> 2. 의문사 when, where, what, how를 한 번씩 사용할 것
> 3. 동사 do, go, leave, ride를 한 번씩 사용할 것

A: Have you decided (1) _____ for the holidays?

B: Yes. I'm going to go to Jeju-do. But I haven't decided (2) _____ there.

A: I've heard horse riding is very exciting.

B: Really? That sounds good, but I don't know (3) _____ a horse.

A: Don't worry about it. The clerks will help you.

B: You're right. How about you? What are you going to do during the holidays?

A: I'm thinking of visiting Busan.

B: Sounds great. When are you going to leave?

A: I haven't decided (4) _____ . I have to finish my project first.

다음 우리말과 일치하도록 각 문장을 바르게 영작하시오.

01
_____
기쁨의 눈물이 내 볼에 흘러내리고 있다.

02
_____
나는 정말 기쁘고 황홀하다.

03
_____
☆ 내가 새라면, 나는 날아오를 텐데.

04
_____
나는 주위를 둘러본다.

05
_____
우리 오케스트라의 다른 단원들이 서로 껴안고 있다.

06
_____
우리의 연주회가 이제 막 끝났고 모든 사람들이 일어서서 우리에게 큰 박수를 보내고 있다.

07
_____
☆ 우리 중 아무도 이런 날이 올 거라고 예상하지 못했다.

08
_____
그것은 긴 여정이었다.

09
_____
내 이름은 Andrea이고 나는 Recycled Orchestra(재활용 오케스트라)의 바이올린 연주자이다.

10
_____
그것이 왜 재활용 오케스트라로 불리냐고?

11
_____
☆ 그것은 우리의 악기들이 쓰레기 매립지에서 나온 물건들로 만들어져 있기 때문이다.

12
_____
그것이 오케스트라가 Landfill Harmonic Orchestra로도 알려진 이유이다.

13
_____
오케스트라의 우리들 대부분은 파라과이의 작은 마을인 카테우라 출신이다.

14
_____
우리 마을에는 거대한 쓰레기 매립지가 있다.

15
_____
몇몇 사람들은 심지어 카테우라 자체가 거대한 쓰레기 매립지라고 말한다.

16
_____
우리들 중 많은 이들이 가난하다.

17
_____
우리 마을에는 희망과 꿈이 많지 않았다.

18
_____
☆ 그러나 우리가 Favio Chávez 선생님을 만났을 때 모든 것이 바뀌기 시작했다.

19
_____
Favio 선생님은 환경 교육가이자 음악가였다.

20
_____
그는 우리에게 음악을 가르치고 싶어 했지만, 큰 문제가 있었다.

21
_____
온 마을에 악기가 단지 몇 개뿐이었다.

22

_____

☆ 우리는 새 악기를 살 형편이 안 되었다.

23

_____

그러나 Favio 선생님은 포기하지 않았다.

24

_____

그는 우리가 쓰레기 매립지에서 나온 물건들로 악기를 만들 수 있다고 말했다.

25

_____

☆ Nicholas라는 이름의 재주가 뛰어난 남자가 이 생각을 실행에 옮길 수 있었다.

26

_____

그는 기름통으로 바이올린을 만들었다.

27

_____

그는 수도관을 플루트로 바꾸었다.

28

_____

우리는 또 다른 문제가 있었다.

29

_____

☆ 아무도 악기를 연주하는 법을 몰랐다.

30

_____

☆ 우리는 심지어 악보를 읽는 법도 알지 못했다.

31

_____

Favio 선생님은 엄청난 인내심을 가지고 우리를 가르쳤다.

32

_____

점차로, 우리는 악기로 어떤 소리를 만들어 내기 시작했다.

33

_____

나는 아직도 우리가 연주했던 첫 곡을 기억한다.

34

_____

그 곡은 매우 짧고 대부분은 음이 맞지 않았다.

35

_____

하지만 그것은 우리에게는 가장 아름다운 곡이었다.

36

_____

우리는 마음속에 새로운 희망을 느꼈다.

37

_____

그때부터, 우리는 매일 연습을 하기 위해 모였다.

38

_____

어느 날, Favio 선생님은 우리에게 엄청난 소식을 말해 주었다.

39

_____

우리는 공연을, 진짜 공연을 하게 될 것이었다!

40

_____

그리고 우리는 지금 여기 수백 명의 사람들 앞에 있다.

41

_____

그들은 우리의 음악을 사랑한다.

42

_____

☆ 세상은 우리에게 쓰레기를 보내지만, 우리는 음악을 돌려보낸다!

[01-02] 다음 글을 읽고, 물음에 답하시오.

　　Tears of joy are rolling down my cheeks. I'm so ①happy and thrilling. If I were a bird, I ②would fly. I look around. The other members in my orchestra ③are hugging one another. Our concert ④has just finished and everyone is standing and ⑤giving us a big hand. None of us ever expected that this day would come. It has been a long journey.

01 윗글의 밑줄 친 ①~⑤ 중 어법상 틀린 것은?

①　　　　②　　　　③　　　　④　　　　⑤

02 윗글의 내용과 일치하지 <u>않는</u> 것은?

① 글쓴이는 기쁨의 눈물을 흘리고 있다.
② 글쓴이의 오케스트라의 단원들은 서로 껴안고 있다.
③ 글쓴이의 오케스트라는 막 연주회를 끝냈다.
④ 모든 사람들이 일어서서 글쓴이의 오케스트라에게 큰 박수를 보내고 있다.
⑤ 글쓴이는 언젠가 이런 날이 올 거라고 예상했다.

[03-05] 다음 글을 읽고, 물음에 답하시오.

　　①My name is Andrea and I'm a violinist in the Recycled Orchestra. ②There are several kinds of musical instruments in the orchestra. ③Why is it called the Recycled Orchestra? ④It's because our musical instruments are made of objects from a landfill. ⑤That's why it's also known ____ⓐ____ the Landfill Harmonic Orchestra.

　　Most of us in the orchestra are from Cateura, a small town ____ⓑ____ Paraguay. There is a huge landfill in our town. Some people even say that Cateura itself is a giant landfill. Many of us are poor. There weren't many hopes and dreams in our town. Everything began to change, however, when we met Favio Chávez.

03 윗글의 문장 ①~⑤ 중 글의 흐름과 <u>관계없는</u> 것은?

①　　　　②　　　　③　　　　④　　　　⑤

04 윗글의 빈칸 ⓐ와 ⓑ에 알맞은 말이 순서대로 짝 지어진 것은?

① as – at　　　② as – in　　　③ to – in
④ for – to　　　⑤ for – at

05 윗글을 읽고 답할 수 <u>없는</u> 질문은?

① Which instrument does Andrea play in the orchestra?
② What are their musical instruments made of?
③ Where is Andrea from?
④ What do some people even say about Cateura?
⑤ When did Andrea first meet Favio Chávez?

[06-08] 다음 글을 읽고, 물음에 답하시오.

　　Favio was an environmental educator and a musician. He wanted to _____ⓐ_____, but there was a big problem. There were only (A)|a few / a little| musical instruments in the whole town. We couldn't afford (B)|buying / to buy| new ones. But Favio didn't give up. He said that we could make musical instruments with objects from the landfill. A talented man (C)|naming / named| Nicholas was able to put this idea into practice. He made violins from oil drums. He turned water pipes into flutes.

06 윗글의 빈칸 ⓐ에 들어갈 말로 알맞은 것은?

① teach us music

② show us a concert

③ play the music for us

④ compose a song for us

⑤ make musical instruments

07 윗글의 (A)~(C)에서 어법상 알맞은 말이 바르게 짝 지어진 것은?

	(A)	(B)	(C)
①	a few	– buying	– named
②	a few	– to buy	– naming
③	a few	– to buy	– named
④	a little	– buying	– named
⑤	a little	– to buy	– naming

08 다음 영어 뜻풀이에 해당하는 단어 중 윗글에서 찾을 수 없는 것은?

① action rather than ideas

② to be able to pay for something

③ an act of traveling from one place to another

④ an area where waste is buried under the ground

⑤ related to the natural conditions in which people, animals and plants live

[09-11] 다음 글을 읽고, 물음에 답하시오.

We had another problem. No one knew ⓐ_____ play musical instruments. We didn't even know _____ ⓑ read music. ①Favio taught us with great patience. Step by step, we began to make some sounds on our instruments. ②I still remember the first piece of music that we played. It was very short and mostly out of tune. But it was the most beautiful music to us. We felt a new hope in our hearts. ③From then on, we gathered to practice every day.

④One day, Favio told us some great news. We were going to have a concert, a real concert!

And here we are now in front of hundreds of people. ⑤They love our music. The world sends us trash, but we send back music!

09 윗글의 빈칸 ⓐ와 ⓑ에 공통으로 들어갈 말로 알맞은 것은?

① what to ② how to ③ when to

④ where to ⑤ why to

10 윗글의 밑줄 친 문장 ①~⑤에 대해 잘못 설명한 사람은?

① 재훈: with great patience는 '엄청난 인내심을 가지고'라는 의미야.

② 세미: that은 관계대명사로 which로 바꿔 쓸 수 있지만 생략할 수는 없어.

③ 기호: to practice는 '~하기 위해서'라는 목적의 의미를 나타내는 to부정사야.

④ 유진: 4형식 문장으로, us는 간접목적어이고 some great news가 직접목적어야.

⑤ 소윤: They는 앞 문장의 hundreds of people을 가리켜.

11 윗글의 내용과 일치하는 것은?

① Favio didn't have any problem in teaching them.

② They couldn't read music, but they could play musical instruments.

③ The first piece of music that they played was short but perfect.

④ The writer didn't like the first piece of music that they played.

⑤ They practiced every day after they played the first piece of music.

서술형

12 다음 글에서 어법상 틀린 부분을 모두 찾아 바르게 고쳐 쓰시오.

Tears of joy are rolling down my cheeks. I'm so happy and thrilled. If I were a bird, I will fly. I look around. The other members in my orchestra is hugging one another. Our concert has just finished and everyone is standing and given us a big hand. None of us ever expected that this day would come. It has been a long journey.

(1) _____ → _____
(2) _____ → _____
(3) _____ → _____

13 다음 글을 아래와 같이 요약할 때 빈칸에 알맞은 말을 쓰시오.

Favio was an environmental educator and a musician. He wanted to teach us music, but there was a big problem. There were only a few musical instruments in the whole town. We couldn't afford to buy new ones. But Favio didn't give up. He said that we could make musical instruments with objects from the landfill. A talented man named Nicholas was able to put this idea into practice. He made violins from oil drums. He turned water pipes into flutes.

▼

Favio wanted to teach us _____, but there were _____
in the whole town. Favio came up with an idea. The idea was to make _____
_____.
Nicholas put this idea _____,
and it was successful.

14 다음 글의 밑줄 친 우리말을 [조건]에 맞게 영작하시오.

My name is Andrea and I'm a violinist in the Recycled Orchestra. 왜 그것은 재활용 오케스트라로 불리는가? It's because our musical instruments are made of objects from a landfill.

[조건]   1. call을 이용하여 영작할 것
         2. 대소문자를 구별하고 문장 부호를 정확히 쓸 것

→ _____

[15-16] 다음 글을 읽고, 물음에 답하시오.

We had another problem. No one knew how to play musical instruments. We didn't even know how to read music. Favio taught us with great patience. Step by step, we began to make some sounds on our instruments. I still remember the first piece of music that we played. It was very short and mostly out of tune. But it was the most beautiful music to us. We felt a new hope in our hearts. From then on, we gathered to practice every day.

15 윗글의 밑줄 친 another problem이 무엇인지 우리말로 쓰시오.

→ _____

16 윗글의 내용과 일치하도록 다음 대화를 완성하시오.

A: How was the first piece of music they played?
B: (1) _____
A: How did they feel in their hearts when they played it?
B: (2) _____
A: What did they do after then?
B: (3) _____

서술형 100% TEST

01 다음 빈칸에 알맞은 단어를 [조건]에 맞게 쓰시오.

I think my group members need more _____ to finish the science project.

[조건]
1. The word starts with p.
2. The word has 8 letters.
3. The word means "the ability to stay calm and accept a delay or suffering without complaining."

02 다음 대화의 빈칸에 알맞은 말을 [보기]에서 골라 쓰시오. (필요시 형태를 바꿀 것)

[보기] one another   be able to   step by step
take part in   out of tune

A: I'm going to (1) _____ the talent show tomorrow.

B: Sounds great!

A: Yeah, but I have a problem.

B: What is it?

A: I'm going to play the guitar, but my guitar is (2) _____. It sounds strange.

B: I think my uncle (3) _____ help you.

A: Really? Thank you so much.

03 다음 상황을 읽고, 마지막 질문에 대한 답을 [조건]에 맞게 쓰시오.

You meet your friend on your way home. Your friend asks you to play soccer together this Saturday. You can't play soccer that day because you have to visit your grandparents. In this situation, what will you say to your friend?

[조건]
1. love와 but을 포함한 거절 표현을 사용할 것
2. 거절의 이유를 포함하여 두 문장으로 답할 것

→ _____

[04-05] 다음 대화를 읽고, 물음에 답하시오.

A: Jiho, what are you reading?

B: I'm reading a book about a baseball player named Jim Abbott.

A: Oh, the man who was born without a right hand?

B: That's right. He tried really hard and even won the MVP award.

A: Yeah. His story was made into a movie. I'm going to watch it this Saturday.

B: Really? What's the title?

A: *Our Hero*. 나는 그것을 보는 게 정말 기대돼.

B: Can I join you, Ann?

A: Sure. See you then.

04 위 대화의 밑줄 친 우리말을 괄호 안의 단어들을 사용하여 영작하시오.

→ _____

(really, looking)

05 위 대화의 내용과 일치하도록 다음 글을 완성하시오.

Jiho is reading a _____ about Jim Abbott. Jim Abbott doesn't have a _____. But he tried really hard and became a great _____. Ann says his story was made into a _____, *Our Hero*. Ann and Jiho are going to watch it together _____.

06 다음 [조건]에 맞게 대화를 완성하시오.

> [조건] • 괄호 안의 단어들 중 필요 없는 단어를 한 개씩 빼고 배열하여 문장을 완성할 것

A: Alex, I'm going to take part in a singing contest next Monday.

B: That's great, Sumin!

A: You (1) _____,
right? (how, play, sing, know, the, guitar, to)

B: Yes, I've played the guitar for 3 years.

A: Great. Can you (2) _____
_____? (while, in, play, sing, the, guitar, for, I, the, contest)

B: I'm sorry, but I can't. I hurt my hand in gym class yesterday.

A: Oh! (3) _____.
(sorry, hear, I'm, to, that, happy)

B: Thanks. But I'll be there to cheer for you.

07 다음 대화를 읽고, 주어진 질문에 완전한 영어 문장으로 답하시오.

A: Minho, did you finish the math homework?

B: Not yet. Math is difficult.

A: Yes, but it's interesting, too.

B: Then can you help me with my math homework, Sally?

A: I'd love to, but I can't. I have to take care of my brother.

(1) What does Minho think about math?

→ _____

(2) Why can't Sally help Minho with his math homework?

→ _____

08 다음 가정법 문장은 직설법 문장으로, 직설법 문장은 가정법 문장으로 바꿔 쓰시오.

(1) If I had the book, I could lend it to you.

→ As _____,

_____.

(2) As he doesn't live in Seoul, I can't see him every day.

→ If _____,

_____.

09 다음 우리말과 같도록 괄호 안의 말을 이용하여 영작하시오.

(1) 그녀는 그에게 언제 그 고양이에게 먹이를 주는지 말했다.

→ _____
(tell, to, feed)

(2) 그 경주를 위해 무엇을 준비해야 하는지 내게 알려 줘.

→ _____
(let, to, prepare, the race)

(3) Brian은 그 표들을 어디서 사야 할지 알아냈다.

→ _____
(find out, to, buy)

10 자연스러운 흐름이 되도록 다음 [조건]에 맞게 문장을 완성하시오.

> [조건] 1. <A>와 <B>에서 각각 한 단어씩 골라 쓸 것
> 2. 각각 3단어로 쓸 것

⟨A⟩	⟨B⟩
when how why	use arrive cook
where what	do start

(1) The manager explained _____
the coffee machine.

(2) What should we do next? Please tell us _____
_____.

(3) I've forgotten when we should arrive at the airport. Do you know _____?

11 다음 우리말을 [조건]에 맞게 영작하시오.

> [조건] 1. 가정법 과거 문장으로 쓸 것
> 2. 괄호 안의 말을 이용할 것

(1) 내게 100만 달러가 있다면, 나는 전 세계를 여행할 수 있을 텐데.
(have a million dollars, travel)

→ _____

(2) 내가 그의 주소를 안다면, 나는 그에게 선물을 보낼 텐데.
(know, send, a gift)

→ _____

12 다음 대화에서 Laura의 상황을 나타내는 문장을 가정법 과거를 이용하여 쓰시오.

> **Mark**: It's sunny today! Let's go on a picnic, Laura.
> **Laura**: I'm sorry, but I can't. I'm too busy.

→ If Laura _____,
she _____.

13 다음 중 어법상 틀린 문장을 두 개 골라 기호를 쓴 후, 문장을 바르게 고쳐 쓰시오.

> ⓐ His history class is not bored.
> ⓑ Please tell me where to going after school.
> ⓒ If I lived on a farm, I could raise this horse.
> ⓓ I'm going to get my face painted at that time.

( ) → _____
( ) → _____

14 다음 [조건]에 맞게 대화를 완성하시오.

> [조건] 1. 각각 「의문사+to부정사」의 형태로 쓸 것
> 2. 대화에 사용된 동사를 사용할 것

> A: Let's get ready for Mom's birthday party.
> B: Okay. Please tell me (1) _____ the balloons.
> A: Stick them on the wall. I don't know (2) _____ the birthday cake in.
> B: Bring it in when the lights are turned off.
> A: Okay. I'm going to make some cookies. Do you know (3) _____ them?
> B: Of course. Let's make them together.

15 다음 빈칸에 알맞은 말을 자유롭게 완성하시오.

(1) If I had a flying carpet, _____
_____.

(2) If I won the lottery, _____
_____.

(3) If I were an astronaut, _____
_____.

[16-17] 다음 글을 읽고, 물음에 답하시오.

> Favio was an environmental educator and a musician. (1)(teach, he, to, us, wanted, music), but there was a big problem. There were only a few musical instruments in the whole town. (2)(afford, we, buy, new, couldn't, to, ones) But Favio didn't give up. He said that we could make musical instruments with objects from the landfill. A talented man named Nicholas (3)(into, was, this, able, practice, put, to, idea). He made violins from oil drums. He turned water pipes into flutes.

16 윗글의 (1)~(3)의 괄호 안의 단어들을 바르게 배열하여 쓰시오.

(1) _____

(2) _____

(3) _____

17 What was Favio's idea about musical instruments?

→ _____

_____

18 다음 대화의 빈칸에 알맞은 말을 [보기]에서 골라 쓰시오.

[보기]
- That is a wonderful story.
- Why is the orchestra called the Recycled Orchestra?
- How do you feel now?
- What are they doing now?
- What is the Recycled Orchestra?

Reporter: Congratulations!
(1) _____

Andrea: I feel thrilled. We just performed our first concert.

Reporter: (2) _____

Andrea: That's because our musical instruments are made of objects from a landfill.

Reporter: That's amazing.

Andrea: Yeah. None of us knew how to play musical instruments, but Favio taught us with great patience.

Reporter: (3) _____

19 다음 글에서 어법상 틀린 문장을 두 개 찾아 문장을 바르게 고쳐 쓰시오.

My name is Andrea and I'm a violinist in the Recycled Orchestra. Why is it called the Recycled Orchestra? It's because of our musical instruments are made of objects from a landfill. That's why it's also known as the Landfill Harmonic Orchestra. Most of us in the orchestra are from Cateura, a small town in Paraguay. There is a huge landfill in our town. Some people even say that Cateura themselves is a giant landfill.

(1) _____

(2) _____

20 다음 편지글의 내용과 일치하도록 아래 대화를 완성하시오.

Dear Admiral Yi Sun-sin,

I'm Sumin. I really respect you because you never gave up in difficult situations. You saved the country and the people. It was amazing that you won the battle with only 12 ships. If I had a time machine, I would go to meet you! I'd like to ask you how to make geobukseon. You're my hero. Thank you.

Sincerely yours,
Sumin

A: Sumin, who is the person you respect most?
B: Admiral Yi Sun-sin.
A: Why do you respect him?
B: (1) _____
A: What did he do?
B: (2) _____
(3) _____
A: What would you like to ask him if you met him?
B: (4) _____

01 다음 중 짝 지어진 단어의 관계가 나머지와 <u>다른</u> 것은? [3점]

① win – lose　　　② joy – sorrow

③ huge – giant　　④ remember – forget

⑤ patience – impatience

02 다음 단어의 영어 뜻풀이가 알맞지 <u>않은</u> 것은? [4점]

① expect: to be able to pay for something

② cheek: either side of the face below the eyes

③ journey: an act of traveling from one place to another

④ environmental: related to the natural conditions in which people, animals and plants live

⑤ orchestra: a group of musicians playing many different kinds of musical instruments

03 다음 빈칸에 공통으로 들어갈 말로 알맞은 것은? [3점]

> • Please _____ out your books and open them at page 10.
> • Who will _____ care of your dogs while you're away?

① put　　　② have　　　③ take

④ hurt　　　⑤ stick

04 다음 중 밑줄 친 단어가 서로 <u>다른</u> 의미로 쓰인 것을 <u>모두</u> 고르면? [4점]

① The cheese was cut into small <u>pieces</u>.
　 Two <u>pieces</u> of the puzzle were left.

② The <u>band</u> played some Beatles songs.
　 Bora plays the drums in the rock <u>band</u>.

③ Kevin hurt his leg in the <u>gym</u> class.
　 When it rains, we play basketball in the <u>gym</u>.

④ Why don't we take a taxi to <u>save</u> time?
　 He tried to <u>save</u> the country and the people.

⑤ I will <u>stick</u> this movie poster on the wall.
　 She bought two stamps to <u>stick</u> on the letter.

05 다음 대화의 빈칸에 들어갈 말로 알맞은 것은? [4점]

> A: You look happy today. What's going on?
> B: I'm so excited. I'm going to go to the beach.
> A: That sounds great!
> B: Yes, _____.

① I think you can swim in the ocean

② I don't want to swim in the ocean

③ I'm not good at swimming in the ocean

④ I'm worried about swimming in the ocean

⑤ I'm really looking forward to swimming in the ocean

06 다음 중 짝 지어진 대화가 자연스럽지 <u>않은</u> 것은? [4점]

① A: What are you going to do tomorrow?
　 B: I'm going to ride my bike.

② A: I hurt my hand in gym class yesterday.
　 B: Oh! I'm sorry to hear that.

③ A: You know how to play the guitar, right?
　 B: Yes, I've played the guitar for 3 years.

④ A: Hey, Bora. Welcome to our rock band.
　 B: Thanks. I'm looking forward to playing in a concert with you.

⑤ A: I'm going to play soccer after school. Do you want to join me?
　 B: Sure, I'd love to. I don't feel well today.

서술형**1**

07 다음 대화의 빈칸에 알맞은 말을 쓰시오. [4점]

> A: What are you gong to do this afternoon?
> B: I'm going to go to the movies. Do you want to join me?
> A: _____
> 　 I have to do my homework.
> B: Okay, then next time.

[08-10] 다음 대화를 읽고, 물음에 답하시오.

> A: Jiho, what are you reading?
> B: I'm reading a book about a baseball player (A) name / named Jim Abbott.
> A: Oh, the man (B) who / whose was born without a right hand?
> B: That's right. He tried really hard and even won the MVP award.
> A: Yeah. His story (C) made / was made into a movie. I'm going to watch it this Saturday.
> B: Really? What's the title?
> A: *Our Hero*. I'm really looking forward to watching it.
> B: Can I join you?
> A: Sure. See you on Saturday.

08 위 대화의 (A)~(C)에서 어법상 알맞은 말이 바르게 짝 지어진 것은? [4점]

	(A)	(B)	(C)
①	name	– who	– made
②	name	– whose	– was made
③	named	– who	– made
④	named	– who	– was made
⑤	named	– whose	– was made

09 위 대화를 읽고 Jim Abbott에 대해 알 수 <u>없는</u> 것은? [4점]

① 야구 선수이다.
② 한 손이 없이 태어났다.
③ 최우수 선수 상을 받았다.
④ 그의 이야기가 영화로 만들어졌다.
⑤ 자서전이 베스트셀러가 되었다.

서술형 **2**

10 위 대화의 내용과 일치하도록 빈칸에 알맞은 말을 쓰시오. [4점]

> Jim Abbott was born _____ _____ _____ _____. He tried really hard and became a great _____ _____.

11 다음 대화의 ①~⑤ 중 주어진 문장이 들어갈 알맞은 곳은? [4점]

> Math is difficult.

> A: Minho, did you finish the math homework? (①)
> B: Not yet. (②)
> A: Yes, but it's interesting, too. (③)
> B: Then can you help me with my math homework? (④)
> A: I'd love to, but I can't. (⑤) I have to take care of my brother.

12 다음 대화의 빈칸에 들어갈 말로 알맞은 것은? [3점]

> A: Let me know _____ next to the sofa.
> B: Well, please put the table next to the sofa.

① what to put
② how to put
③ when to put
④ where to put
⑤ why to put

서술형 **3**

13 다음 문장을 가정법 과거 문장으로 바꿔 쓰시오. [각 2점]

(1) As I don't have enough eggs, I can't bake bread for you.
　→ If _____,
　_____.

(2) As I'm not a super hero, I can't help people in need.
　→ If _____,
　_____.

서술형 **4**

14 다음 괄호 안의 말을 바르게 배열하여 문장을 완성한 후, 우리말로 해석하시오. [4점]

(where, go, let's, to, this Sunday, decide)

→ _____

→ 해석: _____

15 다음 중 어법상 틀린 문장은? [4점]

① I asked him when to have dinner.

② If the baseball cap were cheaper, I would buy it.

③ I was upset because Nick didn't tell me how to do the work.

④ If I am you, I wouldn't wear the red coat.

⑤ If she had enough money, she could buy a new house.

서술형 5

16 다음 [조건]에 맞게 대화를 완성하시오. [각 3점]

> [조건]　1. 각각 to와 의문사를 반드시 포함할 것
> 　　　　2. 대화에 쓰인 표현을 사용할 것

> A: Let's get ready for the party.
> B: Okay. Please tell me (1) _____
> _____.
> A: Stick the balloons on the door. I don't know (2) _____.
> B: Bring the birthday cake in when the lights are turned off.

[17-18] 다음 글을 읽고, 물음에 답하시오.

> Tears of joy ①are rolling down my cheeks. I'm so happy and thrilled. (A)내가 새라면, 나는 날아오를 텐데. I ②look around. The other members in my orchestra are hugging ③one another. Our concert has just finished and everyone is standing and ④giving us a big hand. ⑤None of us ever expected that this day would come. It has been a long journey.

17 윗글의 밑줄 친 ①~⑤의 우리말 뜻이 알맞지 않은 것은? [3점]

① 흘러내리고 있다

② 주위를 둘러보다

③ 각자

④ 우리에게 큰 박수를 보내고 있다

⑤ 우리 중 아무도 예상하지 못했다

서술형 6

18 윗글의 밑줄 친 (A)의 우리말을 [조건]에 맞게 영작하시오. [4점]

> [조건]　1. 가정법 과거 문장으로 쓸 것
> 　　　　2. 8단어로 쓸 것
> 　　　　3. 대소문자를 구별하고 문장 부호를 정확히 쓸 것

→ _____

[19-21] 다음 글을 읽고, 물음에 답하시오.

> My name is Andrea and I'm a violinist in the Recycled Orchestra. ①Why is it called the Recycled Orchestra? It's because our musical instruments are made of objects from a landfill. ②That's why it's also known as the Landfill Harmonic Orchestra.
>
> Most of us in the orchestra ③are from Cateura, a small town in Paraguay. There is a huge landfill in our town. Some people even say that Cateura ④themselves is a giant landfill. Many of us are poor. There weren't many hopes and dreams in our town. Everything ⑤began to change, however, when we met Favio Chávez.

19 윗글의 밑줄 친 ①~⑤ 중 어법상 틀린 것은? [4점]

①　　　②　　　③　　　④　　　⑤

20 윗글의 내용과 일치하지 <u>않는</u> 것은? [4점]

① Andrea plays the violin in the Recycled Orchestra.

② The musical instruments in the Recycled Orchestra are made of objects from a landfill.

③ Cateura is located in Paraguay.

④ There is a huge landfill in Andrea's town.

⑤ Many people in Cateura are rich and they have many hopes.

서술형7

21 다음 질문에 완전한 영어 문장으로 답하시오. [4점]

Q: What is the Recycled Orchestra also known as?

A: _____

22 다음 글의 밑줄 친 ①~⑤ 중 흐름상 어색한 것은? [4점]

Favio was an environmental educator and a musician. ①He wanted to teach us music, but there was a big problem. ②There were only a few musical instruments in the whole town. We couldn't afford to buy new ones. ③But Favio gave up. He said that we could make musical instruments with objects from the landfill. ④A talented man named Nicholas was able to put this idea into practice. ⑤He made violins from oil drums. He turned water pipes into flutes.

[23-25] 다음 글을 읽고, 물음에 답하시오.

We had another problem. (1)No one knew how to play musical instruments. (2)We didn't even know how to read music. Favio taught us with great patience. Step by step, we began to make some sounds on our instruments. I still remember the first piece of music ⓐthat we played. It was very short and mostly out of tune. But it was the most beautiful music to us. We felt a new hope in our hearts. From then on, we gathered to practice every day. One day, Favio told us ⓑsome great news. We were going to have a concert, a real concert!

And here we are now in front of hundreds of people. They love our music. (3)The world sends us trash, but we send back music!

서술형8

23 윗글의 밑줄 친 (1)~(3)을 우리말로 해석하시오. [각 2점]

(1) _____

(2) _____

(3) _____

24 윗글의 밑줄 친 ⓐthat과 쓰임이 같은 것은? [4점]

① It was a bird that broke the window.

② This is my backpack and that's yours.

③ I think that Clare is interested in music.

④ Do you know who that girl in the yellow jacket is?

⑤ The paintings that you showed me were beautiful.

25 윗글의 밑줄 친 ⓑsome great news가 가리키는 것은? [4점]

① 새 악기를 살 수 있다는 소식

② 진짜 공연을 하게 될 거라는 소식

③ 연주했던 첫 곡이 성공적이었다는 소식

④ 유명 오케스트라 공연을 관람할 거라는 소식

⑤ Favio 선생님이 음악을 가르쳐 주기로 했다는 소식

01 다음 빈칸에 공통으로 들어갈 말로 알맞은 것은? [3점]

> • He gave me a _____ of the cheesecake.
> • The pianist performed a new _____ of music recently.

① drum   ② piece   ③ parade
④ battle   ⑤ orchestra

02 다음 빈칸에 알맞은 말을 [보기]에서 골라 쓰시오. [각 2점]

> [보기]   excited   scared   worried   bored

(1) I'm _____ about my dog. He is sick now.
(2) His speech was very long. We were really _____ by it.
(3) Aron was very _____ when he heard a strange sound in the dark.

03 다음 밑줄 친 부분의 우리말 뜻이 알맞지 <u>않은</u> 것은? [3점]

① I <u>wasn't able to</u> focus on studying because of the music. (~할 수 없었다)
② It was a difficult time, but I never <u>gave up</u>. (포기했다)
③ They looked at <u>one another</u> and laughed. (서로)
④ <u>Step by step</u>, I got over my fear and learned to swim. (점차로)
⑤ After our presentation, the teachers <u>gave us a big hand</u>. (우리에게 큰 도움을 줬다)

[서술형1]

04 대화의 밑줄 친 우리말을 [조건]에 맞게 영작하시오. [4점]

> [조건]   1. looking, play, a concert를 이용할 것
>   2. 10단어로 쓸 것

> A: Hey, Bora. Welcome to our rock band.
> B: Thanks. <u>나는 공연에서 너희들과 함께 연주하는 게 기대돼.</u>
> A: We're excited to have a new guitar player.
> B: Great. See you on Friday.

→ _____

05 다음 대화의 빈칸에 들어갈 수 있는 말을 <u>모두</u> 고르면? [4점]

> A: I'm going to visit the museum after school. Do you want to join me?
> B: _____ I have to do my homework.
> A: Okay, then next time.

> ⓐ I'm afraid I can't.   ⓑ Yes, I'd love to.
> ⓒ Of course, I can.   ⓓ I'm with you on that.
> ⓔ I'm sorry, but I can't.   ⓕ I'd love to, but I can't.

① ⓐ, ⓔ   ② ⓐ, ⓔ, ⓕ   ③ ⓑ, ⓒ, ⓓ
④ ⓑ, ⓒ, ⓔ   ⑤ ⓒ, ⓔ, ⓕ

[06-08] 다음 대화를 읽고, 물음에 답하시오.

> A: Alex, I'm going to take part in a singing contest next Monday.
> B: That's great, Sumin!
> A: You know ____ ⓐ ____ to play the guitar, right?
> B: Yes, I've played the guitar for 3 years.
> A: Great. Can you play the guitar ____ ⓑ ____ I sing in the contest?
> B: I'd love to, but I can't. ____ ⓒ ____
> A: Oh! I'm sorry to hear that.
> B: Thanks. But I'll be there to cheer for you.

06 위 대화의 빈칸 ⓐ와 ⓑ에 들어갈 말이 순서대로 짝 지어진 것은? [4점]

① when – while   ② when – unless
③ how – while   ④ how – although
⑤ what – because

07 위 대화의 빈칸 ⓒ에 들어갈 말로 알맞은 것은? [4점]

① I'm happy to help you.

② I like playing the guitar on stage.

③ I'm going to hold a singing contest.

④ I hurt my hand in gym class yesterday.

⑤ I'm also going to take part in the contest.

서술형 2

08 위 대화를 읽고 답할 수 있는 질문을 모두 골라 기호를 쓴 후, 질문에 대한 답을 쓰시오. [5점]

> ⓐ What is Sumin going to do next Monday?
>
> ⓑ How long has Alex played the guitar?
>
> ⓒ What song is Sumin going to sing in the contest?
>
> ⓓ What are they going to do after the conversation?

(　　) → _____

(　　) → _____

[09-10] 다음 대화를 읽고, 물음에 답하시오.

> Linda: Hi, Tony! _____
>
> Tony: I'm going to watch the musical, *Billy Elliot*.
>
> Linda: *Billy Elliot*? _____
>
> Tony: It's about a boy who became a famous dancer. I'm looking forward to watching it.
>
> Linda: Sounds interesting. _____
>
> Tony: Jason Kim. He's a great dancer.
>
> Linda: He's my favorite actor. I watched his musical last year.
>
> Tony: Oh, really? _____
>
> Linda: I'd love to, but I can't. I have volunteer work this weekend.
>
> Tony: Okay. Maybe next time!

09 다음 중 위 대화의 빈칸에 쓰이지 않는 것은? [4점]

① What is it about?

② What's the title?

③ Who is the main actor?

④ Do you want to join me?

⑤ What are you going to do this weekend?

10 위 대화의 내용과 일치하지 않는 것을 모두 고르면? [4점]

① *Billy Elliot* is a musical about a famous dancer.

② Tony can't wait to see the musical, *Billy Elliot*.

③ Jason Kim is Linda's favorite actor.

④ Linda hasn't seen Jason Kim's musical before.

⑤ Tony and Linda are going to watch a musical this weekend.

11 자연스러운 문장이 되도록 다음 단어들을 순서대로 배열할 때, 여섯 번째로 오는 단어는? [3점]

> book, I, put, where, know, didn't, to, the

① to　　　　② know　　　　③ put

④ book　　　⑤ where

서술형 3

12 다음 중 밑줄 친 부분이 어법상 틀린 문장을 두 개 골라 기호를 쓴 후, 틀린 부분을 바르게 고쳐 쓰시오. [4점]

> ⓐ I asked him how to fix the computer.
>
> ⓑ If I were not tired, I would go hiking with Sam.
>
> ⓒ Can you tell me when to taking the medicine?
>
> ⓓ If she has a flying carpet, she could travel all over the world.

(　　) → _____

(　　) → _____

13 다음 빈칸에 들어갈 말로 알맞은 것은? [3점]

> If he _____ the lottery, he could open his own restaurant.

① win ② won ③ wins
④ will win ⑤ has win

14 다음 대화의 빈칸에 알맞은 말이 순서대로 짝 지어진 것은? [4점]

> A: Welcome to my new house.
> B: Thank you for inviting me. Please tell me _____ my coat.
> A: You can hang it on the wall.
> B: I see. Wow! Did you make this apple pie?
> A: Of course.
> B: It looks delicious. Please tell me _____ it.
> A: I'll write down my secret recipe.

① when to put – how to make
② when to put – what to make
③ where to put – how to make
④ where to put – what to make
⑤ what to put – how to make

서술형 **4**

15 다음 우리말과 같도록 괄호 안의 동사를 이용하여 문장을 완성하시오. [3점]

> 만약 내가 애완동물이 있다면, 나는 외롭지 않을 텐데.

→ _____, I woudn't be lonely.
(have)

16 다음 우리말을 영어로 바르게 옮긴 것은? [3점]

> 나는 여기서 무엇을 살지 결정하지 못하겠다.

① I can't decide what buy here.
② I can't decide what to buy here.
③ I can't decide what to buying here.
④ I can't decide what should I buy here.
⑤ I can't decide what to bought here.

[17-19] 다음 글을 읽고, 물음에 답하시오.

> My name is Andrea and I'm a violinist in the Recycled Orchestra. Why is it called the Recycled Orchestra? It's because our musical instruments (A)make / are made of objects from a landfill. That's why it's also known as the Landfill Harmonic Orchestra.
>
> Most of us in the orchestra (B)is / are from Cateura, a small town in Paraguay. There is a huge landfill in our town. Some people even say that Cateura (C)it / itself is a giant landfill. Many of us are poor. There weren't many hopes and dreams in our town. Everything began to change, however, when we met Favio Chávez.

서술형 **5**

17 윗글의 (A)~(C)에서 알맞은 것을 골라 쓰시오. [4점]

(A) _____ (B) _____ (C) _____

서술형 **6**

18 윗글의 내용과 일치하도록 다음 대화의 빈칸에 알맞은 말을 쓰시오. [각 3점]

> A: Andrea, which instrument do you play in the orchestra?
> B: (1) _____
> A: Where are you from?
> B: (2) _____

19 윗글을 읽고 바르게 이해하지 <u>못한</u> 사람은? [4점]

① 미희: Recycled Orchestra라는 이름은 악기를 만든 재료로 인해 지어진 거구나.
② 재준: 카테우라에는 커다란 쓰레기 매립지가 있구나.
③ 윤미: Recycled Orchestra는 Landfill Harmonic Orchestra의 영향을 많이 받았어.
④ 혜정: 재활용 오케스트라 단원들은 파라과이 출신이야.
⑤ 태석: 그들이 Favio 선생님을 만나기 전에는 희망과 꿈이 많지 않았구나.

[20-22] 다음 글을 읽고, 물음에 답하시오.

Favio was an environmental educator and a musician.

(A) But Favio didn't give up.

(B) There were only a few musical instruments in the whole town.

(C) He wanted to teach us music, but there was a big problem.

(D) We couldn't afford to buy new ones.

He said that we could make musical instruments with objects from the landfill. A talented man named Nicholas was able to put ⓐthis idea into practice. He made violins from oil drums. He turned water pipes into flutes.

20 자연스러운 글이 되도록 윗글의 (A)~(D)를 순서대로 배열한 것은? [4점]

① (A) – (B) – (C) – (D) ② (B) – (A) – (C) – (D)

③ (B) – (D) – (A) – (C) ④ (C) – (B) – (D) – (A)

⑤ (C) – (D) – (B) – (A)

서술형7

21 윗글의 밑줄 친 ⓐthis idea가 의미하는 것을 우리말로 쓰시오. [4점]

→ _____

22 윗글을 읽고 답할 수 없는 질문은? [4점]

① What is Favio's job?

② What did Favio want to teach?

③ What was a big problem?

④ How many musical instruments did they need?

⑤ What was Favio's idea about musical instruments?

[23-24] 다음 글을 읽고, 물음에 답하시오.

We had another problem. (①) No one knew how to play musical instruments. We didn't even know how to read music. (②) Step by step, we began to make some sounds on our instruments. (③) I still remember the first piece of music that we played. 그것은 매우 짧고 대부분은 음이 맞지 않았다. But it was the most beautiful music to us. (④) We felt a new hope in our hearts. From then on, we gathered to practice every day. (⑤)

23 윗글의 ①~⑤ 중 주어진 문장이 들어갈 알맞은 곳은? [4점]

Favio taught us with great patience.

①   ②   ③   ④   ⑤

서술형8

24 윗글의 밑줄 친 우리말을 [조건]에 맞게 영작하시오. [4점]

[조건] 1. very, mostly, tune을 반드시 포함할 것
        2. 9단어로 쓸 것

→ _____

서술형9

25 다음 글에서 어법상 틀린 부분을 모두 찾아 바르게 고쳐 쓰시오. [5점]

Dear Admiral Yi Sun-sin,

I'm Sumin. I really respect you because you never gave up in difficult situations. You saved the country and the people. It was amazed that you won the battle with only 12 ships. If I had a time machine, I would go to meet you! I'd like to ask you how make geobukseon. You're my hero. Thank you.

Sincerely yours,

Sumin

(1) _____

(2) _____

01 다음 영어 뜻풀이에 해당하는 단어가 쓰인 문장은? [3점]

> an act of traveling from one place to another

① The giant dinosaur was 6 meters tall.
② Ms. White started her long journey to Spain.
③ Dean can't afford to buy a new pair of sneakers.
④ We have a great interest in environmental issues.
⑤ If we recycle more, we will send less trash to landfills.

서술형 **1**

02 다음 대화의 빈칸에 알맞은 말을 [보기]에서 골라 쓰시오. [각 2점]

| [보기] | out of tune | one another |
| | roll down | get ready for |

(1) A: Let's _____ Sophie's birthday party.
　　B: Okay. I'll decorate the room and bake a cake.
(2) A: Paul is a terrible singer.
　　B: Right. His singing is always _____.

03 다음 중 밑줄 친 부분의 쓰임이 어색한 것은? [4점]

① My cheeks were wet with tears.
② Owls are mostly active at night.
③ This ball is so huge that I can hold it with one hand.
④ I expect this system will make our lives more convenient.
⑤ An old woman explained the way to the building, so we could find it without difficulty.

04 다음 대화의 밑줄 친 부분과 바꿔 쓸 수 있는 것은? [4점]

> A: What are you going to do first?
> B: I'm going to watch a parade at 10:30. Do you want to join me?
> A: I'd love to, but I can't. I'm going to make a mask.

① Yes, I'd love to.　　② I have no idea.
③ I'm sorry to hear that.　④ I'm sorry, but I can't.
⑤ You can say that again.

서술형 **2**

05 자연스러운 대화가 되도록 (A)~(E)를 순서대로 배열하시오. [4점]

> (A) I'd love to, but I can't. I have to do volunteer work.
> (B) Yes, but it's interesting, too.
> (C) Then can you help me with my math homework?
> (D) Minho, did you finish the math homework?
> (E) Not yet. Math is difficult.

(　　) – (　　) – (　　) – (　　) – (　　)

[06-08] 다음 대화를 읽고, 물음에 답하시오.

> A: ①Jiho, what are you reading?
> B: _____ ⓐ _____
> A: Oh, the man who was born without a right hand?
> B: ②That's right. He tried really hard and even won the MVP award.
> A: Yeah. His story was made into a movie. ③I'm going to watch it this Saturday.
> B: Really? What's the title?
> A: *Our Hero.* ④I'm really looking forward to watching it.
> B: ⑤Do you want to join me?
> A: Sure. See you on Saturday.

서술형 3

06 위 대화의 빈칸 ⓐ에 알맞은 말이 되도록 괄호 안의 단어들을 바르게 배열하여 문장을 쓰시오. [4점]

→ _____

(a book, named, about, I'm, Jim Abbott, reading, a baseball player)

07 위 대화의 밑줄 친 ①~⑤ 중 흐름상 어색한 것은? [4점]

①   ②   ③   ④   ⑤

서술형 4

08 위 대화의 내용과 일치하지 <u>않는</u> 것을 <u>모두</u> 골라 기호를 쓴 후, 일치하지 <u>않는</u> 부분을 바르게 고쳐 쓰시오. [4점]

> ⓐ Jim Abbott doesn't have a right hand.
> ⓑ Jim Abbott is a baseball player. He won the MVP award.
> ⓒ Jim Abbott's story was made into a movie.
> ⓓ *Our Hero* is a book about Jim Abbott.
> ⓔ They are going to watch a movie this Sunday.

(   ) _____ → _____

(   ) _____ → _____

09 다음 중 짝 지어진 대화가 자연스럽지 <u>않은</u> 것은? [4점]

① A: I'm going to play soccer. Let's play together.
   B: I'm afraid I can't. I have to visit my grandmother.
② A: You look upset today. What's going on?
   B: I'm so excited. I'm going to travel to Jeju-do.
③ A: I'm going to ride my bike. Do you want to join me?
   B: Yes, I'd love to.
④ A: Can you play the guitar while I sing in the contest?
   B: I'd love to, but I can't. I hurt my hand yesterday.
⑤ A: I'm going to play a water balloon game at the festival. I'm really looking forward to playing it.
   B: Sounds fun.

서술형 5

10 다음 문장을 어법상 바르게 고쳐 문장을 다시 쓰시오. [3점]

> If he know her phone number, he could call her.

→ _____

서술형 6

11 [보기]의 의문사와 괄호 안의 단어를 사용하여 대화를 완성하시오. [각 3점]

[보기]	when	where	what	how

(1) A: Excuse me. You can't park here. Look at the sign over there.
   B: Oh, I'm sorry. I didn't know that. Could you tell me _____? (park)
(2) A: There are lots of T-shirts in this store.
   B: Yeah. I'm not sure _____. (buy)

12 다음 문장에 대해 <u>잘못</u> 설명한 사람은? [4점]

> If I had time to relax, I could enjoy taking a walk.

① 동호: 현재 사실에 반대되는 일을 가정하고 있어.
② 수진: to relax는 time을 수식하는 형용사적 용법의 to부정사야.
③ 나래: enjoy는 목적어로 동명사를 취하기 때문에 taking의 쓰임은 맞아.
④ 진호: take a walk은 '산책하다'라는 의미를 나타내는 표현이야.
⑤ 아인: As I didn't have time to relax, I couldn't enjoy taking a walk.와 같은 의미를 나타내.

13 다음 중 어법상 <u>틀린</u> 문장의 개수는? [4점]

> ⓐ If I were a movie director, I would make a horror movie.
> ⓑ Please tell me when I should feed the dog.
> ⓒ She taught me how to solve the math problem.
> ⓓ If he had a magic lamp, he would make three wishes.

① 0개   ② 1개   ③ 2개   ④ 3개   ⑤ 4개

[14-15] 다음 글을 읽고, 물음에 답하시오.

Tears of joy are rolling down my cheeks. I'm so happy and ____①____. If I were a bird, I ____②____ fly. I look around. The other members in my orchestra are hugging one ____③____. Our concert has just finished and everyone is standing and ____④____ us a big hand. ____⑤____ of us ever expected that this day would come. It has been a long journey.

14 윗글의 빈칸 ①~⑤에 들어갈 말로 알맞지 <u>않은</u> 것은? [3점]

① thrilled   ② will   ③ another
④ giving   ⑤ None

15 윗글의 내용과 일치하는 것은? [4점]

① 오케스트라 단원 모두가 울고 있다.
② 글쓴이는 다른 단원들과 서로 껴안고 있다.
③ 청중들이 기립 박수를 치고 있다.
④ 글쓴이의 오케스트라는 곧 연주회를 시작할 것이다.
⑤ 오케스트라의 단원들은 이런 날이 올 거라고 예상했다.

[16-18] 다음 글을 읽고, 물음에 답하시오.

My name is Andrea and I'm a violinist in the Recycled Orchestra. Why is it called the Recycled Orchestra? _____ⓐ_____ That's why it's also known as the Landfill Harmonic Orchestra.

Most of us in the orchestra are from Cateura, a small town in Paraguay. There is a huge landfill in our town. Some people even say that Cateura itself is a giant landfill. Many of us are poor. There weren't many hopes and dreams in our town. Everything began to change, however, ⓑ<u>when</u> we met Favio Chávez.

서술형7

16 윗글의 빈칸 ⓐ에 들어갈 문장을 [조건]에 맞게 쓰시오. [4점]

[조건]
1. 괄호 안의 단어들 중 필요 없는 한 단어를 빼고 순서대로 배열할 것
2. 대소문자를 구별하고 문장 부호를 정확히 쓸 것

→ _____

_____

(of, it's, our, because, musical, instruments, a, landfill, made, objects, from, are, why)

17 윗글의 밑줄 친 ⓑwhen과 쓰임이 같은 것은? [4점]

① I'll tell you <u>when</u> to stop.
② <u>When</u> did you promise to meet her?
③ <u>When</u> will we know our test results?
④ I loved history <u>when</u> I was a middle school student.
⑤ The police officer asked me <u>when</u> I last saw her.

18 윗글의 내용과 일치하지 <u>않는</u> 것은? [4점]

① Andrea는 바이올린을 연주한다.
② 카테우라는 파라과이에 있다.
③ 카테우라에 큰 쓰레기 매립지가 만들어질 예정이다.
④ 오케스트라 단원들 중 많은 이들이 가난하다.
⑤ 카테우라에는 꿈과 희망이 많지 않았다.

[19-21] 다음 글을 읽고, 물음에 답하시오.

Favio was an environmental educator and a musician. ①He wanted to teach us music, but there was a big problem. ②There was only a few musical instruments in the whole town. ③We couldn't afford to buy new ones. But Favio didn't give up. He said that we could make musical instruments with objects from the landfill. ④A talented man named Nicholas was able to put this idea into practice. He made violins from oil drums. ⑤He turned water pipes into flutes.

19 윗글의 내용과 일치하는 것은? [4점]

① Favio was good at making musical instruments.

② Favio didn't give up teaching them music.

③ There were lots of musical instruments in the whole town.

④ Favio decided to buy new musical instruments.

⑤ Nicholas made violins from water pipes.

서술형 **8**

20 윗글의 밑줄 친 ①~⑤ 중 어법상 **틀린** 것을 골라 바르게 고쳐 쓴 후, **틀린** 이유를 쓰시오. [5점]

(　　) → _____

틀린 이유: _____

_____

_____

서술형 **9**

21 What was Favio's idea about musical instruments? [4점]

→ _____

_____

[22-24] 다음 글을 읽고, 물음에 답하시오.

　　We had another problem. ⓐ아무도 악기를 연주하는 법을 몰랐다. We didn't even know how to read music. ①Favio taught us with great patience. ②Patience is one of the most important qualities people need. ③Step by step, we began to make some sounds on our instruments. ④I still remember the first piece of music that we played. ⑤It was very short and mostly out of tune. But it was the most beautiful music to us. We felt a new hope in our hearts. From then on, we gathered to practice every day. One day, Favio told us some great news. We were going to have a concert, a real concert!

　　And here we are now in front of hundreds of people. They love our music. The world sends us trash, but we send back music!

서술형 **10**

22 윗글의 밑줄 친 ⓐ의 우리말을 [조건]에 맞게 영작하시오. [4점]

[조건]	1. no와 to를 반드시 포함할 것
	2. 8단어로 쓸 것
	3. 대소문자를 구별하고 문장 부호를 정확히 쓸 것

→ _____

23 윗글의 밑줄 친 ①~⑤ 중 글의 흐름과 관계없는 것은? [4점]

①　　　②　　　③　　　④　　　⑤

24 다음 중 윗글에 나오는 단어의 영어 뜻풀이를 **모두** 고르면? [4점]

① mainly, generally

② an area where waste is buried under the ground

③ a person whose job is to teach or educate people

④ an act of traveling from one place to another

⑤ the ability to stay calm and accept a delay or suffering without complaining

25 다음 글의 주제로 알맞은 것은? [4점]

　　This is a bottle shaker. To make it, you need a bottle and buttons. Clean the bottle and put the buttons in the bottle. Close the bottle and decorate it. You can also put different things like rice or sand in it. Different items make different sounds. Listen to my group's bottle shaker.

① 병 세이커 만드는 방법

② 병을 이용한 다양한 예술 작품

③ 병 세이커를 이용한 공연 후기

④ 병을 재활용하는 다양한 방법

⑤ 재료에 따라 병 세이커의 소리가 다른 이유

모의고사

01 다음 단어의 영어 뜻풀이에 해당하지 <u>않는</u> 것은? [3점]

| roll | drone | thrilled | landfill |

① very excited and happy
② either side of the face below the eyes
③ to move along a surface by turning over and over
④ an aircraft without a pilot that is controlled by someone on the ground
⑤ an area where waste is buried under the ground

02 다음 빈칸에 쓰이지 <u>않는</u> 단어는? [3점]

ⓐ Did Amy _____ this note on the bulletin board?
ⓑ I was _____ when a ghost appeared on the screen.
ⓒ In the end I lost my _____ and shouted at David.
ⓓ The players started to _____ to hear the coach's plan.

① stick   ② gather   ③ talented
④ scared   ⑤ patience

03 다음 중 밑줄 친 부분의 쓰임이 어색한 것은? [3점]

① <u>Step by step</u>, the man learned how to live in the forest.
② Dr. Smith didn't <u>give up</u> hope and tried to help the children.
③ We can communicate with <u>one another</u> through social media now.
④ <u>Take care of</u> the eggs from the boiling water after 10 minutes.
⑤ I had a car accident last month and have suffered neck pain <u>from then on</u>.

04 다음 빈칸에 들어갈 말로 알맞은 것은? [3점]

This is a very difficult _____ of music to play.

① loaf   ② slice   ③ piece
④ sheet   ⑤ bundle

[05-06] 다음 대화를 읽고, 물음에 답하시오.

A: Alex, I'm going to take part in a singing contest next Monday.
B: That's great, Sumin!
A: You know how to play the guitar, right?
B: (1) _____
A: Great. Can you play the guitar while I sing in the contest?
B: (2) _____ I hurt my hand in gym class yesterday.
A: Oh! (3) _____
B: Thanks. But I'll be there to cheer for you.

서술형 1

05 위 대화의 빈칸에 알맞은 말을 [보기]에서 골라 쓰시오. [3점]

[보기]
• Yes, I'd love to.
• I'd love to, but I can't.
• I'm sorry to hear that.
• I'm happy to hear that.
• No, I have never played the guitar.
• Yes, I've played the guitar for 3 years.
• I heard you're good at playing the guitar.

(1) _____
(2) _____
(3) _____

06 위 대화의 내용과 일치하는 문장의 개수는? [4점]

ⓐ Sumin is going to sing in the contest next Monday.
ⓑ Alex doesn't know how to play the guitar.
ⓒ Sumin is looking for someone to play the guitar for her.
ⓓ Alex is going to participate in the contest with Sumin.
ⓔ Alex hurt his leg in gym class yesterday.

① 1개   ② 2개   ③ 3개   ④ 4개   ⑤ 5개

서술형 2

07 다음 대화의 내용과 일치하도록 아래 글의 빈칸에 알맞은 말을 쓰시오. [4점]

> A: Hey, Bora. Welcome to our rock band.
> B: Thanks, Tom. I'm looking forward to playing in a concert with you.
> A: We're excited to have a new guitar player.
> B: Great. See you on Friday.

▼

> Bora is a _____ in Tom's rock band. She _____ with the band members.

[08-10] 다음 대화를 읽고, 물음에 답하시오.

> Linda: Hi, Tony! _____ⓐ_____ are you going to do this weekend?
> Tony: I'm going to watch the musical, *Billy Elliot*.
> Linda: *Billy Elliot*? _____ⓑ_____ is it about?
> Tony: It's about a boy _____ⓒ_____ became a famous dancer. I'm looking forward to watching it.
> Linda: Sounds interesting. _____ⓓ_____ is the main actor?
> Tony: Jason Kim. He's a great dancer.
> Linda: He's my favorite actor. I watched his musical last year.
> Tony: Oh, really? Do you want to join me?
> Linda: I'd love to, but I can't. I have volunteer work this weekend.
> Tony: Okay. Maybe next time!

서술형 3

08 위 대화의 빈칸 ⓐ~ⓓ에 알맞은 말을 각각 한 단어로 쓰시오. [각 2점]

ⓐ _____   ⓑ _____

ⓒ _____   ⓓ _____

09 위 대화의 Jason Kim에 대해 알 수 없는 것을 모두 고르면? [4점]

① 뮤지컬 "빌리 엘리어트"의 주연 배우이다.
② 훌륭한 무용수이다.
③ Tony가 가장 좋아하는 배우이다.
④ Linda가 작년에 그의 뮤지컬을 봤다.
⑤ 어렸을 때부터 배우로 활동했다.

서술형 4

10 다음 질문에 대한 답을 완전한 영어 문장으로 쓰시오. [각 2점]

(1) What is Tony going to do this weekend?
→ _____

(2) Why can't Linda join Tony?
→ _____

서술형 5

11 다음 표를 보고, [조건]에 맞게 대화를 완성하시오. [각 2점]

	Time	What to do
Olivia	11:30	watch a parade
Leo	11:30	make a mask

> [조건]   1. 표의 내용과 일치하도록 쓸 것
> 2. (2)는 기대를 나타내는 표현을 사용할 것

> Leo: What are you going to do at 11:30 at the festival?
> Olivia: (1) _____ at that time. I'm really (2) _____ .
> Leo: Sounds fun.
> Olivia: Do you want to join me?
> Leo: (3) _____ I'm going to (4) _____ at that time.

12 다음 밑줄 친 부분을 어법상 바르게 고친 것 중 틀린 것은? [3점]

> • She explained ①how use the app.
> • If I ②am not tired, I would go to the movies.
> • If it is sunny tomorrow, we ③will go on a field trip.
> • Let me know ④where to turning left.
> • If Brian ⑤has more money, he could help children in hospital.

① how to use   ② were not
③ 고칠 필요 없음   ④ where to turn
⑤ 고칠 필요 없음

13 다음 우리말을 영작할 때, 네 번째로 오는 단어는? [3점]

> 너는 이 세탁기를 사용하는 방법을 알고 있니?

① know ② this ③ to
④ use ⑤ how

[14-15] 다음 글을 읽고, 물음에 답하시오.

> Tears of joy are rolling down my cheeks. ⓐI'm so happy and thrilling. ⓑIf I were a bird, I would fly. I look around. ⓒThe other members in my orchestra is hugging one another. Our concert has just finished and everyone is standing and giving us a big hand. None of us ever expected that this day would come. ⓓIt has been a long journey.

14 윗글의 밑줄 친 ⓐ~ⓓ 중 어법상 틀린 문장끼리 짝 지어진 것은? [4점]

① ⓐ, ⓑ ② ⓐ, ⓒ ③ ⓐ, ⓒ, ⓓ
④ ⓑ, ⓒ, ⓓ ⑤ ⓑ, ⓓ

15 윗글의 내용과 일치하는 것은? [4점]

① The writer felt sad and cried.
② The concert disappointed the audience.
③ The writer is one of the members of the orchestra.
④ Most of the audience left their seats right away.
⑤ The writer expected this situation.

[16-17] 다음 글을 읽고, 물음에 답하시오.

> My name is Andrea and I'm a violinist in the Recycled Orchestra. Why is it called the Recycled Orchestra? It's because our musical instruments are made of objects from a landfill. That's why it's also known as the Landfill Harmonic Orchestra.
>
> Most of us in the orchestra are from Cateura, a small town in Paraguay. There is a huge landfill in our town. Some people even say that Cateura ⓐitself is a giant landfill. Many of us are poor. There weren't many hopes and dreams in our town. Everything began to change, however, when we met Favio Chávez.

16 윗글의 밑줄 친 ⓐitself와 쓰임이 같은 것은? [3점]

① She was upset at herself.
② Eric can fix his car himself.
③ I looked at myself in the mirror.
④ Cats clean themselves to remove dirt.
⑤ The man introduced himself to the guests.

서술형 6

17 윗글을 읽고 답할 수 있는 질문을 모두 골라 기호를 쓴 후, 완전한 영어 문장으로 답하시오. [4점]

> ⓐ Which instrument does Andrea play in the orchestra?
> ⓑ What are their musical instruments made of?
> ⓒ Why are most people in Cateura poor?
> ⓓ When did Andrea meet Favio Chávez for the first time?

( ) → _____

( ) → _____

[18-20] 다음 글을 읽고, 물음에 답하시오.

> ①Favio was an environmental educator and a musician. ②He wanted to teach us music, but there was a big problem. ③There were only a few musical instruments in the whole town. We couldn't afford to buy new ones. But Favio didn't give up. ④He said that we could make musical instruments with objects from the landfill. A talented man named Nicholas was able to put this idea into practice. ⑤He made violins from oil drums. He turned water pipes into flutes.

18 윗글의 밑줄 친 ①~⑤에 대한 설명으로 알맞지 <u>않은</u> 것은? [4점]

① Favio는 교육자이자 음악가였다.
② teach us music은 teach music us로 바꿔 쓸 수 있다.
③ a few는 셀 수 있는 명사를 수식하는 수량형용사이다.
④ that은 said의 목적절을 이끄는 접속사로 생략할 수 있다.
⑤ He는 Nicolas를 가리키는데, 그는 재주가 뛰어났다.

서술형7

19 How did Nicholas put Favio's idea into practice? [4점]

→ _____

_____

서술형8

20 다음 [조건]에 맞게 문장을 자유롭게 쓰시오. [4점]

[조건]	1. to be able to pay for something을 뜻하는 단어를 윗글에서 찾을 것
	2. 찾은 단어를 사용해 자유롭게 문장을 쓸 것
	3. 주어와 동사를 포함한 완전한 문장으로 쓸 것

→ _____

[21-22] 다음 글을 읽고, 물음에 답하시오.

ⓐWe had another problem. No one knew how to play musical instruments. ⓑWe didn't even know how to read music. Favio taught us with great patience. (①) Step by step, we began to make some sounds on our instruments. (②) ⓒI still remember the first piece of music what we played. It was very short and mostly out of tune. (③) We felt a new hope in our hearts. ⓓFrom then on, we gathered to practice every day. (④) ⓔOne day, Favio told us some great news. We were going to have a concert, a real concert! (⑤)

21 윗글의 밑줄 친 ⓐ~ⓔ 중 어법상 틀린 것은? [4점]

① ⓐ　　② ⓑ　　③ ⓒ　　④ ⓓ　　⑤ ⓔ

22 윗글의 ①~⑤ 중 주어진 문장이 들어갈 알맞은 곳은? [4점]

But it was the most beautiful music to us.

①　　②　　③　　④　　⑤

[23-24] 다음 대화를 읽고, 물음에 답하시오.

Reporter: Congratulations! How do you feel now?

Andrea: I feel thrilled. We just performed our first concert.

Reporter: What is the orchestra called the Recycled Orchestra?

Andrea: That's because our musical instruments are made of objects from a landfill.

Reporter: That's amazing.

Andrea: Yeah. None of us knew how to play musical instruments, but Favio taught us with great patience.

Reporter: That is a wonderful story.

서술형9

23 위 대화에서 흐름상 어색한 문장을 찾아 바르게 고쳐 쓰시오. [4점]

→ _____

24 위 대화의 내용을 바르게 이해하지 못한 사람은? [4점]

① **Mingi**: Andrea is having a interview.

② **Nari**: Andrea is a member of the Recycled Orchestra.

③ **Jinsu**: The musical instruments of the Recycled Orchestra are made of objects from a landfill.

④ **Jimin**: Only Andrea in the Recycled Orchestra knew how to play musical instruments at first.

⑤ **Yuna**: Favio taught the members of the Recycled Orchestra with great patience.

서술형10

25 자신의 경우라고 가정하여 다음 문장을 자유롭게 완성하시오. [각 2점]

(1) If I had a million dollars, _____

_____ .

(2) If I were an inventor, _____

_____ .

● 틀린 문항을 표시해 보세요.

〈제1회〉대표 기출로 내신 적중 모의고사　　총점 _____ / 100

문항	영역	문항	영역	문항	영역
01	p.10(W)	10	p.14(L&S)	19	pp.30-31(R)
02	p.10(W)	11	p.14(L&S)	20	pp.30-31(R)
03	p.8(W)	12	p.23(G)	21	pp.30-31(R)
04	p.8(W)	13	p.22(G)	22	pp.30-31(R)
05	p.14(L&S)	14	p.23(G)	23	pp.30-31(R)
06	p.13(L&S)	15	pp.22-23(G)	24	pp.30-31(R)
07	p.15(L&S)	16	p.23(G)	25	pp.30-31(R)
08	p.14(L&S)	17	pp.30-31(R)		
09	p.14(L&S)	18	pp.30-31(R)		

〈제2회〉대표 기출로 내신 적중 모의고사　　총점 _____ / 100

문항	영역	문항	영역	문항	영역
01	p.10(W)	10	p.15(L&S)	19	pp.30-31(R)
02	p.10(W)	11	p.23(G)	20	pp.30-31(R)
03	p.8(W)	12	pp.22-23(G)	21	pp.30-31(R)
04	p.14(L&S)	13	p.22(G)	22	pp.30-31(R)
05	p.15(L&S)	14	p.23(G)	23	pp.30-31(R)
06	p.15(L&S)	15	p.22(G)	24	pp.30-31(R)
07	p.15(L&S)	16	p.23(G)	25	p.44(M)
08	p.15(L&S)	17	pp.30-31(R)		
09	p.15(L&S)	18	pp.30-31(R)		

〈제3회〉대표 기출로 내신 적중 모의고사　　총점 _____ / 100

문항	영역	문항	영역	문항	영역
01	p.10(W)	10	p.22(G)	19	pp.30-31(R)
02	p.8(W)	11	p.23(G)	20	pp.30-31(R)
03	p.8(W)	12	p.22(G)	21	pp.30-31(R)
04	p.13(L&S)	13	pp.22-23(G)	22	pp.30-31(R)
05	p.14(L&S)	14	pp.30-31(R)	23	pp.30-31(R)
06	p.14(L&S)	15	pp.30-31(R)	24	pp.30-31(R)
07	p.14(L&S)	16	pp.30-31(R)	25	p.44(M)
08	p.14(L&S)	17	pp.30-31(R)		
09	p.13(L&S)	18	pp.30-31(R)		

〈제4회〉고난도로 내신 적중 모의고사　　총점 _____ / 100

문항	영역	문항	영역	문항	영역
01	p.10(W)	10	p.15(L&S)	19	pp.30-31(R)
02	p.8(W)	11	p.13(L&S)	20	pp.30-31(R)
03	p.8(W)	12	pp.22-23(G)	21	pp.30-31(R)
04	p.8(W)	13	p.23(G)	22	pp.30-31(R)
05	p.15(L&S)	14	pp.30-31(R)	23	p.44(M)
06	p.15(L&S)	15	pp.30-31(R)	24	p.44(M)
07	p.14(L&S)	16	pp.30-31(R)	25	p.22(G)
08	p.15(L&S)	17	pp.30-31(R)		
09	p.15(L&S)	18	pp.30-31(R)		

● 부족한 영역을 점검해 보고 어떻게 더 학습할지 학습 계획을 적어 보세요.

오답 공략
부족한 영역
학습 계획

오답 공략
부족한 영역
학습 계획

오답 공략
부족한 영역
학습 계획

오답 공략
부족한 영역
학습 계획

Lesson 6

Make the World Beautiful

주요 학습 내용	의사소통 기능	감사하기
		A: Thank you for lending me the book. (나에게 책을 빌려줘서 고마워.) B: You're welcome. (천만에.)
		금지하기
		A: You're not allowed to feed the birds here. (여기서 새들에게 먹이를 주면 안 됩니다.) B: I'm sorry. I didn't know that. (죄송합니다. 몰랐어요.)
	언어 형식	so that
		The architect took the curved lines from nature **so that** city people could enjoy them. (그 건축가는 도시 사람들이 즐길 수 있도록 자연에서 곡선을 가져왔다.)
		enough to +동사원형
		It is round and delicate, yet strong **enough to protect** its contents. (그것은 둥글고 부서지기 쉽지만, 내용물을 보호할 만큼 충분히 튼튼하다.)

Words

만점 노트

☆ 자주 출제되는 어휘

* 완벽히 외운 단어는 □ 안에 √표 해 봅시다.

Listen & Speak

□□ add	동 추가하다	
□□ allow☆	동 허락하다, 허용하다 (= permit)	
□□ artwork☆	명 미술품, 예술품	
□□ basic	형 기본적인	
□□ book	동 예약하다, 예매하다	
□□ exhibit	동 전시하다	
□□ flash	명 (카메라) 플래시	
□□ folk village	민속 마을, 민속촌	
□□ lend	동 빌려주다 (↔ borrow)	
□□ on sale	판매 중인	
□□ pick	동 (꽃을) 꺾다	

□□ popular	형 인기 있는
□□ remind	동 상기시키다, 생각나게 하다
□□ show ~ around	~에게 구경시켜 주다
□□ sign	명 표지판
□□ since then	그때부터
□□ total	형 총, 전체의
□□ touch	동 만지다
□□ trip	명 여행, 이동
□□ umbrella stand	우산꽂이
□□ walk around	돌아다니다
□□ wet	형 젖은

Reading

□□ actually	부 실제로, 정말로 (= really)
□□ architect☆	명 건축가, 설계자
□□ beauty	명 아름다움
□□ capture☆	동 담아내다, 표현하다, 포착하다
□□ column	명 기둥
□□ come from	~에서 비롯되다(나오다)
□□ contents	명 내용물, 안에 든 것
□□ curved	형 곡선 모양의, 굽은
□□ delicate☆	형 부서지기 쉬운, 섬세한
□□ exist☆	동 존재하다
□□ example	명 예시, 사례, 보기
□□ expression	명 표현
□□ imagination☆	명 상상력
□□ imitate☆	동 모방하다 (= copy)

□□ indoors	부 실내로, 실내에 (↔ outdoors)
□□ inspiration☆	명 영감
□□ inspire☆	동 영감을 주다
□□ nature☆	명 자연
□□ obvious☆	형 분명한, 명백한 (= clear)
□□ peel	명 (과일·채소의) 껍질
□□ pleasing	형 즐거운, 기분 좋은
□□ roof	명 지붕
□□ sailing boat	돛단배, 범선
□□ shine	동 비추다 (shine – shone – shone)
□□ spaceship	명 우주선
□□ thanks to☆	~ 덕분에
□□ tourist attraction	관광 명소
□□ wave	명 파도, 물결

Language Use

□□ amusement park	놀이공원
□□ foreigner	명 외국인
□□ go through	통과하다
□□ hole	명 구멍
□□ lift	동 들어 올리다

□□ loudly	부 큰 소리로
□□ pass	동 (시험에) 통과하다, 합격하다
□□ ride	명 놀이 기구
□□ shelf	명 선반
□□ stay healthy	건강을 유지하다

Think and Write · Project

□□ garden	명 정원
□□ gym	명 체육관

□□ playground	명 운동장
□□ story	명 (건물의) 층

Words

연습 문제

Answers p. 20

A 다음 단어의 우리말 뜻을 쓰시오.

01 exist _____

02 allow _____

03 architect _____

04 inspire _____

05 basic _____

06 curved _____

07 shine _____

08 delicate _____

09 indoors _____

10 foreigner _____

11 obvious _____

12 example _____

13 capture _____

14 sign _____

15 roof _____

16 artwork _____

17 wave _____

18 pleasing _____

19 remind _____

20 add _____

B 다음 우리말에 해당하는 영어 단어를 쓰시오.

21 예약하다, 예매하다 _____

22 영감 _____

23 전시하다 _____

24 아름다움 _____

25 표현 _____

26 총, 전체의 _____

27 젖은 _____

28 빌려주다 _____

29 (꽃을) 꺾다 _____

30 기둥 _____

31 자연 _____

32 만지다 _____

33 선반 _____

34 우주선 _____

35 상상력 _____

36 모방하다 _____

37 내용물, 안에 든 것 _____

38 (과일·채소의) 껍질 _____

39 들어 올리다 _____

40 (건물의) 층 _____

C 다음 영어 표현의 우리말 뜻을 쓰시오.

01 go through _____

02 on sale _____

03 show ~ around _____

04 since then _____

05 tourist attraction _____

06 stay healthy _____

07 thanks to _____

08 folk village _____

Words Plus
만점 노트

영어 뜻풀이

☐☐	**actually**	실제로, 정말로	used to refer to what is true or real
☐☐	**allow**	허락하다, 허용하다	to let somebody or something do something
☐☐	**architect**	건축가, 설계자	a person who designs buildings
☐☐	**book**	예약하다, 예매하다	to make a reservation for a future time
☐☐	**capture**	담아내다, 표현하다, 포착하다	to represent or describe something very accurately using words or images
☐☐	**column**	기둥	a long post made of steel, stone, etc., used to support a building
☐☐	**contents**	내용물, 안에 든 것	the things that are inside something
☐☐	**curved**	곡선 모양의, 굽은	having the form of a curve
☐☐	**delicate**	부서지기 쉬운, 섬세한	easily broken or damaged
☐☐	**exhibit**	전시하다	to show something in a public place so that people can see it
☐☐	**exist**	존재하다	to be, or to be real
☐☐	**imagination**	상상력	the ability to form pictures or ideas in your mind
☐☐	**imitate**	모방하다	to copy somebody or something
☐☐	**indoors**	실내로, 실내에	inside or into a building
☐☐	**inspiration**	영감	something that gives you ideas about what to do or create
☐☐	**obvious**	분명한, 명백한	easy to see or understand
☐☐	**peel**	(과일·채소의) 껍질	the skin of a fruit
☐☐	**pleasing**	즐거운, 기분 좋은	giving pleasure, enjoyment, or satisfaction
☐☐	**spaceship**	우주선	a vehicle that travels in space, carrying people
☐☐	**wave**	파도, 물결	a raised line of water that moves across the surface of the sea

단어의 의미 관계

- **유의어**
  actually = really (실제로, 정말로)
  obvious = clear (분명한, 명백한)
  allow = permit (허락하다, 허용하다)
  imitate = copy (모방하다)

- **반의어**
  indoors (실내로, 실내에) ↔ outdoors (야외로, 야외에)
  lend (빌려주다) ↔ borrow (빌리다)

- **동사 - 명사**
  imitate (모방하다) – imitation (모조품, 모방)
  attract (마음을 끌다) – attraction (명소, 매력)
  express (표현하다) – expression (표현)
  inspire (영감을 주다) – inspiration (영감)
  imagine (상상하다) – imagination (상상, 상상력)

다의어

- **book** 1. 통 예약하다, 예매하다 2. 명 책
  1. **Book** the concert ticket at least two weeks ago.
     적어도 2주 전에 그 공연 표를 예매해라.
  2. The shelves in his office are filled with **books**.
     그의 사무실 책장은 책으로 가득 차 있다.

- **sign** 1. 명 표지판 2. 통 서명하다
  1. The **sign** in the store window says "OPEN."
     가게 창문의 표지판에 "열림"이라고 쓰여 있다.
  2. **Sign** your name here. 여기에 이름을 서명하세요.

- **pass** 1. 통 (시험에) 통과하다, 합격하다
  2. 통 지나가다, 통과하다 3. 통 건네주다
  1. Jenny **passed** the final exam easily.
     Jenny는 기말고사를 쉽게 통과했다.
  2. Only two trains **pass** the small town.
     오직 두 대의 기차만이 그 소도시를 지나간다.
  3. **Pass** me the salt, please. 소금 좀 건네주세요.

Words Plus
연습 문제

A 다음 뜻풀이에 알맞은 말을 [보기]에서 골라 쓴 후, 우리말 뜻을 쓰시오.

[보기]	exist	exhibit	spaceship	delicate	imagination	allow	architect	inspiration

1 _____ : easily broken or damaged : _____

2 _____ : to be, or to be real : _____

3 _____ : the ability to form pictures or ideas in your mind : _____

4 _____ : to show something in a public place so that people can see it : _____

5 _____ : something that gives you ideas about what to do or create : _____

6 _____ : to let somebody or something do something : _____

7 _____ : a person who designs buildings : _____

8 _____ : a vehicle that travels in space, carrying people : _____

B 다음 짝 지어진 두 단어의 관계가 같도록 빈칸에 알맞은 말을 쓰시오.

1 actually : really = clear : _____

2 borrow : lend = outdoors : _____

3 allow : permit = copy : _____

4 attract : attraction = express : _____

5 imagination : imagine = inspiration : _____

C 다음 빈칸에 알맞은 말을 [보기]에서 골라 쓰시오.

[보기]	contents	obvious	capture	imitate	remind

1 It is _____ that the boy is lying.

2 May I check the _____ of your bag, please?

3 Please _____ me to buy some groceries after work.

4 Thomas can _____ his grandfather's accent perfectly.

5 The artist couldn't _____ the beauty of the mountain in his painting.

D 다음 우리말과 같도록 빈칸에 알맞은 말을 쓰시오.

1 그 상자는 문을 통과하기엔 너무 컸다. → The box was too big to _____ _____ the door.

2 나는 건강을 유지하기 위해 매일 아침 공원에서 조깅한다. → I jog in the park every morning to _____ _____ .

3 새 스마트폰 모델은 현재 A 구역에서 판매 중입니다.

　→ The new smartphone model is _____ _____ in section A now.

4 레인 부츠 덕분에, 나는 거센 빗속을 돌아다닐 수 있었다.

　→ _____ _____ the rain boots, I could walk around in the heavy rain.

5 가능한 한 빨리 나를 방문해라, 그러면 내가 너를 여기저기 구경시켜 줄게.

　→ Visit me as soon as possible, and I'll _____ you _____ .

실전 TEST

01 다음 중 단어의 품사가 나머지와 <u>다른</u> 하나는?

① indoors   ② architect

③ expression   ④ movement

⑤ attraction

02 다음 영어 뜻풀이가 설명하는 단어로 알맞은 것은?

> to make a reservation for a future time

① allow   ② book   ③ capture

④ exist   ⑤ exhibit

03 다음 빈칸에 공통으로 들어갈 알맞은 단어를 쓰시오.

- There was a "CLOSED" _____ on the door of the bakery.
- Don't forget to _____ your name on the document.

→ _____

04 다음 중 밑줄 친 부분의 우리말 뜻이 알맞지 <u>않은</u> 것은?

① Alice likes to <u>walk around</u> in the rain. (돌아다니다)

② Could you <u>show</u> me <u>around</u> your new office?
(~에게 자랑하다)

③ Tickets for the family musical are <u>on sale</u> from May 3. (판매 중인)

④ <u>Thanks to</u> a lot of hard work, the meeting was successful. (~ 덕분에)

⑤ Buckingham Palace is a popular <u>tourist attraction</u> in London. (관광 명소)

05 다음 우리말과 같도록 할 때 빈칸에 들어갈 말로 알맞은 것은?

> 그 피아니스트는 베토벤의 스타일을 모방하려 했다.
> → The pianist tried to _____ the style of Beethoven.

① touch   ② shine   ③ imitate

④ lend   ⑤ attract

06 다음 빈칸에 들어갈 단어로 알맞지 <u>않은</u> 것은?

- Helen will forget to call the doctor if you don't ___①___ her.
- The gallery is going to ___②___ some of Picasso's paintings from next month.
- The wall painting my group drew is very ___③___ to the eye.
- Be careful not to slip on a banana ___④___.
- Ben emptied the ___⑤___ of his bag onto the desk.

① exist   ② exhibit   ③ pleasing

④ peel   ⑤ contents

07 다음 빈칸에 알맞은 말이 순서대로 짝 지어진 것은?

- I can't _____ a world without air and water.
- The artist got her _____ from nature.

① attract – imagine

② attract – attraction

③ imagine – inspire

④ imagine – inspiration

⑤ imitation – imagination

Listen & Speak
핵심 노트

1 감사하기

A: **Thank you for** lending me the book. 　　　　나에게 책을 빌려줘서 고마워.

B: You're welcome. 　　　　천만에.

Thank you for ~.는 '~해 주셔서 감사합니다.'라는 뜻으로 상대방에게 고마움을 표현할 때 사용하는 표현이다. 전치사 for 뒤에는 감사하는 이유가 오며, 보통 명사(구)나 동명사(구)의 형태를 쓴다. 감사에 답할 때는 My pleasure. / It was my pleasure. / You're welcome. 등으로 말할 수 있다.

e.g. • A: **Thank you for** inviting me to your birthday party.
　　　네 생일 파티에 나를 초대해 줘서 고마워.

　　Thank you for your kind invitation. 친절하게 초대해 줘서 고마워.

　　I appreciate your help. 도와주셔서 감사합니다.

　　I'm very grateful (to you) **for** your help.
　　당신의 도움에 정말 감사드립니다.

　　I can't thank you enough. 대단히 고맙습니다.

• B: **My pleasure.** 천만에(요).

　　It was my pleasure.

　　You're welcome.

　　Don't mention it.

시험 포인트 **point**

고마움을 표현하고 그에 답하는 대화가 자연스러운지 파악하는 문제가 자주 출제돼요. 고마움을 나타내는 다양한 표현과 답변을 모두 익혀 두세요.

2 금지하기

A: **You're not allowed to** feed the birds here. 　　여기서 새들에게 먹이를 주면 안 됩니다.

B: I'm sorry. I didn't know that. 　　죄송합니다. 몰랐어요.

You're not allowed to ~.는 '~하는 게 허용되지 않는다.'라는 뜻으로, 상대방에게 어떤 행동을 하지 말라고 금지하는 표현이다. 공공장소에서의 금지 사항을 말할 때 자주 쓰인다.

e.g. • **You're not allowed to** fish here. 여기서 낚시를 하면 안 됩니다.

　　Don't fish here. 여기서 낚시하지 마세요.

　　You shouldn't fish here. 여기서 낚시하지 말아야 해요.

　　You'd better not fish here. 여기서 낚시하지 않는 것이 좋아요.

시험 포인트 **point**

금지하는 표지판이 주어지고 이 상황에서 할 수 있는 알맞은 말이 무엇인지 고르는 문제가 자주 출제되므로 공공장소에서 자주 쓰이는 금지 표지판과 금지하는 표현을 반드시 익혀 두세요.

L&S

Listen & Speak

만점 노트

대화문 해석 보기 >> 90~91쪽

주요 표현
구문 해설

Listen and Speak 1-A

교과서 104쪽

B: Hi, Lisa. ❶ Thank you for ❷ inviting me to your birthday party.

G: ❸ My pleasure. ❹ I'm glad you could come.

B: These flowers are for you. Happy birthday!

G: They are beautiful! Thank you.

Q1. Whose birthday is it?

❶ '~해 줘서 고마워.'라는 뜻으로, 고마움을 나타내는 표현
❷ invite *A* to *B*: A를 B에 초대하다
❸ '천만에.'라는 뜻으로 고마움을 표현하는 말에 답할 때 쓰는 표현
❹ 기쁨을 나타내는 표현

Listen and Speak 1-B

교과서 104쪽

B: Sumin, my train ❶ is leaving ❷ in five minutes.

G: ❸ I hope you enjoyed your trip, Daniel.

B: Of course, I did.

G: ❹ Which place did you like most in my town?

B: ❺ I liked the folk village most.

G: Yeah, it's the most popular place here.

B: I really liked walking around in hanbok. I looked really ❻ cool.

G: I'm glad to hear that.

B: ❼ Thank you for ❽ showing me around.

G: ❾ It was my pleasure. Have a safe trip.

Q2. When is Daniel's train leaving?
Q3. Daniel은 어느 장소가 가장 좋았나요?

❶ 「be동사+동사원형-ing」로 이루어진 현재 진행 시제가 이미 정해져 있는 미래를 표현할 수 있음
❷ ~ 후에
❸ '나는 네가 ~하기를 바란다'라는 의미
❹ Which ~ did you like most?: '너는 어느 ~이 가장 좋았니?'라는 뜻으로, 상대방의 선호를 묻는 표현
❺ 선호를 묻는 질문에 답하는 표현
❻ ⑱ 멋진, 근사한
❼ 고마움을 나타내는 표현
❽ show ~ around: ~에게 구경시켜 주다
❾ 고마움을 표현하는 말에 답할 때 쓰는 표현
　(= My pleasure.)

Listen and Speak 1-C

교과서 104쪽

A: How was the book?

B: ❶ It was great. Thank you for ❷ lending me the book.

A: ❸ You're welcome. It was my pleasure.

Q4. B는 무엇을 고마워하나요?

❶ = the book
❷ lend+간접목적어(me)+직접목적어(the book): ~에게 …을 빌려주다
❸ 고마움을 표현하는 말에 답할 때 쓰는 표현

Listen and Speak 2-A

교과서 105쪽

M: Excuse me. ❶ You're not allowed to bring your umbrella inside.

G: Oh, where ❷ should I put ❸ it?

M: ❹ There is an umbrella stand outside.

G: Okay. I'll put it there. Thank you.

Q5. 소녀는 우산을 어디에 두어야 하나요?

❶ '~하는 게 허용되지 않는다.'라는 뜻으로, 하지 말아야 할 행동을 말할 때 쓰는 표현
❷ 의무를 나타내는 조동사
❸ = my umbrella
❹ There is+단수 명사(구) ~.: ~이 있다.

Listen and Speak 2-B

B: The tickets for the World Music Concert ❶ are on sale now.

G: Really? ❷ Let's ❸ book the tickets online ❹ right away.

B: Okay. Let's see.... There are still tickets left for November 5th.

G: Sounds good. Let's get two student tickets.

B: Oh, ❺ do you mind if I bring my little brother?

G: ❻ Not at all. But it says that ❼ you are not allowed to bring ❽ children under 8.

B: No problem. He's 10.

G: Okay, I'll add one child ticket. The total price is 25 dollars.

B: Great.

G: ❾ I can't wait to see the concert!

Q6. What concert are they going to go?

Q7. How many tickets did they book?

❶ be on sale: 판매 중이다

❷ '~하자'라는 뜻으로, 상대방에게 제안할 때 쓰는 표현

❸ ⑧ 예약하다, 예매하다

❹ 즉시, 곧바로

❺ '제가 ~해도 될까요?'라는 뜻으로, 상대방에게 허락을 구할 때 쓰는 표현

❻ Do you mind if I ~?로 물었을 경우, 허락할 때 쓸 수 있는 표현

❼ 허용되지 않는 행동을 말할 때 쓰는 표현

❽ 8세 미만의 어린이들

❾ I can't wait to+동사원형 ~: '나는 ~하는 것이 정말 기대 돼.'라는 뜻으로, 기대를 나타내는 표현

Listen and Speak 2-C

A: Excuse me. You're not allowed to ❶ feed the birds here.

B: I'm sorry. I didn't know that.

A: Please check the ❷ sign over there.

B: Okay. Thank you.

Q8. B는 무엇을 하고 있었나요?

❶ ⑧ 먹이를 주다

❷ ⑧ 표지판

Real Life Talk > Watch a Video

W: Hello, students! ❶ Thank you for visiting our art museum. This museum opened in 1995. ❷ Since then, it ❸ has exhibited many famous artworks. Today, you will see some famous artworks from the art books. ❹ Before we begin the tour, ❺ let me remind you of a basic rule. You can ❻ take pictures of the artworks, but ❼ you're not allowed to touch ❽ them. Now let's start the tour.

Q9. When did the museum open?

Q10. ❹가 포함된 문장을 해석해 보세요.

❶ 고마움을 나타내는 표현

❷ 그때부터

❸ 현재완료 시제 (계속)

❹ ⑳ ~하기 전에

❺ let+목적어+목적격보어(동사원형): (목적어)가 ~하게 하다
remind A of B: A에게 B를 상기시키다

❻ 사진을 찍다

❼ 허용되지 않는 행동을 말할 때 쓰는 표현

❽ = the artworks

STEP A

우리말과 일치하도록 대화의 빈칸에 알맞은 말을 쓰시오.

주요 표현

1 Listen and Speak 1-A

교과서 104쪽

B: Hi, Lisa. _____ _____ _____ _____ _____ to your birthday party.

G: _____ _____. I'm glad you could come.

B: These flowers are for you. _____ _____!

G: They are beautiful! Thank you.

B: 안녕. Lisa. 네 생일 파티에 나를 초대해 줘서 고마워.
G: 천만에. 나는 네가 와서 기뻐.
B: 이 꽃들은 너를 위한 거야. 생일 축하해!
G: 꽃들이 아름답구나! 고마워.

2 Listen and Speak 1-B

교과서 104쪽

B: Sumin, my train is leaving _____ _____ _____.

G: I hope you enjoyed your trip, Daniel.

B: Of course, I did.

G: _____ _____ _____ _____ _____ in my town?

B: I liked the folk village most.

G: Yeah, it's _____ _____ _____ _____ here.

B: I really liked walking around in hanbok. I _____ _____ _____.

G: I'm glad to hear that.

B: Thank you _____ _____ _____ _____ _____.

G: It was my pleasure. Have a safe trip.

B: 수민아, 내가 타는 기차가 5분 후에 떠나.
G: 나는 네 여행이 즐거웠기를 바라, Daniel.
B: 물론 즐거웠지.
G: 너는 우리 마을에서 어느 장소가 가장 좋았니?
B: 나는 민속촌이 가장 좋았어.
G: 그래. 민속촌은 이곳에서 가장 인기 있는 곳이야.
B: 나는 한복을 입고 돌아다니는 게 정말 좋았어. 내가 정말 멋져 보였어.
G: 그 말을 들으니 기쁘구나.
B: 나에게 여기저기 구경시켜 줘서 고마워.
G: 천만에. 조심해서 가.

3 Listen and Speak 1-C

교과서 104쪽

A: How was the book?

B: It was great. Thank you _____ _____ _____ _____ _____.

A: _____ _____. It was my pleasure.

A: 그 책은 어땠니?
B: 좋았어. 나에게 책을 빌려줘서 고마워.
A: 천만에. 별거 아니야.

4 Listen and Speak 2-A

교과서 105쪽

M: Excuse me. You're _____ _____ _____ _____ your umbrella inside.

G: Oh, where should I put it?

M: There is _____ _____ _____ outside.

G: Okay. I'll put it there. Thank you.

M: 실례합니다. 우산을 안으로 가져오면 안 됩니다.
G: 아, 제가 우산을 어디에 두어야 하나요?
M: 밖에 우산꽂이가 있어요.
G: 알겠습니다. 거기에 둘게요. 감사합니다.

5 Listen and Speak 2-B

B: The tickets for the World Music Concert are _____ _____ now.

G: Really? Let's _____ _____ _____ _____ right away.

B: Okay. Let's see…. There are still tickets left for November 5th.

G: Sounds good. Let's get two student tickets.

B: Oh, _____ _____ _____ _____ _____ bring my little brother?

G: Not at all. But it says that _____ _____ _____ _____ _____ _____ children under 8.

B: No problem. He's 10.

G: Okay, I'll add one child ticket. The total price is 25 dollars.

B: Great.

G: _____ _____ _____ to see the concert!

B: '세계 음악 콘서트' 표가 지금 판매 중이야.

G: 정말? 지금 당장 온라인으로 표를 예매하자.

B: 좋아. 어디 보자…. 11월 5일에 표가 아직 남아 있어.

G: 잘됐다. 학생 표 두 장을 예매하자.

B: 오, 내 남동생을 데려가도 될까?

G: 물론이지. 하지만 8세 미만의 어린이들은 데려오지 못한다고 쓰여 있어.

B: 문제없어. 그(내 남동생)는 10살이야.

G: 그래, 어린이 표 한 장을 추가할게. 총액이 25달러야.

B: 좋아.

G: 나는 콘서트를 보는 게 정말 기대돼!

6 Listen and Speak 2-C

A: Excuse me. You're not allowed to _____ _____ _____ here.

B: I'm sorry. I didn't know that.

A: Please _____ _____ _____ over there.

B: Okay. Thank you.

A: 실례합니다. 여기서 새들에게 먹이를 주면 안 됩니다.

B: 죄송합니다. 몰랐어요.

A: 저쪽에 있는 표지판을 확인해 주세요.

B: 알겠습니다. 감사합니다.

7 Real Life Talk > Watch a Video

W: Hello, students! _____ _____ _____ _____ our art museum. This museum opened in 1995. Since then, it _____ _____ many famous artworks. Today, you will see some famous artworks from the art books. Before we begin the tour, _____ _____ _____ _____ of a basic rule. You can take pictures of the artworks, but _____ _____ _____ _____ _____ them. Now let's start the tour.

W: 안녕하세요, 학생 여러분! 우리 미술관을 방문해 주셔서 감사합니다. 이 미술관은 1995년에 문을 열었습니다. 그때부터 이곳은 많은 유명한 작품을 전시해 왔습니다. 오늘, 여러분은 미술 책에 실린 유명한 작품 몇 점을 보게 될 것입니다. 관람을 시작하기 전에, 기본 규칙을 상기시켜 드리겠습니다. 작품의 사진을 찍을 수는 있지만 만져서는 안 됩니다. 이제 관람을 시작해 봅시다.

Listen & Speak
대화 순서 배열하기

자연스러운 대화가 되도록 순서를 바르게 배열하시오.

1 Listen and Speak 1-A

교과서 104쪽

ⓐ They are beautiful! Thank you.
ⓑ Hi, Lisa. Thank you for inviting me to your birthday party.
ⓒ My pleasure. I'm glad you could come.
ⓓ These flowers are for you. Happy birthday!

(   ) – (   ) – (   ) – (   )

2 Listen and Speak 1-B

교과서 104쪽

ⓐ Of course, I did.
ⓑ I liked the folk village most.
ⓒ Sumin, my train is leaving in five minutes.
ⓓ Which place did you like most in my town?
ⓔ I'm glad to hear that.
ⓕ I hope you enjoyed your trip, Daniel.
ⓖ I really liked walking around in hanbok. I looked really cool.
ⓗ It was my pleasure. Have a safe trip.
ⓘ Yeah, it's the most popular place here.
ⓙ Thank you for showing me around.

(ⓒ) – (   ) – (   ) – (   ) – (   ) – (   ) – (ⓖ) – (   ) – (ⓘ) – (   )

3 Listen and Speak 1-C

교과서 104쪽

ⓐ It was great. Thank you for lending me the book.
ⓑ How was the book?
ⓒ You're welcome. It was my pleasure.

(   ) – (   ) – (   )

4 Listen and Speak 2-A

교과서 105쪽

ⓐ Excuse me. You're not allowed to bring your umbrella inside.
ⓑ There is an umbrella stand outside.
ⓒ Oh, where should I put it?
ⓓ Okay. I'll put it there. Thank you.

(   ) – (   ) – (   ) – (   )

5 Listen and Speak 2-B

교과서 105쪽

ⓐ Sounds good. Let's get two student tickets.

ⓑ Okay. Let's see.... There are still tickets left for November 5th.

ⓒ No problem. He's 10.

ⓓ The tickets for the World Music Concert are on sale now.

ⓔ Oh, do you mind if I bring my little brother?

ⓕ Okay, I'll add one child ticket. The total price is 25 dollars.

ⓖ Not at all. But it says that you are not allowed to bring children under 8.

ⓗ Really? Let's book the tickets online right away.

ⓘ I can't wait to see the concert!

ⓙ Great.

(ⓓ) – (   ) – (   ) – (   ) – (ⓔ) – (   ) – (   ) – (   ) – (ⓘ) – (   )

6 Listen and Speak 2-C

교과서 105쪽

ⓐ Okay. Thank you.

ⓑ Excuse me. You're not allowed to feed the birds here.

ⓒ Please check the sign over there.

ⓓ I'm sorry. I didn't know that.

(   ) – (   ) – (   ) – (   )

7 Real Life Talk > Watch a Video

교과서 106쪽

ⓐ Before we begin the tour, let me remind you of a basic rule.

ⓑ This museum opened in 1995.

ⓒ Hello, students!

ⓓ You can take pictures of the artworks, but you're not allowed to touch them.

ⓔ Since then, it has exhibited many famous artworks.

ⓕ Thank you for visiting our art museum.

ⓖ Today, you will see some famous artworks from the art books.

ⓗ Now let's start the tour.

(ⓒ) – (   ) – (   ) – (   ) – (ⓖ) – (   ) – (   ) – (   )

01 다음 대화의 빈칸에 들어갈 말로 알맞은 것은?

> A: _____ recommending
> the movie.
> B: You're welcome.

① I don't feel like
② Thank you for
③ I'm interested in
④ I'm worried about
⑤ I'm looking forward to

02 다음 대화의 빈칸에 들어갈 말로 알맞은 것을 <u>모두</u> 고르면?

> A: Excuse me. _____
> B: I'm sorry. I didn't know that.

① I'm glad you feed the birds here.
② You shouldn't feed the birds here.
③ I can't wait to feed the birds here.
④ Can you help me feed the birds here?
⑤ You're not allowed to feed the birds here.

03 자연스러운 대화가 되도록 (A)~(D)를 바르게 배열한 것은?

> (A) My pleasure. I'm glad you could come.
> (B) They are beautiful! Thank you.
> (C) Hi, Lisa. Thank you for inviting me to your birthday party.
> (D) These flowers are for you. Happy birthday!

① (A) – (B) – (C) – (D)　② (A) – (C) – (D) – (B)
③ (C) – (A) – (D) – (B)　④ (C) – (B) – (D) – (A)
⑤ (D) – (B) – (A) – (C)

고
난도
04 다음 대화의 밑줄 친 ①~⑤ 중 흐름상 <u>어색한</u> 것은?

> A: ①<u>Excuse me.</u> ②<u>You're allowed to bring your umbrella inside.</u>
> B: Oh, where should I put it?
> A: ③<u>There is an umbrella stand outside.</u>
> B: Okay. ④<u>I'll put it there.</u> ⑤<u>Thank you.</u>

①　　　②　　　③　　　④　　　⑤

[05-06] 다음 대화를 읽고, 물음에 답하시오.

> A: Sumin, my train is leaving in five minutes.
> B: I hope you enjoyed your trip, Daniel.
> A: Of course, I did.
> B: Which place did you like most in my town?
> A: I liked the folk village most.
> B: Yeah, it's the most popular place here.
> A: I really liked walking around in hanbok. I looked really cool.
> B: I'm glad to hear that.
> A: _____
> (you, thank, me, for, showing, around)
> B: It was my pleasure. Have a safe trip.

신
유형
05 위 대화의 빈칸에 알맞은 말이 되도록 괄호 안의 단어들을 배열할 때, 다섯 번째로 오는 단어는?

① me　　　② for　　　③ thank
④ showing　　　⑤ you

06 위 대화의 내용과 일치하지 <u>않는</u> 것은?

① 수민이는 Daniel을 배웅하고 있다.
② Daniel은 수민이가 사는 곳에서 여행을 했다.
③ Daniel은 민속촌이 가장 좋았다.
④ Daniel은 한복을 입고 시원하다고 느꼈다.
⑤ 수민이는 Daniel이 여행을 즐긴 것이 기쁘다.

[07-09] 다음 대화를 읽고, 물음에 답하시오.

Somi: The tickets for the World Music Concert ⓐare on sale now.

Joe: Really? ⓑLet's book the tickets online right away.

Somi: _____①_____ Let's see.... ⓒThere are still tickets left for November 5th.

Joe: _____②_____ Let's get two student tickets.

Somi: Oh, do you mind if I bring my little brother?

Joe: _____③_____ But ⓓit says what you are not allowed to bring children under 8.

Somi: _____④_____ He's 10.

Joe: Okay, I'll add one child ticket. The total price is 25 dollars.

Somi: _____⑤_____

Joe: ⓔI can't wait to see the concert!

07 위 대화의 빈칸 ①~⑤에 들어갈 말로 알맞지 <u>않은</u> 것은?

① Okay.   ② Sounds good.

③ Of course.   ④ No problem.

⑤ Great.

08 위 대화의 밑줄 친 ⓐ~ⓔ 중 어법상 <u>틀린</u> 것은?

① ⓐ   ② ⓑ   ③ ⓒ   ④ ⓓ   ⑤ ⓔ

고난도
09 위 대화의 내용과 일치하지 <u>않는</u> 것은?

① They are booking 3 tickets for the World Music Concert.

② They are going to the concert on November 5th.

③ Somi will bring her little brother to the concert.

④ Somi's brother is under 8.

⑤ Joe is looking forward to seeing the concert.

서술형

[10-11] 다음 글을 읽고, 물음에 답하시오.

Hello, students! Thank you for visiting our art museum. This museum opened in 1995. Since then, it has exhibited many famous artworks. Today, you will see some famous artworks from the art books. Before we begin the tour, let me remind you of <u>a basic rule</u>. You can take pictures of the artworks, but you're not allowed to touch them. Now let's start the tour.

10 윗글의 밑줄 친 <u>a basic rule</u>이 의미하는 것을 우리말로 쓰시오.

→ _____

11 다음 질문에 완전한 영어 문장으로 답하시오.

Where does this talk take place?

→ _____

12 괄호 안의 단어들을 이용하여 대화의 빈칸에 알맞은 문장을 쓰시오. (필요시 형태를 바꿔 쓸 것)

A: Excuse me. Can I ask you a question?

B: Sure, what is it?

A: Am I allowed to use a flash here?

B: Sorry. (1) _____
                              (allow)

A: Okay, I see.

B: (2) _____
                 (thank, understand)

STEP A

1 목적을 나타내는 so that

- The architect took the curved lines from nature **so that** city people could enjoy them.

  그 건축가는 도시 사람들이 즐길 수 있도록 자연에서 곡선을 가져왔다.

- He spoke loudly **so that** everyone could hear him.

  그는 모든 사람들이 들을 수 있도록 큰 소리로 말했다.

- Emily went to bed early **so that** she could get up early.

  Emily는 일찍 일어날 수 있도록 일찍 잠자리에 들었다.

(1) 의미와 형태

so that은 「so that + 주어 + 동사 ~」의 형태로 목적을 나타내는 절을 이끌어, '~하도록, ~하기 위해(서)'라는 의미를 나타낸다. so that이 이끄는 절의 동사는 주로 can/could 또는 will/would와 함께 쓰거나 현재시제로 쓴다.

- Yujin exercises every day **so that** she can stay healthy.

  유진이는 건강을 유지할 수 있도록 매일 운동한다.

- I made some sandwiches **so that** my family could eat them.

  나는 가족이 먹을 수 있도록 샌드위치를 좀 만들었다.

(2) 목적을 나타내기 위해 「to + 동사원형」, 「so as to + 동사원형」, 「in order to + 동사원형」, 「in order that + 주어 + can/may + 동사원형」을 쓸 수도 있다.

- Yujin exercises every day **(so as) to** stay healthy.

  유진이는 건강을 유지하기 위해 매일 운동한다.

- We went to the stadium early **in order to** get good seats.

  우리는 좋은 자리를 얻기 위해 경기장에 일찍 갔다.

- Come early **in order that** you may see him. 네가 그를 만날 수 있도록 일찍 와.

  비교 콤마(,) 다음에 오는 so (that)는 '그래서, 그 결과'라는 의미로, 콤마(,) 앞에 오는 절의 '결과'를 나타낸다.

- I was bored with the movie, **so (that)** I fell asleep. 나는 그 영화가 지루해서 잠이 들었다.

point

시험 포인트

so that과 so ~ that을 구분하는 문제가 자주 출제돼요. 각 형태의 의미를 정확히 기억하세요.

so ~ that

- Last night, Nick was **so** tired **that** he went to bed early.

  어젯밤, Nick은 너무 피곤해서 일찍 잠자리에 들었다.

  [중2 7과]

QUICK CHECK

1 다음 괄호 안에서 알맞은 것을 고르시오.

(1) Mr. White jogs every morning so (what / that) he can stay healthy.

(2) I saved money (in order to / in order that) buy a new bicycle.

(3) Ann never uses plastic bags (so that / so as to) she can protect the environment.

2 자연스러운 문장이 되도록 바르게 연결하시오.

(1) I ran to school　　　•　　　• ⓐ so that Tom can hit it.

(2) Throw the ball slowly　•　　　• ⓑ so that I could be on time.

(3) I should try my best　•　　　• ⓒ so that our soccer team can win the game.

2 형용사/부사+enough to+동사원형

- It is round and delicate, yet strong **enough to** protect its contents.

  그것은 둥글고 부서지기 쉽지만
  내용물을 보호할 만큼 충분히 튼튼하다.

- Eric is smart **enough to** solve difficult math problems.

  Eric은 어려운 수학 문제를 풀 만큼 충분히 똑똑하다.

- The boy is not tall **enough to reach** the top shelf.

  그 소년은 선반의 맨 위에 닿을 만큼 충분히 키가 크지 않다.

(1) 의미와 형태

「형용사/부사+enough to+동사원형」은 '~할 만큼(~하기에) 충분히 …한(하게)'이라는 의미를 나타낸다.

- This ladder is long **enough to** reach the shelf.

  이 사다리는 선반에 닿을 만큼 충분히 길다.

- I couldn't run fast **enough to** catch up with her.

  나는 그녀를 따라잡을 만큼 충분히 빨리 달릴 수 없었다.

(2) to부정사의 의미상의 주어가 문장의 주어와 다를 경우, to부정사 앞에 「for+목적격」을 써서 의미상의 주어를 나타낸다.

- The ball is small **enough for me to** carry in my bag. 이 공은 내가 가방에 넣어 다닐 만큼 충분히 작다.

시험 포인트 **point**

「형용사/부사+enough to+동사원형」, 「so+형용사/부사+that+주어+can+동사원형」, 「too+형용사/부사+to+동사원형」의 형태와 의미를 파악하는 문제가 자주 출제돼요. 각 표현의 형태와 의미 차이를 정확히 기억하세요.

한 단계 더!

「형용사/부사+enough to+동사원형」은 「so+형용사/부사+that+주어+can+동사원형」으로 바꿔 쓸 수 있다.

- He is smart **enough to** solve the problem. 그는 그 문제를 풀 만큼 충분히 똑똑하다.

  = He is **so** smart **that** he **can** solve the problem.

비교 「too+형용사/부사+to+동사원형」은 '너무 ~해서 …할 수 없다'라는 뜻으로, 「so+형용사/부사+that+주어+can't+동사원형」으로 바꿔 쓸 수 있다.

- I'm **too** tired **to** clean my room. 나는 너무 피곤해서 내 방을 청소할 수 없다.

  = I'm **so** tired **that** I **can't** clean my room.

QUICK CHECK

1 다음 괄호 안에서 알맞은 것을 고르시오.

(1) Helen is old (too / enough) to go to school.
(2) My bag is big (so / enough) to carry 10 books.
(3) Thomas was (brave enough / enough brave) to run after the thief.

2 다음 문장의 밑줄 친 부분을 바르게 고쳐 쓰시오.

(1) He is enough diligent to write a diary every day. → _____
(2) My sister is strong enough moving these boxes. → _____
(3) This toy car is small enough fit in my pocket. → _____

G Grammar
연습 문제

1 목적을 나타내는 so that

A 다음 괄호 안에서 알맞은 것을 고르시오.

1 Please be quiet so (that / which) I can read a book.

2 Henry lowered his voice (so / to) that Jane couldn't hear him.

3 Leave a note for me (in / so) that I can remember to take my glasses.

4 Why don't you start out early (so that / so as to) you don't have to hurry?

B [보기]에서 알맞은 말을 골라 so that을 사용하여 문장을 완성하시오.

[보기]	he could bake a cake	he could catch the first bus	he could understand them

1 Jack ran fast _____.

2 Peter took baking classes _____.

3 I explained the class rules to him clearly _____.

C 다음 우리말과 같도록 괄호 안의 말을 바르게 배열하여 문장을 완성하시오.

1 그녀는 건강을 유지할 수 있도록 규칙적으로 운동한다. (stay, she, can, so, healthy, that)
   → She exercises regularly _____.

2 우리는 일출을 볼 수 있도록 일찍 일어났다. (so, see, we, the sunrise, that, could)
   → We got up early _____.

3 그는 제시간에 그곳에 도착하기 위해 택시를 탔다. (to, so, get, on time, there, as)
   → He took a taxi _____.

4 Mike는 그녀가 길을 찾을 수 있도록 그녀에게 지도를 주었다. (that, find, so, she, could, the way)
   → Mike gave her a map _____.

5 나는 신선한 공기를 느끼기 위해 창문을 열었다. (to, the fresh air, in, feel, order)
   → I opened the windows _____.

D 다음 밑줄 친 부분의 의미에 유의하여 문장을 우리말로 해석하시오.

1 Emily drinks warm milk <u>so that she can sleep well</u>.
   → _____

2 Hosu saved money <u>so that he could travel with his friends</u>.
   → _____

3 Bill spoke loudly <u>so that everyone could hear him</u>.
   → _____

2 형용사/부사 + enough to + 동사원형

A 다음 괄호 안의 단어들을 바르게 배열하여 문장을 완성하시오.

1 This classroom is _____ 50 students in it. (enough, have, to, big)

2 Sam was _____ in public. (to, speak, brave, enough)

3 They are _____ themselves. (old, to, enough, look, after)

4 Yuna is _____ the English book. (enough, smart, understand, to)

5 Terry is _____ the roller coaster. (old, ride, to, enough, not)

B 다음 문장에서 어법상 <u>틀린</u> 부분을 바르게 고쳐 문장을 다시 쓰시오.

1 My dog was fast enough to catching the ball.
→ _____

2 Judy is wise enough give advice to her friends.
→ _____

3 The rope is strong enough holding my weight.
→ _____

4 Robin was not enough rich to lend his friend the money.
→ _____

C 다음 문장과 같은 의미를 나타내도록 enough를 사용하여 바꿔 쓰시오.

1 I was so hungry that I could eat a whole pizza.
→ _____

2 The string is so long that it can go around the house.
→ _____

3 He was so lucky that he could get the job.
→ _____

D 다음 우리말과 같도록 괄호 안의 말을 사용하여 문장을 쓰시오.

1 Amy는 3개 언어를 말할 만큼 충분히 똑똑하다. (smart, three languages)
→ _____

2 보라의 영어는 외국인과 이야기를 나눌 만큼 충분히 유창하다. (good, talk, a foreigner)
→ _____

3 그 코트는 그녀가 입기에 충분히 크다. (big, her, wear)
→ _____

실전 TEST

[01-02] 다음 빈칸에 들어갈 말로 알맞은 것을 고르시오.

01 John went to bed early _____ he could get up early.

① or ② but ③ so that
④ since ⑤ instead

02 Jessica is smart _____ to solve difficult math problems.

① so ② too ③ very
④ much ⑤ enough

03 다음 괄호 안에 주어진 단어들을 배열하여 문장을 완성할 때 알맞은 것은?

The window was closed (in, wind, the, blow, that, couldn't, cold, so).

① so in that the cold wind couldn't blow
② so the cold wind that couldn't blow in
③ that so the cold wind couldn't blow in
④ so that couldn't the cold wind blow in
⑤ so that the cold wind couldn't blow in

[04-05] 두 문장의 의미가 같도록 할 때, 빈칸에 들어갈 말로 알맞은 것을 고르시오.

한 단계 | 더!

04 The basketball player is so tall that she can reach the ceiling.
→ The basketball player is tall _____ to reach the ceiling.

① so ② very ③ even
④ too ⑤ enough

05 She studied science hard to get a good grade.
→ She studied science hard _____ she could get a good grade.

① as ② if ③ although
④ since ⑤ so that

한 단계 | 더!

06 다음 빈칸에 알맞은 말이 순서대로 짝 지어진 것은?

• I could not run fast _____ to catch up with Sara.
• Andrew is _____ talented that he can win the talent show.

① too – so ② too – too
③ enough – so ④ enough – too
⑤ so – enough

신유형

[07-08] 다음 우리말을 영어로 옮길 때, 빈칸에 쓰이지 않는 단어를 고르시오.

07 Tom은 스트레스를 풀 수 있도록 요가 수업을 듣는다.
→ Tom _____ yoga classes _____ that he _____ _____ his stress.

① so ② can ③ to
④ takes ⑤ relieve

08 그녀는 권투 시합에서 이길 정도로 충분히 강하다.
→ She is _____ _____ to _____ the boxing _____.

① win ② match ③ strong
④ too ⑤ enough

09 다음 중 어법상 <u>틀린</u> 문장은?

① He hurried so that wouldn't be late.

② She practiced hard so as to win the game.

③ Robert searched the Internet in order to buy some clothes.

④ My brother went to the supermarket to buy some milk.

⑤ Julia turns on the radio at 7 o'clock so that she can listen to her favorite program.

10 다음 밑줄 친 부분을 어법에 맞게 고친 것 중 <u>틀린</u> 것은?

① She is old enough <u>make</u> her own decisions.
　→ to make

② Jiho ran fast enough <u>to won</u> the race.
　→ to win

③ Nick was <u>enough clever</u> to correct the error.
　→ clever enough

④ They are rich enough <u>to donating</u> lots of money.
　→ donate

⑤ The sofa wasn't <u>strong enough of us</u> to sit on.
　→ strong enough for us

11 다음 문장의 밑줄 친 부분과 바꿔 쓸 수 있는 것은?

My father turned off the TV <u>in order to sleep well</u>.

① when he could sleep well

② so that he could sleep well

③ but he couldn't sleep well

④ because he didn't sleep well

⑤ although he couldn't sleep well

12 다음 중 빈칸에 들어갈 말이 나머지와 <u>다른</u> 하나는?

① Joan was absent from school yesterday _____ she was very sick.

② Amy studied hard _____ that she could pass the exam.

③ Simon saved money _____ as to buy a birthday gift for Judy.

④ I was _____ tired that I couldn't clean the backyard.

⑤ We took a taxi _____ that we could get there on time.

13 주어진 문장과 같은 의미를 나타내는 것은?

Yumi is so rich that she can buy the house.

① Yumi is rich enough to buy the house.

② Yumi is very rich, but she can't buy the house.

③ Since Yumi was very rich, she could buy the house.

④ Yumi is too rich to buy the house.

⑤ Yumi buys the house so that she can be rich.

14 다음 단어들을 자연스러운 문장이 되도록 배열할 때, 여섯 번째로 오는 단어는?

Minho, that, he, them, collected, donate, could, used clothes, so

① so　　　② he　　　③ donate

④ could　　⑤ that

15 다음 문장에 대한 설명으로 옳은 것을 <u>모두</u> 고르면?

> Lena is kind enough to help her poor neighbor.

① Lena is kind so that she can help her poor neighbor.로 바꿔 쓸 수 있다.
② kind와 enough의 위치를 바꿔 쓸 수 있다.
③ 「형용사+enough to+동사원형」의 구문이 쓰였다.
④ 'Lena는 어려운 이웃을 도울 만큼 충분히 친절하다.'로 해석한다.
⑤ kind enough to help는 too kind to help로 바꿔 쓸 수 있다.

[16-17] 다음 우리말을 영어로 바르게 옮긴 것을 고르시오.

16 빵이 타지 않도록 주의해서 보세요.

① Watch the bread closely so as to not burn.
② Watch the bread closely so does it not burn.
③ Watch the bread closely so that does not burn.
④ Watch so closely that the bread does not burn.
⑤ Watch closely so that the bread does not burn.

17 이 방은 50명을 수용할 만큼 충분히 크다.

① This room is too large to hold 50 people.
② This room is large enough to hold 50 people.
③ This room is large enough that hold 50 people.
④ This room is enough large to hold 50 people.
⑤ This room is so large that it cannot hold 50 people.

18 다음 ①~⑤ 중 enough가 들어가기에 알맞은 곳은?

> It (①) is (②) warm (③) to wear (④) short sleeves (⑤).

19 다음 중 어법상 <u>틀린</u> 것을 바르게 고친 것끼리 짝 지어진 것은?

> ⓐ I gave him a map so as that he wouldn't get lost.
> ⓑ I'll put the books in alphabetical order so that you can find them easily.
> ⓒ I was so tired that I almost fell asleep at the meeting.
> ⓓ The girl is not tall enough to reaching the top shelf.

① ⓐ so as that → so that
② ⓑ so that → in order to
③ ⓐ so as that → so that
 ⓓ to reaching → to reach
④ ⓑ so that → in order to
 ⓓ tall enough → enough tall
⑤ ⓒ so → 삭제
 ⓓ to reaching → to reach

20 다음 우리말과 같도록 괄호 안의 단어들을 배열하여 문장을 완성할 때, 추가해야 하는 단어는?

> 내 여동생은 대학에 갈 만큼 충분히 나이가 들었다.
> (is, my, sister, old, to, college, to, younger, go)

① so   ② too   ③ far
④ much   ⑤ enough

21 다음 그림을 보고, [조건]에 맞게 문장을 완성하시오.

> [조건]   1. enough를 포함할 것
>   2. 괄호 안의 말을 사용할 것

(1)   (2)

(1) Minho is _____.
           (strong, lift)
(2) The mouse is _____.
           (small, go through)

22 Lucy가 각 행동을 한 목적을 나타내도록 [보기]의 말을 이용하여 문장을 완성하시오. (so를 포함할 것)

> [보기]   she could donate them
>   she could feel the fresh air
>   everyone could hear her speech

(1) Lucy opened the window _____
_____.
(2) Lucy spoke loudly _____
_____.
(3) Lucy collected old items _____
_____.

23 다음 우리말과 같도록 괄호 안의 말을 사용하여 영작하시오.

(1) 그 사다리는 천장에 닿을 만큼 충분히 길다.
    (ladder, long, reach the ceiling)
    → _____
(2) 이 가방은 두 개의 농구공을 담을 만큼 충분히 크지 않다.
    (bag, big, carry two basketballs)
    → _____
(3) 그 스마트폰은 나의 할머니께서 사용하시기에 충분히 쉽다.
    (smartphone, easy, my grandmother, use)
    → _____

24 다음 문장을 우리말로 해석하시오.

(1) Tony swims every morning so that he can stay healthy.
    → _____
(2) Julie is smart enough to solve difficult puzzles.
    → _____
(3) The movie was so funny that I watched it twice.
    → _____

한 단계 | 더!

25 주어진 문장과 같은 의미를 나타내도록 enough를 사용하여 문장을 바꿔 쓰시오.

(1) Mary is so wise that she can advise her older sister.
    → _____
(2) The old man was so rich that he could buy several cars.
    → _____
(3) It was so windy that we could fly a kite.
    → _____

26 괄호 안의 단어들을 바르게 배열하여 문장을 완성하시오.

(1) Fred saved money _____
_____.
    (his, so, with, could, travel, he, friends, that)
(2) The boy is _____
_____.
    (to, enough, not, reach, tall, the bookshelf)
(3) The pants are _____
_____.
    (for, long, to, her, enough, wear)

STEP
A

자연이 도시를 만나다

Nature Meets City

01 '예술이 자연을 모방한다'라는 표현을 들어 본 적이 있는가?

02 많은 예술가들이 그들의 아이디어와 영감을 그들 주변의 세상에서 얻는다.

03 이는 자연계가 아름다운 곳이기 때문이다.

04 자연의 형태는 보기에 매우 좋다.

05 예를 들면 왼쪽의 달걀을 봐라.

06 아름답지 않은가?

07 그것은 둥글고 부서지기 쉽지만, 내용물을 보호할 만큼 충분히 튼튼하다.

08 달걀처럼 생긴 건물을 상상할 수 있는가?

09 이러한 형태의 건물이 런던에는 실제로 존재한다.

10 자연은 세계의 많은 건축가들에게 영감을 주어 왔다.

11 이것은 스페인에 있는 사그라다 파밀리아 성당이다.

12 그것은 세계에서 가장 유명한 성당 중의 하나이다.

13 성당 안에 있는 아름다운 높은 기둥들을 봐라.

14 그것들은 나무처럼 보인다. 그렇지 않은 가?

15 유명한 건축가인 Antoni Gaudi는 사그라다 파밀리아 성당에 나무의 형태를 사용했다.

16 그렇게 해서 그는 자연의 아름다움을 실내로 가져왔다.

17 앞의 두 예시에서 우리는 무엇이 건축가에게 영감을 주었는지 쉽게 알 수 있다.

---

01 Have you heard of the expression, "Art imitates nature"?
현재완료 시제 의문문: Have(Has)+주어+과거분사 ~?

02 Many artists get their ideas and inspirations from the world around them.
= many artists

03 This is because the natural world is a beautiful place.
이것은 ~이기 때문이다 (because 뒤에는 이유가 이어짐)

04 The shapes in nature are very pleasing to the eye.
문장의 주어   즐거운, 기분 좋은 (현재분사 형태의 형용사)

05 For example, look at the egg on the left.
= For instance   ~을 보다
(예를 들어)

06 Isn't it beautiful?

07 It is round and delicate, yet strong enough to protect its contents.
= the egg   접속사 (그렇지만)   형용사(strong)+enough to+동사원형: ~할 만큼 충분히 …한

08 Can you imagine a building that looks like an egg?
선행사   that은 주격 관계대명사

09 Such a building actually exists in London.
= a building that looks like an egg

10 Nature has inspired many architects around the world.
have(has)+과거분사: 현재완료 (계속)

11 This is the Sagrada Familia in Spain.

= the Sagrada Familia
12 It is one of the most famous churches in the world.
one of the+최상급(most famous)+복수 명사(churches):
가장 ~한 … 중의 하나

13 Look at the beautiful tall columns inside the church.
명령문 (동사원형으로 시작)

14 They look like trees, don't they?
= the beautiful tall columns   부가의문문: 앞의 일반동사 look이
긍정이므로 부정문으로 쓰임

15 The famous architect, Antoni Gaudi, used the
└ = ┘동격 관계
shape of trees in the Sagrada Familia.

16 That's how he brought the beauty of nature indoors.
That's how+주어+동사 ~: 그것이 ~한 방법이다, 그런 식으로 ~하는 것이다

17 In the first two examples, we can easily see what inspired the architect.
런던의 달걀처럼 생긴 건물,   쉽게   의문사 what이 이끄는 명사절
사그라다 파밀리아 성당   (see의 목적어 역할)

18 But in the next example from Australia, this is not so obvious.
= what inspired the architect

18 하지만 호주의 다음 예시에서는 이것이 그다지 명확하지 않다.

19 Jørn Utzon, the architect of the Sydney Opera House, took a shape from nature and added his imagination.
└ = ┘ 동격 관계
take A from B: B에서 A를 가져오다

19 시드니 오페라 하우스의 건축가인 Jørn Utzon은 자연에서 형태를 가져와 자신의 상상력을 더했다.

20 Can you guess what inspired him?
의문사 what이 이끄는 명사절 (guess의 목적어 역할)

20 무엇이 그에게 영감을 주었는지 추측할 수 있는가?

21 Many people think that it is the waves in the ocean or a sailing boat.
접속사 (that이 이끄는 명사절이 think의 목적어 역할)

21 많은 사람들은 그것이 바다의 파도나 돛단배라고 생각한다.

22 But interestingly, the inspiration came from an orange.
문장 전체를 수식하는 부사
come from: ~에서 비롯되다(나오다)

22 하지만 흥미롭게도, 그 영감은 오렌지에서 비롯되었다.

23 Look at the roof closely.
명령문

23 지붕을 자세히 봐라.

24 Can you see the peels of an orange?

24 오렌지의 껍질들이 보이는가?

25 When orange lights are shone on the building, you can see the peels more clearly.
접속사 (~할 때)   수동태: be동사 + 과거분사
clearly(⊕ 명확하게)의 비교급: 더 명확하게

25 오렌지색 조명이 건물을 비추면, 껍질들을 더 명확하게 볼 수 있다.

26 What about Korea?

26 한국은 어떤가?

27 Have you ever been to Dongdaemun Design Plaza in Seoul?
Have you (ever) been to + 장소?: 너는 ~에 가 본 적이 있니?

27 서울의 동대문 디자인 플라자에 가 본 적이 있는가?

28 Many people think that the building looks like a giant spaceship.
접속사   look like: ~처럼 보이다

28 많은 사람들은 그 건물이 거대한 우주선처럼 보인다고 생각한다.

29 But the architect, Zaha Hadid, took the curved lines from nature so that city people could enjoy them.
└ = ┘ 동격 관계   ~하도록, ~하기 위해(서)

29 하지만 건축가인 Zaha Hadid는 도시 사람들이 즐길 수 있도록 자연에서 곡선을 가져왔다.

30 Thanks to its special design, it has become a popular tourist attraction in Seoul.
= Dongdaemun Design Plaza   have(has) + 과거분사: 현재완료

30 이 특별한 디자인 덕분에, 그것(동대문 디자인 플라자)은 서울의 인기 있는 관광 명소가 되었다.

31 As you can see, many buildings try to capture the beauty of nature in their design.
try + to부정사: ~하려고 노력하다(애쓰다)

31 보는 바와 같이, 많은 건물들이 디자인에 자연의 아름다움을 담아내려고 한다.

32 They are perfect examples of "Nature meets city."

32 그것들(그 건물들)은 '자연이 도시를 만나다'의 완벽한 예이다.

33 If you were an architect, what would you choose from nature?
가정법 과거(If + 주어 + 동사의 과거형 ~, 주어 + 조동사의 과거형 + 동사원형)의 주절이 의문문으로 쓰인 형태

33 만약 당신이 건축가라면, 자연에서 무엇을 선택할 텐가?

Reading
빈칸 채우기

우리말 뜻과 일치하도록 교과서 본문의 문장을 완성하시오.

중요 문장

01 _____ _____ _____ of the expression, "Art imitates nature"?

01 '예술이 자연을 모방한다'라는 표현을 들어 본 적이 있는가?

02 Many artists get _____ _____ _____ _____ from the world around them.

02 많은 예술가들이 그들의 아이디어와 영감을 그들 주변의 세상에서 얻는다.

03 _____ _____ _____ the natural world is a beautiful place.

03 이는 자연계가 아름다운 곳이기 때문이다.

04 _____ _____ _____ _____ _____ are very pleasing to the eye.

04 자연의 형태는 보기에 매우 좋다.

05 _____ _____ , look at the egg on the left.

05 예를 들면 왼쪽의 달걀을 봐라.

06 _____ _____ _____ ?

06 아름답지 않은가?

07 It is round and delicate, yet _____ _____ _____ _____ its contents.

07 그것은 둥글고 부서지기 쉽지만, 내용물을 보호할 만큼 충분히 튼튼하다.

08 Can you imagine a building that _____ _____ an egg?

08 달걀처럼 생긴 건물을 상상할 수 있는가?

09 Such a building _____ _____ _____ London.

09 이러한 형태의 건물이 런던에는 실제로 존재한다.

10 Nature _____ _____ many architects around the world.

10 자연은 세계의 많은 건축가들에게 영감을 주어 왔다.

11 This is the Sagrada Familia _____ _____ .

11 이것은 스페인에 있는 사그라다 파밀리아 성당이다.

12 It is one of _____ _____ _____ _____ in the world.

12 그것은 세계에서 가장 유명한 성당 중의 하나이다.

13 Look at the _____ _____ _____ inside the church.

13 성당 안에 있는 아름다운 높은 기둥들을 봐라.

14 They look like trees, _____ _____ ?

14 그것들은 나무처럼 보인다. 그렇지 않은가?

15 The famous architect, Antoni Gaudi, used _____ _____ _____ _____ in the Sagrada Familia.

15 유명한 건축가인 Antoni Gaudi는 사그라다 파밀리아 성당에 나무의 형태를 사용했다.

16 That's how he brought _____ _____ _____ indoors.

16 그렇게 해서 그는 자연의 아름다움을 실내로 가져왔다.

17 In the first two examples, we can easily see _____ _____ _____ .

17 앞의 두 예시에서 우리는 무엇이 건축가에게 영감을 주었는지 쉽게 알 수 있다.

18 But in the next example from Australia, this is _____ _____
_____.

19 Jørn Utzon, the architect of the Sydney Opera House, took a shape from nature and _____ _____ _____.

20 _____ _____ _____ what inspired him?

21 Many people think that it is the waves in the ocean or _____
_____ _____.

22 But interestingly, the inspiration _____ _____ an orange.

23 Look at the roof _____.

24 Can you see _____ _____ of an orange?

25 When orange lights are shone on the building, you can see the peels
_____ _____.

26 _____ _____ Korea?

27 _____ _____ _____ _____ _____
Dongdaemun Design Plaza in Seoul?

28 Many people think that the building looks like _____ _____
_____.

29 But the architect, Zaha Hadid, _____ _____ _____
_____ from nature so that city people could enjoy them.

30 Thanks to its special design, it has become _____ _____
_____ _____ in Seoul.

31 As you can see, many buildings _____ _____ _____ the beauty of nature in their design.

32 They are _____ _____ of "Nature meets city."

33 If you were an architect, _____ _____ _____ _____
from nature?

18 하지만 호주의 다음 예시에서는 이것이 그다지 명확하지 않다.

19 시드니 오페라 하우스의 건축가인 Jørn Utzon은 자연에서 형태를 가져와 자신의 상상력을 더했다.

20 무엇이 그에게 영감을 주었는지 추측할 수 있는가?

21 많은 사람들은 그것이 바다의 파도나 돛단 배라고 생각한다.

22 하지만 흥미롭게도, 그 영감은 오렌지에서 비롯되었다.

23 지붕을 자세히 봐라.

24 오렌지의 껍질들이 보이는가?

25 오렌지색 조명이 건물을 비추면, 껍질들을 더 명확하게 볼 수 있다.

26 한국은 어떤가?

27 서울의 동대문 디자인 플라자에 가 본 적이 있는가?

28 많은 사람들은 그 건물이 거대한 우주선처럼 보인다고 생각한다.

29 하지만 건축가인 Zaha Hadid는 도시 사람들이 즐길 수 있도록 자연에서 곡선을 가져왔다.

30 이 특별한 디자인 덕분에, 그것(동대문 디자인 플라자)은 서울의 인기 있는 관광 명소가 되었다.

31 보는 바와 같이, 많은 건물들이 디자인에 자연의 아름다움을 담아내려고 한다.

32 그것들(그 건물들)은 '자연이 도시를 만나다'의 완벽한 예이다.

33 만약 당신이 건축가라면, 자연에서 무엇을 선택할 텐가?

STEP
A

글의 내용과 문장의 어법에 맞게 괄호 안에서 알맞은 어휘를 고르시오.

01 Have you (hear / heard) of the expression, "Art imitates nature"?

02 Many artists (get / gets) their ideas and inspirations from the world around them.

03 This is (because of / because) the natural world is a beautiful place.

04 The shapes in nature (are / is) very pleasing to the eye.

05 (For example / As a result), look at the egg on the left.

06 Isn't it (beautiful / beautifully)?

07 It is round and delicate, yet strong enough (protect / to protect) its contents.

08 Can you imagine a building (that / what) looks like an egg?

09 Such a building actually (exist / exists) in London.

10 Nature has inspired (many / much) architects around the world.

11 (This is / These are) the Sagrada Familia in Spain.

12 It is one of the most famous (church / churches) in the world.

13 Look at the beautiful tall columns (inside / indoors) the church.

14 They look like trees, (don't / doesn't) they?

15 The famous architect, Antoni Gaudi, used the shape of trees (in / on) the Sagrada Familia.

16 That's (how / why) he brought the beauty of nature indoors.

17 In the first two examples, we can (easy / easily) see what inspired the architect.

18   But in the next example from Australia, this is not so (obvious / obviously).

19   Jørn Utzon, the architect of the Sydney Opera House, took a shape from nature and (added / removed) his imagination.

20   Can you guess (what / who) inspired him?

21   Many people think (that / which) it is the waves in the ocean or a sailing boat.

22   But (interesting / interestingly), the inspiration came from an orange.

23   Look at the roof (wisely / closely).

24   Can you see the peels of an (apple / orange)?

25   When orange lights are shone on the building, you can see the peels (more / much) clearly.

26   What (of / about) Korea?

27   Have you ever been (to / from) Dongdaemun Design Plaza in Seoul?

28   Many people think that the building (looks / looks like) a giant spaceship.

29   But the architect, Zaha Hadid, took the curved lines from nature (that / so that) city people could enjoy them.

30   (Thanks to / Thanks for) its special design, it has become a popular tourist attraction in Seoul.

31   As you can see, many buildings try (capture / to capture) the beauty of nature in their design.

32   They are perfect examples of "(Architect / Nature) meets city."

33   If you (are / were) an architect, what would you choose from nature?

Reading
틀린 문장 고치기

밑줄 친 부분이 내용이나 어법상 바르면 ○, 어색하면 ✕에 표시하고 고쳐 쓰시오.

01 Have you <u>hear</u> of the expression, "Art imitates nature"? ○ ✕

02 Many artists get their ideas and inspirations from the world around <u>it</u>. ○ ✕

03 This is because the natural world <u>are</u> a beautiful place. ○ ✕

04 The shapes in nature are very <u>pleased</u> to the eye. ○ ✕

05 For example, <u>look at</u> the egg on the left. ○ ✕

06 <u>Isn't it</u> beautiful? ○ ✕

07 It is round and delicate, yet <u>enough strong</u> to protect its contents. ○ ✕

08 Can you imagine a building that <u>look</u> like an egg? ○ ✕

09 Such a building actually <u>exist</u> in London. ○ ✕

10 Nature <u>has inspired</u> many architects around the world. ○ ✕

11 This is the Sagrada Familia <u>to</u> Spain. ○ ✕

12 It is one of the <u>more</u> famous churches in the world. ○ ✕

13 Look at the <u>beautiful tall columns</u> inside the church. ○ ✕

14 They look <u>for</u> trees, don't they? ○ ✕

15 <u>The famous architect, Antoni Gaudi,</u> used the shape of trees in the Sagrada Familia. ○ ✕

16 <u>That's how</u> he brought the beauty of nature indoors. ○ ✕

17 In the first two examples, we can easily see <u>what</u> inspired the architect. ○ ✕

18   But in the next example from Australia, this is <u>not so obvious</u>.   ⬜ O ⬜ X

19   Jørn Utzon, the <u>architecture</u> of the Sydney Opera House, took a shape from nature and   ⬜ O ⬜ X
       added his imagination.

20   Can you guess <u>what inspired to him</u>?   ⬜ O ⬜ X

21   Many people think that it is the waves in the ocean <u>but</u> a sailing boat.   ⬜ O ⬜ X

22   But interestingly, the <u>inspire</u> came from an orange.   ⬜ O ⬜ X

23   Look at the roof <u>closely</u>.   ⬜ O ⬜ X

24   Can you see <u>the peels of an orange</u>?   ⬜ O ⬜ X

25   When orange lights are shone on the building, you can see the peels <u>more clear</u>.   ⬜ O ⬜ X

26   <u>What of</u> Korea?   ⬜ O ⬜ X

27   <u>Have you ever been to</u> Dongdaemun Design Plaza in Seoul?   ⬜ O ⬜ X

28   Many people think <u>which</u> the building looks like a giant spaceship.   ⬜ O ⬜ X

29   But the architect, Zaha Hadid, took the curved lines from nature <u>such that</u> city people could   ⬜ O ⬜ X
       enjoy them.

30   <u>Thanks to</u> its special design, it has become a popular tourist attraction in Seoul.   ⬜ O ⬜ X

31   <u>While</u> you can see, many buildings try to capture the beauty of nature in their design.   ⬜ O ⬜ X

32   They are perfect examples of <u>"Nature meets city."</u>   ⬜ O ⬜ X

33   If you were an architect, what <u>will</u> you choose from nature?   ⬜ O ⬜ X

STEP A

주어진 단어를 바르게 배열하여 문장을 쓰시오.

01 '예술이 자연을 모방한다'라는 표현을 들어 본 적이 있는가? (you / the expression, / have / heard of / "Art imitates nature")
→

02 많은 예술가들이 그들의 아이디어와 영감을 그들 주변의 세상에서 얻는다.
(inspirations / from the world / get / around them / their ideas / and / many artists)
→

03 이는 자연계가 아름다운 곳이기 때문이다. (is / because / is / this / the natural world / a beautiful place)
→

04 자연의 형태는 보기에 매우 좋다. (very / the shapes / are / to the eye / in nature / pleasing)
→

05 예를 들면 왼쪽의 달걀을 봐라. (the egg / for example, / on the left / look at)
→

06 아름답지 않은가? (beautiful / isn't / it)
→

07 그것은 둥글고 부서지기 쉽지만, 내용물을 보호할 만큼 충분히 튼튼하다.
(it / yet / to protect / round / delicate, / strong / its contents / is / enough / and)
→

08 달걀처럼 생긴 건물을 상상할 수 있는가? (looks / that / imagine / a building / can / like / an egg / you)
→

09 이러한 형태의 건물이 런던에는 실제로 존재한다. (such / exists / actually / a building / in London)
→

10 자연은 세계의 많은 건축가들에게 영감을 주어 왔다. (many architects / has inspired / around the world / nature)
→

11 이것은 스페인에 있는 사그라다 파밀리아 성당이다. (this / the Sagrada Familia / in Spain / is)
→

12 그것은 세계에서 가장 유명한 성당 중의 하나이다. (it / of / most / the / famous churches / one / in the world / is)
→

13 성당 안에 있는 아름다운 높은 기둥들을 봐라. (columns / the beautiful tall / look at / inside the church)
→

14 그것들은 나무처럼 보인다, 그렇지 않은가? (like / they / trees, / look / they / don't)
→

15 유명한 건축가인 Antoni Gaudi는 사그라다 파밀리아 성당에 나무의 형태를 사용했다.
(Antoni Gaudi, / the shape of / used / in the Sagrada Familia / the famous architect, / trees)
→

16 그렇게 해서 그는 자연의 아름다움을 실내로 가져왔다. (how / brought / the beauty / of / that's / he / indoors / nature)
→

17 앞의 두 예시에서 우리는 무엇이 건축가에게 영감을 주었는지 쉽게 알 수 있다.
(easily / inspired / we / see / in the first two examples, / can / what / the architect)
→

18 하지만 호주의 다음 예시에서는 이것이 그다지 명확하지 않다.

(is / in the next example / not / but / obvious / so / from Australia, / this)

→

19 시드니 오페라 하우스의 건축가인 Jørn Utzon은 자연에서 형태를 가져와 자신의 상상력을 더했다.

(added / the architect / took / a shape / and / Jørn Utzon, / of the Sydney Opera House, / from nature / his imagination)

→

20 무엇이 그에게 영감을 주었는지 추측할 수 있는가? (can / him / guess / inspired / you / what)

→

21 많은 사람들은 그것이 바다의 파도나 돛단배라고 생각한다.

(is / the waves / or / many people / that / it / in the ocean / think / a sailing boat)

→

22 하지만 흥미롭게도, 그 영감은 오렌지에서 비롯되었다. (an orange / came / but / the inspiration / from / interestingly,)

→

23 지붕을 자세히 봐라. (at / the roof / look / closely)

→

24 오렌지의 껍질들이 보이는가? (you / the peels / see / of / can / an orange)

→

25 오렌지색 조명이 건물을 비추면, 껍질들을 더 명확하게 볼 수 있다.

(more / see / are shone / orange lights / can / clearly / on the building, / you / the peels / when)

→

26 한국은 어떤가? (about / Korea / what)

→

27 당신은 서울의 동대문 디자인 플라자에 가 본 적이 있는가? (ever / you / in Seoul / been / to / have / Dongdaemun Design Plaza)

→

28 많은 사람들은 그 건물이 기대한 우주선처럼 보인다고 생각한다.

(looks / a giant spaceship / that / think / the building / many people / like)

→

29 하지만 건축가인 Zaha Hadid는 도시 사람들이 즐길 수 있도록 자연에서 곡선을 가져왔다.

(city people / Zaha Hadid, / enjoy / from nature / could / the architect, / the curved lines / took / but / so that / them)

→

30 이 특별한 디자인 덕분에, 그것은 서울의 인기 있는 관광 명소가 되었다.

(it / its special design, / a popular tourist attraction / thanks to / has become / in Seoul)

→

31 보는 바와 같이, 많은 건물들이 디자인에 자연의 아름다움을 담아내려고 한다.

(try / the beauty / can / see, / of nature / you / many buildings / as / to capture / in their design)

→

32 그것들은 '자연이 도시를 만나다'의 완벽한 예이다. (examples / of / they / "Nature meets city." / are / perfect)

→

33 만약 당신이 건축가라면, 자연에서 무엇을 선택할 텐가?

(were / choose / you / if / what / would / you / from nature / an architect,)

→

[01-03] 다음 글을 읽고, 물음에 답하시오.

Have you heard of the expression, "_____"? Many artists get their ideas and inspirations from the world around them. This is (A) why / because the natural world is a beautiful place. The shapes in nature (B) is / are very pleasing to the eye. For example, look at the egg on the left. Isn't it beautiful? It is round and delicate, yet (C) enough strong / strong enough to protect its contents. Can you imagine a building that looks like an egg? Such a building actually exists in London.

01 윗글의 빈칸에 들어갈 말로 가장 알맞은 것은?

① Art inspires nature
② The big art is our life
③ Art imitates nature
④ Nature is the true law
⑤ Nature looks like an artist

02 윗글의 (A), (B), (C)에서 알맞은 것끼리 짝 지어진 것은?

	(A)	(B)	(C)
①	because	– is	– strong enough
②	why	– is	– enough strong
③	because	– are	– strong enough
④	why	– is	– strong enough
⑤	because	– are	– enough strong

03 윗글의 글쓴이와 의견이 다른 것은?

① 많은 예술가들이 아이디어를 그들 주변의 세상에서 얻는다.
② 자연계는 아름답다.
③ 자연의 형태는 보기에 매우 좋다.
④ 달걀은 아름답진 않지만, 내용물을 보호할 만큼 충분히 튼튼하다.
⑤ 런던에는 달걀처럼 생긴 건물이 있다.

[04-07] 다음 글을 읽고, 물음에 답하시오.

Nature ⓐhas inspired many architects around the world. This is the Sagrada Familia in Spain. It is one of the most famous churches in the world.
(A) They look like trees, don't they?
(B) Look at the beautiful tall columns inside the church.
(C) That's how he brought the beauty of nature indoors.
(D) The famous architect, Antoni Gaudi, used the shape of trees in the Sagrada Familia.

04 자연스러운 글이 되도록 (A)~(D)를 바르게 배열한 것은?

① (A) – (C) – (B) – (D)   ② (B) – (A) – (D) – (C)
③ (B) – (C) – (A) – (D)   ④ (C) – (A) – (B) – (D)
⑤ (C) – (B) – (D) – (A)

05 윗글의 밑줄 친 ⓐ의 현재완료와 용법이 같은 것은?

① I have never eaten French food.
② Jimin has been to Canada before.
③ Anna has just finished her homework.
④ Tom has seen a famous movie star.
⑤ I have known Judy since I was a little child.

06 윗글에서 다음 영어 뜻풀이에 해당하는 단어를 찾아 쓰시오.

a person who designs buildings

→ _____

07 윗글을 읽고 답할 수 <u>없는</u> 질문은?

① What has inspired many architects?

② Where is the Sagrada Familia located?

③ What do the columns inside the Sagrada Familia look like?

④ What are the columns inside the Sagrada Familia made of?

⑤ What shape did Antoni Gaudi use in the Sagrada Familia?

09 윗글의 빈칸 ⓐ에 들어갈 말로 알맞은 것은?

① natural ② famous ③ interesting

④ beautiful ⑤ obvious

10 윗글의 빈칸 ⓑ에 들어갈 말로 알맞은 것은?

① to ② on ③ for

④ from ⑤ of

[08-12] 다음 글을 읽고, 물음에 답하시오.

In the first two examples, we can easily see what inspired the architect. But in the next example from Australia, this is not so ___ⓐ___. Jørn Utzon, the architect of the Sydney Opera House, took a shape ___ⓑ___ nature and added his imagination. (①) Can you guess what inspired him? (②) But interestingly, the inspiration came from an orange. (③) Look at the roof closely. (④) Can you see the peels of an orange? (⑤) When orange lights are shone on the building, you can see the peels more clearly.

08 윗글의 앞에 나왔을 내용으로 가장 알맞은 것은?

① 호주의 관광 명소로 유명한 건축물들 소개

② Jørn Utzon의 어린 시절 일화

③ 다른 나라의 오페라 하우스와 시드니 오페라 하우스의 비교

④ 시드니 오페라 하우스의 지붕 묘사

⑤ 다른 건축물들과 각 건축가가 영감을 받은 대상의 예시

11 윗글의 ①~⑤ 중 주어진 문장이 들어갈 알맞은 곳은?

> Many people think that it is the waves in the ocean or a sailing boat.

① ② ③ ④ ⑤

12 윗글을 읽고 알 수 있는 것은?

① 호주에서 가장 유명한 건축물

② Jørn Utzon이 시드니 오페라 하우스를 완공한 연도

③ 많은 관광객이 시드니 오페라 하우스를 찾는 이유

④ 시드니 오페라 하우스의 건축가가 영감을 받은 것

⑤ 시드니 오페라 하우스에 비추는 조명의 개수

STEP
A

[13-16] 다음 글을 읽고, 물음에 답하시오.

What about Korea? ① Have you ever been to Dongdaemun Design Plaza in Seoul? Many people think ⓐ that the building ② looks like a giant spaceship. But ③ the architect, Zaha Hadid, took the curved lines from nature ④ so as to city people could enjoy them. ⑤ Thanks to its special design, ⓑ it has become a popular tourist attraction in Seoul.

13 윗글의 밑줄 친 ①~⑤ 중 어법상 틀린 것은?

①   ②   ③   ④   ⑤

14 윗글의 밑줄 친 ⓐthat과 쓰임이 같은 것은?

① Do you want this bag or that one?
② Is that your grandfather over there?
③ I wish you wouldn't say things like that.
④ Julia told me that she missed the school bus this morning.
⑤ This is the picture that was painted by my uncle.

15 윗글의 밑줄 친 ⓑ가 가리키는 것은?

① Korea
② Dongdaemun Design Plaza
③ a giant spaceship
④ the curved line
⑤ a popular tourist attraction

16 윗글의 내용과 일치하지 않는 것은?

① 동대문 디자인 플라자는 한국의 서울에 있다.
② 많은 사람들은 동대문 디자인 플라자를 보고 우주선을 떠올린다.
③ Zaha Hadid는 동대문 디자인 플라자의 건축가이다.
④ Zaha Hadid는 자연에서 재료를 가져와 동대문 디자인 플라자를 건축했다.
⑤ 동대문 디자인 플라자는 인기 있는 관광 명소이다.

[17-19] 다음 글을 읽고, 물음에 답하시오.

As you can see, many buildings try to capture the beauty of nature in their design. They are perfect examples of "Nature meets city." If you were an architect, what would you choose from _____?

고신도 유형

17 윗글의 밑줄 친 As와 같은 뜻으로 쓰인 것의 개수는?

ⓐ My uncle works as a tour guide.
ⓑ Jenny spilled the water as she was getting up.
ⓒ As you know, David is moving to California soon.
ⓓ As I felt tired, I took a taxi instead of walking home.

① 0개   ② 1개   ③ 2개
④ 3개   ⑤ 4개

18 윗글의 빈칸에 들어갈 말로 알맞은 것은?

① building   ② beauty   ③ nature
④ design   ⑤ example

19 윗글을 읽고 바르게 추론한 사람은?

① 보라: 이 글의 앞에는 건물의 디자인에 자연의 아름다움이 담긴 예가 언급되었겠네.
② 은재: 많은 건축물들이 환경친화적 재료를 사용하는 이유를 알겠어.
③ 수연: 도시의 건축은 자연환경을 파괴하니 자제해야 해.
④ 가영: 자연 속에 도시를 세워야 해.
⑤ 우빈: 건축물이 자연을 닮으면 많은 관광객이 보러 와.

[20-21] 다음 글을 읽고, 물음에 답하시오.

Have you heard of the expression, "Art imitates nature"? Many artists get their ideas and inspirations from the world around them. This is because the natural world is a beautiful place. The shapes in nature are very pleasing to the eye. For example, look at the egg on the left. Isn't it beautiful? 그것은 둥글고 부서지기 쉽지만, 그것의 내용물을 보호할 만큼 충분히 튼튼하다. Can you imagine a building that looks like an egg? Such a building actually exists in London.

20 윗글의 밑줄 친 우리말과 같도록 [조건]에 맞게 문장을 쓰시오.

> [조건]　1. 주어진 단어를 바르게 배열할 것
> 　　　　2. 콤마(,)를 포함할 것
> 　　　　3. 대소문자를 구별하고 문장 부호를 정확히 쓸 것

> it, round, to, its, contents, yet, is, strong, and, enough, delicate, protect

→ _____

_____

21 윗글을 읽고 쓴 다음 노트를 완성하시오.

> **"Art imitates _____"**
> • **Main Idea:** Many artists get _____
> 　　　_____ _____ _____
> 　　　from the world around them.
> • **Reason:** The natural world is a _____
> 　　　_____.
> • **Example:** A building in London looks like a(n)
> 　　　_____.

[22-23] 다음 글을 읽고, 물음에 답하시오.

ⓐNature has inspired many architects around the world. ⓑThis is the Sagrada Familia in Spain. ⓒIt is one of the most famous church in the world. Look at the beautiful tall columns inside the church. ⓓThey look like trees, aren't they? ⓔThe famous architect, Antoni Gaudi, used the shape of trees in the Sagrada Familia. That's how he brought the beauty of nature indoors.

22 윗글의 밑줄 친 ⓐ~ⓔ 중 어법상 틀린 것을 두 개 찾아 기호를 쓴 후, 문장을 바르게 고쳐 쓰시오.

(　　) → _____

(　　) → _____

23 윗글을 아래와 같이 요약할 때, 빈칸에 알맞은 말을 윗글에서 찾아 쓰시오.

고/난도

> Antoni Gaudi took the _____ _____
> _____ from nature when he built the
> _____ inside the Sagrada Familia. In this
> way, the _____ _____ _____ was
> brought _____ by him.

24 다음 글을 읽고, 밑줄 친 ⓐ와 ⓑ를 우리말로 해석하시오.

> What about Korea? Have you ever been to Dongdaemun Design Plaza in Seoul? Many people think that the building looks like a giant spaceship. ⓐBut the architect, Zaha Hadid, took the curved lines from nature so that city people could enjoy them. ⓑThanks to its special design, it has become a popular tourist attraction in Seoul.

ⓐ _____

ⓑ _____

After You Read_B

The Sagrada Familia
- Location: Spain
- Architect: Antoni Gaudi
- ❶ Its beautiful tall columns ❷ look like trees.
- The architect brought the beauty of nature ❸ indoors.

The Sydney Opera House
- Location: Australia
- Architect: Jørn Utzon
- The architect ❹ was inspired by an orange.

Dongdaemun Design Plaza
- Location: Korea
- Architect: Zaha Hadid
- The architect ❺ took the curved lines from nature.
- It is a popular ❻ tourist attraction in Seoul.

샤그라다 파밀리아 성당
- 위치: 스페인
- 건축가: Antoni Gaudi
- 그것의 아름답고 높은 기둥은 나무처럼 보인다.
- 건축가는 자연의 아름다움을 실내로 가져왔다.

시드니 오페라 하우스
- 위치: 호주
- 건축가: Jørn Utzon
- 건축가는 오렌지에서 영감을 받았다.

동대문 디자인 플라자
- 위치: 한국
- 건축가: Zaha Hadid
- 건축가는 자연에서 곡선을 가져왔다.
- 그것은 서울의 인기 있는 관광 명소이다.

❶ The Sagrada Familia의 소유격을 가리킴
❷ look like + 명사(구): ~처럼 보이다　　　　❸ (부) 실내로
❹ 「be동사 + 과거분사 + by」로 이루어진 수동태 문장
❺ take A from B: B에서 A를 가져오다　　　　❻ 관광 명소

Think and Write_Step 2

I go to Boram Middle School in Suwon. My school has a ❶ 4-story building. It also has a large playground, a gym and a small garden. The garden is ❷ on top of the school building. We grow some vegetables there ❸ so that we can have fresh food. My favorite place is the bench under the big tree. I ❹ love sitting there and ❺ talking with my friends. I like my school very much.

나는 수원에 있는 보람중학교에 다닌다. 우리 학교에는 4층짜리 건물이 있다. 우리 학교에는 또한 넓은 운동장과 체육관, 작은 정원이 있다. 정원은 학교 건물 옥상에 있다. 우리는 신선한 음식을 먹을 수 있도록 그곳에서 채소를 기른다. 내가 가장 좋아하는 장소는 커다란 나무 아래에 있는 벤치이다. 나는 그곳에 앉아서 친구들과 이야기하는 것을 아주 좋아한다. 나는 우리 학교가 아주 좋다.

❶ story는 '(건물의) 층'이라는 뜻의 명사로, 두 개의 명사(4, story)가 하이픈(-)으로 연결되어 하나의 형용사처럼 building을 수식
❷ ~의 꼭대기에　　　　❸ ~하도록, ~하기 위해(서) (목적)
❹ love는 목적어로 to부정사와 동명사를 모두 취할 수 있는 동사
❺ love의 목적어인 sitting there와 talking with my friends가 and에 의해 병렬 구조로 연결됨

Project_Step 2

This is my house. It ❶ looks like a tree. The roof opens ❷ so that I can get fresh air and sunshine ❸ all the time. ❹ You know what? My house can move ❺ around.

이것은 나의 집이야. 내 집은 나무처럼 보여. 내가 항상 신선한 공기를 얻고 햇빛을 받을 수 있도록 지붕이 열려. 그거 아니? 내 집은 움직일 수 있어.

❶ look like + 명사(구): ~처럼 보이다　　　　❷ ~하도록, ~하기 위해(서) (목적)
❸ 항상, 내내, 줄곧
❹ '그거 아니?'라는 뜻으로 재미있거나 놀라운 것을 말하려 할 때 사용하는 표현
❺ (부) 이리저리, 여기저기

실전 TEST

[01-02] 다음 글을 읽고, 물음에 답하시오.

The Sagrada Familia
- Location: Spain
- Architect: Antoni Gaudi
- Its beautiful tall columns look _____(A)_____ trees.
- The architect brought the beauty of nature indoors.

The Sydney Opera House
- Location: Australia
- Architect: Jørn Utzon
- The architect was inspired _____(B)_____ an orange.

Dongdaemun Design Plaza
- Location: Korea
- Architect: Zaha Hadid
- The architect took the curved lines _____(C)_____ nature.
- It is a popular tourist attraction in Seoul.

01 윗글의 빈칸 (A), (B), (C)에 들어갈 말이 바르게 짝 지어진 것은?

	(A)	(B)	(C)
①	at	– up	– to
②	at	– by	– from
③	like	– in	– to
④	like	– by	– from
⑤	for	– in	– into

02 윗글을 읽고 알 수 <u>없는</u> 것은?

① 사그라다 파밀리아 성당이 있는 나라
② 시드니 오페라 하우스의 건축가
③ 시드니 오페라 하우스 외관의 색
④ 동대문 디자인 플라자의 건축가
⑤ 동대문 디자인 플라자가 있는 도시

[03-04] 다음 글을 읽고, 물음에 답하시오.

I go to Boram Middle School in Suwon. My school has a 4-story building. It also has a large playground, a gym and a small garden. The garden is on top of the school building. <u>우리는 신선한 음식을 먹을 수 있도록 그곳에서 채소를 기른다.</u> My favorite place is the bench under the big tree. I love sitting there and talking with my friends. I like my school very much.

서술형

03 윗글의 밑줄 친 우리말과 같도록 주어진 단어들을 바르게 배열하여 문장을 쓰시오.

> grow, there, we, fresh food, some vegetables, we, so, can, that, have

→ _____

_____

04 윗글의 내용과 일치하지 <u>않는</u> 것은?

① 보람중학교는 수원에 있다.
② 보람중학교에는 4층짜리 건물, 운동장, 체육관, 정원이 있다.
③ 정원은 4층짜리 건물 옆에 있다.
④ 글쓴이가 가장 좋아하는 곳은 큰 나무 아래에 있는 벤치이다.
⑤ 글쓴이는 벤치에서 친구들과 이야기하는 것을 좋아한다.

신유형

05 다음 글의 빈칸에 들어갈 수 <u>없는</u> 단어는?

This is my house. It _____ like a tree. The roof opens so _____ I can get fresh air and sunshine all the _____. You know what? My house can move _____.

① that　　② time　　③ looks
④ nature　　⑤ around

W Words
고득점 맞기

01 다음 중 짝 지어진 두 단어의 관계가 [보기]와 같지 <u>않은</u> 것은?

[보기]   helpful – useful

① clear – obvious   ② really – actually
③ allow – permit   ④ indoors – outdoors
⑤ imitate – copy

02 다음 중 단어의 품사가 나머지와 <u>다른</u> 하나는?

① popular   ② pleasing   ③ curved
④ basic   ⑤ actually

03 다음 단어의 영어 뜻풀이의 빈칸에 들어갈 말로 알맞은 것은?

architect: a person who designs _____

① buildings   ② artworks   ③ shelves
④ contents   ⑤ clothes

04 다음 빈칸에 들어갈 말이 순서대로 짝 지어진 것은?

• Thanks _____ Richard, I found this great bookstore.
• Could you show me _____ when I visit your hometown?

① out – of   ② to – away
③ to – around   ④ with – away
⑤ with – around

05 다음 빈칸에 공통으로 들어갈 말을 한 단어로 쓰시오.

• In order to get the festival tickets, you have to _____ in advance.
• I have to return this _____ to the school library by July 6th.

→ _____

06 다음 빈칸에 들어갈 말로 알맞은 것은?

I love taking pictures of _____ such as mountains and beaches.

① story   ② nature   ③ example
④ design   ⑤ spaceship

고/단도
07 다음 중 밑줄 친 단어에 대한 설명으로 알맞지 <u>않은</u> 것은?

① They're checking the <u>contents</u> of the box.
(the things that are inside something)
② The needle was slightly <u>curved</u> at the end.
(having the form of a curve)
③ Babies have very <u>delicate</u> skin, so be careful.
(easily broken or damaged)
④ Joe believes that ghosts really <u>exist</u>.
(to be, or to be real)
⑤ Add the lemon <u>peel</u> to the olive oil and boil for 2 minutes. (the seed of a fruit)

08 괄호 안의 우리말과 같도록 빈칸에 알맞은 말을 쓰시오.

These shoes are _____ _____ at most department stores these days.
(이 신발은 요즘 대부분의 백화점에서 판매 중이다.)

09 다음 빈칸에 들어가지 <u>않는</u> 단어는?

> ⓐ We admired the _____ of the sunset.
> ⓑ The country has a _____ population of about 100 million.
> ⓒ Could you _____ Paul about dinner on Friday?
> ⓓ He has a unique ability to _____ any sound he hears.

① total   ② imitate   ③ remind
④ shine   ⑤ beauty

고
난도 신
유형
10 다음 영어 뜻풀이에 해당하는 단어가 쓰인 문장은?

> to represent or describe something very accurately using words or images

① Please do not touch the statue.
② He gave several examples to show that he is right.
③ It is impossible to capture her beauty in a painting.
④ Use the flash when you're taking pictures indoors.
⑤ The roof of the temple was held up by a row of thick stone columns.

11 다음 빈칸에 들어갈 말을 [보기]에서 골라 쓰시오.

> [보기]   express   expression
>   attract   attraction

(1) Namsan Seoul Tower is a popular tourist _____ in Seoul.
(2) Do you know the _____, "I have butterflies in my stomach"?
(3) The stores have many interesting items, so they _____ many people.

12 다음 중 두 단어의 관계가 같은 것끼리 짝 지어진 것은?

> ⓐ usual – usually   ⓑ express – expression
> ⓒ polite – politely   ⓓ move – movement
> ⓔ differ – different   ⓕ imagine – imagination

① ⓐ, ⓑ, ⓒ   ② ⓐ, ⓒ, ⓔ
③ ⓑ, ⓒ, ⓔ   ④ ⓑ, ⓓ, ⓕ
⑤ ⓒ, ⓔ, ⓕ

13 다음 중 밑줄 친 단어의 쓰임이 알맞지 <u>않은</u> 것은?

① Huge <u>waves</u> were breaking on the shore.
② Could you <u>lend</u> me your pen?
③ Lucy gets <u>pleasure</u> from helping others.
④ His early childhood <u>inspiration</u> him to write his first novel.
⑤ I went straight up to the door and knocked <u>loudly</u>.

고
난도
14 다음 중 밑줄 친 단어의 의미가 서로 같은 것은?

① You should not <u>pick</u> the flowers in the park.
   <u>Pick</u> your favorite number from 1 to 10.
② David hurt his hand in the <u>gym</u> class.
   Let's play in the <u>gym</u> when it rains.
③ The movie is based on a true <u>story</u>.
   The building is 20 <u>stories</u> high.
④ Could you <u>pass</u> me the pepper, please?
   Yujin practiced every day to <u>pass</u> the dance audition.
⑤ On my way to school, two <u>foreigners</u> asked me the way to City Hall.
   About 40 million <u>foreigners</u> visited the U.S. last year.

Listen & Speak

영작하기

우리말과 일치하도록 대화를 바르게 영작하시오.

1 Listen and Speak 1-A

B: _____

G: _____

B: _____

G: _____

해석   교과서 104쪽

B: 안녕, Lisa. 네 생일 파티에 나를 초대해
　 줘서 고마워.

G: 천만에. 나는 네가 와서 기뻐.

B: 이 꽃들은 너를 위한 거야. 생일 축하해!

G: 꽃들이 아름답구나! 고마워.

2 Listen and Speak 1-B

B: _____

G: _____

B: _____

G: _____

G: _____

B: _____

G: _____

B: _____

G: _____

B: _____

G: _____

교과서 104쪽

B: 수민아, 내가 타는 기차가 5분 후에 떠나.

G: 나는 네 여행이 즐거웠기를 바라, Daniel.

B: 물론 즐거웠지.

G: 너는 우리 마을에서 어느 장소가 가장 좋았
　 니?

B: 나는 민속촌이 가장 좋았어.

G: 그래, 민속촌은 이곳에서 가장 인기 있는 곳
　 이야.

B: 나는 한복을 입고 돌아다니는 게 정말 좋았
　 어. 내가 정말 멋져 보였어.

G: 그 말을 들으니 기쁘구나.

B: 나에게 여기저기 구경시켜 줘서 고마워.

G: 천만에. 조심해서 가.

3 Listen and Speak 1-C

A: _____

B: _____

A: _____

교과서 104쪽

A: 그 책은 어땠니?

B: 좋았어. 나에게 책을 빌려줘서 고마워.

A: 천만에. 별거 아니야.

4 Listen and Speak 2-A

M: _____

G: _____

M: _____

G: _____

교과서 105쪽

M: 실례합니다. 우산을 안으로 가져오면 안 됩
　 니다.

G: 아, 제가 우산을 어디에 두어야 하나요?

M: 밖에 우산꽂이가 있어요.

G: 알겠습니다. 거기에 둘게요. 감사합니다.

5 Listen and Speak 2-B

교과서 105쪽

B: _____

G: _____

B: _____

G: _____

B: _____

G: _____

B: _____

G: _____

B: _____

G: _____

B: _____

G: _____

해석

B: '세계 음악 콘서트' 표가 지금 판매 중이야.

G: 정말? 지금 당장 온라인으로 표를 예매하자.

B: 좋아. 어디 보자…. 11월 5일에 표가 아직 남아 있어.

G: 잘됐다. 학생 표 두 장을 예매하자.

B: 오, 내 남동생을 데려가도 될까?

G: 물론이지. 하지만 8세 미만의 어린이들은 데려오지 못한다고 쓰여 있어.

B: 문제없어. 그(내 남동생)는 10살이야.

G: 그래, 어린이 표 한 장을 추가할게. 총액이 25달러야.

B: 좋아.

G: 나는 콘서트를 보는 게 정말 기대돼!

6 Listen and Speak 2-C

교과서 105쪽

A: _____

B: _____

A: _____

B: _____

A: 실례합니다. 여기서 새들에게 먹이를 주면 안 됩니다.

B: 죄송합니다. 몰랐어요.

A: 저쪽에 있는 표지판을 확인해 주세요.

B: 알겠습니다. 감사합니다.

7 Real Life Talk > Watch a Video

교과서 106쪽

W: _____

_____

_____

_____

_____

_____

_____

W: 안녕하세요, 학생 여러분!

우리 미술관을 방문해 주셔서 감사합니다.

이 미술관은 1995년에 문을 열었습니다.

그때부터 이곳은 많은 유명한 작품을 전시해 왔습니다.

오늘, 여러분은 미술 책에 실린 유명한 작품 몇 점을 보게 될 것입니다.

관람을 시작하기 전에, 기본 규칙을 상기시켜 드리겠습니다.

작품의 사진을 찍을 수는 있지만 만져서는 안 됩니다.

이제 관람을 시작해 봅시다.

01 다음 중 짝 지어진 대화가 자연스럽지 <u>않은</u> 것은?

① A: Excuse me. You shouldn't fly a drone here.
B: Okay, I see.

② A: These flowers are for you. Happy birthday!
B: They're beautiful. Thank you.

③ A: You're not allowed to drink soda here.
B: Thank you for understanding.

④ A: Am I allowed to use a flash?
B: Sorry. You're not allowed to use a flash here.

⑤ A: Thank you for inviting me to your birthday party.
B: My pleasure. I'm glad you could come.

02 다음 대화의 밑줄 친 부분의 의도로 알맞은 것은?

A: Excuse me. <u>You're not allowed to bring your umbrella inside.</u>
B: Oh, where should I put it?
A: There is an umbrella stand outside.

① giving opinions
② agreeing with someone
③ asking someone for advice
④ telling someone how to do something
⑤ telling someone not to do something

03 다음 대화의 빈칸에 들어갈 말로 알맞은 것은?

A: How was the book?
B: It was great. _____
A: You're welcome. It was my pleasure.

① I hope you enjoyed the book.
② I'm looking forward to reading it.
③ Thank you for lending me the book.
④ I was not interested in the book at all.
⑤ I should return it to the library this week.

[04-05] 다음 대화를 읽고, 물음에 답하시오.

A: Sumin, my train is leaving in five minutes.
B: I hope you enjoyed your trip, Daniel.
A: Of course, I did.
B: Which place did you like most in my town?
A: I liked the folk village most.
B: Yeah, it's the most popular place here.
A: I really liked walking around in hanbok. I looked really cool.
B: I'm glad to hear that.
A: Thank you for showing me around.
B: _____ Have a safe trip.

04 위 대화의 빈칸에 들어갈 말로 알맞지 <u>않은</u> 것은?

① My pleasure.　　　② You're welcome.
③ Don't mention it.　　④ It was my pleasure.
⑤ I'm with you on that.

05 위 대화를 읽고 답할 수 있는 질문은?

① How many days did Daniel travel?
② What did Daniel eat in Sumin's town?
③ When will Sumin visit Daniel's town?
④ Which place did Daniel like most in Sumin's town?
⑤ How long does it take to get to Daniel's town by train?

06 다음 글의 빈칸에 들어갈 말로 알맞은 것은?

Hello, students! Thank you for visiting our art museum. Today, you will see some famous artworks from the art books. Before we begin the tour, let me remind you of a basic rule. You can take pictures of the artworks, but _____ _____. Now let's start the tour.

① you can also touch them
② make sure you touch them
③ I'm looking forward to touching them
④ I'm happy that you touched them
⑤ you're not allowed to touch them

07 다음 대화의 빈칸에 알맞은 말을 [조건]에 맞게 쓰시오.

> [조건] 1. [보기]에서 필요 없는 두 단어를 제외한 나머지 단어들을 사용할 것
> 2. 필요하면 단어의 형태를 바꿀 것
> 3. 대소문자를 구별하고 문장 부호를 정확히 쓸 것

[보기] help cake make thank
sorry me you for a at

A: How was your mom's birthday party?

B: It was great. _____

_____

A: My pleasure.

[08-10] 다음 대화를 읽고, 물음에 답하시오.

Somi: The tickets for the World Music Concert are on sale now.

Joe: Really? Let's book the tickets online right away.

Somi: Okay. Let's see.... There are still tickets left for November 5th.

Joe: Sounds good. Let's get two student tickets.

Somi: Oh, do you mind if I bring my little brother?

Joe: Not at all. But it says that you are not allowed to bring children under 8.

Somi: No problem. He's 10.

Joe: Okay, I'll add one child ticket. The total price is 25 dollars.

Somi: Great.

Joe: I can't wait to see the concert!

08 Which tickets are on sale now?

→ _____

09 Which children are Somi and Joe not allowed to bring to the concert?

→ _____

고
난도
10 위 대화의 내용과 일치하도록 다음 글을 완성하시오.

Somi and Joe are booking _____ _____ for the World Music Concert on _____ 5th. Somi is going to _____ _____ _____ _____. He can go to the concert because fortunately he's 10.

11 다음 대화의 빈칸에 알맞은 말을 [보기]에서 골라 쓰시오.

[보기] • Can I ask you a question?
• Do you have any questions?
• I'm sorry to hear that.
• Thank you for understanding.
• You'd better eat snacks here.
• You're not allowed to eat snacks here.

A: Excuse me. (1) _____

B: Sure, what is it?

A: Am I allowed to eat snacks?

B: Sorry. (2) _____

A: Okay, I see.

B: (3) _____

01 다음 우리말을 영어로 옮길 때, 여덟 번째로 오는 단어는?

그는 바이올린 연주자가 될 수 있도록 바이올린을 켜는 것을 매우 열심히 연습한다.

① he   ② violin   ③ so
④ can   ⑤ that

02 다음 괄호 안에 주어진 단어들을 배열하여 문장을 완성할 때 알맞은 것은?

The kitten is _____.
(hand, enough, small, fit, my, in, to)

① enough small to fit in my hand
② enough small fit in my to hand
③ small enough fit in my to hand
④ small enough fit to hand in my
⑤ small enough to fit in my hand

03 다음 중 영어를 우리말로 잘못 옮긴 것은?

① He set the alarm so that he could get up at 6 a.m.
  → 그는 아침 6시에 일어날 수 있도록 알람을 맞췄다.
② She drank warm milk, so she slept well.
  → 그녀는 잠을 잘 자기 위해서 따뜻한 우유를 마셨다.
③ My sister turned the music down so that I could read a book.
  → 내 여동생은 내가 책을 읽을 수 있도록 음악 소리를 줄였다.
④ We should hurry in order to be there in time.
  → 우리는 그곳에 제시간에 도착하기 위해 서둘러야 한다.
⑤ It was so dark that we could hardly see.
  → 너무 어두워서 우리는 거의 볼 수 없었다.

신유형
04 다음 중 어법상 옳은 문장의 개수는?

ⓐ He is not enough old to take care of himself.
ⓑ She reads web comics so that she can relieve her stress.
ⓒ The heater is hot enough to cause burns, so be careful.
ⓓ The water in the lake was clean enough for us to drink.
ⓔ You should keep milk in the refrigerator so that stays fresh.

① 0개   ② 1개   ③ 2개
④ 3개   ⑤ 4개

05 다음 빈칸에 공통으로 들어갈 말로 알맞은 것은?

• Let's get there early _____ that we can get good seats.
• There are no more chairs, _____ we'll have to stand.

① if   ② so   ③ such
④ since   ⑤ enough

06 다음 중 어법상 틀린 부분을 바르게 고친 것은?

The sofa was not enough comfortable for me to sit on.

① was → were
② enough → too enough
③ enough comfortable → comfortable enough
④ comfortable → comfortably
⑤ for me → of me

07 다음 빈칸에 알맞은 말이 순서대로 짝 지어진 것은?

> Semi swims every day _____ she can stay healthy. She is strong _____ lift heavy boxes.

① so – enough

② so that – enough to

③ so that – enough too

④ so as to – too enough

⑤ in order to – enough to

08 주어진 문장과 같은 의미를 나타내는 것은?

> I left home early to catch the first train.

① I left home early since I caught the first train.

② I left home early because I caught the first train.

③ I left home too early to catch the first train.

④ I left home early so that I could catch the first train.

⑤ Although I left home early, I couldn't catch the first train.

09 짝 지어진 두 문장의 의미가 서로 <u>다른</u> 것은?

① Rick is tall enough to reach the top shelf.
　 Rick is so tall that he can reach the top shelf.

② My grandmother is too weak to work in her garden.
　 My grandmother is so weak that she can't work in her garden.

③ Linda is strong enough to carry the chairs.
　 Linda is so strong that she can carry the chairs.

④ The boy studies several languages so that he can be a tour guide.
　 The boy studies several languages in order to be a tour guide.

⑤ Kate's son is old enough to go to kindergarten.
　 Kate's son is too old to go to kindergarten.

10 다음 중 문장에 대한 설명이 알맞지 <u>않은</u> 것을 <u>모두</u> 고르면?

① The pizza was big enough for four people to eat.
　 → '그 피자는 네 사람이 먹을 만큼 충분히 컸다.'로 해석한다.

② Please be quiet so that I can concentrate on the book.
　 → so that은 '결과'를 나타내는 절을 이끈다.

③ I spoke slowly so that Kevin could understand my Korean.
　 → I spoke too slowly for Kevin to understand my Korean.으로 바꿔 쓸 수 있다.

④ The monkey climbed up a banana tree so that he could eat the bananas.
　 → The monkey so climbed up a banana tree that he could eat the bananas.로 바꿔 쓸 수 있다.

⑤ This suitcase is small enough to carry on the plane.
　 → 「형용사+enough to+동사원형」은 '~할 만큼 충분히 …한'이라는 뜻을 나타낸다.

11 다음 문장을 [보기]의 문장과 연결할 때 so that을 써서 자연스러운 문장이 되는 것을 찾아 기호를 쓰시오.

(1) Close the door. 　　　　　　 (　　　)

(2) He parked the car in the shadow. 　 (　　　)

(3) Mr. Brown booked the window seat. 　 (　　　)

[보기] 　ⓐ He could see the nice view.
　　　　ⓑ It wouldn't get too hot.
　　　　ⓒ The cold air doesn't come in.

12 다음 우리말을 영어로 쓸 때, 빈칸에 쓰이지 <u>않는</u> 단어는?

> 이 탁자는 내가 옮길 만큼 충분히 작다.
> → This table is _____ _____ _____ _____ _____ carry.

① to　　　　② too　　　　③ small

④ for　　　　⑤ enough

서술형

13 다음 그림을 보고, [조건]에 맞게 문장을 완성하시오.

> [조건] 1. 각 학생이 돈을 저축한 목적이 되도록 쓸 것
>   2. so that과 could를 포함할 것

(1)

Jane saved money _____

_____.

(2)

Minho saved money _____

_____.

한 단계 더!

14 다음 문장을 [조건]에 맞게 바꿔 쓰시오.

> [조건] 1. enough를 사용할 것
>   2. 주어와 동사를 포함한 완전한 문장으로 쓸 것

(1) The stadium is so large that it can hold 3,000 people.

→ _____

(2) Sora is so brave that she can go into the Ghost House.

→ _____

(3) The skirt was so cheap that Amy could buy it.

→ _____

15 짝 지어진 세 문장의 의미가 같도록 괄호 안의 표현을 사용하여 문장을 완성하시오.

(1) Lucas studied hard to pass the final exam.

= Lucas studied hard _____

_____. (in order to)

= Lucas studied hard _____

_____. (so that, could)

(2) Bora ran fast to catch the last bus.

= Bora ran fast _____

_____. (so as to)

= Bora ran fast _____

_____. (so that, could)

16 다음 우리말과 같도록 [조건]에 맞게 영작하시오.

> [조건] 1. [보기]에서 알맞은 단어를 골라 사용할 것
>   2. enough를 사용할 것

> [보기]   understand   hold   lift

(1) 그 바구니는 모든 공들을 담을 만큼 충분히 크다.

→ _____

(2) John은 그 바위를 들 만큼 충분히 힘이 세다.

→ _____

(3) 이 책은 내 남동생이 이해할 만큼 충분히 쉽다.

→ _____

17 자신의 목표를 이루기 위해 했던 일 두 가지를 [보기]와 같이 so that을 사용하여 완전한 문장으로 쓰시오.

> [보기] I played the guitar every day so that I could join the school band.

(1) _____

_____

(2) _____

_____

다음 우리말과 일치하도록 각 문장을 바르게 영작하시오.

01
_____

'예술이 자연을 모방한다'라는 표현을 들어 본 적이 있는가?

02
_____

☆ 많은 예술가들이 그들의 아이디어와 영감을 그들 주변의 세상에서 얻는다.

03
_____

이는 자연계가 아름다운 곳이기 때문이다.

04
_____

자연의 형태는 보기에 매우 좋다.

05
_____

예를 들면 왼쪽의 달걀을 봐라.

06
_____

아름답지 않은가?

07
_____

☆ 그것은 둥글고 부서지기 쉽지만, 내용물을 보호할 만큼 충분히 튼튼하다.

08
_____

당신은 달걀처럼 생긴 건물을 상상할 수 있는가?

09
_____

이러한 형태의 건물이 런던에는 실제로 존재한디.

10
_____

자연은 세계의 많은 건축가들에게 영감을 주어 왔다.

11
_____

이것은 스페인에 있는 사그라다 파밀리아 성당이다.

12
_____

그것은 세계에서 가장 유명한 성당 중의 하나이다.

13
_____

성당 안에 있는 아름다운 높은 기둥들을 봐라.

14
_____

그것들은 나무처럼 보인다, 그렇지 않은가?

15
_____

☆ 유명한 건축가인 Antoni Gaudi는 사그라다 파밀리아 성당에 나무의 형태를 사용했다.

16
_____

그렇게 해서 그는 자연의 아름다움을 실내로 가져왔다.

17

_____

☆ 앞의 두 예시에서 우리는 무엇이 건축가에게 영감을 주었는지 쉽게 알 수 있다.

18

_____

하지만 호주의 다음 예시에서는 이것이 그다지 명확하지 않다.

19

_____

☆ 시드니 오페라 하우스의 건축가인 Jørn Utzon은 자연에서 형태를 가져와 자신의 상상력을 더했다.

20

_____

당신은 무엇이 그에게 영감을 주었는지 추측할 수 있는가?

21

_____

많은 사람들은 그것이 바다의 파도나 돛단배라고 생각한다.

22

_____

하지만 흥미롭게도, 그 영감은 오렌지에서 비롯되었다.

23

_____

지붕을 자세히 봐라.

24

_____

당신은 오렌지의 껍질들이 보이는가?

25

_____

오렌지색 조명이 건물을 비추면, 당신은 껍질들을 더 명확하게 볼 수 있다.

26

_____

한국은 어떤가?

27

_____

당신은 서울의 동대문 디자인 플라자에 가 본 적이 있는가?

28

_____

많은 사람들은 그 건물이 거대한 우주선처럼 보인다고 생각한다.

29

_____

☆ 하지만 건축가인 Zaha Hadid는 도시 사람들이 즐길 수 있도록 자연에서 곡선을 가져왔다.

30

_____

이 특별한 디자인 덕분에, 그것은 서울의 인기 있는 관광 명소가 되었다.

31

_____

☆ 보는 바와 같이, 많은 건물들이 디자인에 자연의 아름다움을 담아내려고 한다.

32

_____

그것들은 '자연이 도시를 만나다'의 완벽한 예이다.

33

_____

만약 당신이 건축가라면, 자연에서 무엇을 선택할 텐가?

Reading
고득점 맞기

[01-03] 다음 글을 읽고, 물음에 답하시오.

Have you heard of the expression, "Art imitates nature"? ① Many artists get their ideas and inspirations from the world around them. This is because the natural world is a beautiful place. ② The shapes in nature are very pleasing to the eye. ③ For example, look at the egg on the left. Isn't it beautiful? ④ It is round and delicate, yet weak enough to protect its contents. Can you imagine a building _____ looks like an egg? ⑤ Such a building actually exists in London.

01 윗글의 밑줄 친 ①~⑤ 중 흐름상 어색한 것은?

①   ②   ③   ④   ⑤

02 윗글의 빈칸에 들어갈 수 있는 것을 모두 고르면?

① who   ② that   ③ which
④ where   ⑤ what

03 다음 영어 뜻풀이에 해당하는 단어 중 윗글에서 찾을 수 없는 것은?

① to be, or to be real
② easily broken or damaged
③ to copy somebody or something
④ the things that are inside something
⑤ to let somebody or something do something

[04-06] 다음 글을 읽고, 물음에 답하시오.

Nature has inspired many architects around the world. This is the Sagrada Familia in Spain. ⓐ It is one of the most famous churches in the world. Look at the beautiful tall columns inside the church. ⓑ They look like trees, don't they? The famous architect, Antoni Gaudi, used the shape of trees in the Sagrada Familia. That's _____ he brought the beauty of nature indoors.

04 윗글의 밑줄 친 ⓐ와 ⓑ가 각각 가리키는 것이 순서대로 짝지어진 것은?

① nature – churches
② nature – the beautiful tall columns
③ the Sagrada Familia – churches
④ the Sagrada Familia – the beautiful tall columns
⑤ Spain – the beautiful tall columns

05 윗글의 빈칸에 들어갈 말로 알맞은 것은?

① how   ② why   ③ because
④ when   ⑤ what

06 윗글의 내용과 일치하지 <u>않는</u> 것은?

① Many architects have been inspired by nature.
② The Sagrada Familia is in Spain.
③ The Sagrada Familia is famous around the world.
④ The columns outside the Sagrada Familia look like trees.
⑤ Antoni Gaudi was inspired by trees when he built the columns for the Sagrada Familia.

[07-09] 다음 글을 읽고, 물음에 답하시오.

In the first two examples, we can (A) closely / easily see ①what inspired the architect. But in the next example from Australia, this is not so obvious. Jørn Utzon, the architect of the Sydney Opera House, ②took a shape from nature and add his imagination. Can you guess ③what it inspired him? Many people think (B) which / that it is the waves in the ocean or a sailing boat. But interestingly, the (C) imagination / inspiration came from an orange. ④Look at the roof closely. Can you see the peels of an orange? When orange lights are shone on the building, ⑤you can see the peels more clearly.

07 윗글의 (A), (B), (C)에서 알맞은 것끼리 짝 지어진 것은?

	(A)	(B)	(C)
①	closely	– that	– inspiration
②	closely	– which	– imagination
③	easily	– that	– imagination
④	easily	– which	– inspiration
⑤	easily	– that	– inspiration

08 윗글의 밑줄 친 ①~⑤ 중 어법상 틀린 것을 모두 고르면?

①　　　②　　　③　　　④　　　⑤

09 윗글을 읽고 답할 수 없는 질문은?

① Who was the architect of the Sydney Opera House?
② What was the architect of the Sydney Opera House inspired by?
③ What do many people think the architect of the Sydney Opera House was inspired by?
④ How high is the Sydney Opera House?
⑤ When can you see the orange peels more clearly on the Sydney Opera House?

[10-12] 다음 글을 읽고, 물음에 답하시오.

What about Korea? Have you ever (A) been / were to Dongdaemun Design Plaza in Seoul? Many people think that the building looks like a giant spaceship. But the architect, Zaha Hadid, took the curved lines from nature (B) in order to / so that city people could enjoy them. Thanks to its special design, it has become a popular tourist attraction in Seoul. As you can see, many buildings try to capture the beauty of nature in their design. They are perfect examples of "Nature meets city." If you were an architect, what (C) would / will you choose from nature?

10 윗글의 (A), (B), (C)에서 어법상 알맞은 말이 바르게 짝 지어진 것은?

	(A)	(B)	(C)
①	been	– in order to	– would
②	been	– so that	– will
③	been	– so that	– would
④	were	– in order to	– will
⑤	were	– so that	– would

11 윗글을 두 단락으로 나눌 때, 두 번째 단락이 시작되는 첫 네 단어를 쓰시오.

→ _____

12 윗글을 읽고 알 수 없는 것은?

① 동대문 디자인 플라자가 있는 도시의 이름
② 많은 사람들이 동대문 디자인 플라자를 보며 떠올리는 것
③ 동대문 디자인 플라자의 건축가의 이름
④ 동대문 디자인 플라자의 건축가가 자연에서 곡선을 가져온 목적
⑤ 동대문 디자인 플라자의 용도

서술형

[13-14] 다음 글을 읽고, 물음에 답하시오.

Have you heard of the expression, "Art imitates nature"? <u>Many artists get their ideas and inspirations from the world around them.</u> This is because the natural world is a beautiful place. The shapes in nature is very pleasing to the eye. For example, look at the egg on the left. Isn't it beautiful? It is round and delicate, yet strong enough to protect its contents. Can you imagine a building what looks like an egg? Such a building actually exists in London.

13 윗글의 밑줄 친 문장을 우리말로 해석하시오.

→ _____

14 윗글에서 어법상 틀린 문장을 <u>모두</u> 찾아 문장을 바르게 고쳐 쓰시오.

(1) _____

(2) _____

[15-16] 다음 글을 읽고, 물음에 답하시오.

In the first two examples, we can easily see what inspired the architect. But in the next example from Australia, this is not so obvious. Jørn Utzon, the architect of the Sydney Opera House, took a shape from nature and added his imagination. 당신은 무엇이 그에게 영감을 주었는지 추측할 수 있는가? Many people think that it is the waves in the ocean or a sailing boat. But interestingly, the inspiration came from an orange. Look at the roof closely. Can you see the peels of an orange? When orange lights are shone on the building, you can see the peels more clearly.

15 윗글의 밑줄 친 우리말과 같도록 [조건]에 맞게 영작하시오.

[조건]	1. [보기]의 단어들 중 필요한 것만 골라서 쓸 것
	2. 주어와 동사를 포함한 완전한 문장으로 쓸 것
	3. 대소문자를 구별하고 문장 부호를 정확히 쓸 것

[보기]	that	what	you	his	him
	I	can	will	guess	wonder
	inspiration	inspired	inspiring		

→ _____

16 윗글을 요약한 아래 글을 완성하시오.

Many people think that the Sydney Opera House was inspired by _____ _____.

But what inspired the architect of the Sydney Opera House was _____.

17 다음 글을 읽고, 주어진 질문에 완전한 영어 문장으로 답하시오.

What about Korea? Have you ever been to Dongdaemun Design Plaza in Seoul? Many people think that the building looks like a giant spaceship. But the architect, Zaha Hadid, took the curved lines from nature so that city people could enjoy them. Thanks to its special design, it has become a popular tourist attraction in Seoul.

(1) What do many people think Dongdaemun Design Plaza looks like?

→ _____

(2) Why did Zaha Hadid take the curved lines from nature?

→ _____

01 다음 영어 뜻풀이에 모두 해당하는 단어를 쓰시오.

- a set of printed sheets of paper that are held together inside a cover
- to make a reservation for a future time

→ _____

02 [보기]에서 알맞은 단어를 골라 문장을 완성하시오.

[보기]	inspire	inspiration
	express	expression
	imitate	imitation

(1) The parrot can _____ my voice.

(2) Do you know the _____, "Time is money"?

(3) The artist got her _____ from the world around her.

03 다음 그림을 보고, [조건]에 맞게 대화를 완성하시오.

[조건]　1. 괄호 안의 단어를 이용하여 총 6단어의 문장으로 쓸 것
　　　　2. 주어와 동사를 포함한 완전한 문장으로 쓸 것

A: Excuse me. _____
　　　　　　　　　　　　(allow, here)
B: I'm sorry. I didn't know that.
A: Please check the sign over there.
B: Okay. Thank you.

04 괄호 안의 말을 이용하여 대화를 완성하시오.

A: How was the book?
B: It was great. _____
　　　　　　　　　　　　(lend me the book)
A: You're welcome. It was my pleasure.

05 다음 미술관에서 허용되는 것과 허용되지 않는 것을 우리 말로 쓰시오.

　　This museum opened in 1995. Since then, it has exhibited many famous artworks. Today, you will see some famous artworks from the art books. Before we begin the tour, let me remind you of a basic rule. You can take pictures of the artworks, but you're not allowed to touch them. Now let's start the tour.

(1) 허용되는 것: _____

(2) 허용되지 않는 것: _____

고
난도
[06-07] 다음 상황을 읽고, 마지막 질문에 대한 답을 [조건]에 맞게 쓰시오.

06　Your friend helped you plant some flowers in your garden. What will you say to your friend?

[조건]　1. Thank로 문장을 시작할 것
　　　　2. 대소문자를 구별하고 문장 부호를 정확히 쓸 것

→ _____

07　You work as a librarian in the library. You see a boy eating snacks. You have to tell him not to eat them. What will you say to him?

[조건]　1. you와 allow를 이용할 것
　　　　2. 주어와 동사를 포함한 완전한 문장으로 쓸 것

→ _____

08 다음 Daniel의 일기를 읽고, 아래 대화를 완성하시오.

> August 20
> I'm back home today. It was a great trip. I liked the folk village most. I really liked walking around in hanbok. I looked really cool. I said thank you to Sumin for showing me around.

Daniel: Sumin, my train is leaving in five minutes.
Sumin: I hope you enjoyed your trip.
Daniel: Of course, I did.
Sumin: Which place did you like most in my town?
Daniel: (1) _____
Sumin: Yeah, it's the most popular place here.
Daniel: (2) _____
I looked really cool.
Sumin: I'm glad to hear that.
Daniel: (3) _____
Sumin: It was my pleasure. Have a safe trip.

09 다음 중 어법상 틀린 문장을 두 개 찾아 기호를 쓴 후, 문장을 바르게 고쳐 쓰시오.

ⓐ His painting is good enough to sell.
ⓑ You should be in a hurry so that you won't be late for the club meeting.
ⓒ It was enough warm to eat out this evening.
ⓓ David practices playing the guitar very hard in order that win the contest.
ⓔ I collected used books so as to donate them.

( ) → _____
_____
( ) → _____
_____

10 다음 우리말과 같도록 [조건]에 맞게 영작하시오.

[조건] 1. [보기]에서 알맞은 단어를 두 개씩 골라 쓸 것 (필요하면 형태를 바꿀 것)
2. so that을 사용할 것

[보기] pass go study catch

(1) Ben은 시험에 통과할 수 있도록 열심히 공부한다.
→ _____
(2) Amy는 첫 기차를 탈 수 있도록 일찍 잠자리에 들었다.
→ _____

11 다음 글에서 어법상 틀린 부분을 두 개 찾아 바르게 고쳐 쓰시오.

This is Dream Amusement Park. Hosu is tall enough to got on the ride. Sumi isn't bravery enough to go into the Ghost House. Minho's English is good enough to talk with a foreigner.

(1) _____ → _____
(2) _____ → _____

12 다음 상황에서 할 수 있는 말을 so that을 사용하여 완성하시오.

(1)
Bora wants to make a cake for her mother's birthday. You think that taking baking classes is a good idea.

→ Bora, take _____
_____.

(2)
You are reading a book and your brother, Giho is watching TV in the living room. He turns the volume up and you can't concentrate on your book.

→ Giho, please turn _____
_____.

13 다음 괄호 안의 단어들을 바르게 배열하여 문장을 완성하시오.

(1) _____

(smart, is, to, difficult, solve, the, enough, Peter, quiz)

(2) _____

(enough, Amy, the, to, lift, box, is, strong, not)

14 다음 [조건]에 맞게 문장을 자유롭게 완성하시오.

> [조건]　1. 앞뒤 문맥상 의미가 통하도록 쓸 것
> 　　　　2. so that을 사용할 것

(1) We should exercise every day _____

_____.

(2) Write a diary _____

_____.

(3) Open the windows often _____

_____.

[15-16] 다음 글을 읽고, 물음에 답하시오.

　Have you heard of the expression, "Art imitates nature"? Many artists get their ideas and inspirations from the world around them. This is because the natural world is a beautiful place. The shapes in nature are very pleasing to the eye. For example, look at the egg on the left. Isn't it beautiful? <u>It is round and delicate, yet strong enough to protect its contents.</u> Can you imagine a building that looks like an egg? Such a building actually exists in London.

15 윗글의 밑줄 친 문장을 우리말로 해석하시오.

→ _____

16 윗글의 내용과 일치하도록 다음 질문에 완전한 영어 문장으로 답하시오.

(1) Why do many artists get their ideas and inspirations from the world around them?

→ _____

_____

(2) In which city can we find a building that looks like an egg?

→ _____

_____

[17-18] 다음 글을 읽고, 물음에 답하시오.

　<u>자연은 세계의 많은 건축가들에게 영감을 주어 왔다.</u> This is the Sagrada Familia in Spain. It is one of the most famous churches in the world. Look at the beautiful tall columns inside the church. They look like trees, don't they? The famous architect, Antoni Gaudi, used the shape of trees in the Sagrada Familia. That's how he brought the beauty of nature indoors.

17 윗글의 밑줄 친 우리말을 [조건]에 맞게 영작하시오.

> [조건]　1. 동사 inspire를 이용해 현재완료 시제로 쓸 것
> 　　　　2. many와 around를 포함할 것

→ _____

18 윗글의 내용과 일치하도록 다음 대화를 완성하시오.

Reporter:	How did you bring the beauty of nature indoors?
Antoni Gaudi:	I used (1) _____ in the Sagrada Familia.
Reporter:	Where did you apply the shape to?
Antoni Gaudi:	Look at (2) _____.
Reporter:	Oh, they look like trees!

[19-20] 다음 글을 읽고, 물음에 답하시오.

In the first two examples, we can easily see what inspired the architect. But in the next example from Australia, ⓐthis is not so obvious. Jørn Utzon, the architect of the Sydney Opera House, took a shape from nature and added his imagination. Can you guess what inspired him? Many people think that it is the waves in the ocean or a sailing boat. But interestingly, the inspiration came from an orange. Look at the roof closely. Can you see the peels of an orange? When orange lights are shone on the building, you can see the peels more clearly.

19 윗글의 밑줄 친 ⓐthis가 가리키는 것을 윗글에서 찾아 4단 어로 쓰시오.

→ _____

20 윗글의 내용과 일치하도록 다음 문장을 완성하시오.

Jørn Utzon, the _____ of the Sydney Opera House, was inspired by _____.

[21-22] 다음 글을 읽고, 물음에 답하시오.

What about Korea? Have you ever been to Dongdaemun Design Plaza in Seoul? Many people think that the building looks at a giant spaceship. But the architect, Zaha Hadid, took the curved lines from nature so that city people could enjoy them. Thanks for its special design, it has become a popular tourist attraction in Seoul.

21 윗글에서 문맥상 어색한 문장을 두 개 찾아 바르게 고쳐 쓰시오.

(1) _____

_____

(2) _____

_____

22 윗글의 내용을 요약한 다음 문장을 완성하시오.

Zaha Hadid took _____ and used them in Dongdaemun Design Plaza in order that _____ them.

23 다음 글을 읽고, 'I'가 되어 인터뷰 질문에 대한 답을 완전한 영어 문장으로 쓰시오.

I go to Boram Middle School in Suwon. My school has a 4-story building. It also has a large playground, a gym and a small garden. The garden is on top of the school building. We grow some vegetables there so that we can have fresh food. My favorite place is the bench under the big tree. I love sitting there and talking with my friends. I like my school very much.

(1) What does your school have?

→ _____

(2) Where is the garden?

→ _____

(3) What is your favorite place?

→ _____

01 다음 중 짝 지어진 단어의 관계가 [보기]와 같은 것은? [3점]

> [보기]　　　　　allow – permit

① like – dislike
② obvious – clear
③ begin – finish
④ lend – borrow
⑤ indoors – outdoors

02 다음 중 영어 뜻풀이가 알맞지 <u>않은</u> 것은? [3점]

① actually: used to refer to what is true or real
② delicate: having the form of a curve
③ contents: the things that are inside something
④ pleasing: giving pleasure, enjoyment, or satisfaction
⑤ column: a long post made of steel, stone, etc., used to support a building

03 다음 빈칸에 공통으로 들어갈 말로 알맞은 것은? [4점]

> • If you _____ the museum tickets now, you can get a discount.
> • The Adventures of Tom Sawyer is a _____ by Mark Twain.

① sign
② touch
③ book
④ pick
⑤ pass

04 다음 빈칸에 들어가지 <u>않는</u> 단어는? [4점]

> ⓐ The gallery will _____ Van Gogh's paintings from next month.
> ⓑ Lucy taught me some _____ dance steps.
> ⓒ The artist usually gets his _____ from nature.
> ⓓ Bill doesn't _____ his feelings to others.

① express
② basic
③ imitate
④ inspiration
⑤ exhibit

05 다음 대화의 빈칸에 들어갈 말로 알맞은 것은? [3점]

> A: How was the movie?
> B: It was great. _____ recommending it.
> A: You're welcome. It was my pleasure.

① Sorry for
② Thank you for
③ I'm good at
④ I'm interested in
⑤ I'm looking forward to

[06-07] 다음 글을 읽고, 물음에 답하시오.

> Hello, students! Thank you for visiting our art museum. This museum opened in 1995. Since then, it has exhibited many famous artworks.
> (A) You can take pictures of the artworks, but you're not allowed to touch them.
> (B) Today, you will see some famous artworks from the art books.
> (C) Before we begin the tour, let me remind you of a basic rule.
> (D) Now let's start the tour.

06 자연스러운 흐름이 되도록 (A)~(D)를 바르게 배열한 것은? [4점]

① (A) – (B) – (D) – (C)
② (A) – (C) – (B) – (D)
③ (B) – (C) – (A) – (D)
④ (B) – (D) – (A) – (C)
⑤ (D) – (A) – (B) – (C)

07 윗글을 읽고 알 수 <u>없는</u> 것은? [4점]

① 말을 하고 있는 장소
② 미술관이 개관한 연도
③ 미술관에서 전시하고 있는 작품 수
④ 미술관에서의 사진 촬영에 관한 규칙
⑤ 미술관에서 금지된 행동

[서술형 1]

08 괄호 안의 말을 이용하여 대화의 빈칸에 알맞은 문장을 쓰시오. [4점]

> A: Hi, Lisa. _____
>
> _____
>
> (thank, invite, your birthday party)
> B: My pleasure. I'm glad you could come.
> A: These flowers are for you. Happy birthday!
> B: They are beautiful! Thank you.

[09-10] 다음 대화를 읽고, 물음에 답하시오.

> A: The tickets for the World Music Concert are on sale now.
> B: Really? Let's book the tickets online right away.
> A: Okay. Let's see.... ①There are still tickets left for November 5th.
> B: Sounds good. ②Let's get two student tickets.
> A: Oh, do you mind if I bring my little brother?
> B: Not at all. ③But it says that you are allowed to bring children under 8.
> A: No problem. He's 10.
> B: Okay, I'll add one child ticket. ④The total price is 25 dollars.
> A: Great.
> B: ⑤I can't wait to see the concert!

09 위 대화의 밑줄 친 ①~⑤ 중 흐름상 어색한 것은? [4점]

① ② ③ ④ ⑤

[서술형 2]

10 위 대화의 내용과 일치하도록 다음 문장을 완성하시오. [4점]

> They booked two student tickets and _____ _____ _____ for the World Music Concert on _____ _____.

[11-12] 다음 빈칸에 들어갈 말로 알맞은 것을 고르시오. [각 3점]

11
> Anna turned on the TV _____ she could watch the comedy show.

① however   ② although   ③ so that
④ in fact   ⑤ in order to

12
> William is smart _____ to solve the difficult puzzle.

① too   ② for   ③ so
④ that   ⑤ enough

13 다음 중 어법상 틀린 문장은? [4점]

① I'm saving money so that I can donate it to the poor.
② I practice playing tennis very hard to win the tennis match.
③ Jason got up early so as to catch the first train.
④ I stayed at home in order to finish my art homework.
⑤ Amy drank warm milk so that could sleep well.

[서술형 3]

14 다음 우리말과 같도록 괄호 안의 표현을 사용하여 문장을 쓰시오. [각 3점]

(1) 그는 내게 동네를 구경시켜 줄 만큼 충분히 친절했다.
　　(kind, show me around the town)
　　→ _____

(2) 그녀는 그 무거운 상자를 들어 올릴 만큼 충분히 힘이 세다.
　　(strong, lift the heavy box)
　　→ _____

[15-17] 다음 글을 읽고, 물음에 답하시오.

Have you heard of the expression, "Art imitates nature"? Many artists get their ideas and inspirations from the world around them. ⓐThis is because the natural world is a beautiful place. The shapes in nature are very pleasing to the eye. ___ⓑ___, look at the egg on the left. Isn't it beautiful? (A)It is round and delicate, yet strong enough protect its contents. (B)Can you imagine a building that look like an egg? Such a building actually exists in London.

서술형 **4**

15 윗글의 밑줄 친 ⓐThis가 가리키는 것을 우리말로 쓰시오. [4점]

→ _____

_____

16 윗글의 빈칸 ⓑ에 들어갈 말로 알맞은 것은? [4점]

① In fact   ② In addition   ③ However
④ Instead   ⑤ For example

서술형 **5**

17 윗글의 밑줄 친 (A)와 (B)의 문장을 어법상 바르게 고쳐 쓰시오. [각 3점]

(A) → _____

_____

(B) → _____

_____

[18-20] 다음 글을 읽고, 물음에 답하시오.

Nature has (A)captured / inspired many architects around the world. This is the Sagrada Familia in Spain. It is one of the most famous churches in the world. Look at the beautiful tall columns inside the church. They look ⓐlike trees, don't they? The famous architect, Antoni Gaudi, used the shape of (B)leaves / trees in the Sagrada Familia. That's how he brought the beauty of nature (C)indoors / outdoors.

18 윗글의 (A)~(C)에서 글의 흐름상 알맞은 단어가 바르게 짝 지어진 것은? [4점]

       (A)   (B)   (C)
① captured – leaves – indoors
② captured – trees – indoors
③ inspired – leaves – outdoors
④ inspired – trees – indoors
⑤ inspired – trees – outdoors

19 윗글의 밑줄 친 ⓐlike와 쓰임이 같은 것은? [4점]

① I like baseball, but my sister loves basketball.
② The boy was acting like a little child.
③ Judy doesn't like to spend her evenings in front of the TV.
④ I'd like to hear your opinion on the subject.
⑤ What kind of club activity do you like best?

20 윗글을 읽고 알 수 있는 것을 모두 고르면? [4점]

① 사그라다 파밀리아 성당이 있는 나라
② 사그라다 파밀리아 성당이 인기 있는 이유
③ 사그라다 파밀리아 성당 안에 있는 기둥의 개수
④ Antoni Gaudi가 사그라다 파밀리아 성당의 기둥을 만들 때 영감을 받은 것
⑤ Antoni Gaudi가 사그라다 파밀리아 성당을 지은 이유

[21-23] 다음 글을 읽고, 물음에 답하시오.

In the first two examples, we can easily see what ⓐ(inspire) the architect. But in the next example from Australia, this is not so obvious. Jørn Utzon, the architect of the Sydney Opera House, took a shape from nature and ⓑ(add) his imagination. Can you guess what inspired him? Many people think that it is the waves in the ocean or a sailing boat. But ⓒ(interest), the inspiration came from an orange. Look at the roof closely. Can you see the peels of an orange? When orange lights are shone on the building, you can see the peels more clearly.

21 윗글의 ⓐ~ⓒ의 괄호 안의 단어를 알맞은 형태로 바꾼 것끼리 짝 지어진 것은? [4점]

	ⓐ	ⓑ	ⓒ
①	inspired	– added	– interestingly
②	inspired	– was added	– interestingly
③	inspired	– added	– interesting
④	was inspired	– added	– interestingly
⑤	was inspired	– was added	– interesting

서술형 6
22 윗글을 요약한 아래 글을 완성하시오. [4점]

Many people think that _____ _____ inspired the architect of the Sydney Opera House. However, he was actually inspired by _____.

서술형 7
23 윗글을 읽고 답할 수 있는 질문을 골라 기호를 쓰고, 완전한 문장으로 답하시오. [5점]

ⓐ What was the architect inspired by in the first two examples?
ⓑ In which country can we see the Sydney Opera House?
ⓒ Why did the architect of the Sydney Opera House take a shape from nature?
ⓓ Why did the architect of the Sydney Opera House add his imagination?

(   ) → _____

[24-25] 다음 글을 읽고, 물음에 답하시오.

This is my house. ①It looks like a tree. ②The tree has survived for many years. ③The roof opens so that I can get fresh air and sunshine all the time. ④You know what? ⑤My house can move around.

24 윗글의 밑줄 친 ①~⑤ 중 글의 흐름상 관계없는 문장은? [4점]

①   ②   ③   ④   ⑤

서술형 8
25 윗글의 'I'가 지호(Jiho)일 때, 윗글의 내용과 일치하도록 다음 대화를 완성하시오. [4점]

Jiho: Welcome to my house.
Ella: Wow, your house is amazing!
Jiho: Thanks. What does it look like?
Ella: Well, it (1) _____.
Jiho: Right. Look at the roof. It opens in order to (2) _____.
Ella: That's great! What else is special about your house?
Jiho: My house can (3) _____.

01 다음 중 짝 지어진 단어의 관계가 나머지와 다른 하나는? [3점]

① attract – attraction
② local – location
③ inspire – inspiration
④ imitate – imitation
⑤ express – expression

02 다음 중 밑줄 친 부분의 우리말 뜻이 알맞지 않은 것은? [3점]

① I take yoga classes to stay healthy.
　　　　　　　　　　　　(건강을 유지하다)
② Let me show you around this town.
　　　　(~에게 구경시켜 주다)
③ Thanks to the map, we could find the way easily.
　(~ 덕분에)
④ The ball is too big to go through the hole.
　　　　　　　　　　(내려가다)
⑤ This tower has become a famous tourist attraction in my hometown. 　　　(관광 명소)

03 다음 중 밑줄 친 단어의 쓰임이 어색한 것은? [4점]

① Please remind me to post this letter.
② The boy touched the worm on his hand.
③ Liszt's music is very pleased to the ear.
④ I was moved by the beauty of the scenery.
⑤ This glass is very delicate, so be careful with it.

04 다음 대화의 빈칸에 들어갈 말로 알맞은 것은? [4점]

> A: Excuse me. _____ bring your umbrella inside.
> B: Oh, where should I put it?
> A: There is an umbrella stand outside.
> B: Okay. I'll put it there. Thank you.

① I'm going to
② Make sure you
③ I'm trying to
④ I would like to
⑤ You're not allowed to

05 다음 중 짝 지어진 대화가 자연스럽지 않은 것은? [4점]

① A: You're not allowed to feed the birds here.
　 B: I'm sorry. I didn't know that.
② A: How was your mom's birthday party?
　 B: It was great. Thank you for helping me make a cake.
③ A: Excuse me. Can I ask you a question?
　 B: Sure, what is it?
④ A: These flowers are for you. Happy birthday!
　 B: They are beautiful. I'm sorry to hear that.
⑤ A: Am I allowed to bring a pet?
　 B: Sorry. You're not allowed to bring a pet here.

[06-07] 다음 대화를 읽고, 물음에 답하시오.

> A: Sumin, my train is leaving in five minutes.
> B: I hope you enjoyed your trip, Daniel.
> A: _____①_____
> B: Which place did you like most in my town?
> A: _____②_____
> B: Yeah, it's the most popular place here.
> A: I really liked walking around in hanbok.
> _____③_____
> B: _____④_____
> A: Thank you for showing me around.
> B: _____⑤_____ Have a safe trip.

06 위 대화의 ①~⑤에 들어갈 말로 알맞지 않은 것은? [4점]

① Of course, I did.
② I liked the folk village most.
③ I looked really cool.
④ I'm glad to hear that.
⑤ I'm with you on that.

서술형 1

07 위 대화의 내용과 일치하도록 다음 글을 완성하시오. [4점]

> Daniel had a trip in Sumin's town. He liked the _____ _____ most. He really liked _____ _____ in _____.

[08-09] 다음 글을 읽고, 물음에 답하시오.

Hello, students! Thank you for visiting our art museum. This museum opened in 1995. Since then, it has exhibited many famous artworks. Today, you will see some famous artworks from the art books. Before we begin the tour, let me remind you of a basic rule. You can take pictures of the artworks, but you're not allowed to touch them. Now let's start the tour.

서술형 **2**

08 윗글의 내용과 일치하도록 빈칸에 알맞은 말을 쓰시오. [4점]

Q: Where does this talk take place?
A: It takes place at a(n) _____ .

09 윗글의 내용을 잘못 이해한 학생을 모두 고르면? [4점]

① 예나: 미술관은 1995년에 문을 열었어.
② 민준: 미술관은 많은 유명한 작품을 전시해 왔어.
③ 도야: 미술 책에 실린 작품은 아직 없어.
④ 우주: 작품의 사진을 찍어서는 안 돼.
⑤ 소영: 작품을 만지지 않도록 유의해야 해.

10 다음 빈칸에 들어갈 말이 순서대로 짝 지어진 것은? [3점]

• I lent my bike to Mike so _____ he could ride it in the park.
• Tim is old _____ to ride the roller coaster.

① that – too
② that – enough
③ what – enough
④ which – much
⑤ which – enough

서술형 **3**

11 다음 우리말과 같도록 괄호 안의 말을 사용하여 영작하시오. [각 3점]

(1) Sue는 그 야구 경기를 볼 수 있도록 TV를 켰다. (so that)

→ _____

(2) 이 책은 내가 읽을 만큼 충분히 쉽다. (enough, for)

→ _____

_____

12 다음 중 어법상 틀린 문장을 모두 고르면? [4점]

① I listen to piano music so that I can relieve my stress.
② We should turn off the light in order to save electricity.
③ Rachel is not enough tall to touch the shelf.
④ Mr. Johns spoke clearly so as to everybody could understand his speech.
⑤ The cheesecake is large enough for five people to eat.

13 다음 중 빈칸에 so가 들어갈 수 있는 것끼리 짝 지어진 것은? [4점]

ⓐ Amy saved money _____ that she could buy a present for her nephew.
ⓑ You should put on sunscreen in order not _____ get sunburn.
ⓒ I came home early _____ as to eat dinner with my family.
ⓓ Wash your sneakers with this soap _____ make them clean.

① ⓐ, ⓑ
② ⓐ, ⓒ
③ ⓐ, ⓑ, ⓒ
④ ⓑ, ⓒ
⑤ ⓒ, ⓓ

서술형**4**

14 다음 우리말을 [조건]에 맞게 영작하시오. [4점]

[조건]   1. [보기]에서 필요한 단어 3개를 골라 사용할 것

2. 10단어로 쓸 것

[보기]	so	too	enough
	go	run	come
	in	out	through

그 개는 그 구멍을 통과할 만큼 충분히 작았다.

→ _____

[15-17] 다음 글을 읽고, 물음에 답하시오.

①Nature has inspired many architects around the world. This is the Sagrada Familia in Spain. ⓐ그것은 세계에서 가장 유명한 성당 중의 하나이다. ②Look at the beautiful tall columns inside the church. ③They look like trees, aren't they? ④The famous architect, Antoni Gaudi, used the shape of trees in the Sagrada Familia. ⑤That's how he brought the beauty of nature indoors.

15 윗글의 밑줄 친 ①~⑤ 중 어법상 **틀린** 것은? [4점]

①   ②   ③   ④   ⑤

서술형**5**

16 윗글의 밑줄 친 ⓐ의 우리말을 [조건]에 맞게 영작하시오. [4점]

[조건]   1. 괄호 안의 단어들을 이용할 것

2. 대소문자를 구별하고 문장 부호를 정확히 쓸 것

→ _____

(famous, church, in)

서술형**6**

17 윗글을 아래와 같이 요약할 때, 빈칸에 알맞은 말을 윗글에서 찾아 쓰시오. [4점]

Antoni Gaudi took the _____ _____ _____ from nature when he built the the Sagrada Familia. In this way, the _____ _____ _____ was brought indoors by him.

[18-20] 다음 글을 읽고, 물음에 답하시오.

In the first two examples, we can ___ⓐ___ see what inspired the architect. But in the next example from Australia, this is not so obvious. Jørn Utzon, the architect of the Sydney Opera House, took a shape from nature and added his imagination. Can you guess what inspired him? Many people think that it is the waves in the ocean or a sailing boat. But ___ⓑ___, the inspiration came from an orange. Look at the roof ___ⓒ___. Can you see the peels of an orange? When orange lights are shone on the building, you can see the peels more ___ⓓ___.

18 윗글의 빈칸 ⓐ~ⓓ에 들어가지 **않는** 단어는? [4점]

① closely   ② easily

③ clearly   ④ hardly

⑤ interestingly

서술형**7**

19 윗글을 요약한 다음 문장을 완성하시오. [4점]

The _____ of the Sydney Opera House was inspired by a(n) _____ and added _____ _____.

---

144   Lesson 6   Make the World Beautiful

20 윗글을 읽고 알 수 있는 것은? [4점]

① 앞에 나온 두 예시 건물이 있는 나라

② 앞에 나온 두 예시 건물을 지은 건축가의 이름

③ 매년 시드니 오페라 하우스를 찾는 관광객의 수

④ 많은 사람들이 시드니 오페라 하우스를 보고 건축가에게 영감을 주었다고 생각하는 것

⑤ 시드니 오페라 하우스의 건축가가 지붕 건설에 사용한 기법

[21-22] 다음 글을 읽고, 물음에 답하시오.

What about Korea? (①) Have you ever been to Dongdaemun Design Plaza in Seoul? (②) But the architect, Zaha Hadid, took the curved lines from nature (A) so as to / so that city people could enjoy them. (③) Thanks to its special design, it has become a popular tourist attraction in Seoul. (④)

 (B) As / Although you can see, many buildings try to capture the beauty of nature in their design. (⑤) They are perfect examples of "Nature meets city." (C) If / Unless you were an architect, what would you choose from nature?

21 윗글의 ①~⑤ 중 주어진 문장이 들어갈 알맞은 곳은? [4점]

Many people think that the building looks like a giant spaceship.

①　　　　②　　　　③　　　　④　　　　⑤

22 윗글의 (A)~(C)에서 알맞은 것끼리 짝 지어진 것은? [4점]

　　　　(A)　　　　(B)　　　　(C)

① so as to – As　　　 – If

② so as to – Although – Unless

③ so that　– As　　　 – If

④ so that　– As　　　 – Unless

⑤ so that　– Although – If

[23-25] 다음 글을 읽고, 물음에 답하시오.

(A) It also has a large playground, a gym and a small garden.

(B) My school has a 4-story building.

(C) We grow some vegetables there so that we can have fresh food.

(D) The garden is on top of the school building.

(E) I go to Boram Middle School in Suwon.

My favorite place is the bench under the big tree. I love sitting there and talking with my friends. I like my school very much.

*I = Bora

23 자연스러운 글이 되도록 (A)~(E)를 바르게 배열한 것은? [4점]

① (A) – (B) – (D) – (E) – (C)

② (A) – (E) – (B) – (D) – (C)

③ (B) – (A) – (D) – (E) – (C)

④ (E) – (A) – (B) – (C) – (D)

⑤ (E) – (B) – (A) – (D) – (C)

24 윗글을 쓴 목적으로 알맞은 것은? [4점]

① 자신의 학교를 소개하려고

② 학교의 건물을 묘사하려고

③ 학교의 축제를 광고하려고

④ 학교에서 기른 채소를 판매하려고

⑤ 학교 시설에 관해 건의하려고

서술형8

25 윗글의 내용과 일치하도록 다음 대화를 완성하시오. [5점]

Mike: What does your school have?

Bora: My school has ＿＿＿＿＿＿. It also has ＿＿＿＿＿, ＿＿＿＿＿ and ＿＿＿＿＿.

Mike: A small garden? What do you grow there?

Bora: We grow some vegetables so that ＿＿＿ ＿＿＿＿＿＿＿＿＿.

Mike: Sounds great!

01 다음 영어 뜻풀이에 해당하는 단어가 쓰인 것은? [3점]

> inside or into a building

① It's good to express your feelings.
② Don't imitate my body movements.
③ Let's go indoors and eat something.
④ The sign on the wall said "Wash your hands."
⑤ Please move the books onto the second shelf.

02 다음 빈칸에 들어가지 <u>않는</u> 단어는? [4점]

> ⓐ My back hurt and I can't _____ anything for a while.
> ⓑ Tom studied really hard to _____ the exam.
> ⓒ They are checking the _____ of the bag.
> ⓓ The _____ of this building are made of stone.

① lift   ② loudly   ③ columns
④ pass   ⑤ contents

서술형1
03 다음 우리말과 같도록 빈칸에 알맞은 말을 쓰시오. [각 2점]

(1) Where did your idea _____ _____?
   (네 아이디어는 어디에서 비롯되었니?)

(2) Clare's new book is _____ _____ at most bookstores now.
   (Clare의 새 책이 지금 대부분의 서점에서 판매 중이다.)

04 다음 대화의 빈칸에 들어갈 말로 알맞은 것은? [4점]

> A: How was your grandfather's birthday party?
> B: It was great. _____
> A: You're welcome.

① I made this cake for you.
② I hope you enjoyed the party.
③ I wanted to hold a party for him.
④ Thank you for helping me make a cake.
⑤ I wanted to invite you to his birthday party.

[05-06] 다음 대화를 읽고, 물음에 답하시오.

> A: The tickets for the World Music Concert are on sale now.
> B: Really? Let's book the tickets online right away.
> A: Okay. Let's see.... There are still tickets left for November 5th.
> B: Sounds good. Let's get two student tickets.
> A: Oh, do you mind if I bring my little brother?
> B: Not at all. But it says that you are not allowed to bring children under 8.
> A: _____ He's 10.
> B: Okay, I'll add one child ticket. The total price is 25 dollars.

05 위 대화의 빈칸에 들어갈 말로 알맞은 것은? [4점]

① Why not?   ② No problem.
③ My pleasure.   ④ That's too bad.
⑤ Sorry, I didn't know that.

서술형2
06 위 대화의 내용과 일치하도록 예매한 표에 관한 정보를 완성하시오. [4점]

> **World Music Concert**
> • Date _____ 5
> • Number of Tickets Students: _____
>   Children: _____
> • Total Price _____

[07-08] 다음 대화를 읽고, 물음에 답하시오.

> A: Excuse me. (①) Can I ask you a question? (②)
> B: Sure, what is it? (③)
> A: Am I allowed to use a flash? (④)
> B: Sorry. (⑤)
> A: Okay, I see.
> B: _____

07 위 대화의 ①∼⑤ 중 주어진 문장이 들어갈 알맞은 곳은? [4점]

> You're not allowed to use a flash here.

①   ②   ③   ④   ⑤

08 위 대화의 빈칸에 들어갈 말로 알맞은 것은? [4점]

① You like taking pictures.

② Things will be better soon.

③ Please take a picture for me.

④ Thank you for understanding.

⑤ I'm worried about using the flash.

09 다음 글의 내용과 일치하는 것은? [4점]

> Hello, students! Thank you for visiting our art museum. This museum opened in 1995. Since then, it has exhibited many famous artworks. Today, you will see some famous artworks from the art books. Before we begin the tour, let me remind you of a basic rule. You can take pictures of the artworks, but you're not allowed to touch them. Now let's start the tour.

① 미술관을 방문한 학생이 이야기하고 있다.

② 미술관이 개관했을 때는 유명한 작품이 없었다.

③ 미술관의 작품 몇 점은 미술 책에 실려 있다.

④ 미술관에서는 사진 촬영이 금지되어 있다.

⑤ 미술관의 일부 작품은 만져 볼 수 있다.

10 다음 중 어법상 옳은 문장은? [4점]

① Andy never uses plastic bottles to that he can protect the environment.

② Rosa saved money in order buy Yujin's birthday present.

③ Wendy studies very hard to getting better grades.

④ My father swims every morning so to stay healthy.

⑤ I went to bed early so that I could get up early next morning.

[서술형 **3**]

11 다음 그림을 보고, enough와 [보기]에서 고른 단어를 두 개씩 사용하여 글을 완성하시오. [각 2점]

[보기]	good	tall	brave
	go	get	talk

> This is Dream Amusement Park. Hosu is (1) _____ on the ride. Sumi isn't (2) _____ into the Ghost House. Minho's English is (3) _____ with a foreigner.

[서술형 **4**]

12 다음 [조건]에 맞게 문장을 바꿔 쓰시오. [각 3점]

> [조건]　　1. 괄호 안의 말을 반드시 사용할 것
> 　　　　2. 대소문자를 구별하고 문장 부호를 정확히 쓸 것

(1) Ms. Brown went to the train station in order to pick up her sister. (so that, could)

→ _____

(2) I was so tired that I fell asleep at the dinner table. (enough)

→ _____

13 다음 중 어법상 틀린 문장의 개수는? [4점]

> ⓐ I made some sandwiches in order to give them to Helen.
> ⓑ The ribbon is long enough to wrap around the gift.
> ⓒ We collected old clothes so that we could donate them.
> ⓓ The boat is not big enough to hold all of us.

① 0개　　② 1개　　③ 2개　　④ 3개　　⑤ 4개

[14-16] 다음 글을 읽고, 물음에 답하시오.

Have you heard of the expression, "Art imitates nature"? (①) This is because the natural world is a beautiful place. (②) The shapes in nature are very pleasing to the eye. (③) For example, look at the egg on the left. (④) Isn't it beautiful? (⑤) It is round and delicate, yet strong ____ⓐ____ to protect its contents. ⓑ(you, looks, a, imagine, that, building, like, an, can, egg)? Such a building actually exists in London.

14 윗글의 ①~⑤ 중 주어진 문장이 들어갈 알맞은 곳은? [4점]

Many artists get their ideas and inspirations from the world around them.

①   ②   ③   ④   ⑤

15 윗글의 빈칸 ⓐ에 들어갈 단어가 사용된 문장은? [4점]

① Are you able to imitate a monkey?

② Lukas is old enough to work and earn money.

③ Julian is the best football player in school.

④ We stood up in order to get a better view.

⑤ I need your help since there is too much work to do.

서술형 5

16 윗글의 ⓑ의 괄호 안에 주어진 단어들을 바르게 배열하여 문장을 완성하시오. [4점]

→ _____ ?

[17-18] 다음 글을 읽고, 물음에 답하시오.

Nature has inspired many architects around the world. This is the Sagrada Familia in Spain. It is one of the most famous churches in the world. Look at the beautiful tall columns inside the church. They look like trees, don't they? The famous architect, Antoni Gaudi, used the shape of trees in the Sagrada Familia. That's how he brought the beauty of _____ indoors.

17 윗글의 빈칸에 들어갈 말로 알맞은 것은? [3점]

① city   ② nature   ③ column

④ church   ⑤ architecture

서술형 6

18 윗글을 읽고 답할 수 있는 질문을 모두 골라 기호를 쓰고, 완전한 문장으로 답하시오. [5점]

ⓐ What have many architects around the world been inspired by?

ⓑ How high are the columns inside the Sagrada Familia?

ⓒ What do the columns inside the Sagrada Familia look like?

ⓓ Why did Antoni Gaudi build the Sagrada Familia?

(   ) → _____

(   ) → _____

[19-21] 다음 글을 읽고, 물음에 답하시오.

In the first two examples, we can easily ____ⓐ____ what inspired the architect. But in the next example from Australia, ①this is very obvious. Jørn Utzon, the architect of the Sydney Opera House, ②took a shape from nature and added his imagination. ③Can you guess what inspired him? Many people think that it is ④the waves in the ocean or a sailing boat.

But interestingly, the inspiration ⑤came from an orange. Look at the roof closely. Can you see the peels of an orange? When orange lights are shone on the building, you can _____ ⓑ _____ the peels more clearly.

19 윗글의 빈칸 ⓐ와 ⓑ에 공통으로 들어갈 말로 알맞은 것은? [3점]

① know   ② see   ③ learn

④ think   ⑤ take

20 윗글의 밑줄 친 ①~⑤ 중 글의 흐름상 어색한 것은? [4점]

①   ②   ③   ④   ⑤

(서술형 **7**)

21 윗글의 내용과 일치하도록 위의 건축물을 소개하는 글을 완성하시오. [3점]

```
            The Sydney Opera House
• Location: _____
• _____ : Jørn Utzon
Jørn Utzon was inspired by a(n) _____ .
```

[22-24] 다음 글을 읽고, 물음에 답하시오.

What about Korea? Have you ever been _____ Dongdaemun Design Plaza in Seoul? Many people think that the building looks _____ a giant spaceship. 하지만 건축가인 Zaha Hadid는 도시 사람들이 그것들을 즐길 수 있도록 자연에서 곡선을 가져왔다. Thanks to its special design, it has become a popular tourist attraction _____ Seoul.

As you can see, many buildings try to capture the beauty of nature in their design. They are perfect examples _____ "Nature meets city." If you were an architect, what would you choose from nature?

22 윗글의 빈칸에 쓰이지 <u>않는</u> 것은? [4점]

① to   ② in   ③ into

④ like   ⑤ of

(서술형 **8**)

23 윗글의 밑줄 친 우리말과 같도록 [조건]에 맞게 문장을 완성하시오. [4점]

```
[조건]   1. so that과 괄호 안의 말을 사용할 것
         2. 콤마(,)를 두 번 사용할 것
```

→ But _____

_____ .

(took, the curved lines, enjoy)

24 다음 중 윗글에 나오는 단어의 영어 뜻풀이를 <u>모두</u> 고르면? [3점]

① easy to see or understand

② easily broken or damaged

③ to copy somebody or something

④ a vehicle that travels in space, carrying people

⑤ to represent or describe something very accurately using words or images

(서술형 **9**)

25 다음 글의 밑줄 친 우리말과 같도록 [보기]에서 두 단어를 제외한 나머지 단어들을 바르게 배열하여 문장을 완성하시오. [4점]

```
[보기]
and, opens, I, that, too, sunshine, can, get, air,
the, roof, all, time, so, as, fresh, the
```

```
   This is my house. It looks like a tree. 지붕은 내
가 항상 신선한 공기를 얻고 햇빛을 받을 수 있도록 열려.
You know what? My house can move around.
```

→ _____

_____

01 주어진 단어의 영어 뜻풀이에 해당하지 <u>않는</u> 것은? [3점]

wave	exhibit	exist	inspiration

① to be, or to be real

② the things that are inside something

③ something that gives you ideas about what to do or create

④ to show something in a public place so that people can see it

⑤ a raised line of water that moves across the surface of the sea

---

서술형 **1**

02 [보기]의 단어를 이용하여 문장을 완성하시오. [각 2점] (필요시 형태를 바꿀 것)

[보기]	attract	express	imagine

(1) These flowers are brightly colored in order to _____ butterflies.

(2) The fantasy novel came from the author's _____ about the future world.

(3) I'd like to _____ my thanks for your kindness.

---

03 다음 중 밑줄 친 단어의 의미가 서로 같은 것은? [4점]

① Will you <u>peel</u> the potatoes?
Remove the <u>peel</u> from the banana.

② Please <u>sign</u> your name here.
The <u>sign</u> on the gate said "Keep Out."

③ I don't know which color to <u>pick</u>.
Don't <u>pick</u> roses in the park.

④ The play is based on a true <u>story</u>.
Her new house has four <u>stories</u> including an attic.

⑤ I'd like to <u>book</u> three tickets to Busan.
It was impossible for me to <u>book</u> a seat for the music festival.

---

04 다음 중 밑줄 친 부분의 쓰임이 어색한 것은? [3점]

① Babies' shoes are <u>with sale</u> in that store.

② Could you <u>show</u> me <u>around</u> your new house?

③ You'd better not <u>walk around</u> alone at night.

④ <u>Thanks to</u> you, I could finish my science project on time.

⑤ <u>Go through</u> this gate, and you'll see the kitchen.

---

05 다음 대화의 밑줄 친 부분의 의도로 알맞은 것은? [3점]

A: How was the book?
B: It was great. <u>Thank you for lending me the book.</u>
A: You're welcome. It was my pleasure.

① greeting someone ② expressing worry

③ showing appreciation ④ passing along a request

⑤ responding to good or bad news

서술형 **2**

06 다음 표지판을 보고, [조건]에 맞게 대화를 완성하시오. [각 2점]

[조건]	1. (1)에는 괄호 안의 말을 이용하여 총 8단어의 문장으로 쓸 것
	2. (2)에는 괄호 안의 단어들을 바르게 배열할 것

A: Excuse me. (1) _____
_____ (allow, fly a drone, here)
B: I'm sorry. I didn't know that.
A: Please (2) _____.
(sign, there, check, the, over)
B: Okay. Thank you.

07 다음 중 짝 지어진 대화가 자연스럽지 <u>않은</u> 것은? [4점]

① A: Thank you for inviting me to your birthday party.
　　 B: My pleasure. I'm glad you could come.
② A: Do you mind if I bring my sister to the concert?
　　 B: Not at all.
③ A: Excuse me. You shouldn't drink soda here.
　　 B: Okay, I see.
④ A: Am I allowed to touch the artwork?
　　 B: Sorry. You're allowed to touch the artwork here.
⑤ A: Thank you for helping me arrange the books on the shelves.
　　 B: You're welcome. It was my pleasure.

08 자연스러운 대화가 되도록 (A)~(D)를 바르게 배열한 것은? [3점]

(A) Okay. I'll put it there. Thank you.
(B) Oh, where should I put it?
(C) Excuse me. You're not allowed to bring your umbrella inside.
(D) There is an umbrella stand outside.

---

① (A) – (B) – (C) – (D)　　② (A) – (C) – (D) – (B)
③ (C) – (A) – (D) – (B)　　④ (C) – (B) – (D) – (A)
⑤ (D) – (B) – (A) – (C)

[09-10] 다음 대화를 읽고, 물음에 답하시오.

A: Sumin, my train is leaving in five minutes.
B: ①I hope you enjoy your trip, Daniel.
A: Of course, I did.
B: ②Which place did you like most in my town?
A: I liked the folk village most.
B: ③Yeah, it's the most popular place here.
A: I really liked walking around in hanbok. ④I looked really cool.
B: I'm glad to hear that.
A: ⑤Thank you for showing me around.
B: It was my pleasure. Have a safe trip.

서술형3

09 위 대화의 밑줄 친 ①~⑤ 중 흐름상 어색한 문장을 찾아 번호를 쓴 후, 문장을 바르게 고쳐 쓰시오. [4점]

(　　　) → _____

10 위 대화를 읽고 알 수 <u>없는</u> 것은? [4점]

① when Daniel's train is leaving
② the place Daniel liked most
③ the most popular place in Sumin's town
④ what Daniel really liked
⑤ the color of hanbok that Daniel wore

11 다음 중 밑줄 친 말의 쓰임이 알맞은 것끼리 짝 지어진 것은? [3점]

ⓐ Ms. White left the door open so <u>that</u> she could hear the baby.
ⓑ Joe wrote down Fred's birthday in his diary in <u>as</u> that he wouldn't forget it.
ⓒ The man in front of me was <u>so</u> tall that I couldn't see the movie.
ⓓ Nari goes to bed early so <u>as that</u> get plenty of sleep.

---

① ⓐ, ⓑ　　　　② ⓐ, ⓒ　　　　③ ⓐ, ⓓ
④ ⓑ, ⓒ　　　　⑤ ⓒ, ⓓ

12 다음 문장에 대해 <u>잘못</u> 설명한 사람은? [3점]

This book is easy enough for us to understand.

---

① 지민: 「형용사+enough to+동사원형」의 표현이 쓰였어.
② 세나: easy와 enough의 위치는 바꿀 수 없어.
③ 우진: This book is so easy that we can understand it.으로 바꿔 쓸 수 있어.
④ 지현: to understand의 의미상의 주어는 「for+목적격」으로 써야 하므로 for us의 쓰임은 맞아.
⑤ 승민: too ~ to ... 구문을 이용하여 바꿔 쓸 수 있어.

서술형 **4**

13 다음 우리말과 같도록 [조건]에 맞게 영작하시오. [각 3점]

> [조건]   1. so that을 사용할 것
>   2. 과거시제로 쓸 것

(1) 나는 수학을 공부하는 데 집중할 수 있도록 TV를 껐다.

→ _____

(2) 내 남동생은 새 자전거를 살 수 있도록 돈을 저축했다.

→ _____

서술형 **5**

14 다음 [조건]에 맞게 문장을 자유롭게 완성하시오. [각 3점]

> [조건]   1. 문장의 주어는 괄호 안의 형용사에 해당하는
>   대상으로 쓸 것(사람, 사물 등)
>   2. 괄호 안의 형용사, enough, to를 반드시 포
>   함할 것

(1) _____

(big)

(2) _____

(interesting)

[15-17] 다음 글을 읽고, 물음에 답하시오.

> Have you heard of the ___@___, "Art imitates nature"? Many artists get their ideas and inspirations from the world around them. This is (A) because / why the natural world is a beautiful place. The ___ⓑ___ in nature are very pleasing to the eye. (B) For example / In fact, look at the egg on the left. Isn't it beautiful? It is round and delicate, (C) so / yet strong enough to protect its contents. Can you imagine a building that looks ___ⓒ___ an egg? Such a building ___ⓓ___ exists in London.

15 윗글의 빈칸 @~ⓓ에 들어가지 <u>않는</u> 단어는? [4점]

① shapes　　② like　　③ expression

④ too　　⑤ actually

16 윗글의 (A)~(C)에서 글의 흐름상 알맞은 말이 바르게 짝 지어진 것은? [4점]

	(A)	(B)	(C)
①	because	For example	so
②	because	For example	yet
③	because	In fact	so
④	why	For example	so
⑤	why	In fact	yet

서술형 **6**

17 Where do many artists get their ideas and inspirations? [4점]

→ _____

[18-21] 다음 글을 읽고, 물음에 답하시오.

> Nature has inspired many architects around the world. This is the Sagrada Familia in Spain. ①It is one of the most famous church in the world. Look at the beautiful tall columns inside the church. ②They look like trees, don't they? The famous architect, Antoni Gaudi, used the shape of trees in the Sagrada Familia. That's how he brought the beauty of nature indoors.
>
> ③In the first two examples, we can easily see what inspired the architect. But in the next example from Australia, this is not so obvious. Jørn Utzon, the architect of the Sydney Opera House, took a shape from nature and added his imagination. Can you guess what inspired him? ④Many people think that it is the waves in the ocean or a sailing boat. But interestingly, the inspiration came from an orange. Look at the roof closely. Can you see the peels of an orange? ⑤When orange lights are shone on the building, you can see the peels more clearly.

18 윗글의 밑줄 친 ①~⑤ 중 어법상 <u>틀린</u> 문장의 개수는? [4점]

① 0개　　② 1개　　③ 2개　　④ 3개　　⑤ 4개

서술형 7

19 윗글의 the Sagrada Familia와 the Sydney Opera House의 공통점을 우리말로 쓰시오. [4점]

→ _____

서술형 8

20 윗글의 내용과 일치하도록 다음 대화를 완성하시오. [4점]

A: What inspired each _____?
B: Antoni Gaudi used _____
   in the Sagrada Familia. You can see the
   shape in _____ inside
   the church.
A: Oh, I see. What about the Sydney Opera
   House?
B: Jørn Utzon was inspired by _____.
A: That's interesting!

21 윗글을 잘못 이해하고 있는 사람은? [4점]

① 수현: 사그라다 파밀리아 성당 안의 기둥에서 Antoni Gaudi
   가 영감 받은 대상을 쉽게 찾아볼 수 있구나.
② 시원: Antoni Gaudi는 그가 영감을 받은 대상의 아름다움을
   실내로 가져왔어.
③ 지원: 시드니 오페라 하우스를 보면 건축가가 무엇에서 영감을
   받았는지 누구나 쉽게 알 수 있어.
④ 기우: Jørn Utzon은 영감을 받은 대상에 자신의 상상력을 더
   했구나.
⑤ 현주: 시드니 오페라 하우스에 오렌지색 조명이 비춰지면 건축
   가가 영감을 받은 것을 더 명확하게 볼 수 있어.

[22-23] 다음 글을 읽고, 물음에 답하시오.

What about Korea? Have you ever been to Dongdaemun Design Plaza in Seoul? Many people think that the building looks like ①a giant spaceship. But the architect, Zaha Hadid, took the curved lines from nature so that city people ②could enjoy them. Thanks to its ③ordinary design, it has become a popular tourist attraction in Seoul.

As you can see, many buildings try to capture ④the beauty of nature in their design. They are ⑤perfect examples of "Nature meets city." If ⓐ(were, you, would, choose, you, from, what, an, architect, nature)?

22 윗글의 밑줄 친 ①~⑤ 중 흐름상 어색한 것은? [4점]

①   ②   ③   ④   ⑤

서술형 9

23 윗글의 ⓐ의 괄호 안에 주어진 단어들을 바르게 배열하여 문장을 완성하시오. [4점]

→ If _____,
   _____?

[24-25] 다음 글을 읽고, 물음에 답하시오.

I go to Boram Middle School in Suwon. My school has a 4-story building. It also has a large playground, a gym and a small garden. The garden is on top of the school building. We grow some vegetables there so what we can have fresh food. My favorite place is the bench under the big tree. I love sitting there and talking with my friends. I like my school very much.

*I = Mina

서술형 10

24 윗글에서 어법상 틀린 부분을 찾아 바르게 고쳐 쓰시오. [4점]

_____ → _____

25 Which one is NOT true about Boram Middle School? [4점]

① It is in Suwon.
② It has a garden on top of the school building.
③ Students grow vegetables in the large playground.
④ Mina likes the bench under the big tree most.
⑤ Mina likes her school a lot.

● 틀린 문항을 표시해 보세요.

● 부족한 영역을 점검해 보고 어떻게 더 학습할지 학습 계획을 적어 보세요.

〈1회〉 대표 기출로 내신 **적중** 모의고사　　　　총점 _____ / 100

문항	영역	문항	영역	문항	영역
01	p.84(W)	10	p.89(L&S)	19	pp.104-105(R)
02	p.84(W)	11	p.96(G)	20	pp.104-105(R)
03	p.84(W)	12	p.97(G)	21	pp.104-105(R)
04	p.82(W)	13	p.96(G)	22	pp.104-105(R)
05	p.88(L&S)	14	p.97(G)	23	pp.104-105(R)
06	p.89(L&S)	15	pp.104-105(R)	24	p.118(M)
07	p.89(L&S)	16	pp.104-105(R)	25	p.118(M)
08	p.88(L&S)	17	pp.104-105(R)		
09	p.89(L&S)	18	pp.104-105(R)		

오답 공략
부족한 영역
학습 계획

〈2회〉 대표 기출로 내신 **적중** 모의고사　　　　총점 _____ / 100

문항	영역	문항	영역	문항	영역
01	p.84(W)	10	pp.96-97(G)	19	pp.104-105(R)
02	p.82(W)	11	pp.96-97(G)	20	pp.104-105(R)
03	p.82(W)	12	pp.96-97(G)	21	pp.104-105(R)
04	p.88(L&S)	13	p.96(G)	22	pp.104-105(R)
05	p.87(L&S)	14	p.97(G)	23	p.118(M)
06	p.88(L&S)	15	pp.104-105(R)	24	p.118(M)
07	p.88(L&S)	16	pp.104-105(R)	25	p.118(M)
08	p.89(L&S)	17	pp.104-105(R)		
09	p.89(L&S)	18	pp.104-105(R)		

오답 공략
부족한 영역
학습 계획

〈3회〉 대표 기출로 내신 **적중** 모의고사　　　　총점 _____ / 100

문항	영역	문항	영역	문항	영역
01	p.84(W)	10	p.96(G)	19	pp.104-105(R)
02	p.82(W)	11	p.97(G)	20	pp.104-105(R)
03	p.82(W)	12	pp.96-97(G)	21	pp.104-105(R)
04	p.88(L&S)	13	pp.96-97(G)	22	pp.104-105(R)
05	p.89(L&S)	14	pp.104-105(R)	23	pp.104-105(R)
06	p.89(L&S)	15	pp.104-105(R)	24	pp.104-105(R)
07	p.87(L&S)	16	pp.104-105(R)	25	p.118(M)
08	p.87(L&S)	17	pp.104-105(R)		
09	p.89(L&S)	18	pp.104-105(R)		

오답 공략
부족한 영역
학습 계획

〈4회〉 고난도로 내신 **적중** 모의고사　　　　총점 _____ / 100

문항	영역	문항	영역	문항	영역
01	p.84(W)	10	p.88(L&S)	19	pp.104-105(R)
02	p.84(W)	11	p.96(G)	20	pp.104-105(R)
03	p.84(W)	12	p.97(G)	21	pp.104-105(R)
04	p.82(W)	13	p.96(G)	22	pp.104-105(R)
05	p.88(L&S)	14	p.97(G)	23	pp.104-105(R)
06	p.89(L&S)	15	pp.104-105(R)	24	p.118(M)
07	p.87(L&S)	16	pp.104-105(R)	25	p.118(M)
08	p.88(L&S)	17	pp.104-105(R)		
09	p.88(L&S)	18	pp.104-105(R)		

오답 공략
부족한 영역
학습 계획

Lesson

7

Feel the Wonder

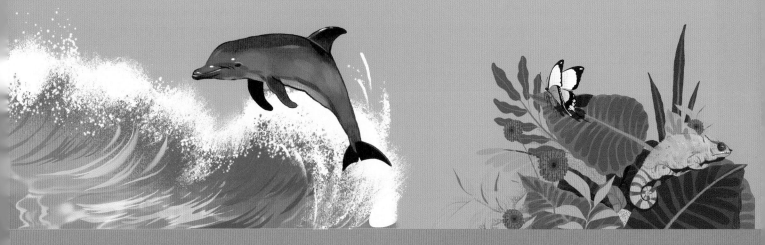

주요 학습 내용	의사소통 기능	궁금함 표현하기	A: **I wonder** where the bus stop is. (나는 버스 정류장이 어디에 있는지 궁금해.) B: It's in front of the police station. (그곳은 경찰서 앞에 있어.)
		보고하기	A: Is there anything interesting? (뭔가 재미있는 게 있니?) B: **This article says** scientists have discovered a new planet. (이 기사에 따르면 과학자들이 새로운 행성을 발견했대.)
	언어 형식	소유격 관계대명사	This small fish **whose** favorite food is clams uses a tool to open them. (가장 좋아하는 먹이가 조개인 이 작은 물고기는 조개를 열기 위해 도구를 사용한다.)
		시간을 나타내는 접속사	Humpback whales stand on their tails **while** they sleep. (혹등고래는 잠을 자는 동안 꼬리로 서 있다.)

학습 단계 PREVIEW					
STEP **A**	Words	Listen & Speak	Grammar	Reading	기타 지문
STEP **B**	Words	Listen & Speak	Grammar	Reading	서술형 100% TEST
내신 적중 모의고사	제 **1** 회	제 **2** 회	제 **3** 회	제 **4** 회	

STEP A

교과서 핵심 내용 학습 및 실전 TEST 구간

Words

만점 노트

☆ 자주 출제되는 어휘

* 완벽히 외운 단어는 □ 안에 √표 해 봅시다.

Listen & Speak

☐☐ article☆	똉 (신문·잡지의) 기사		☐☐ scenery	똉 경치, 풍경
☐☐ autumn leaves	단풍		☐☐ someday	傳 언젠가
☐☐ average	똉 평균의		☐☐ temperature	똉 기온
☐☐ be covered with	~으로 덮여 있다		☐☐ the South Pole☆	(지구의) 남극
☐☐ camel	똉 낙타		☐☐ this time of year	이맘때는, 이맘때쯤이면
☐☐ complete	똉 완료하다 똉 완전한		☐☐ weather forecast☆	일기 예보
☐☐ discover☆	똉 발견하다		☐☐ wonder☆	똉 궁금하다, 궁금해하다
☐☐ go without	~ 없이 지내다			똉 경이, 경탄, 놀라움
☐☐ planet	똉 행성			

Reading

☐☐ appear	똉 나타나다 (↔ disappear)		☐☐ nearby☆	傳 가까이에, 근처에
☐☐ blow	똉 (입으로) 불다 (blow – blew – blown)		☐☐ ocean☆	똉 대양, 바다
☐☐ breath	똉 숨, 호흡		☐☐ probably	傳 아마도 (= perhaps)
☐☐ breathe☆	똉 숨을 쉬다		☐☐ serve	똉 (음식을) 제공하다, 차려 주다
☐☐ calculate☆	똉 계산하다		☐☐ smash☆	똉 때려 부수다, 깨뜨리다
☐☐ clam	똉 조개		☐☐ species☆	똉 (분류상의) 종
☐☐ completely	傳 완전히		☐☐ spot☆	똉 발견하다, 찾아내다
☐☐ deep	똉 깊은			(spot-spotted-spotted)
☐☐ distance	똉 거리		☐☐ surface☆	똉 수면, 표면
☐☐ dive	똉 (물속으로) 뛰어들다		☐☐ take a look at	~을 (한번) 보다
☐☐ fall asleep	잠들다		☐☐ tail☆	똉 (동물의) 꼬리
☐☐ fool☆	똉 속이다, 기만하다		☐☐ tightly	傳 단단히, 꽉
☐☐ give up	포기하다		☐☐ tool☆	똉 도구
☐☐ hide	똉 숨다, 숨기다 (hide-hid-hidden)		☐☐ under	똉 ~ 아래에
☐☐ in the end	마침내, 결국		☐☐ up to	~까지
☐☐ millions of	수많은		☐☐ whale	똉 고래

Language Use

☐☐ abroad	傳 해외에(서)		☐☐ mop	똉 대걸레로 닦다
☐☐ foreigner	똉 외국인		☐☐ shiny	똉 빛나는, 반짝거리는
☐☐ friendly	똉 친절한, 상냥한		☐☐ vacuum	똉 진공청소기로 청소하다
☐☐ monster	똉 괴물		☐☐ wish	똉 소원, 소망

Think and Write · Project

☐☐ Arctic	똉 북극 (지방)		☐☐ octopus	똉 문어
☐☐ enemy	똉 적, 적군		☐☐ round	똉 둥근, 원형의
☐☐ fact	똉 사실		☐☐ several	똉 몇몇의
☐☐ fat	똉 지방		☐☐ surround	똉 둘러싸다

Words
연습 문제

A 다음 단어의 우리말 뜻을 쓰시오.

01 tightly _____

02 scenery _____

03 completely _____

04 mop _____

05 breath _____

06 vacuum _____

07 several _____

08 Arctic _____

09 nearby _____

10 spot _____

11 tool _____

12 friendly _____

13 fool _____

14 discover _____

15 clam _____

16 tail _____

17 wonder _____

18 appear _____

19 probably _____

20 smash _____

B 다음 우리말에 해당하는 영어 단어를 쓰시오.

21 (입으로) 불다 _____

22 행성 _____

23 평균의 _____

24 (분류상의) 종 _____

25 숨다, 숨기다 _____

26 수면, 표면 _____

27 숨을 쉬다 _____

28 (음식을) 제공하다 _____

29 적, 적군 _____

30 거리 _____

31 깊은 _____

32 계산하다 _____

33 기온 _____

34 해외에(서) _____

35 둘러싸다 _____

36 언젠가 _____

37 고래 _____

38 둥근, 원형의 _____

39 일기 예보 _____

40 (지구의) 남극 _____

C 다음 영어 표현의 우리말 뜻을 쓰시오.

01 millions of _____

02 up to _____

03 in the end _____

04 take a look at _____

05 go without _____

06 give up _____

07 be covered with _____

08 this time of year _____

STEP A

영어 뜻풀이

☐☐ Arctic	북극 (지방)	the area around the North Pole
☐☐ blow	(입으로) 불다	to send out air from the mouth
☐☐ breathe	숨을 쉬다	to move air into and out of your lungs
☐☐ calculate	계산하다	to find a number, answer, etc. by using mathematical processes
☐☐ clam	조개	a type of sea creature with a shell in two parts that can close together
☐☐ discover	발견하다	to see, find, or become aware of something for the first time
☐☐ distance	거리	the amount of space between two places or things
☐☐ dive	뛰어들다, 다이빙하다	to jump into water, especially with your arms and head going in first
☐☐ forecast	예측, 예보	a statement about what you think is going to happen in the future
☐☐ hide	숨다	to go to or stay at a place where you cannot be seen or found
☐☐ million	100만, 수많은	the number 1,000,000
☐☐ serve	(음식을) 제공하다, 차려 주다	to give food or drink to someone, usually in a restaurant
☐☐ smash	때려 부수다, 깨뜨리다	to break something into many pieces
☐☐ species	(분류상의) 종	a set of animals or plants that have similar characteristics to each other
☐☐ spot	발견하다, 찾아내다	to see or notice someone or something that is difficult to see or find
☐☐ surface	수면, 표면	the upper layer of an area of land or water
☐☐ tightly	단단히, 꽉	closely and firmly
☐☐ tool	도구	a piece of equipment you use with your hands for a particular task
☐☐ whale	고래	a very large mammal that lives in the sea
☐☐ wonder	경이, 경탄, 놀라움	a feeling of surprise and admiration for something very beautiful or new

단어의 의미 관계

- **유의어**
  completely = totally (완전히)
  fact = truth (사실)
  probably = perhaps (아마도)

- **반의어**
  appear (나타나다) ↔ disappear (사라지다)
  tightly (단단히, 꽉) ↔ loosely (느슨하게)

- **형용사 – 부사**
  easy (쉬운) – easily (쉽게)
  complete (완전한) – completely (완전히)
  tight (단단한, 꽉 끼는) – tightly (단단히, 꽉)

- **명사 – 형용사**
  friend (친구) – friendly (친절한, 상냥한)
  wonder (경탄, 놀라움) – wonderful (놀라운)

다의어

- **spot** 1. 통 발견하다, 찾아내다 2. 명 장소, 위치 3. 명 얼룩

  1. He could **spot** a police car behind him.
     그는 그의 뒤에서 경찰차를 발견할 수 있었다.
  2. This looks like a nice **spot** for a picnic.
     이곳은 소풍하기에 좋은 장소처럼 보인다.
  3. There were mud **spots** on my hat.
     내 모자에 진흙 얼룩이 있었다.

- **fool** 1. 통 속이다, 기만하다 2. 명 바보

  1. Don't be **fooled** by her appearance.
     그녀의 외모에 속지 마.
  2. I feel like a **fool** when I make a stupid mistake.
     나는 어리석은 실수를 할 때 내가 바보처럼 느껴진다.

- **complete** 1. 통 완료하다, 끝마치다 2. 형 완전한

  1. I need one more piece to **complete** the puzzle.
     나는 퍼즐을 완료하는 데 한 조각이 더 필요하다.
  2. The room was a **complete** mess.
     그 방은 완전 엉망진창이었다.

Words Plus

연습 문제

A 다음 뜻풀이에 알맞은 말을 [보기]에서 골라 쓴 후, 우리말 뜻을 쓰시오.

[보기]	smash	distance	serve	forecast	tool	tightly	dive	clam

1 _____ : closely and firmly : _____

2 _____ : the amount of space between two places or things : _____

3 _____ : to give food or drink to someone, usually in a restaurant : _____

4 _____ : a piece of equipment you use with your hands for a particular task : _____

5 _____ : to break something into many pieces : _____

6 _____ : a type of sea creature with a shell in two parts that can close together : _____

7 _____ : to jump into water, especially with your arms and head going in first : _____

8 _____ : a statement about what you think is going to happen in the future : _____

B 다음 짝 지어진 두 단어의 관계가 같도록 빈칸에 알맞은 말을 쓰시오.

1 fact : truth = perhaps : _____

2 loosely : tightly = _____ : disappear

3 tight : tightly = complete : _____

4 wonder : wonderful = friend : _____

C 다음 빈칸에 알맞은 말을 [보기]에서 골라 쓰시오.

[보기]	average	wonder	breath	spot	surface

1 I can't _____ any mistakes in this report.

2 Monica took a deep _____ to calm down.

3 The _____ age of the participants in the marathon was 35 years old.

4 Thomas saw a big fish swimming under the _____ of the water.

5 When my niece saw Santa Claus, her eyes were filled with _____.

D 다음 우리말과 같도록 빈칸에 알맞은 말을 쓰시오.

1 그 차는 6명까지 탈 수 있다. → The car holds _____ _____ six people.

2 나는 이 프로젝트가 끝날 때까지 포기하지 않을 것이다. → I won't _____ _____ until this project is finished.

3 설악산은 이맘때 아주 아름답다. → Mt. Seorak is very beautiful _____ _____ _____ .

4 일주일 동안 물 없이 지내는 것은 불가능하다. → It is impossible to _____ _____ water for a week.

5 이 사진을 한번 보고 Ann과 Lisa를 찾아봐.

→ _____ _____ _____ _____ this photo and find Ann and Lisa.

실전 TEST

01 다음 중 단어의 품사가 다른 하나는?

① article ② breathe ③ clam
④ ocean ⑤ scenery

02 다음 영어 뜻풀이에 알맞은 단어는?

to go to or stay at a place where you cannot be seen or found

① hide ② dive ③ appear
④ vacuum ⑤ blow

03 다음 빈칸에 공통으로 들어갈 말로 알맞은 것은?

• Experience makes even _____s wise.
• Don't let his kind smile _____ you.

① land ② book ③ calculate
④ fool ⑤ forecast

04 다음 중 밑줄 친 부분의 우리말 뜻이 알맞지 않은 것은?

① Can I take a look at your old pictures?
(~을 찾다)
② Luke's novels gave pleasure to millions of readers.
(수많은)
③ If you want to achieve your goal, keep going and don't give up. (포기하다)
④ In the end, they decided to spend Christmas at home. (결국)
⑤ It is impossible for a person to go without food and water for forty days. (~ 없이 지내다)

05 다음 우리말과 같도록 할 때 빈칸에 들어갈 말로 알맞은 것은?

지구 표면의 거의 10%가 얼음으로 덮여 있다.
→ Nearly 10% of the Earth's _____ is covered by ice.

① fact ② surface ③ species
④ breath ⑤ Arctic

고
^{난도}
06 다음 문장의 밑줄 친 단어와 같은 의미로 쓰인 것은?

This is the best spot to take a picture.

① Olivia has an ink spot on her skirt.
② He knows a good spot to park the car.
③ I expected to spot a deer in the woods.
④ Remove the spot on your white blouse.
⑤ You can easily spot the colorful lanterns in the light festival.

07 다음 대화의 빈칸에 들어갈 말로 알맞은 것은?

A: What are you doing?
B: I'm trying to _____ how much money I'll need on vacation.

① dive ② mop ③ complete
④ surround ⑤ calculate

08 괄호 안의 우리말과 같도록 빈칸에 알맞은 말을 쓰시오.

The temperature went _____ _____ 37℃ yesterday.
(어제 기온이 섭씨 37도까지 올라갔다.)

L&S Listen & Speak
핵심 노트

1 궁금함 표현하기

A: **I wonder** where the bus stop is.

B: It's in front of the police station.

나는 버스 정류장이 어디에 있는지 궁금해.

그곳은 경찰서 앞에 있어.

I wonder ~.는 '나는 ~이 궁금하다.'라는 뜻으로 어떤 것에 대해 궁금함을 나타낼 때 사용하는 표현이다. I wonder 뒤에는 「의문사＋주어＋동사」의 의문사절이나 「if/whether＋주어＋동사」의 if절 또는 whether절이 이어진다.

e.g.
- A: **I wonder** how high this mountain is. 나는 이 산이 얼마나 높은지 궁금해.
  B: It's about 2,000m high. 그것은 높이가 약 2,000미터야.
- A: **I wonder** how long the Amazon River is. 나는 아마존강이 얼마나 긴지 궁금해.
  B: It's about 7,000km long. 그것은 길이가 약 7,000킬로미터야.
- **I wonder** how long camels can go without water in the desert.
  나는 낙타들이 사막에서 물 없이 얼마나 오래 지낼 수 있는지 궁금해.
- **I wonder** if you can help me.
  나는 네가 나를 도와줄 수 있는지 궁금해.
- **I'm curious about** the art director of this movie.
  나는 이 영화의 미술 감독이 궁금해.

> **시험 포인트** **point**
> I wonder 다음에 오는 의문사절이나 if/whether절의 어순에 유의하세요. 또한 I wonder 뒤에 이어지는 궁금해하는 내용의 답을 파악하는 문제도 자주 출제돼요.

2 보고하기

A: Is there anything interesting?

B: **This article says** scientists have discovered a new planet.

뭔가 재미있는 게 있니?

이 기사에 따르면 과학자들이 새로운 행성을 발견했대.

This article says ~.는 '이 기사에 따르면 ~.'이라는 뜻으로 어딘가에서 보거나 들은 내용을 상대방에게 보고하거나 전달할 때 사용하는 표현이다. 정보 제공자에 따라 This article 대신 The Internet, The book, People, Someone 등을 쓸 수 있다.

e.g.
- **The weather forecast says** it'll be rainy in the afternoon.
  일기 예보에서 오후에 비가 올 거래.
- **The Internet says** the shortest hiking course takes about two hours.
  인터넷에 따르면 가장 짧은 등산 코스가 약 두 시간 정도 걸린대.
- **The book says** the blue whale is about 30m long.
  그 책에 따르면 대왕고래는 길이가 30미터 정도래.
- **People says** more foreigners are learning Korean.
  사람들에 따르면 더 많은 외국인들이 한국어를 배우고 있대.

> **시험 포인트** **point**
> 보거나 들은 내용의 출처가 어디인지와 보고하거나 전달하는 내용이 무엇인지 파악하는 문제가 자주 출제돼요.

Listen and Speak 1-A

교과서 122쪽

B: We're ❶ almost ❷ at the top of the mountain.

G: ❸ I wonder how high this mountain is.

B: It's about 2,000m high.

G: Wow! This is a really high mountain.

B: Yes, it is. ❹ Let's keep going.

❶ ⓟ 거의

❷ ~의 꼭대기에

❸ I wonder ~.는 '나는 ~이 궁금하다.'라는 뜻으로, I wonder 뒤에 의문사가 이끄는 절이 뒤따르는 경우 「의문사(+형용사) +주어+동사」의 어순으로 씀

❹ Let's+동사원형 ~.: ~하자.
keep+동명사: 계속 ~하다

Q1. 소녀는 무엇을 궁금해하나요?

Listen and Speak 1-B

교과서 122쪽

B: Look at the baby penguins on TV. They're so cute.

G: Yes, but they ❶ look very cold out there.

B: Yeah, the South Pole is ❷ the coldest place on Earth.

G: ❸ I wonder how cold it is there.

B: ❹ The average temperature is about -58℃ in July and -26℃ in December.

G: Oh, then, July is ❺ colder than December there. Interesting!

B: Yes. ❻ Although it's very cold there, it doesn't snow much.

G: That's interesting, too!

❶ look+형용사: ~해 보이다
부사 very는 형용사 cold를 수식

❷ coldest는 형용사 cold의 최상급
the+형용사의 최상급: 가장 ~한

❸ 궁금함을 나타내는 표현으로, 「I wonder+의문사(how)+형용사(cold)+주어(it)+동사(is) ~.」의 어순으로 쓰인 문장
it: 날씨를 나타내는 비인칭 주어
there = the South Pole(남극)

❹ 평균 기온

❺ 형용사의 비교급(colder)+than ~: ~보다 더 …한

❻ 웹 (비록) ~이지만

Q2. 남극은 12월과 7월 중 어느 달이 더 추운가요?

Q3. ❻이 포함된 문장을 해석해 보세요.

Listen and Speak 1-C

교과서 122쪽

A: We're finally here.

B: Yes, I'm so ❶ excited. Let's ❷ look around.

A: ❸ I wonder where the bus stop is.

B: It's ❹ in front of the police station.

A: You're right. Let's go.

❶ 주어 I가 감정을 느끼는 것이므로 과거분사 형태의 형용사인 excited 사용

❷ 둘러보다

❸ 「I wonder+의문사(where)+주어(the bus stop)+동사(is).」의 어순으로 쓰인 문장

❹ ~ 앞에

Q4. Where is the bus stop?

Listen and Speak 2-A

교과서 123쪽

B: The weather is so nice outside.

G: Yeah. ❶ How about going on a picnic this afternoon?

B: Good idea. ❷ Can you check the weather?

G: Oh, no! ❸ The weather forecast says it'll be rainy in the afternoon.

B: Let's go another time, then.

❶ How about+동명사 ~?는 '~하는 게 어떠니?'라는 뜻으로, 제안할 때 사용하는 표현 / go on a picnic: 소풍을 가다

❷ Can you ~?는 상대방에게 요청할 때 사용하는 표현

❸ The weather forecast says ~.는 '일기 예보에 따르면 ~.'이라는 뜻으로, 보거나 들은 내용을 보고하거나 전달하는 표현 / says 뒤에 목적절을 이끄는 접속사 that이 생략됨 / it: 날씨를 나타내는 비인칭 주어

Q5. 지금 날씨가 어떤가요?

Listen and Speak 2-B

B: Sumin, ❶ what are you going to do on Sunday?

G: I'm going to go hiking. ❷ Do you want to join me?

B: I'd love to. Where do you want to go?

G: ❸ I'm thinking of going to Namsan.

B: Oh, the scenery there is so beautiful ❹ this time of year.

G: Right. I heard ❺ that ❻ it's covered with red autumn leaves now.

B: Great. ❼ How long does the shortest hiking course take?

G: ❽ The Internet says it takes about two hours.

B: Okay, see you on Sunday!

Q6. 남산의 가장 짧은 등산 코스는 시간이 얼마나 걸리나요?

Q7. When are they going to Namsan? → They are going to Namsan _____.

❶ What are you going to do?: 너는 무엇을 할 거니? (계획을 묻는 표현) / 요일(Sunday) 앞에는 전치사 on을 사용

❷ 함께 하고 싶은지 묻는 표현

❸ I'm thinking of + 동명사 ~.: 나는 ~할 생각이다.

❹ 이맘때는, 이맘때쯤이면

❺ 명사절을 이끄는 접속사로 생략 가능

❻ be covered with: ~으로 덮여 있다

❼ How long does ~ take?: ~이 얼마나 걸리니? (소요 시간을 묻는 표현)

❽ 인터넷에서 본 정보를 보고하거나 전달하는 표현

Listen and Speak 2-C

A: ❶ What are you doing?

B: I'm reading the newspaper.

A: ❷ Is there anything interesting?

B: ❸ This article says scientists have discovered a new planet.

Q8. B가 읽고 있는 기사의 내용은 무엇인가요?

❶ 너는 무엇을 하고 있니? (현재진행형이 쓰인 의문문)

❷ Is there ~?: ~이 있니? / -thing으로 끝나는 대명사(anything)는 형용사(interesting)가 뒤에서 수식함

❸ 기사에서 본 정보를 보고하거나 전달하는 표현 / that이 생략된 절에 「have + 과거분사(discovered)」의 현재완료가 쓰임

Real Life Talk > Watch a Video

Suji: Check out this picture!

Tony: Wow! The camels are walking ❶ in a line in the desert.

Suji: Yeah. The desert looks very hot and dry.

Tony: ❷ I wonder how long camels can go without water in the desert.

Suji: Let's ❸ find out on the Internet.

Tony: Okay. ❹ The Internet says they can go about two weeks without water.

Suji: Wow, that's amazing! Camels are really interesting animals.

Tony: I ❺ want to travel with ❻ them in the desert someday.

Q9. What are the camels in the picture doing?

Q10. 두 사람은 인터넷에서 무엇에 관해 찾아보았나요?

❶ 한 줄로

❷ 궁금함을 나타내는 표현으로, 「I wonder + 의문사(how) + 형용사(long) + 주어(camels) + 동사(can go) ~.」의 어순으로 쓰인 문장
go without: ~ 없이 지내다

❸ 찾아보다, 발견하다

❹ 인터넷에서 본 정보를 보고하거나 전달하는 표현
they = camels
without ⓟ ~ 없이

❺ want는 to부정사를 목적어로 취하는 동사

❻ = camels

Listen & Speak
빈칸 채우기

우리말과 일치하도록 대화의 빈칸에 알맞은 말을 쓰시오.

주요 표현

1 Listen and Speak 1-A

B: We're almost _____ _____ _____ of the mountain.

G: _____ _____ _____ _____ this mountain is.

B: It's about 2,000m high.

G: Wow! This is a really high mountain.

B: Yes, it is. Let's _____ _____.

 해석

교과서 122쪽

B: 우리는 산 정상에 거의 다 왔어.

G: 나는 이 산이 얼마나 높은지 궁금해.

B: 이 산은 높이가 약 2,000미터야.

G: 와! 이 산은 정말 높은 산이구나.

B: 응, 맞아. 계속 올라가자.

2 Listen and Speak 1-B

B: Look at the baby penguins on TV. They're so cute.

G: Yes, but they _____ _____ _____ out there.

B: Yeah, the South Pole is _____ _____ _____ on Earth.

G: I wonder _____ _____ _____ _____ there.

B: The average temperature is about -58℃ in July and -26℃ in December.

G: Oh, then, July _____ _____ _____ December there. Interesting!

B: Yes. _____ _____ _____ _____ there, it doesn't snow much.

G: That's interesting, too!

교과서 122쪽

B: 텔레비전에 나온 아기 펭귄들을 봐. 아주 귀여워.

G: 응, 하지만 그들은 저곳에서 매우 추워 보여.

B: 그래. 남극은 지구상에서 가장 추운 곳이야.

G: 나는 그곳이 얼마나 추운지 궁금해.

B: 평균 기온이 7월에는 약 섭씨 영하 58도이고, 12월에는 약 섭씨 영하 26도야.

G: 오, 그러면 그곳은 12월보다 7월이 더 춥구나. 흥미롭다!

B: 응, 비록 그곳은 매우 춥지만 눈은 많이 내리지 않아.

G: 그것도 흥미롭다!

3 Listen and Speak 1-C

A: We're finally here.

B: Yes, I'm so excited. Let's _____ _____.

A: I wonder _____ _____ _____ _____ _____.

B: It's _____ _____ _____ the police station.

A: You're right. Let's go.

교과서 122쪽

A: 우리는 마침내 여기에 왔어.

B: 그래. 나는 매우 신이 나. 우리 둘러보자.

A: 나는 버스 정류장이 어디에 있는지 궁금해.

B: 그곳은 경찰서 앞에 있어.

A: 네 말이 맞네. 가자.

4 Listen and Speak 2-A

B: The weather is so nice outside.

G: Yeah. _____ _____ _____ _____ on a picnic this afternoon?

B: Good idea. _____ _____ _____ the weather?

G: Oh, no! _____ _____ _____ _____ it'll be rainy in the afternoon.

B: Let's go another time, then.

교과서 123쪽

B: 바깥 날씨가 아주 좋아.

G: 그래. 오늘 오후에 소풍 가는 게 어때?

B: 좋은 생각이야. 날씨를 확인해 줄래?

G: 오, 이런! 일기 예보에서 오후에 비가 올 거래.

B: 그러면 다음에 가자.

5 Listen and Speak 2-B

B: Sumin, what are you going to do on Sunday?

G: _____ _____ _____ _____ _____. Do you want to join me?

B: _____ _____ _____. Where do you want to go?

G: I'm _____ _____ _____ _____ Namsan.

B: Oh, the scenery there is so beautiful this time of year.

G: Right. I heard that _____ _____ _____ red autumn leaves now.

B: Great. How long does the shortest hiking course take?

G: _____ _____ _____ it takes about two hours.

B: Okay, see you on Sunday!

해석

B: 수민아, 너는 일요일에 무엇을 할 거니?

G: 나는 등산을 갈 거야. 나와 함께 가겠니?

B: 그러고 싶어. 너는 어디로 가고 싶니?

G: 나는 남산에 가려고 생각 중이야.

B: 오, 매년 이맘때 그곳 경치는 아주 아름답지.

G: 맞아. 지금 빨간 단풍잎으로 덮여 있다고 들었어.

B: 좋아. 가장 짧은 등산 코스는 얼마나 걸리니?

G: 인터넷 정보에 따르면 약 두 시간 정도 걸린대.

B: 알겠어, 일요일에 봐!

6 Listen and Speak 2-C

A: _____ _____ _____ _____?

B: I'm reading the newspaper.

A: Is there _____ _____?

B: This article says scientists _____ _____ _____ _____ _____.

A: 너는 무엇을 하고 있니?

B: 나는 신문을 읽고 있어.

A: 재미있는 내용이 있니?

B: 이 기사에 따르면 과학자들이 새로운 행성을 발견했대.

7 Real Life Talk > Watch a Video

Suji: Check out this picture!

Tony: Wow! The camels _____ _____ _____ _____ _____ in the desert.

Suji: Yeah. The desert looks _____ _____ _____ _____.

Tony: I wonder _____ _____ without water in the desert.

Suji: Let's find out on the Internet.

Tony: Okay. _____ _____ _____ they can go about two weeks without water.

Suji: Wow, that's amazing! Camels are really interesting animals.

Tony: I _____ _____ _____ with them in the desert someday.

수지: 이 사진을 봐!

Tony: 와! 낙타들이 사막에서 한 줄로 걸어가고 있네.

수지: 응. 사막은 매우 덥고 건조해 보여.

Tony: 나는 낙타들이 사막에서 물 없이 얼마나 오래 지낼 수 있는지 궁금해.

수지: 인터넷에서 찾아보자.

Tony: 그래. 인터넷 정보에 따르면 낙타는 물 없이 2주 정도 지낼 수 있대.

수지: 와, 굉장하다! 낙타는 정말 흥미로운 동물이구나.

Tony: 나는 언젠가 사막에서 그들과 함께 여행하고 싶어.

Listen & Speak

대화 순서 배열하기

자연스러운 대화가 되도록 순서를 바르게 배열하시오.

1 Listen and Speak 1-A

교과서 122쪽

ⓐ Yes, it is. Let's keep going.
ⓑ We're almost at the top of the mountain.
ⓒ It's about 2,000m high.
ⓓ Wow! This is a really high mountain.
ⓔ I wonder how high this mountain is.

(   ) – (ⓔ   ) – (   ) – (   ) – (   )

2 Listen and Speak 1-B

교과서 122쪽

ⓐ Look at the baby penguins on TV. They're so cute.
ⓑ I wonder how cold it is there.
ⓒ Yeah, the South Pole is the coldest place on Earth.
ⓓ Yes. Although it's very cold there, it doesn't snow much.
ⓔ Yes, but they look very cold out there.
ⓕ The average temperature is about -58℃ in July and -26℃ in December.
ⓖ Oh, then, July is colder than December there. Interesting!
ⓗ That's interesting, too!

(ⓐ   ) – (ⓔ   ) – (   ) – (   ) – (   ) – (   ) – (ⓓ   ) – (   )

3 Listen and Speak 1-C

교과서 122쪽

ⓐ Yes, I'm so excited. Let's look around.
ⓑ You're right. Let's go.
ⓒ We're finally here.
ⓓ It's in front of the police station.
ⓔ I wonder where the bus stop is.

(ⓒ   ) – (   ) – (   ) – (   ) – (   )

4 Listen and Speak 2-A

교과서 123쪽

ⓐ Let's go another time, then.
ⓑ Yeah. How about going on a picnic this afternoon?
ⓒ Oh, no! The weather forecast says it'll be rainy in the afternoon.
ⓓ Good idea. Can you check the weather?
ⓔ The weather is so nice outside.

(   ) – (   ) – (   ) – (   ) – (   )

5 Listen and Speak 2-B

교과서 123쪽

ⓐ I'd love to. Where do you want to go?

ⓑ The Internet says it takes about two hours.

ⓒ Sumin, what are you going to do on Sunday?

ⓓ Oh, the scenery there is so beautiful this time of year.

ⓔ Right. I heard that it's covered with red autumn leaves now.

ⓕ I'm thinking of going to Namsan.

ⓖ I'm going to go hiking. Do you want to join me?

ⓗ Okay, see you on Sunday!

ⓘ Great. How long does the shortest hiking course take?

(ⓒ) – (ⓖ) – ( ) – ( ) – ( ) – ( ) – (ⓘ) – ( ) – ( )

6 Listen and Speak 2-C

교과서 123쪽

ⓐ This article says scientists have discovered a new planet.

ⓑ What are you doing?

ⓒ I'm reading the newspaper.

ⓓ Is there anything interesting?

( ) – ( ) – ( ) – ( )

7 Real Life Talk > Watch a Video

교과서 124쪽

ⓐ I wonder how long camels can go without water in the desert.

ⓑ Let's find out on the Internet.

ⓒ Wow, that's amazing! Camels are really interesting animals.

ⓓ Check out this picture!

ⓔ Wow! The camels are walking in a line in the desert.

ⓕ Okay. The Internet says they can go about two weeks without water.

ⓖ I want to travel with them in the desert someday.

ⓗ Yeah. The desert looks very hot and dry.

(ⓓ) – ( ) – ( ) – (ⓐ) – ( ) – ( ) – ( ) – (ⓖ)

01 다음 대화의 빈칸에 들어갈 말로 알맞은 것은?

A: _____

B: It's about 2,000m high.

① I wonder how high this mountain is.

② What is the smallest country in the world?

③ I don't know how fast the cheetah can run.

④ I'm thinking of going to the beach this weekend.

⑤ The book says the blue whale is about 30m long.

02 자연스러운 대화가 되도록 순서대로 배열한 것은?

(A) What are you doing?

(B) Is there anything interesting?

(C) This article says scientists have discovered a new planet.

(D) I'm reading the newspaper.

① (A) – (C) – (D) – (B)

② (A) – (D) – (B) – (C)

③ (C) – (A) – (D) – (B)

④ (D) – (B) – (A) – (C)

⑤ (D) – (C) – (A) – (B)

03 다음 대화의 밑줄 친 우리말을 영어로 옮길 때 마지막에 오는 단어는?

A: 나는 도서관이 어디에 있는지 궁금해.

B: It's in front of the police station.

① is   ② the   ③ where

④ library   ⑤ wonder

04 다음 대화의 밑줄 친 ①~⑤ 중 흐름상 어색한 것은?

A: ①The weather is so nice outside.

B: Yeah. ②How about going on a picnic this afternoon?

A: ③Good idea. ④Can you check the weather?

B: Oh, no! ⑤The weather forecast says it'll be sunny in the afternoon.

A: Let's go another time, then.

①   ②   ③   ④   ⑤

[05-07] 다음 대화를 읽고, 물음에 답하시오.

Giho: Sally, ①look at the baby penguins on TV. They're so cute.

Sally: Yes, but they ②look very cold out there.

Giho: Yeah, the South Pole is ③the coldest place on Earth.

Sally: ④I wonder how cold is it there.

Giho: The average temperature is about -58℃ in July and -26℃ in December.

Sally: Oh, then, July is _____ December there. Interesting!

Giho: Yes. ⑤Although it's very cold there, it doesn't snow much.

Sally: That's interesting, too!

05 위 대화의 밑줄 친 ①~⑤ 중 어법상 틀린 것은?

①   ②   ③   ④   ⑤

06 위 대화의 빈칸에 들어갈 말로 알맞은 것은?

① warmer than   ② colder than

③ hotter than   ④ as warm as

⑤ as cold as

07 위 대화를 읽고 답할 수 <u>없는</u> 질문은?

① What are they watching on TV?
② Where is the coldest place on Earth?
③ What does Sally wonder?
④ What is the average temperature in the South Pole in December?
⑤ Why doesn't it snow much in the South Pole?

[08-09] 다음 대화를 읽고, 물음에 답하시오.

Suji: Check out this picture!
Tony: Wow! The camels are walking in a line in the desert.
Suji: Yeah. The desert looks very hot and dry.
Tony: I wonder _____ camels can go without water in the desert.
Suji: Let's find out on the Internet.
Tony: Okay. The Internet says they can go about two weeks without water.
Suji: Wow, that's amazing! Camels are really interesting animals.
Tony: I want to travel with them in the desert someday.

08 위 대화의 빈칸에 들어갈 말로 알맞은 것은?

① how far   ② how often
③ how high   ④ how many
⑤ how long

09 위 대화의 내용과 일치하지 <u>않는</u> 것은?

① 사진 속 낙타들은 사막에서 한 줄로 걸어가고 있다.
② 두 사람은 궁금한 점을 동물에 관한 책에서 찾아보았다.
③ 두 사람이 찾은 정보에 따르면 낙타는 물 없이 2주 정도를 지낼 수 있다.
④ 수지는 낙타가 흥미로운 동물이라고 생각한다.
⑤ Tony는 언젠가 사막에서 낙타와 여행하고 싶어 한다.

10 다음 괄호 안의 말을 바르게 배열하여 대화의 빈칸에 알맞은 말을 쓰시오.

A: _____
(how, wonder, I, Jupiter, big, is)
B: The Internet says Jupiter is over 11 times bigger than Earth.

[11-12] 다음 대화를 읽고, 물음에 답하시오.

A: Sumin, what are you going to do on Sunday?
B: I'm going to go hiking. (1) _____
A: I'd love to. Where do you want to go?
B: I'm thinking of going to Namsan.
A: Oh, the scenery there is so beautiful this time of year.
B: Right. (2) _____
A: Great. How long does the shortest hiking course take?
B: (3) _____
A: Okay, see you on Sunday!

11 위 대화의 빈칸에 알맞은 말을 [보기]에서 골라 쓰시오.

[보기] • Do you want to join me?
        • The Internet says it takes about two hours.
        • I heard that it's covered with red autumn leaves now.

(1) _____
(2) _____
(3) _____

12 다음 질문에 완전한 영어 문장으로 답하시오.

Q: What are they going to do on Sunday?
A: _____

STEP A

1 소유격 관계대명사

- This small fish **whose** favorite food is clams uses a tool to open them.
  선행사
  가장 좋아하는 먹이가 조개인 이 작은 물고기는 조개를 열기 위해 도구를 사용한다.

- The man **whose** painting is in the museum is my uncle.
  선행사
  미술관에 그림이 있는 그 남자는 우리 삼촌이다.

- I met a girl **whose** name is the same as mine.
  선행사
  나는 나와 이름이 같은 소녀를 만났다.

소유격 (대)명사 대신 쓰여 소유격 역할을 하는 관계대명사를 소유격 관계대명사라고 하며, 선행사에 상관없이 whose를 사용한다. 소유격 관계대명사 whose는 생략할 수 없으며, whose가 이끄는 관계대명사절은 바로 앞의 선행사를 수식한다.

- I know the boy. His uncle is a famous movie star.
  → I know the boy **whose** uncle is a famous movie star.
  나는 삼촌이 유명한 영화배우인 소년을 안다.

- Robin has a cat. Its tail is long.
  → Robin has a cat **whose** tail is long.
  Robin은 꼬리가 긴 고양이 한 마리가 있다.

비교 의문사 whose(누구의)와 혼동하지 않도록 유의한다.

- **Whose** bag is this? 이것은 누구의 가방이니?
- I don't know **whose** keys they are. 나는 그것들이 누구의 열쇠인지 모른다.

point

시험 포인트
어떤 관계대명사가 쓰여야 하는지 묻는 문제가 자주 출제돼요. 주격 관계대명사, 목적격 관계대명사와 구별할 수 있도록 각 관계대명사의 쓰임을 정확하게 알아야 해요.

주격 관계대명사
- They are the people **who** take part in the 4 Deserts Race.
  그들은 '4 Deserts Race'에 참가하는 사람들이다.
  [중2 4과]

목적격 관계대명사
- Chris found the bicycle **that** he lost yesterday.
  Chris는 어제 잃어버린 자전거를 찾았다.
  [중2 7과]

QUICK CHECK

1 다음 괄호 안에서 알맞은 것을 고르시오.

(1) The girl (whose / who) arm is broken is Olivia.

(2) Ms. Brown is the teacher (whom / whose) I respect the most.

(3) I had dinner at the restaurant (which / whose) owner is French.

2 다음 문장에서 소유격 관계대명사 whose가 들어갈 위치를 고르시오.

(1) I met (ⓐ) an old man (ⓑ) hair (ⓒ) was (ⓓ) gray.

(2) The family (ⓐ) has (ⓑ) a dog (ⓒ) name (ⓓ) is Max.

(3) The woman (ⓐ) job (ⓑ) is (ⓒ) photographing famous people (ⓓ) is my neighbor.

2 시간을 나타내는 접속사

- Humpback whales stand on their tails **while** they sleep. 혹등고래는 잠을 자는 동안 꼬리로 서 있는다.
- The tuskfish blows on the sand **until** a clam appears. tuskfish는 조개가 나타날 때까지 모래에 입김을 분다.
- We had dinner **after** we watched a movie. 우리는 영화를 본 후에 저녁을 먹었다.

(1) 시간을 나타내는 접속사에는 when(~할 때), before(~하기 전에), after(~한 후에), while(~하는 동안에), until(~할 때까지), since(~한 이후로) 등이 있다. 시간을 나타내는 접속사는 부사절을 이끌며, 접속사 뒤에는 「주어 + 동사 ~」로 이루어진 절이 이어진다.

- She always wears a hat **when** she works in the garden.
  그녀는 정원에서 일할 때 항상 모자를 쓴다.
- You should take a shower **after** you exercise.
  운동을 한 후에 너는 샤워를 해야 한다.
- Someone called **while** you were out. 네가 외출한 동안 누군가 전화를 했다.
- The children played **until** it got dark. 아이들은 어두워질 때까지 놀았다.
- I haven't heard from them **since** they went to Germany.
  나는 그들이 독일에 간 이후로 그들에게서 소식을 듣지 못했다.

(2) 시간을 나타내는 접속사가 이끄는 절은 주절의 앞이나 뒤에 올 수 있다. **주의!** until과 since가 이끄는 절은 주절의 앞에 잘 오지 않아요.

- You should take a shower **after** you exercise.
  After you exercise, you should take a shower.

(3) 시간을 나타내는 접속사가 이끄는 부사절은 미래의 의미일지라도 현재시제로 쓴다.

- **When** I *get* to the airport, I'll call you.
  내가 공항에 도착하면, 네게 전화할게.

---

point

시험 포인트
시간을 나타내는 접속사를 문맥에 맞게 사용하는 문제가 자주 출제되므로 각 접속사의 의미를 정확히 알아두어야 해요. 또한, 시간의 접속사가 이끄는 부사절은 미래의 의미일지라도 현재시제로 쓴다는 것을 기억하세요.

시간을 나타내는 접속사 when

- **When** Rahul was in middle school, he acted in a school play.
  Rahul이 중학생이었을 때, 그는 학교 연극에서 연기를 했다.
  [중1 6과]

이유를 나타내는 접속사 since

- It couldn't be real gold **since** it was too light.
  그것은 너무 가벼웠기 때문에 진짜 금일 리가 없었나.
  [중3 4과]

QUICK CHECK

1 다음 괄호 안에서 문맥상 자연스러운 것을 고르시오.

(1) My sweater got smaller (when / until) I washed it in hot water.
(2) (Before / After) he packed his baggage, he left for a business trip.
(3) My dad has worked in a bank (while / since) I was young.

2 다음 문장에서 부사절에 밑줄을 치고, 밑줄 친 부분의 의미를 우리말로 쓰시오.

(1) Let's wait until the snow stops. _____
(2) Before I left the room, I turned off the lights. _____
(3) I was really happy when I passed the audition. _____

연습 문제

1 소유격 관계대명사

A 다음 괄호 안에서 알맞은 것을 고르시오.

1 I know a girl (whom / whose) dream is to be a famous dancer.

2 The wallet (which / whose) Joan found on the street isn't mine.

3 I met a child (that / whose) grandfather is a science teacher.

4 I like people (who / whose) are kind to others.

5 Bill saw a snake (whose / which) color was red.

B 다음 문장의 밑줄 친 부분이 어법상 <u>틀렸으면</u> 바르게 고쳐 쓰시오.

1 Mary has a cat <u>that</u> eyes are blue. → _____

2 I found the boy <u>whose</u> was walking his dogs. → _____

3 We talked about a man <u>who</u> son is a tennis player. → _____

4 A girl <u>whose</u> name is Emma is sitting on the bench. → _____

5 The fish <u>whose</u> my brother caught was very big. → _____

C 다음 두 문장을 관계대명사 whose를 사용하여 한 문장으로 연결하시오.

1 The woman called the police. Her bike was stolen.
→ The woman _____.

2 Look at the octopus. Its head is round.
→ Look at the octopus _____.

3 Do you know the student? His name is Paul Anderson.
→ Do you know _____?

D 다음 우리말과 같도록 괄호 안의 말을 바르게 배열하여 문장을 완성하시오.

1 나는 차가 고장 난 여자를 도왔다.
→ I helped _____.
(car, down, a woman, whose, broke)

2 나는 가장 좋아하는 과목이 수학인 친구가 있다.
→ I have _____.
(Math, whose, is, a friend, subject, favorite)

3 Rapunzel은 머리카락이 아주 긴 아름다운 공주이다.
→ Rapunzel is a _____.
(is, very, beautiful, whose, princess, long, hair)

2 시간을 나타내는 접속사

A 다음 우리말과 같도록 [보기]에서 알맞은 접속사를 골라 쓰시오.

[보기]	after	before	until	since	while

1 우리는 12살 이후로 서로 알고 지내고 있다.

→ We have known each other _____ we were 12.

2 너는 내가 없는 동안 내 개를 돌봐 줄 수 있니?

→ Can you take care of my dog _____ I'm away?

3 나는 점심을 먹은 후에 Sam과 축구를 했다.

→ _____ I had lunch, I played soccer with Sam.

4 당근이 부드러워질 때까지 볶아라.

→ Fry the carrots _____ they become soft.

B 다음 괄호 안에서 문맥상 자연스러운 것을 고르시오.

1 Brush your teeth (before / after) you go to bed.

2 I waited in front of the door (because / until) someone came out.

3 She was listening to music (while / unless) she was driving to work.

C 다음 문장에서 어법상 또는 문맥상 <u>틀린</u> 부분을 찾아 바르게 고쳐 쓰시오.

1 When she will come home, she will clean the living room.   _____ → _____

2 During he lived in London, many friends visited him.   _____ → _____

3 My sister and I mopped the floor up to it looked shiny.   _____ → _____

D 다음 우리말과 같도록 괄호 안의 말을 바르게 배열하여 문장을 완성하시오.

1 Kevin이 내게 전화했을 때 나는 텔레비전을 보고 있었다.

→ _____, I was watching TV.

　(Kevin, when, me, called)

2 그는 휴가에서 돌아온 이후로 바빴다.

→ He _____ from holiday.

　　(came back, has, since, busy, he, been)

3 우리는 놀이공원에 가기 전에 아침을 먹었다.

→ We had breakfast _____.

　　　　(we, to, before, the amusement park, went)

4 Sally는 언니가 거실을 진공청소기로 청소하는 동안 창문을 닦았다.

→ Sally _____.

　　　(while, the living room, the windows, her sister, vacuumed, cleaned)

01 다음 우리말을 영어로 옮길 때 빈칸에 들어갈 말로 알맞은 것은?

> 그들은 눈이 녹을 때까지 집에 머물렀다.
> → They stayed at home _____ the snow melted.

① as   ② until   ③ when
④ after   ⑤ since

[02-03] 다음 빈칸에 들어갈 말로 알맞은 것을 고르시오.

02 I saw Terry _____ I was waiting for the train.

① if   ② that   ③ until
④ while   ⑤ though

03 I have a friend _____ grandmother is a famous painter.

① that   ② who   ③ whom
④ which   ⑤ whose

[04-05] 다음 빈칸에 알맞은 말이 순서대로 짝 지어진 것을 고르시오.

04
• You should wait on the sidewalk _____ the traffic light is red.
• Wash vegetables carefully _____ you eat them.

① until – before   ② until – after
③ when – before   ④ when – unless
⑤ before – after

05
• I have two books _____ were written by Roald Dahl.
• I interviewed a woman _____ dog is more than 20 years old.

① whose – that   ② whose – which
③ which – who   ④ which – whose
⑤ who – whose

[06-07] 다음 우리말을 영어로 바르게 옮긴 것을 고르시오.

06 그는 7살 때 이후로 바이올린을 연주해 왔다.

① He has played the violin since he is 7.
② He has played the violin after he was 7.
③ He has played the violin until he was 7.
④ He has played the violin since he was 7.
⑤ He has played the violin before he was 7.

07 Joseph은 별명이 Spiderman인 남자를 만났다.

① Joseph met a man nickname was Spiderman.
② Joseph met a man his nickname was Spiderman.
③ Joseph met a man that nickname was Spiderman.
④ Joseph met a man which nickname was Spiderman.
⑤ Joseph met a man whose nickname was Spiderman.

08 다음 중 밑줄 친 When(when)의 쓰임이 나머지 넷과 다른 것은?

① I don't know when we can visit her.
② When I was young, I learned Spanish.
③ Brian was very small when he was born.
④ My eyes feel dry when I use my smartphone.
⑤ When it gets dark, you can see the stars shining.

09 다음 두 문장을 한 문장으로 바르게 연결한 것은?

This is the tiger. Its eyes are green.

① This is the tiger that eyes are green.
② This is the tiger which eyes are green.
③ This is the tiger whom eyes are green.
④ This is the tiger whose eyes are green.
⑤ This is the tiger whose its eyes are green.

10 다음 밑줄 친 부분 중 어법상 틀린 것은?

I ①will help you ②with your work ③when I ④will finish ⑤mine.

①   ②   ③   ④   ⑤

11 다음 우리말과 같도록 괄호 안의 단어들을 배열하여 문장을 완성할 때, 여섯 번째로 오는 단어는?

그 수의사는 다리가 부러진 나의 개를 치료했다.
(my, vet, leg, the, was, whose, broken, healed, dog)

① dog   ② leg   ③ whose
④ my   ⑤ was

12 다음 문장과 문맥상 의미가 같은 것은?

David takes a walk after he has breakfast.

① After David takes a walk, he has breakfast.
② David has breakfast before he takes a walk.
③ David takes a walk before he has breakfast.
④ David takes a walk and he has breakfast.
⑤ David takes a walk as he has breakfast.

13 다음 문장에서 어법상 틀린 부분을 찾아 바르게 고쳐 쓰시오.

The woman whom bag was stolen went to the police station.

_____ → _____

14 다음 중 빈칸에 들어갈 관계대명사가 나머지 넷과 다른 것은?

① I saw a cat _____ nose was very flat.
② I know the woman _____ hair is brown.
③ He is the author _____ books became hit movies.
④ Here are the sheep _____ wool is very expensive.
⑤ I like this desk _____ my uncle made for me.

15 다음 우리말과 같도록 할 때 빈칸에 들어갈 말로 알맞지 않은 것은?

나는 버스를 기다리는 동안 Jamie를 만났다.
→ I met Jamie __①__ __②__ __③__ __④__ __⑤__ the bus.

① before   ② I   ③ was
④ waiting   ⑤ for

[16-17] 다음 빈칸에 공통으로 알맞은 말을 고르시오.

16 • Jason has lived in this town _____ he was 10.
   • I came in the room quietly _____ I didn't want to wake the baby up.

① since   ② while   ③ when
④ until   ⑤ before

17 • They won't say _____ names are on the list.
   • Daisy _____ uncle is a famous inventor is my best friend.

① what   ② who   ③ that
④ which   ⑤ whose

18 다음 중 어법상 **틀린** 문장은?

① Jessie learned French after she moved to Paris.
② We will go camping when the weather is nice.
③ Don't use your smartphone during you drive.
④ Let's keep walking until we find the hidden treasure.
⑤ I haven't seen him since I had lunch with him last Saturday.

19 다음 밑줄 친 부분을 어법상 바르게 고친 것 중 **틀린** 것은?

① I met a girl that name is Anna. (→ whom)
② Let's find the rabbit which fur is thick. (→ whose)
③ The turtle is an animal whose has a hard shell. (→ that)
④ The necklace whose she is wearing is made of gold. (→ which)
⑤ The reporter interviewed the swimmer whose won the gold medal. (→ who)

20 다음 중 밑줄 친 부분의 쓰임이 같은 것끼리 짝 지어진 것은?

ⓐ Do you know whose laptop that is?
ⓑ I know a boy whose dream is to be a famous ballet dancer.
ⓒ A reindeer is an animal whose horns look like branches.
ⓓ I wonder whose story was chosen for the school play.

① ⓐ, ⓑ   ② ⓐ, ⓒ   ③ ⓑ, ⓒ
④ ⓑ, ⓓ   ⑤ ⓒ, ⓓ

21 다음 두 문장에 대한 설명으로 **틀린** 것은?

ⓐ Paul helped a man whose arm was broken.
ⓑ When I get home, my dog always sits in front of the door.

① ⓐ의 whose는 a man을 선행사로 하는 소유격 관계대명사이다.
② ⓐ의 whose는 that으로 바꿔 쓸 수 있다.
③ ⓐ의 whose는 생략할 수 없다.
④ ⓑ의 when은 접속사로 쓰였다.
⑤ ⓑ는 주절과 부사절의 위치를 바꿔도 같은 의미를 나타낸다.

22 다음 중 어법상 옳은 문장의 개수는?

ⓐ Heat the butter until turns to brown.
ⓑ After he finished exercising, he took a shower.
ⓒ Pinocchio is a cute doll whose wish is to become a boy.
ⓓ The paintings whose Mr. Clark showed to me were beautiful.
ⓔ Close the windows before you leave the room.

① 0개   ② 1개   ③ 2개   ④ 3개   ⑤ 4개

23 다음 괄호 안의 말을 바르게 배열하여 문장을 다시 쓴 후, 문장을 우리말로 해석하시오.

(1) They played basketball (got, until, it, dark).

→ _____

→ 해석: _____

(2) She read a newspaper (was, the baby, while, sleeping).

→ _____

→ 해석: _____

(3) You have to eat something (you, this medicine, before, take).

→ _____

→ 해석: _____

24 다음 두 문장을 관계대명사를 사용하여 한 문장으로 바꿔 쓰시오.

(1) Ted has a dog. Its ears are very long.

→ Ted _____ .

(2) A girl is flying a drone. Her name is Melisa.

→ A girl _____ .

25 다음 우리말과 같도록 [조건]에 맞게 문장을 완성하시오.

[조건]　1. [보기]에서 알맞은 말을 골라 사용할 것

　　　　2. 시제를 정확히 쓸 것

　　　　3. 대소문자를 구별할 것

[보기]　　visit me　　go to bed　　work out

(1) Amy가 나를 방문했을 때, 나는 꽃에 물을 주고 있었다.

→ _____ ,

I was watering the flowers.

(2) Emma는 운동한 후에 매우 피곤했다.

→ Emma felt very tired _____ .

(3) 지나는 잠자리에 들기 전에 양치질하는 것을 결코 잊지 않는다.

→ Jina never forgets to brush her teeth _____

_____ .

26 다음 우리말과 같도록 [조건]에 맞게 영작하시오.

[조건]　1. 알맞은 관계대명사를 사용할 것

　　　　2. 괄호 안의 말을 이용할 것

(1) 머리카락이 길고 곱슬곱슬한 소녀는 Kate다.

→ _____

(the girl, hair, curly)

(2) 나는 나를 위해 요리를 할 수 있는 로봇을 갖고 싶다.

→ _____

(want, a robot, for)

(3) 깃털이 주황색인 앵무새를 봐.

→ _____

(the parrot, feathers)

27 다음 그림을 보고, 각 상자에서 알맞은 말을 하나씩 골라 문장을 완성하시오.

until	vacuumed	cleaning
while	looked	very shiny
after	finished	the living room

(1) Jiho cleaned the window _____ his dad

_____ .

(2) His younger sister mopped the floor _____

it _____ .

(3) _____ they _____ ,

his mom put flowers on the table.

바다 아래에

Under the Sea

01 우리 행성의 3분의 2는 대양들로 덮여 있다.

01 <u>3분의 2</u> 　　　　　 수동태: be동사＋과거분사＋by＋행위자
Two-thirds of our planet is covered by oceans.
주어: 분수＋of＋명사구　　　　 of 뒤의 명사(구)에 수 일치

02 대양들은 신기한 것으로 가득 차 있으며 수많은 종의 서식지이다.

02 　　　　　　　　　　　　　　　(they)
They are full of wonder and are home to millions of species.
= Oceans 　└ be full of: ～으로 가득 차다

03 매일 우리는 대양들에 관한 새로운 것들을 배우고 있다.

03 Every day, we are learning new things about them.
　　　　　　　　　　현재진행형:
　　　　　　　　　　be동사의 현재형＋동사원형-ing

04 몇몇 흥미로운 바다 동물들을 알아보자.

04 Let's find out about some interesting sea animals.
　　　　 알아보다, 찾다

05 좋은 꿈 꿔라

05 Sweet Dreams

06 여러분은 그림 속 이 고래들이 무엇을 하고 있는지 추측할 수 있는가?

06 Can you guess what these whales are doing in the picture?
　　　　 간접의문문: 의문사(what)＋주어(these whales)＋동사(are doing) ～
　　　　 (guess의 목적어 역할)

07 그것들은 무리를 지어 서 있는 것처럼 보인다.

07 It looks like they are standing up in a group.
　　　 look like: ～처럼 보이다 (뒤에 절이 온 경우임)

08 그러나 그것들은 실제로는 잠을 자고 있다!

08 But they are actually sleeping!

09 혹등고래는 잠을 자는 동안 꼬리로 서 있는다.

09 Humpback whales stand on their tails while they sleep.
　　　　　　　　　　　　　　　 ～하는 동안에 (시간 접속사)

10 그것들은 수면 근처에서 잠을 잔다.

10 They sleep near the surface.
= Humpback whales

11 그것들은 물고기가 아니기 때문에 숨을 쉬기 위해 위로 나올 필요가 있다.

11 Since they are not fish, they need to come up to breathe.
～이기 때문에 (이유 접속사)　　　 need to＋동사원형: 　부사적 용법의 to부정사
　　　　　　　　　　　　　　　 ～할 필요가 있다 　(목적)

12 또한 그것들은 완전히 잠들지 않는다.

12 Also, they don't fall asleep completely.
　　　　　　　　 잠들다

13 그것들은 잠에서 깨면 심호흡을 하러 물 밖으로 나왔다가 바다로 다시 뛰어든다.

13 　　　　　　　　　　　　　　　　　　　　　 명 숨, 호흡
When they wake up, they come out of the water for a deep breath
～할 때 (시간 접속사)　　　　　　　 전 ～을 위해, ～하러

and dive back into the sea.

14 맛있게 먹어라

14 Enjoy Your Meal

15 만약 물고기가 똑똑하지 않다고 생각한다면 tuskfish를 한번 봐라.

15 　　　　　 (that)　　　　　　 ～을 (한번) 보다
If you think fish are not smart, take a look at the tuskfish.
만약 ～라면　 fish의 복수형
(조건 접속사) 　(fish는 단수형과 복수형이 동일함)

16 This small fish [whose favorite food is clams] uses a tool to open them.
소유격 관계대명사
= clams
주어
동사
부사적 용법의 to부정사 (목적)

16 가장 좋아하는 먹이가 조개인 이 작은 물고기는 조개를 열기 위해 도구를 사용한다.

17 Clams usually hide under the sand, so they cannot be easily discovered.
= clams
(접) 그래서
조동사가 포함된 수동태:
조동사 + be + 과거분사

17 조개는 대개 모래 아래에 숨어 있어서 쉽게 발견될 수 없다.

18 The tuskfish blows on the sand until a clam appears.
~할 때까지 (시간 접속사)

18 tuskfish는 조개가 나타날 때까지 모래에 입김을 분다.

19 The clam is closed tightly, so the fish cannot eat it.
(접) 그래서
수동태: be동사 + 과거분사
= the clam

19 조개가 단단히 닫혀 있어서 물고기는 그것을 먹을 수 없다.

20 But the tuskfish doesn't give up.

20 그러나 tuskfish는 포기하지 않는다.

21 It smashes the clam against a rock.
= The tuskfish
smash A against B: A를 B에 내리치다

21 tuskfish는 조개를 바위에 내리친다.

22 In the end, the clam opens and dinner is served.
= dinner is ready

22 마침내 조개가 열리고 밥상이 차려진다.

23 One, Two, Three, Jump!

23 하나, 둘, 셋, 뛰어라!

24 You have probably seen a bird fly down to the sea to catch a fish.
지각동사(see) + 목적어(a bird) + 동사원형(fly)
fish의 단수형
현재완료: have + 과거분사 (경험)
부사적 용법의 to부정사 (목적)

24 여러분은 아마 새가 물고기를 잡기 위해 바다로 날아 내려가는 것을 본 적이 있을 것이다.

25 But have you ever seen a fish jump out of the water to catch a bird?
Have you ever + 과거분사 ~?:
너는 ~해 본 적이 있니?
부사적 용법의 to부정사 (목적)

25 그러나 물고기가 새를 잡기 위해 물 밖으로 뛰어오르는 것을 본 적이 있는가?

26 Well, birds have to be careful when a giant trevally is around.
have to + 동사원형:
~해야 한다
~할 때 (시간 접속사)

26 자, giant trevally가 주변에 있을 때 새들은 조심해야 한다.

27 This fish can grow up to 170cm and 80kg.

27 이 물고기는 170센티미터에 80킬로그램까지 자랄 수 있다.

28 But don't let its size fool you.
(동) 속이다, 기만하다
사역동사(let) + 목적어(its size) + 동사원형(fool): (목적어)가 ~하게 하다

28 그러나 그 크기에 속지 마라.

29 This fish is quick and smart.

29 이 물고기는 빠르고 똑똑하다.

30 It can spot a flying bird and calculate its speed and distance.
and에 의해 병렬 연결
현재분사 (명사 bird 수식)

30 그것은 날고 있는 새를 발견하고 그 새의 속도와 거리를 계산할 수 있다.

31 When the bird flies nearby, the giant trevally jumps out of the water and
~할 때 (시간 접속사)
out of + 명사: ~ 밖으로

catches it.
= the bird

31 새가 가까이에 날고 있을 때, giant trevally는 물 밖으로 뛰어올라 새를 잡는다.

빈칸 채우기

우리말 뜻과 일치하도록 교과서 본문의 문장을 완성하시오.

중요 문장

01 Two-thirds of our planet _____ _____ _____ oceans.

01 우리 행성의 3분의 2는 대양들로 덮여 있다.

02 They are full of wonder and are home to _____ _____ species.

02 대양들은 신기한 것으로 가득 차 있으며 수많은 종의 서식지이다.

03 Every day, we _____ _____ new things about them.

03 매일 우리는 대양들에 관한 새로운 것들을 배우고 있다.

04 _____ _____ _____ about some interesting sea animals.

04 몇몇 흥미로운 바다 동물들을 알아보자.

05 Sweet _____

05 좋은 꿈 꿔라

06 _____ _____ _____ what these whales are doing in the picture?

06 여러분은 그림 속 이 고래들이 무엇을 하고 있는지 추측할 수 있는가?

07 It looks like they are standing up _____ _____ _____.

07 그것들은 무리를 지어 서 있는 것처럼 보인다.

08 But they _____ _____ _____!

08 그러나 그것들은 실제로는 잠을 자고 있다!

09 Humpback whales _____ _____ _____ _____ while they sleep.

09 혹등고래는 잠을 자는 동안 꼬리로 서 있는다.

10 They sleep _____ _____ _____.

10 그것들은 수면 근처에서 잠을 잔다.

11 Since they are not fish, they need to come up _____ _____.

11 그것들은 물고기가 아니기 때문에 숨을 쉬기 위해 위로 나올 필요가 있다.

12 Also, they _____ _____ _____ _____.

12 또한 그것들은 완전히 잠들지 않는다.

13 When they wake up, they _____ _____ _____ _____ _____ for a deep breath and dive back into the sea.

13 그것들은 잠에서 깨면 심호흡을 하러 물 밖으로 나왔다가 바다로 다시 뛰어든다.

14 _____ Your Meal

14 맛있게 먹어라

15 If you think fish are not smart, _____ _____ _____ the tuskfish.

15 만약 물고기가 똑똑하지 않다고 생각한 다면 tuskfish를 한번 봐라.

16 This small fish _____ _____ _____ _____
   _____ uses a tool to open them.

16 가장 좋아하는 먹이가 조개인 이 작은 물고기는 조개를 열기 위해 도구를 사용한다.

17 Clams usually hide under the sand, so they _____ _____
   _____ _____ .

17 조개는 대개 모래 아래에 숨어 있어서 쉽게 발견될 수 없다.

18 The tuskfish blows on the sand _____ _____ _____
   _____ .

18 tuskfish는 조개가 나타날 때까지 모래에 입김을 분다.

19 The clam _____ _____ _____ , so the fish cannot eat it.

19 조개가 단단히 닫혀 있어서 물고기는 그것을 먹을 수 없다.

20 But the tuskfish _____ _____ _____ .

20 그러나 tuskfish는 포기하지 않는다.

21 It _____ the clam _____ a rock.

21 tuskfish는 조개를 바위에 내리친다.

22 _____ _____ _____ , the clam opens and dinner is
   served.

22 마침내 조개가 열리고 밥상이 차려진다.

23 One, Two, Three, _____ !

23 하나, 둘, 셋, 뛰어라!

24 You have probably seen a bird fly down to the sea _____ _____
   _____ _____ .

24 여러분은 아마 새가 물고기를 잡기 위해 바다로 날아 내려가는 것을 본 적이 있을 것이다.

25 But _____ _____ _____ _____ a fish jump out of the
   water to catch a bird?

25 그러나 물고기가 새를 잡기 위해 물 밖으로 뛰어오르는 것을 본 적이 있는가?

26 Well, birds _____ _____ _____ _____ when a giant
   trevally is around.

26 자, giant trevally가 주변에 있을 때 새들은 조심해야 한다.

27 This fish can _____ _____ _____ 170cm and 80kg.

27 이 물고기는 170센티미터에 80킬로그램까지 자랄 수 있다.

28 But don't _____ _____ _____ _____ you.

28 그러나 그 크기에 속지 마라.

29 This fish is _____ _____ _____ .

29 이 물고기는 빠르고 똑똑하다.

30 It can spot a flying bird and calculate _____ _____ _____
   _____ .

30 그것은 날고 있는 새를 발견하고 그것(그 새)의 속도와 거리를 계산할 수 있다.

31 _____ _____ _____ _____ _____ , the giant
   trevally jumps out of the water and catches it.

31 새가 가까이에 날고 있을 때, giant trevally는 물 밖으로 뛰어올라 새를 잡는다.

바른 어휘 · 어법 고르기

글의 내용과 문장의 어법에 맞게 괄호 안에서 알맞은 어휘를 고르시오.

01 (Second-three / Two-thirds) of our planet is covered by oceans.

02 They are (full / empty) of wonder and are home to millions of species.

03 Every day, we are learning new things about (it / them).

04 Let's find out (about / at) some interesting sea animals.

05 Sweet (Dreams / Food)

06 Can you guess (what / that) these whales are doing in the picture?

07 It looks (as / like) they are standing up in a group.

08 But they are actually (slept / sleeping)!

09 Humpback whales stand on their tails (while / during) they sleep.

10 They sleep (near / far from) the surface.

11 (Until / Since) they are not fish, they need to come up to breathe.

12 Also, they don't fall (sleep / asleep) completely.

13 When they (wake up / sleep), they come out of the water for a deep breath and dive back into the sea.

14 (Cook / Enjoy) Your Meal

15 (If / Unless) you think fish are not smart, take a look at the tuskfish.

16 This small fish (whose / whom) favorite food is clams uses a tool to open them.

17 Clams usually hide under the sand, so they (can / cannot) be easily discovered.

18   The tuskfish blows on the sand (before / until) a clam appears.

19   The clam is closed tightly, so the fish cannot eat (it / them).

20   But the tuskfish (gives up / doesn't give up).

21   It (protects / smashes) the clam against a rock.

22   In the end, the clam opens and dinner (is served / serves).

23   One, Two, Three, (Dive / Jump)!

24   You have probably seen a bird (fly / to fly) down to the sea to catch a fish.

25   But have you ever (saw / seen) a fish jump out of the water to catch a bird?

26   Well, birds have to be (careful / carefully) when a giant trevally is around.

27   This fish can grow (up / up to) 170cm and 80kg.

28   But don't let its size (fool / fooled) you.

29   This fish is (slow / quick) and smart.

30   It can spot a flying bird and calculate (its / their) speed and distance.

31   When the bird flies nearby, the giant trevally jumps out of the water and (catches / catch) it.

틀린 문장 고치기

밑줄 친 부분이 내용이나 어법상 바르면 ○, 어색하면 ✕에 표시하고 고쳐 쓰시오.

01 Two-thirds of our planet <u>covered</u> by oceans.　　　　　○ ✕

02 They are full of wonder and <u>is</u> home to millions of species.　　　　　○ ✕

03 Every day, we are learning new things about <u>them</u>.　　　　　○ ✕

04 Let's <u>finding out</u> about some interesting sea animals.　　　　　○ ✕

05 Sweet <u>Dreams</u>　　　　　○ ✕

06 Can you guess what these whales <u>is</u> doing in the picture?　　　　　○ ✕

07 It <u>looks</u> they are standing up in a group.　　　　　○ ✕

08 But they <u>are actually sleeping</u>!　　　　　○ ✕

09 Humpback whales stand on their <u>back</u> while they sleep.　　　　　○ ✕

10 They sleep <u>near</u> the surface.　　　　　○ ✕

11 <u>Although</u> they are not fish, they need to come up to breathe.　　　　　○ ✕

12 Also, they don't fall asleep <u>complete</u>.　　　　　○ ✕

13 <u>Before</u> they wake up, they come out of the water for a deep breath and dive back into the sea.　　○ ✕

14 <u>Enjoys</u> Your Meal　　　　　○ ✕

15 <u>As</u> you think fish are not smart, take a look at the tuskfish.　　　　　○ ✕

16 This small fish whose favorite food is clams <u>uses</u> a tool to open them.　　　　　○ ✕

17 Clams usually hide under the sand, so they <u>cannot be easily discover</u>.　　　　　○ ✕

18 The tuskfish blows on the sand until a clam <u>disappears</u>.   ⭕ ✕

19 The clam is <u>open</u> tightly, so the fish cannot eat it.   ⭕ ✕

20 But the tuskfish <u>doesn't give up</u>.   ⭕ ✕

21 It smashes the clam <u>against</u> a rock.   ⭕ ✕

22 In the end, the clam opens and dinner <u>serves</u>.   ⭕ ✕

23 One, Two, Three, <u>Jump</u>!   ⭕ ✕

24 You have probably seen a bird fly down to the sea <u>catch</u> a fish.   ⭕ ✕

25 But have you ever seen a fish <u>jumps</u> out of the water to catch a bird?   ⭕ ✕

26 Well, birds have to be careful <u>when</u> a giant trevally is around.   ⭕ ✕

27 This fish can <u>grows</u> up to 170cm and 80kg.   ⭕ ✕

28 But don't let its size <u>fooling</u> you.   ⭕ ✕

29 This fish is <u>quick and smart</u>.   ⭕ ✕

30 It can spot a flying bird and <u>calculates</u> its speed and distance.   ⭕ ✕

31 When the bird flies nearby, the giant trevally jumps <u>out of</u> the water and catches it.   ⭕ ✕

주어진 단어를 바르게 배열하여 문장을 쓰시오.

01 우리 행성의 3분의 2는 대양들로 덮여 있다. (of / oceans / our planet / by / two-thirds / is covered)

→

02 그것들(대양들)은 신기한 것으로 가득 차 있으며 수많은 종의 서식지이다.

(are / home / wonder / are / full of / and / species / they / to / millions of)

→

03 매일 우리는 그것들(대양들)에 관한 새로운 것들을 배우고 있다. (new things / every day, / are learning / about them / we)

→

04 몇몇 흥미로운 바다 동물들을 알아보자. (sea animals / about / some interesting / find out / let's)

→

05 좋은 꿈 꿔라 (Dreams / Sweet)

→

06 여러분은 그림 속 이 고래들이 무엇을 하고 있는지 추측할 수 있는가?

(these whales / can / what / are doing / in the picture / guess / you)

→

07 그것들은 무리를 지어 서 있는 것처럼 보인다. (it / in a group / are standing up / looks like / they)

→

08 그러나 그것들은 실제로는 잠을 자고 있다! (are / but / actually sleeping / they)

→

09 혹등고래는 잠을 자는 동안 꼬리로 서 있는다. (sleep / while / stand / humpback whales / on their tails / they)

→

10 그것들은 수면 근처에서 잠을 잔다. (near / sleep / they / the surface)

→

11 그것들은 물고기가 아니기 때문에 숨을 쉬기 위해 위로 나올 필요가 있다.

(come up / they / since / they / not / need to / to breathe / are / fish,)

→

12 또한 그것들은 완전히 잠들지 않는다. (fall asleep / also, / completely / they / don't)

→

13 그것들은 잠에서 깨면 심호흡을 하러 물 밖으로 나왔다가 바다로 다시 뛰어든다.

(and / when / into the sea / out of the water / they / wake up, / they / dive back / come / for a deep breath)

→

14 맛있게 먹어라 (Your / Enjoy / Meal)

→

15 만약 물고기가 똑똑하지 않다고 생각한다면 tuskfish를 한번 봐라.

(you / take a look at / if / fish / smart, / are not / the tuskfish / think)

→

16 가장 좋아하는 먹이가 조개인 이 작은 물고기는 그것들(조개)을 열기 위해 도구를 사용한다.

(whose / a tool / this small fish / uses / to open / favorite food / is / them / clams)

→

17 조개는 대개 모래 아래에 숨어 있어서 쉽게 발견될 수 없다.

(cannot / hide / clams / under the sand, / they / be easily discovered / so / usually)

→

18 tuskfish는 조개가 나타날 때까지 모래에 입김을 분다. (appears / until / the tuskfish / blows / a clam / on the sand)

→

19 조개가 단단히 닫혀 있어서 물고기는 그것을 먹을 수 없다. (it / cannot / is closed / the clam / eat / tightly, / so / the fish)

→

20 그러나 tuskfish는 포기하지 않는다. (doesn't / the tuskfish / but / give up)

→

21 그것(tuskfish)은 조개를 바위에 내리친다. (the clam / it / a rock / smashes / against)

→

22 마침내 조개가 열리고 밥상이 차려진다. (the clam / and / is served / in the end, / opens / dinner)

→

23 하나, 둘, 셋, 뛰어라! (One, / Jump / Three, / Two,)

→

24 여러분은 아마 새가 물고기를 잡기 위해 바다로 날아 내려가는 것을 본 적이 있을 것이다.

(to catch / a bird / you / a fish / have probably seen / fly down / to the sea)

→

25 그러나 물고기가 새를 잡기 위해 물 밖으로 뛰어오르는 것을 본 적이 있는가?

(jump / to catch / have you ever seen / a bird / a fish / out of the water / but)

→

26 자, giant trevally가 주변에 있을 때 새들은 조심해야 한다.

(when / birds / well, / be careful / a giant trevally / around / is / have to)

→

27 이 물고기는 170센티미터에 80킬로그램까지 자랄 수 있다. (170cm and 80kg / grow / this fish / up to / can)

→

28 그러나 그 크기에 속지 마라. (fool / its size / don't / let / you / but)

→

29 이 물고기는 빠르고 똑똑하다. (smart / quick / is / and / this fish)

→

30 그것은 날고 있는 새를 발견하고 그것(그 새)의 속도와 거리를 계산할 수 있다.

(spot / and / it / its speed and distance / can / a flying bird / calculate)

→

31 새가 가까이에 날고 있을 때, giant trevally는 물 밖으로 뛰어올라 새를 잡는다.

(jumps / the giant trevally / nearby, / flies / when / the bird / catches / it / out of the water / and)

→

[01-03] 다음 글을 읽고, 물음에 답하시오.

Two-thirds of our planet (A) is / are covered by oceans. They are full _____ⓐ_____ wonder and are home to millions _____ⓑ_____ species. Every day, we are (B) learned / learning new things about them. Let's find out about some interesting sea animals.

01 윗글의 (A)와 (B)에서 알맞은 것을 골라 쓰시오.

(A) _____ (B) _____

02 윗글의 빈칸 ⓐ와 ⓑ에 공통으로 들어갈 말로 알맞은 것은?

① in ② at ③ of
④ for ⑤ with

03 윗글 다음에 이어질 내용으로 가장 알맞은 것은?

① 바닷속의 신기한 지형
② 흥미로운 바다 동물들
③ 바다 동물의 진화 과정
④ 바다에 얽힌 신화와 전설
⑤ 인류가 바다를 이용해 온 예

[04-06] 다음 글을 읽고, 물음에 답하시오.

Can you guess what these whales are doing in the picture? (①) It looks like they are standing up in a group. (②) Humpback whales stand on their tails while they sleep. (③) They sleep near the surface. _____ⓐ_____ they are not fish, they need to come up to breathe. (④) Also, they don't fall asleep completely. (⑤) When they wake up, they come out of the water for a deep breath and dive back into the sea.

04 윗글의 ①~⑤ 중 주어진 문장이 들어갈 알맞은 곳은?

But they are actually sleeping!

①   ②   ③   ④   ⑤

05 윗글의 빈칸 ⓐ에 들어갈 알맞은 접속사는?

① While ② Before ③ Since
④ Unless ⑤ Although

06 윗글의 혹등고래에 대한 내용과 일치하지 않는 것은?

① 잠을 자는 동안 꼬리로 서 있다.
② 수면 근처에서 잠을 잔다.
③ 숨을 쉬기 위해 물 밖으로 나와야 한다.
④ 완전히 잠들지 않는다.
⑤ 잠에서 깨자마자 물속 깊이 헤엄쳐 내려간다.

[07-11] 다음 글을 읽고, 물음에 답하시오.

If you think fish are not smart, take a look at the tuskfish. This small fish _____ⓐ_____ favorite food is clams uses a tool to open them. Clams usually hide under the sand, so they cannot be easily (A) covered / discovered. The tuskfish blows on the sand until a clam (B) appears / disappears. The clam is closed tightly, so the fish cannot eat ⓑit. But the tuskfish _____ⓒ_____. It smashes the clam against a rock. In the end, the clam (C) opens / is closed and dinner is served.

07 윗글의 빈칸 ⓐ에 들어갈 말로 알맞은 것은?

① who ② that ③ which
④ what ⑤ whose

08 윗글의 (A)~(C)에서 문맥상 알맞은 말이 바르게 짝 지어진 것은?

| | (A) | (B) | (C) |

① discovered – disappears – is closed

② covered – appears – opens

③ discovered – appears – opens

④ covered – disappears – is closed

⑤ discovered – appears – is closed

09 윗글의 밑줄 친 ⓑit이 가리키는 것은?

① a rock ② dinner

③ the sand ④ the clam

⑤ the tuskfish

10 윗글의 빈칸 ⓒ에 들어갈 말로 알맞은 것은?

① doesn't give up

② spreads the sand

③ doesn't use a tool

④ doesn't want to eat it

⑤ tries to hide the clam

11 윗글을 읽고 tuskfish에 관해 알 수 있는 것은?

① 서식 환경

② 평균 수명

③ 이용하는 도구

④ 하루에 먹는 먹이의 양

⑤ 천적으로부터 자신을 보호하는 방법

[12-16] 다음 글을 읽고, 물음에 답하시오.

You ①have probably seen a bird fly down to the sea to catch a fish. But have you ever seen a fish ②to jump out of the water to catch a bird? Well, birds ___(A)___ when a giant trevally is around. This fish ③can grow up to 170cm and 80kg. But don't let ⓐits size fool you. This fish is quick and smart. ⓑIt can spot a ④flying bird and calculate ⓒits speed and distance. ⑤When the bird flies nearby, the giant trevally jumps out of the water and catches ⓓit.

12 윗글의 밑줄 친 ①~⑤ 중 어법상 틀린 것은?

① ② ③ ④ ⑤

13 윗글의 빈칸 (A)에 들어갈 말로 알맞은 것은?

① have to be careful

② use an interesting tool

③ can catch the fish easily

④ have no natural enemies

⑤ should communicate with each other

14 윗글의 밑줄 친 ⓐ~ⓓ 중 giant trevally를 가리키는 것끼리 짝 지어진 것은?

① ⓐ, ⓑ ② ⓐ, ⓑ, ⓓ ③ ⓑ, ⓒ

④ ⓑ, ⓒ, ⓓ ⑤ ⓒ, ⓓ

15 다음 영어 뜻풀이에 해당하는 단어를 윗글에서 찾아 쓰시오.

> to find a number, answer, etc. by using mathematical processes

→ _____

16 윗글을 읽고 giant trevally에 대해 바르게 이해하지 <u>못한</u> 사람은?

① 민주: 물고기인데 물 밖으로 뛰어 오를 수 있네.

② 세준: 170센티미터에 80킬로그램까지 자랄 수 있다니 큰 물고기구나.

③ 서희: 크기가 큰데도 느리지 않아.

④ 가연: 날고 있는 새의 속도와 거리를 계산할 수 있어.

⑤ 준수: 새를 유인해서 물속으로 뛰어들게 하는 게 정말 신기해.

[17-21] 다음 글을 읽고, 물음에 답하시오.

Can you guess what these whales are doing in the picture? It ①<u>looks like</u> they are standing up in a group. But they are actually sleeping! Humpback whales stand on their tails ____(A)____ they sleep. They sleep near the surface. Since they are not fish, they need to come up ⓐ<u>to breathe</u>. Also, they ②<u>don't fall asleep completely</u>. When they wake up, they come out of the water for a deep breath and dive back into the sea.

If you think fish are not smart, ③<u>take a look at the</u> tuskfish. This small fish whose favorite food is clams ____ⓑ____ a tool to open them. Clams usually hide under the sand, so they cannot be easily discovered. The tuskfish blows on the sand ____(B)____ a clam appears. The clam is closed tightly, so the fish cannot eat it. But the tuskfish ④<u>doesn't give up</u>. It smashes the clam against a rock. ⑤<u>In the end</u>, the clam opens and dinner is served.

17 윗글의 밑줄 친 ①~⑤의 우리말 뜻이 알맞지 <u>않은</u> 것은?

① ~처럼 보이다

② 완전히 잠들지 않는다

③ ~을 돌보다

④ 포기하지 않는다

⑤ 마침내

18 윗글의 빈칸 (A)와 (B)에 알맞은 접속사가 순서대로 짝 지어진 것은?

	(A)	(B)		(A)	(B)
①	before	– after	②	unless	– until
③	while	– until	④	unless	– after
⑤	while	– though			

19 윗글의 밑줄 친 ⓐ<u>to breathe</u>와 쓰임이 같은 것은?

① She wants some bread <u>to eat</u>.

② It is important <u>to protect</u> nature.

③ Jina's dream is <u>to become</u> a pilot.

④ They all agreed <u>to go</u> to the beach.

⑤ I went to the library <u>to return</u> some books.

20 윗글의 빈칸 ⓑ에 들어갈 use의 형태로 알맞은 것은?

① used

② uses

③ is used

④ are used

⑤ are using

21 윗글을 읽고 답할 수 <u>없는</u> 질문은?

① Where do humpback whales sleep?

② Why do humpback whales come out of the water?

③ How many hours do humpback whales sleep a day?

④ Where do clams usually hide?

⑤ How does the tuskfish open the clam?

22 다음 글에 나온 혹등고래가 자는 모습을 우리말로 설명하시오.

> Can you guess what these whales are doing in the picture? It looks like they are standing up in a group. But they are actually sleeping! Humpback whales stand on their tails while they sleep. They sleep near the surface. Since they are not fish, they need to come up to breathe.

→ _____

[23-24] 다음 글을 읽고, 물음에 답하시오.

> If you think fish are not smart, take a look at the tuskfish. 가장 좋아하는 먹이가 조개인 이 작은 물고기는 그것들을 열기 위해 도구를 사용한다. Clams usually hide under the sand, so they cannot be easily discovered. The tuskfish blows on the sand until a clam appears. The clam is closed tightly, so the fish cannot eat it. But the tuskfish doesn't give up. It smashes the clam against a rock. In the end, the clam opens and dinner is served.

고/단도
23 윗글의 밑줄 친 우리말과 같도록 [조건]에 맞게 문장을 쓰시오.

> [조건]   1. 알맞은 관계대명사를 사용할 것
>   2. 괄호 안의 단어를 사용할 것

→ _____

_____

(small, food, clams, a tool)

24 다음 질문에 완전한 영어 문장으로 답하시오.

(1) Where do clams usually hide?

→ _____

(2) How does the tuskfish open the clam?

→ _____

[25-27] 다음 글을 읽고, 물음에 답하시오.

> You have probably seen a bird fly down to the sea to catch a fish. ⓐ그러나 물고기가 새를 잡기 위해 물 밖으로 뛰어오르는 것을 본 적이 있는가? Well, birds have to be careful when a giant trevally is around. This fish can grow up to 170cm and 80kg. ⓑBut don't let its size fool you. This fish is quick and smart. It can spot a flying bird and calculate its speed and distance. When the bird flies nearby, the giant trevally jumps out of the water and catches it.

25 윗글의 밑줄 친 ⓐ의 우리말과 같도록 주어진 말을 바르게 배열하여 문장을 완성하시오.

> have, catch, but, you, a fish, ever, to, seen, jump, the water, a bird, out of

→ _____

_____

고/단도
26 윗글의 밑줄 친 ⓑ와 의미가 통하도록 다음 문장의 빈칸에 알맞은 말을 쓰시오.

→ The fish is very _____ ,

but it is _____ .

27 How does the giant trevally catch a flying bird? Answer in English.

→ _____

_____

After You Read_A

I learned about oceans today. ❶ Two-thirds of our planet is covered by oceans. ❷ They are home to ❸ millions of species. ❹ There are many interesting facts about sea animals. ❺ For example, humpback whales stand on their tails ❻ while they sleep, and they sleep ❼ near the surface.

나는 오늘 대양에 대해 배웠다. 우리 행성의 3분의 2는 대양으로 덮여 있다. 대양은 수많은 종의 서식지이다. 바다 동물들에 관한 재미있는 사실이 많이 있다. 예를 들어, 혹등고래는 잠을 자는 동안 꼬리로 서 있고, 수면 근처에서 잠을 잔다.

❶ Two-thirds: 3분의 2 / 주어가 「분수＋of＋명사」인 경우 동사는 of 뒤의 명사의 수에 일치시킨다.

❷ = Oceans

❸ 수많은

❹ There are＋복수 명사(many interesting facts) ~.: ~이 있다.

❺ 예를 들어 (= For instance)

❻ ~하는 동안에 (시간 접속사)

❼ (전) ~에서 가까이

Think and Write_Step 1_동영상 Script

Beluga whale: Hello, I'm a beluga whale. I live in the Arctic Ocean. ❶ It's very cold. So my skin is very thick and ❷ about half of my body is fat. I also have a round head. ❸ When I'm hungry, I usually eat fish and clams. I'm white ❹ all over, so people also ❺ call me the white whale. ❻ When I ❼ was born, I was gray. But ❽ when I grew up, my body became white! I can make several sounds. I use these sounds to talk to other whales. Yes, we can communicate!

Octopus: Hello, I'm an octopus. I live on the ocean floor. ❾ I'm different from other ocean animals ❿ in many ways. I have no bones so I can move around easily in the ocean. I have eight arms. My favorite food is small fish. I can change the color of my skin ⓫ to hide from my enemies. ⓬ When I meet an enemy, I ⓭ shoot out dark black ink and swim away. Oh, one more thing. The color of my blood is blue.

Beluga 고래: 안녕하세요, 저는 Beluga 고래예요. 저는 북극해에 살아요. 북극해는 매우 추워요. 그래서 제 피부는 매우 두껍고 제 몸의 절반 정도는 지방이랍니다. 저는 또한 동그란 머리를 가졌어요. 저는 배가 고플 때 주로 물고기와 조개를 먹어요. 저는 온몸이 하얘서, 사람들은 저를 흰고래라고도 불러요. 태어났을 때 저는 회색이었어요. 하지만 자라자 제 몸은 흰색이 되었어요! 저는 몇몇 소리를 낼 수 있어요. 저는 이러한 소리들을 다른 고래들과 이야기할 때 사용해요. 맞아요, 우리는 의사소통을 할 수 있어요!

문어: 안녕하세요, 저는 문어예요. 저는 바다 바닥에 살아요. 저는 많은 면에서 다른 바다 동물들과 다르답니다. 저는 뼈가 없어서 바다에서 쉽게 돌아다닐 수 있어요. 저는 팔이 8개예요. 제가 가장 좋아하는 먹이는 작은 물고기예요. 저는 적으로부터 숨기 위해 피부색을 바꿀 수 있어요. 적을 만나면 저는 먹물을 내뿜고 헤엄쳐 가 버리지요. 오, 한 가지 더 있어요. 제 피 색깔은 파란색이에요.

❶ = The Arctic Ocean

❷ about (부) 약, 대략 / 주어가 「half＋of＋명사(my body)」인 경우 동사는 of 뒤의 명사의 수에 일치시킨다.

❸, ❻, ❽, ⓬ ~할 때 (시간 접속사)

❹ 전체에 걸쳐, 도처에

❺ call＋목적어(me)＋목적격보어(the white whale): (목적어)를 ~라고 부르다

❼ be born: 태어나다

❾ be different from: ~과 다르다

❿ 많은 면에서

⓫ '~하기 위해서'라는 의미의 목적을 나타내는 부사적 용법의 to부정사

⓭ 내뿜다

My Fun Animal: Beluga whale

I will introduce the beluga whale. It lives in the Arctic Ocean. It has a round head. It usually eats fish and clams. An interesting fact ❶ about the beluga whale is ❷ that it is white all over. ❸ That's why people call ❹ it the white whale. ❺ When it is born, it is gray. But ❻ when it grows up, its body becomes white! I ❼ want to see this animal ❽ with my own eyes!

My Fun Animal: Octopus

I will introduce the octopus. It lives on the ocean floor. It has no bones so it can move around easily in the ocean. It usually eats small fish. An interesting fact ❾ about the octopus is ❿ that it can change the color of its skin ⓫ to hide from its enemies. ⓬ When it meets an enemy, it shoots out dark black ink and swims away. I ⓭ want to see this animal with my own eyes!

나의 재미있는 동물: Beluga 고래

저는 Beluga 고래를 소개할게요. 그것은 북극해에 살아요. 그것은 동그란 머리를 가졌어요. 그것은 주로 물고기와 조개를 먹어요. Beluga 고래에 관한 흥미로운 사실은 온몸이 하얗다는 거예요. 그것이 사람들이 Beluga 고래를 흰고래라고 부르는 이유예요. Beluga 고래는 태어날 때 회색이에요. 하지만 자라면, 몸은 흰색이 돼요! 저는 제 눈으로 이 동물을 보고 싶어요!

나의 재미있는 동물: 문어

저는 문어를 소개할게요. 그것은 바다 바닥에서 살아요. 그것은 뼈가 없어서 바다에서 쉽게 돌아다닐 수 있어요. 그것은 주로 작은 물고기를 먹어요. 문어에 관한 흥미로운 사실은 적으로부터 숨기 위해 문어가 피부색을 바꿀 수 있다는 거예요. 그것은 적을 만나면, 먹물을 내뿜고 헤엄쳐 가 버리지요. 저는 제 눈으로 이 동물을 보고 싶어요!

❶, ❾ ⓟ ~에 관한
❸ That's why ~.: (그것이) ~한 이유이다.
❺, ❻, ⓬ ~할 때 (시간 접속사)
❽ 내 두 눈으로
❷, ❿ 보어로 쓰인 명사절을 이끄는 접속사
❹ = the beluga whale
❼, ⓭ want는 to부정사를 목적어로 취하는 동사
⓫ 부사적 용법의 to부정사 (목적)

- The Pacific Ocean is ❶ the largest and deepest ocean.
- The Atlantic Ocean is ❷ the second largest ocean.
- The Indian Ocean has ❸ the greatest number of plant and animal species.
- The Southern Ocean is a really cold ocean. You can find penguins there.
- The Arctic Ocean is ❹ the smallest of the five oceans.

· 태평양은 가장 크고 깊은 대양이다.
· 대서양은 두 번째로 큰 대양이다.
· 인도양에는 가장 많은 식물과 동물 종이 있다.
· 남극해는 정말 추운 대양이다. 그곳에서 펭귄을 발견할 수 있다.
· 북극해는 다섯 개의 대양 중 가장 작다.

❶ 형용사 large와 deep의 최상급 표현이 and로 연결되어 있음
❷ the + 서수(second) + 형용사의 최상급(largest): ~ 번째로 …한
❸ 가장 많은
❹ the smallest: 형용사 small의 최상급 표현 / of: ~ 중에서 (최상급에서 범위를 한정함)

Arctic Ocean

This is the smallest of the five oceans. It is very cold. It ❶ is surrounded by ❷ Europe, Asia and North America. Polar bears live around here!

북극해

이것은 다섯 개의 대양 중에서 가장 작다. 이 대양은 매우 춥다. 이 대양은 유럽, 아시아, 북아메리카에 둘러싸여 있다. 북극곰이 여기 주변에 산다!

❶ be surrounded by: ~에 둘러싸여 있다
❷ A, B and C로 열거함

실전 TEST

[01-02] 다음 글을 읽고, 물음에 답하시오.

I learned about oceans today. <u>우리 행성의 3분의 2는 대양으로 덮여 있다.</u> They are home to millions of species. There are many interesting facts about sea animals. _____, humpback whales stand on their tails while they sleep, and they sleep near the surface.

서술형 **1**

01 윗글의 밑줄 친 우리말과 같도록 괄호 안의 단어들을 이용하여 문장을 완성하시오.

→ _____ by oceans.
   (of, planet, cover)

02 윗글의 빈칸에 들어갈 말로 알맞은 것은?

① However   ② Instead   ③ As a result
④ In addition   ⑤ For example

[03-05] 다음 글을 읽고, 물음에 답하시오.

Hello, I'm a beluga whale. I live in the Arctic Ocean. It's very cold. So my skin is very thick and about half of my body is fat. (①) I also have a round head. (②) When I'm hungry, I usually eat fish and clams. (③) I'm white all over, so people also call me the white whale. (④) When I was born, I was gray. (⑤) I can make several sounds. I use these sounds to talk to other whales. Yes, we can _____!

03 윗글의 ①~⑤ 중 주어진 문장이 들어갈 알맞은 곳은?

| But when I grew up, my body became white! |

①   ②   ③   ④   ⑤

고
난도
04 윗글의 빈칸에 들어갈 말로 알맞은 것은?

① jump high
② communicate
③ catch fish easily
④ be friends with humans
⑤ travel up to 130km a day

05 윗글의 beluga 고래에 대한 내용과 일치하지 <u>않는</u> 것은?

① 매우 추운 바다에 산다.
② 피부가 매우 두껍다.
③ 동그란 머리를 가졌다.
④ 주로 물고기와 조개를 먹는다.
⑤ 태어났을 때부터 온몸이 하얗다.

[06-08] 다음 글을 읽고, 물음에 답하시오.

Hello, I'm an octopus. I live on the ocean floor. I'm different ___ⓐ___ other ocean animals in many ways. (so, bones, move around, I, have, no, I, can, easily) in the ocean. I have eight arms. My favorite food is small fish. I can change the color of my skin to hide ___ⓑ___ my enemies. When I meet an enemy, I shoot out dark black ink and swim away. Oh, one more thing. The color of my blood is blue.

06 윗글의 빈칸 ⓐ와 ⓑ에 공통으로 들어갈 말로 알맞은 것은?

① on   ② of   ③ in
④ with   ⑤ from

서술형 **2**

07 윗글의 괄호 안의 말을 바르게 배열하여 쓰시오.

→ _____

08 윗글을 읽고 문어에 대해 알 수 <u>없는</u> 것은?

① 사는 곳   ② 평균 수명

③ 피의 색깔   ④ 가장 좋아하는 먹이

⑤ 천적을 방어하는 방법

[09-10] 다음 글을 읽고, 물음에 답하시오.

I will ①introduce the beluga whale. It lives in the Arctic Ocean. It has a round head. It ②usually eats fish and clams. An interesting fact about the beluga whale is that it is white ③all over. That's ④because people call it the white whale. _____ⓐ_____ it is born, it is gray. But _____ⓑ_____ it grows up, its body becomes white! I want to see this animal ⑤with my own eyes!

09 윗글의 밑줄 친 ①~⑤ 중 흐름상 어색한 것은?

①   ②   ③   ④   ⑤

10 윗글의 빈칸 ⓐ와 ⓑ에 공통으로 알맞은 접속사는?

① If(if)   ② When(when)

③ While(while)   ④ Before(before)

⑤ Though(though)

[11-12] 다음 글을 읽고, 물음에 답하시오.

I will introduce the octopus. It lives on the ocean floor. It has no bones so it can move around easily in the ocean. It usually eats small fish. An interesting fact <u>about</u> the octopus is that it can change the color of its skin to hide from its enemies. When it meets an enemy, it shoots out dark black ink and swims away. I want to see this animal with my own eyes!

고/난도

11 윗글의 밑줄 친 about과 의미가 같은 것끼리 짝 지어진 것은?

ⓐ The repair of my bike will cost <u>about</u> $50.

ⓑ I'm looking for books <u>about</u> climate change.

ⓒ Fry the onion and garlic for <u>about</u> two minutes.

ⓓ When are you going to start the history project <u>about</u> Hangeul?

① ⓐ, ⓑ   ② ⓐ, ⓒ   ③ ⓐ, ⓑ, ⓓ

④ ⓑ, ⓓ   ⑤ ⓒ, ⓓ

[서술형3]

12 What does the octopus do when it meets an enemy? Answer in English.

→ _____

[13-14] 다음 글을 읽고, 물음에 답하시오.

Arctic Ocean

This is the (A)(small) of the five oceans. It is very cold. It (B)(surround) by Europe, Asia and North America. Polar bears live around here!

[서술형4]

13 윗글의 (A)와 (B)의 괄호 안의 말을 알맞은 형태로 바꿔 쓰시오.

(A) _____   (B) _____

고/난도

14 윗글을 읽고 답할 수 있는 질문은?

① How large is the Arctic Ocean?

② How deep is the Arctic Ocean?

③ Do people live in the Arctic Ocean?

④ Which animals live around the Arctic Ocean?

⑤ How many islands are found in the Arctic Ocean?

W Words
고득점 맞기

01 다음 중 짝 지어진 두 단어의 관계가 [보기]와 <u>다른</u> 것은?

> [보기]　　　　　　　easy – easily

① tight – tightly　　　② final – finally
③ actual – actually　　④ friend – friendly
⑤ complete – completely

02 다음 영어 뜻풀이의 빈칸에 들어갈 말로 알맞은 것은?

> blow: to send out _____ from the mouth

① air　　　　　② water　　　　③ food
④ things　　　⑤ pieces

03 다음 영어 뜻풀이에 <u>모두</u> 해당하는 단어는?

> • a particular area or place
> • to see or notice someone or something that is difficult to see or find

① store　　　　② spot　　　　③ park
④ land　　　　⑤ matter

04 다음 중 밑줄 친 부분의 쓰임이 알맞지 <u>않은</u> 것은?

① The ship can carry <u>up of</u> 10 tons.
② The weather is very cold <u>this time of year</u>.
③ Let's <u>take a look at</u> some wild animals that live in the jungle.
④ The super star receives <u>millions of</u> fan letters every month.
⑤ Clare didn't <u>give up</u> her dream and practiced playing the piano every day.

05 다음 빈칸에 들어가지 <u>않는</u> 단어는?

> • After I _____ the living room, my sister mopped the floor.
> • The master _____ all the vases except one with a hammer.
> • Dean _____ deeply before he started to speak again.
> • The scientists _____ how to predict an earthquake.

① smashed　　② vacuumed　　③ breathed
④ served　　　⑤ discovered

06 다음 빈칸에 공통으로 들어갈 단어를 주어진 철자로 시작하여 쓰시오.

> • Don't be such a _____!
> • The boy tries to _____ other people about his age.
> • Like a _____, I told my secret to everybody.

→ f_____

07 다음 대화의 빈칸에 들어갈 말로 알맞은 것은?

> A: Do you know where she _____ the treasure?
> B: No, but I've heard she made a map. If we find the map, we can find the treasure.

① dived　　　② hid　　　　③ wondered
④ appeared　　⑤ completed

08 괄호 안의 우리말과 같도록 빈칸에 알맞은 말을 쓰시오.

> How long can camels _____ _____ water?
> (낙타는 얼마 동안 물 없이 지낼 수 있니?)

09 다음 밑줄 친 단어와 바꿔 쓸 수 있는 것은?

I completely forgot that it's Sam's birthday today.

① nearby   ② tightly   ③ friendly
④ probably   ⑤ totally

[10-11] 다음 빈칸에 들어갈 말이 순서대로 짝 지어진 것을 고르시오.

10 ⓐ My car is parked _____, so we can walk there.
     ⓑ Dessert will be _____ after you finish your meals.
     ⓒ Computers can _____ the total price much faster than we can.

① nearby – served – calculate
② abroad – surrounded – appear
③ nearby – surrounded – calculate
④ abroad – served – appear
⑤ nearby – served – appear

11 ⓐ The temperature in July goes up _____ 42℃ in this area.
     ⓑ Take a closer look _____ this painting.
     ⓒ Ann spent the afternoon looking _____ the town.

① for – at – with
② for – for – with
③ to – at – around
④ to – for – around
⑤ to – at – with

12 다음 중 단어의 영어 뜻풀이가 알맞지 <u>않은</u> 것은?

① surface: the upper layer of an area of land or water
② clam: a type of sea creature with a shell in two parts that can close together
③ calculate: to find a number, answer, etc. by using mathematical processes
④ smash: to jump into water, especially with your arms and head going in first
⑤ wonder: a feeling of surprise and admiration for something very beautiful or new

13 다음 빈칸에 들어갈 말을 [보기]에서 골라 쓰시오.

[보기]   distance   fact   enemy
         wonder   speed   species
         planet   tail   whale

(1) Measure the _____ between the two points.
(2) Some plant and animal _____ are found only in the Amazon rainforest.
(3) Her eyes grew with _____ when she saw the Grand Canyon.

고_{난도} 신_{유형}
14 다음 영어 뜻풀이에 해당하는 단어가 쓰인 문장은?

a piece of equipment you use with your hands for a particular task

① Heat the oven to a temperature of 230℃.
② This tool can be used in a variety of ways.
③ Mr. Brown's wish is to run his own restaurant.
④ Everyone should take part in protecting our planet.
⑤ The pond's surface was covered with red autumn leaves.

STEP
B

우리말과 일치하도록 대화를 바르게 영작하시오.

1 Listen and Speak 1-A

B: _____

G: _____

B: _____

G: _____

B: _____

해석   교과서 122쪽

B: 우리는 산 정상에 거의 다 왔어.

G: 나는 이 산이 얼마나 높은지 궁금해.

B: 그것(이 산)은 높이가 약 2,000미터야.

G: 와! 이것(이 산)은 정말 높은 산이구나.

B: 응, 맞아. 계속 올라가자.

2 Listen and Speak 1-B

B: _____

G: _____

B: _____

G: _____

B: _____

G: _____

B: _____

G: _____

교과서 122쪽

B: 텔레비전에 나온 아기 펭귄들을 봐. 아주 귀여워.

G: 응, 하지만 그들은 저곳에서 매우 추워 보여.

B: 그래, 남극은 지구상에서 가장 추운 곳이야.

G: 나는 그곳이 얼마나 추운지 궁금해.

B: 평균 기온이 7월에는 약 섭씨 영하 58도이고 12월에는 약 섭씨 영하 26도야.

G: 오, 그러면 그곳은 12월보다 7월이 더 춥구나. 흥미롭다!

B: 응. 비록 그곳은 매우 춥지만 눈은 많이 내리지 않아.

G: 그것도 흥미롭다!

3 Listen and Speak 1-C

A: _____

B: _____

A: _____

B: _____

A: _____

교과서 122쪽

A: 우리는 마침내 여기에 왔어.

B: 그래, 나는 매우 신이 나. 우리 둘러보자.

A: 나는 버스 정류장이 어디에 있는지 궁금해.

B: 그곳은 경찰서 앞에 있어.

A: 네 말이 맞네. 가자.

4 Listen and Speak 2-A

B: _____

G: _____

B: _____

G: _____

B: _____

교과서 123쪽

B: 바깥 날씨가 아주 좋아.

G: 그래. 오늘 오후에 소풍 가는 게 어때?

B: 좋은 생각이야. 날씨를 확인해 줄래?

G: 오, 이런! 일기 예보에서 오후에 비가 올 거래.

B: 그러면 다음에 가자

5 Listen and Speak 2-B

B: _____

G: _____

B: _____

G: _____

B: _____

G: _____

B: _____

G: _____

B: _____

G: _____

B: _____

교과서 123쪽

해석

B: 수민아, 너는 일요일에 무엇을 할 거니?

G: 나는 등산을 갈 거야. 나와 함께 가겠니?

B: 그러고 싶어. 넌 어디로 가고 싶니?

G: 나는 남산에 가려고 생각 중이야.

B: 오, 매년 이맘때 그곳 경치는 아주 아름답지.

G: 맞아. 지금 빨간 단풍잎으로 덮여 있다고 들었어.

B: 좋아. 가장 짧은 등산 코스는 얼마나 걸리니?

G: 인터넷 정보에 따르면 약 두 시간 정도 걸린대.

B: 알겠어, 일요일에 봐!

6 Listen and Speak 2-C

A: _____

B: _____

A: _____

B: _____

교과서 123쪽

A: 너는 무엇을 하고 있니?

B: 나는 신문을 읽고 있어.

A: 재미있는 내용이 있니?

B: 이 기사에 따르면 과학자들이 새로운 행성을 발견했대.

7 Real Life Talk > Watch a Video

Suji: _____

Tony: _____

Suji: _____

Tony: _____

Suji: _____

Tony: _____

Suji: _____

Tony: _____

교과서 124쪽

수지: 이 사진을 봐!

Tony: 와! 낙타들이 사막에서 한 줄로 걸어가고 있네.

수지: 응. 사막은 매우 덥고 건조해 보여.

Tony: 나는 낙타들이 사막에서 물 없이 얼마나 오래 지낼 수 있는지 궁금해.

수지: 인터넷에서 찾아보자.

Tony: 그래. 인터넷 정보에 따르면 그들은(낙타는) 물 없이 2주 정도 지낼 수 있대.

수지: 와, 굉장하다! 낙타는 정말 흥미로운 동물이구나.

Tony: 나는 언젠가 사막에서 그들과 함께 여행하고 싶어.

STEP
B

[01-02] 다음 대화를 읽고, 물음에 답하시오.

A: Look at the baby penguins on TV. They're so cute.

B: Yes, but they look very cold out there.

A: Yeah, the South Pole is the coldest place on Earth.

B: _____

A: The average temperature is about -58℃ in July and -26℃ in December.

B: Oh, then, July is colder than December there. Interesting!

A: Yes. Although it's very cold there, it doesn't snow much.

B: That's interesting, too!

01 위 대화의 빈칸에 들어갈 말로 알맞은 것은?

① How can we go there?

② I wonder how cold it is there.

③ What other animals live there?

④ The book says polar bears are endangered.

⑤ I'm curious about why the South Pole is so cold.

02 위 대화의 내용과 일치하면 T, 일치하지 않으면 F로 표시할 때, 순서대로 짝 지어진 것은?

ⓐ They are watching TV.

ⓑ December is the coldest month in the South Pole.

ⓒ It snows a lot in the South Pole.

ⓓ They don't know where the coldest place in the world is.

① T – T – F – F　② T – F – T – F　③ T – F – F – F

④ F – T – F – F　⑤ F – F – T – T

[03-04] 다음 대화를 읽고, 물음에 답하시오.

A: Sumin, what are you going to do on Sunday?

B: I'm going to go hiking. Do you want to join me, Brian?

A: I'd love to. (①)

B: I'm thinking of going to Namsan. (②)

A: Oh, the scenery there is so beautiful this time of year. (③)

B: Right. I heard that it's covered with red autumn leaves now. (④)

A: Great. How long does the shortest hiking course take?

B: The Internet says it takes about two hours. (⑤)

A: Okay, see you on Sunday!

03 위 대화의 ①~⑤ 중 주어진 문장이 들어갈 알맞은 곳은?

Where do you want to go?

①　　　②　　　③　　　④　　　⑤

04 위 대화를 바르게 이해하지 못한 사람은?

① 시윤: 두 사람은 일요일에 만나겠네.

② 민재: 지금 계절은 가을이구나.

③ 보라: 수민이는 원하는 정보를 인터넷에서 찾았어.

④ 지우: Brian은 남산에 대해 아는 것이 전혀 없구나.

⑤ 세진: 남산의 가장 짧은 등산 코스가 약 두 시간 정도 걸리네.

05 다음 중 짝 지어진 대화가 자연스럽지 않은 것은?

① A: I wonder what the smallest country is in the world.

　B: Let's find out on the Internet.

② A: This mountain is about 2,000m high.

　B: Wow! It is a really high mountain.

③ A: I wonder where the bus stop is.

　B: You can take the No. 1005 bus.

④ A: What is the longest river in the world?

　B: I think it's the Amazon River.

⑤ A: Is there anything interesting in the newspaper?

　B: This article says scientists have discovered a new planet.

06 다음 대화의 빈칸에 알맞은 말을 [보기]에서 골라 쓰시오.

A: (1) _____

B: Yeah. How about going on a picnic this afternoon?

A: (2) _____ Can you check the weather?

B: Oh, no! (3) _____

A: Let's go another time, then.

[보기]
- Good idea.
- Let's keep going.
- The weather is so nice outside.
- The weather is very cold outside.
- The weather forecast says it'll be rainy in the afternoon.
- The newspaper says the weather was good yesterday.

07 다음 대화의 밑줄 친 우리말을 [조건]에 맞게 영작하시오.

[조건]
1. 괄호 안의 단어들 중 필요 없는 두 단어는 빼고 사용할 것
2. 대소문자를 구별하고 문장 부호를 정확히 쓸 것

A: 나는 에베레스트산이 얼마나 높은지 궁금해.

B: The Internet says it is about 8,850m high.

→ _____

(how, I, long, wonder, Mt. Everest, high, is, what)

08 다음 기사 정보를 읽고, 대화를 완성하시오.

The blue whale is the largest animal in the world. It is about 30m long.

▼

A: Which is (1) _____?

B: It's the blue whale.

A: I wonder (2) _____ it is.

B: The article says (3) _____
_____.

A: That's amazing!

[09-10] 다음 대화를 읽고, 물음에 답하시오.

Suji: Check out this picture!

Tony: Wow! The camels are walking in a line in the desert.

Suji: Yeah. The desert looks very hot and dry.

Tony: I wonder how long camels can go without water in the desert.

Suji: Let's find out on the Internet.

Tony: Okay. The Internet says they can go about two weeks without water.

Suji: Wow, that's amazing! Camels are really interesting animals.

Tony: I want to travel with them in the desert someday.

09 다음 질문에 완전한 영어 문장으로 답하시오.

Q: What are the camels in the picture doing?

A: _____

10 위 대화의 내용과 일치하도록 다음 글을 완성하시오.

Tony wonders how long camels can go without water in the desert. According to (1) _____, camels (2) _____ _____. Tony wants to (3) _____.

Grammar
고득점 맞기

01 다음 빈칸에 들어갈 수 <u>없는</u> 것은?

Lucy is a pianist whose _____.

① house is in Busan
② brother is a composer
③ pet is a colorful parrot
④ her concerts are always sold out
⑤ portrait is in the gallery

[02-03] 다음 빈칸에 알맞은 말이 순서대로 짝 지어진 것을 고르시오.

02 • The novels _____ J. K. Rowling wrote are read in many countries.
• We are looking for students _____ can do volunteer work on Sundays.
• Helen is the girl _____ sneakers are red and white.

① whose – who – that
② whose – which – which
③ that – who – which
④ which – who – whose
⑤ which – that – whom

03 • _____ you were out, someone knocked on the door.
• Do not start eating _____ the food is served to everyone.
• We have to protect our planet _____ it's too late.

① While – until – before
② Unless – since – after
③ While – since – before
④ Unless – until – before
⑤ While – until – after

04 다음 두 문장을 한 문장으로 바르게 연결한 것은?

Chris is my neighbor. His dog is very big.

① Chris is my neighbor that dog is very big.
② Chris is my neighbor what dog is very big.
③ Chris is my neighbor whom dog is very big.
④ Chris is my neighbor whose dog is very big.
⑤ Chris is my neighbor whose his dog is very big.

05 다음 우리말을 영어로 옮길 때, 사용하지 <u>않는</u> 단어를 모두 고르면?

내가 롤러스케이트 한 켤레를 산 후에 Joan이 내게 그것을 타는 법을 보여 줄 것이다.
→ _____ a pair of roller skates, Joan will show me how to ride them.

① I   ② after   ③ will
④ buy   ⑤ before

06 다음 중 밑줄 친 부분을 생략할 수 <u>없는</u> 것을 모두 고르면?

① Look at the boy <u>whose</u> hair is blond.
② Mary is wearing a hat <u>which</u> her mom made.
③ Do you remember <u>what</u> you had for dinner?
④ The picture <u>which</u> you're looking at is my favorite.
⑤ The people <u>who</u> live in this village are very friendly.

07 다음 [보기]의 밑줄 친 when과 쓰임이 같은 것은?

[보기] The bell rang <u>when</u> I turned on the radio.

① Could you tell me <u>when</u> to arrive?
② <u>When</u> does your new song come out?
③ I want to know <u>when</u> the bridge was built.
④ He asked me <u>when</u> the summer vacation started.
⑤ My voice becomes very low <u>when</u> I speak in public.

08 다음 밑줄 친 부분 중 어법상 옳은 것은?

① I know a girl <u>that</u> mother is a famous scientist.

② Don't put off until tomorrow <u>which</u> you can do today.

③ The bicycle <u>what</u> I bought last week is already broken.

④ The horse <u>whose</u> nose is white belongs to Mr. Moore.

⑤ Have you seen a man <u>whom</u> looks like the person in this photo?

고
난도

09 다음 중 두 문장의 밑줄 친 부분의 의미가 같은 것은?

① He met many foreigners <u>while</u> he was abroad.
  <u>While</u> Kelly is outgoing, her twin sister is shy.

② The baby kept crying <u>until</u> his mom arrived.
  Let's wait inside the building <u>until</u> the rain stops.

③ They have been friends <u>since</u> they were 12.
  We canceled the picnic <u>since</u> Peter had a bad cold.

④ I wonder <u>if</u> Robert knows the truth.
  <u>If</u> you have any questions, feel free to contact us.

⑤ Do you remember <u>when</u> the car accident happened?
  <u>When</u> my eyes are tired, I close them for a moment.

10 다음 대화의 밑줄 친 ①~⑤ 중 어법상 틀린 것은?

A: Did you go to the flea market ①<u>which</u> was held in Green Park?

B: Yes, I did. ②<u>There were</u> lots of useful items ③<u>that</u> were almost new.

A: Great. Did you get anything from the market?

B: Yes, I did. I bought a blue backpack ④<u>which</u> pocket was very big. What about you?

A: Well, I wanted ⑤<u>to go</u> there, but I couldn't. I had to take care of my little brother.

11 다음 중 빈칸에 whose를 쓸 수 <u>없는</u> 것은?

① Do you know _____ smartphone it is?

② Look at the car _____ is covered with dust.

③ Shrek is a friendly monster _____ body is green.

④ The boy _____ eyes are green is Jane's cousin.

⑤ Would you show me a shirt _____ sleeves are short?

고
난도

12 다음 중 어법상 틀린 문장끼리 짝 지어진 것은?

ⓐ We went to a town whose bus system was convenient.

ⓑ A shoplifter is a person whose steals things from a shop.

ⓒ Can you take care of my cats during I'm in the hospital?

ⓓ After Rosa read the fantasy novels, she lent them to Colin.

① ⓐ, ⓑ   ② ⓑ, ⓒ   ③ ⓑ, ⓓ

④ ⓑ, ⓒ, ⓓ   ⑤ ⓒ, ⓓ

고
난도 신
유형

13 다음 중 문장에 대한 설명을 바르게 말하지 <u>못한</u> 사람을 <u>모두</u> 고르면?

① Look at the monkey whose tail is 13cm long.
  → 보미: 선행사가 동물인 the monkey이므로 whose를 which로 바꿔야 해.

② I'll tell them the news after they will finish their work.
  → 지원: 시간의 부사절은 미래의 의미를 현재시제로 나타내므로 will을 삭제해야 해.

③ Emma waited outside until the department store opened.
  → 가람: until은 '~할 때까지'라는 의미의 시간을 나타내는 접속사야.

④ Since this Tuesday is a holiday, we don't have to go to school.
  → 민서: Since는 When으로 바꿔 써도 같은 의미를 나타내.

⑤ This donation will be used for families whose homes were destroyed by the storm.
  → 준민: whose는 소유격 관계대명사로 whose가 이끄는 관계대명사절이 선행사 families를 수식해.

서술형

14 다음 두 문장을 관계대명사를 사용하여 한 문장으로 연결하여 쓰시오.

(1) I met a boy. His dream is to be a scientist.

→ _____

(2) Can you see the man? His arm is broken.

→ _____

(3) I'm looking for a book. I borrowed it from Bill yesterday.

→ _____

(4) Look at the spiders. Their shapes are all similar.

→ _____

15 다음 우리말과 같도록 [조건]에 맞게 문장을 완성하시오.

[조건] 1. [보기]의 접속사 중 하나를 골라 사용할 것
         2. 괄호 안의 말을 이용할 것
         3. 시제를 정확하게 쓸 것

[보기] after   if   when   because
        until   while   since   before

(1) 내가 너에게 멈추라고 말할 때까지 계속 가.
(keep, go, tell, stop)

→ _____

(2) 그녀는 스페인을 떠난 후에 자신의 이름을 바꾸었다.
(change, name, leave)

→ _____

_____

(3) 나는 태어난 이후로 서울에서 살아 왔다. (live, be born)

→ _____

_____

(4) Lucas가 정원에서 꽃에 물을 줄 때 나는 설거지를 했다.
(wash, the dishes, water, the flowers)

→ _____

_____

16 다음 중 어법상 틀린 문장을 모두 찾아 기호를 쓴 후, 문장을 바르게 고쳐 쓰시오.

ⓐ The woman we met yesterday is a lawyer.

ⓑ I want to visit the British Museum while I will be in London.

ⓒ Our soccer team won the every game after Jacob joined our team.

ⓓ Charlotte is a wise spider whose best friend is Wilbur.

ⓔ The present whose my aunt sent to me hasn't arrived yet.

(   ) → _____

_____

(   ) → _____

_____

17 주어진 [조건]에 맞게 다음 대화를 완성하시오.

[조건] 1. 괄호 안의 말을 바르게 배열할 것
         2. (1)과 (3)은 [보기]의 접속사 중 하나를 골라 사용할 것
         3. (2)는 알맞은 관계대명사를 사용할 것

[보기]   after   while   since

A: I'm home, Mom.

B: Oh, Mike. I fell asleep for a while. Did you go out with Lucky?

A: Yes, Mom. (1) _____, (were, you, sleeping) I walked Lucky around the park.

B: Sounds great! You're a good boy.

A: In the park, (2) _____

_____. (a dog, I, were, saw, short, very, legs) It was really cute.

B: Great. Will you have lunch now?

A: Well, (3) _____

_____.

(I'll, lunch, I, have, take, a shower)

다음 우리말과 일치하도록 각 문장을 바르게 영작하시오.

01

_____

우리 행성의 3분의 2는 대양들로 덮여 있다.

02

_____

☆ 그것들(대양들)은 신기한 것으로 가득 차 있으며 수많은 종의 서식지이다.

03

_____

매일 우리는 그것들(대양들)에 관한 새로운 것들을 배우고 있다.

04

_____

몇몇 흥미로운 바다 동물들을 알아보자.

05

_____

좋은 꿈 꿔라

06

_____

여러분은 그림 속 이 고래들이 무엇을 하고 있는지 추측할 수 있는가?

07

_____

그것들은 무리를 지어 서 있는 것처럼 보인다.

08

_____

그러나 그것들은 실제로는 잠을 자고 있다!

09

_____

☆ 혹등고래는 잠을 자는 동안 꼬리로 서 있는다.

10

_____

그것들은 수면 근처에서 잠을 잔다.

11

_____

그것들은 물고기가 아니기 때문에 숨을 쉬기 위해 위로 나올 필요가 있다.

12

_____

또한 그것들은 완전히 잠들지 않는다.

13

_____

☆ 그것들은 잠에서 깨면 심호흡을 하러 물 밖으로 나왔다가 바다로 다시 뛰어든다.

14

_____

맛있게 먹어라

15

_____

만약 물고기가 똑똑하지 않다고 생각한다면 tuskfish를 한번 봐라.

16

_____

☆ 가장 좋아하는 먹이가 조개인 이 작은 물고기는 그것들(조개)을 열기 위해 도구를 사용한다.

17

_____

조개는 대개 모래 아래에 숨어 있어서 쉽게 발견될 수 없다.

18

_____

☆ tuskfish는 조개가 나타날 때까지 모래에 입김을 분다.

19

_____

조개가 단단히 닫혀 있어서 물고기는 그것을 먹을 수 없다.

20

_____

그러나 tuskfish는 포기하지 않는다.

21

_____

☆ 그것(tuskfish)은 조개를 바위에 내리친다.

22

_____

마침내 조개가 열리고 밥상이 차려진다.

23

_____

하나, 둘, 셋, 뛰어라!

24

_____

여러분은 아마 새가 물고기를 잡기 위해 바다로 날아 내려가는 것을 본 적이 있을 것이다.

25

_____

그러나 물고기가 새를 잡기 위해 물 밖으로 뛰어오르는 것을 본 적이 있는가?

26

_____

☆ 자, giant trevally가 주변에 있을 때 새들은 조심해야 한다.

27

_____

이 물고기는 170센티미터에 80킬로그램까지 자랄 수 있다.

28

_____

그러나 그 크기에 속지 마라.

29

_____

이 물고기는 빠르고 똑똑하다.

30

_____

그것은 날고 있는 새를 발견하고 그것(새)의 속도와 거리를 계산할 수 있다.

31

_____

☆ 새가 가까이에 날고 있을 때, giant trevally는 물 밖으로 뛰어올라 그것(새)을 잡는다.

[01-04] 다음 글을 읽고, 물음에 답하시오.

①Two-thirds of our planet are covered by oceans. They are full of wonder and are home to millions of species. ②Every day, we are learning new things about them. Let's find out about some interesting sea animals.

③Can you guess what these whales are doing in the picture? ④It looks likely they are standing up in a group. But they are actually _____ⓐ_____! Humpback whales stand on their tails (A)| until / while | they sleep. They sleep near the surface. (B)| Since / After | they are not fish, they need to come up to breathe. ⑤Also, they don't fall asleep completely. (C)| When / Unless | they wake up, they come out of the water for a deep breath and dive back into the sea.

01 윗글의 빈칸 ⓐ에 들어갈 말로 알맞은 것은?

① eating   ② sleeping
③ playing   ④ swimming
⑤ breathing

02 윗글의 (A), (B), (C)에 알맞은 말이 순서대로 짝 지어진 것은?

	(A)	(B)	(C)
①	while	After	Unless
②	until	Since	Unless
③	while	Since	When
④	until	After	When
⑤	while	Since	Unless

고 신
단도 유형
03 윗글의 밑줄 친 ①~⑤ 중 어법상 **틀린** 문장의 개수는?

① 0개   ② 1개   ③ 2개
④ 3개   ⑤ 4개

04 윗글을 읽고 알 수 **없는** 것을 **모두** 고르면?

① 지구에서 대양이 차지하는 비율
② 가장 깊은 바다의 깊이
③ 혹등고래의 잠자는 모습
④ 혹등고래가 물고기가 아닌 이유
⑤ 혹등고래가 잠에서 깨면 물 밖으로 나오는 이유

[05-09] 다음 글을 읽고, 물음에 답하시오.

①Since you think fish are not smart, take a look at the tuskfish. This small fish ②which favorite food is clams ③uses a tool ⓐto open them. Clams usually hide under the sand, so they cannot be easily discovered. The tuskfish blows on the sand _____ⓑ_____. The clam ④is closed tightly, so the fish cannot eat it. But the tuskfish doesn't give up. It smashes the clam against a rock. In the end, the clam opens and dinner ⑤serves.

05 윗글의 밑줄 친 ①~⑤를 바르게 고치지 **못한** 것은?

① Since → If
② which → whose
③ uses → use
④ is closed tightly → 고칠 필요 없음
⑤ serves → is served

06 윗글의 밑줄 친 ⓐto open과 쓰임이 같은 것은?

① Kevin wishes to make his dream come true someday.

② I have something to tell you about the school festival.

③ It's difficult for me to wake up early on Sundays.

④ The badminton player practiced very hard to win the competition.

⑤ My club members decided to do wall paintings as volunteer work.

07 윗글의 빈칸 ⓑ에 들어갈 말로 알맞은 것은?

① while a clam is moving

② until a clam appears

③ after a clam disappears

④ unless a clam passes by

⑤ because a clam has hard shells

08 다음 영어 뜻풀이에 해당하는 단어 중 윗글에서 찾을 수 없는 것은?

① to send out air from the mouth

② to break something into many pieces

③ the upper layer of an area of land or water

④ to see, find, or become aware of something for the first time

⑤ a piece of equipment you use with your hands for a particular task

09 윗글의 내용과 일치하는 것은?

① The tuskfish is a giant fish.

② The tuskfish doesn't like eating clams.

③ Clams are usually found between rocks.

④ It is impossible for tuskfish to find clams.

⑤ The tuskfish uses a rock to open clams.

[10-12] 다음 글을 읽고, 물음에 답하시오.

You have probably seen a bird fly down to the sea to catch a fish. But have you ever seen a fish jump out of the water to catch a bird? (①) Well, birds have to be careful when a giant trevally is around. (②) This fish can grow up to 170cm and 80kg. (③) This fish is quick and smart. (④) It can spot a flying bird and calculate its speed and distance. (⑤) When the bird flies nearby, the giant trevally jumps out of the water and catches it.

10 윗글의 ①~⑤ 중 주어진 문장이 들어갈 알맞은 곳은?

> But don't let its size fool you.

①   ②   ③   ④   ⑤

11 윗글의 밑줄 친 spot과 의미가 같은 것은?

① There was a big spot on the curtain.

② We're looking for a good spot for the picnic.

③ You should wash the spot from the T-shirt.

④ I think this is the best spot to hold a flea market.

⑤ I could spot you easily in the audience because you were wearing a big hat.

12 윗글을 읽고 답할 수 없는 질문은?

① How big can the giant trevally grow?

② What can the giant trevally calculate?

③ What is the giant trevally's favorite food?

④ How does the giant trevally catch the bird?

⑤ Why do birds have to be careful when a giant trevally is around?

서술형

[13-14] 다음 글을 읽고, 물음에 답하시오.

(can, whales, what, these, guess, doing, are, you) in the picture? It looks like they are standing up in a group. But they are actually sleeping! Humpback whales stand on their tails while they sleep. They sleep near the surface. Since they are not fish, they need to come up to breathe. Also, they don't fall asleep completely. When they wake up, they come out of the water for a deep breath and dive back into the sea.

13 윗글의 괄호 안의 단어들을 바르게 배열하여 문장을 완성하시오.

→ _____

14 다음 질문에 완전한 영어 문장으로 답하시오.

Q: Why do humpback whales come out of the water when they wake up?

A: _____

[15-16] 다음 글을 읽고, 물음에 답하시오.

If you think fish are not smart, take a look at the tuskfish. This small fish which favorite food is clams uses a tool to open them. Clams usually hide under the sand, so they cannot easily discover. The tuskfish blows on the sand until a clam appears. The clam is closed tightly, so the fish cannot eat it. But the tuskfish doesn't give up. It smashes the clam against a rock. In the end, the clam opens and dinner is served.

고
/난도
15 윗글에서 어법상 틀린 문장을 두 개 찾아 문장을 바르게 고쳐 쓰시오.

(1) _____

(2) _____

16 윗글의 내용과 일치하도록 다음 대화를 완성하시오.

A: Have you heard of the tuskfish?
B: No, I haven't. Can you tell me about it?
A: Sure. (1) _____
   is clams.
B: Clams? Well, clams usually hide under the sand. How does the tuskfish find a clam?
A: This fish (2) _____
   _____.
B: That's interesting!
A: Yeah. But the clam is closed tightly, so the fish (3) _____.
B: Oh, the tuskfish is very smart!

고
/난도
17 다음 글을 읽고, giant trevally에 대한 표를 완성하시오.

Have you ever seen a fish jump out of the water to catch a bird? Well, birds have to be careful when a giant trevally is around. This fish can grow up to 170cm and 80kg. But don't let its size fool you. This fish is quick and smart. It can spot a flying bird and calculate its speed and distance. When the bird flies nearby, the giant trevally jumps out of the water and catches it.

Giant Trevally

how big	(1) It can _____ _____.
how smart	(2) It can spot a flying bird and _____ _____.
how to catch the bird	(3) _____ _____

서술형 100% TEST

01 다음 빈칸에 알맞은 단어를 [조건]에 맞게 쓰시오.

You need to _____ through the nose, not through the mouth.

> [조건] 1. The word starts with "b."
> 2. The word has 7 letters.
> 3. The word means "to move air into and out of your lungs."

고
난도

02 주어진 문장의 밑줄 친 단어를 포함하는 문장을 [조건]에 맞게 영작하시오.

> [조건] 1. 주어진 문장의 spot과 같은 의미로 쓸 것
> 2. 주어와 동사를 포함한 완전한 문장으로 쓸 것

It is not easy to <u>spot</u> stars at night in a city.

→ _____

03 다음 문장의 빈칸에 알맞은 말을 [보기]에서 골라 쓴 후, 문장을 우리말로 해석하시오.

> [보기]   millions of   go without
> all over   in the end   up to

(1) How long can humans _____ food?
   → 해석: _____
(2) The trees can grow _____ 30 meters.
   → 해석: _____
(3) This medicine can save _____ lives.
   → 해석: _____

04 다음 지도를 보고, 괄호 안의 단어를 사용하여 대화의 빈칸에 알맞은 문장을 쓰시오.

A: We're finally here.
B: Yes, I'm so excited. Let's look around.
A: _____
   (wonder, where)
B: It's between the café and the bakery.
A: You're right. Let's go.

고
난도

05 다음 대화의 밑줄 친 우리말을 [조건]에 맞게 영작하여 대화를 완성하시오.

> [조건]   1. 괄호 안의 말을 사용할 것
> 2. (1)에는 총 8단어의 문장을 쓸 것
> 3. (2)에는 축약형을 포함한 총 10단어의 문장을 쓸 것

A: The weather is so nice outside.
B: Yeah. (1) <u>오늘 오후에 소풍 가는 게 어때?</u> (how, going)
A: Good idea. Can you check the weather?
B: Oh, no! (2) <u>일기 예보에 따르면 오후에 비가 내릴 거야.</u>
   (the weather forecast, it'll, rainy, in)
A: Let's go another time, then.

(1) _____
(2) _____

06 다음 대화의 내용과 일치하도록 아래 글을 완성하시오.

A: Look at the baby penguins on TV. They're so cute.

B: Yes, but they look very cold out there.

A: Yeah, the South Pole is the coldest place on Earth.

B: I wonder how cold it is there.

A: The average temperature is about -58℃ in July and -26℃ in December.

B: Oh, then, July is colder than December there. Interesting!

A: Yes. Although it's very cold there, it doesn't snow much.

B: That's interesting, too!

▼

The coldest place on Earth is (1) _____ _____. The average temperature is about -58℃ (2) _____ and -26℃ (3) _____. The interesting thing is that July is (4) _____ December there. Also, (5) _____ _____ though it's very cold there.

^고
/난도
07 다음 괄호 안의 말을 바르게 배열하여 대화를 완성하시오.

A: Check out this picture!

B: Wow! (1) _____ _____ (are, in the desert, the camels, in a line, walking)

A: Yeah. The desert looks very hot and dry.

B: (2) _____ _____ (how long, I, camels, go, wonder, water, without, in the desert, can)

A: Let's find out on the Internet.

^고
/난도
08 다음 인터넷 정보와 일치하도록 아래 대화를 완성하시오.

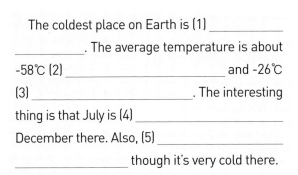

Do you know which planet is the biggest in the solar system? The answer is Jupiter. It is over 11 times bigger than Earth. How amazing!

A: Which is the biggest planet in the solar system?

B: It's Jupiter.

A: I wonder (1) _____.

B: The Internet (2) _____ _____.

A: That's amazing!

09 다음 문장을 어법상 바르게 고쳐 다시 쓰시오.

(1) Dean is the student who nickname is Smile Prince.

→ _____

(2) I want to ride a horse tail is black.

→ _____

(3) We're looking for the girl whose is wearing a blue hat.

→ _____

10 자연스러운 문장이 되도록 빈칸에 알맞은 말을 자유롭게 쓰시오.

(1) When I was young, _____.

(2) _____ until it got dark.

(3) _____ after I have dinner.

11 다음 [조건]에 맞게 문장을 완성하시오.

> [조건]   1. [보기]에서 알맞은 말을 하나씩 골라 사용할 것
>   2. 알맞은 관계대명사를 사용할 것

> [보기]   I do in my free time
>   hobby is rock-climbing
>   top is covered with snow
>   was written by Shakespeare

(1) I met a woman _____

_____ .

(2) Drawing is _____

_____ .

(3) Look at the mountain _____

_____ .

(4) He bought a book _____

_____ .

12 다음 우리말과 같도록 [조건]에 맞게 영작하시오.

> [조건]   1. 괄호 안의 말을 사용할 것
>   2. (1), (2)는 알맞은 관계대명사를 사용할 것
>   3. (3), (4)는 알맞은 접속사를 사용할 것

(1) 몸이 파란색인 Genie는 요술램프 속에 산다.

     (body, in a magic lamp)

     → _____

(2) 스마트폰을 도난당한 그 학생은 경찰을 불렀다.

     (stolen, called, the police)

     → _____

(3) 나는 숙제를 마친 후에 Bill과 테니스를 칠 것이다.

     (finish, play)

     → _____

(4) 우리는 그가 이탈리아에 간 이후로 그에게서 소식을 듣지 못
     했다.

     (heard, went, Italy)

     → _____

13 다음 글의 밑줄 친 우리말과 같도록 [조건]에 맞게 문장을 완성하시오.

> Can you guess what these whales are doing in the picture? It looks like they are standing up in a group. But they are actually sleeping! (1) <u>혹등고래는 그들이 잠을 자는 동안 그들의 꼬리로 서 있는다.</u> They sleep near the surface. (2) <u>그들은 물고기가 아니기 때문에 숨을 쉬기 위해 위로 나올 필요가 있다.</u> Also, they don't fall asleep completely. When they wake up, they come out of the water for a deep breath and dive back into the sea.

> [조건]   1. [보기]에서 알맞은 접속사를 하나씩 골라 사용할 것
>   2. 괄호 안의 말을 사용할 것

> [보기]   if   after   since   while   until   though

(1) Humpback whales _____

_____ . (stand on, tails)

(2) _____ , they

_____ . (need, come up)

[14-16] 다음 글을 읽고, 물음에 답하시오.

> If you think fish are not smart, take a look at the tuskfish. (small fish, favorite food, are, a tool, this, whose, clams, uses, which, is) to open them. Clams usually hide under the sand, so they cannot be easily discovered. The tuskfish blows on the sand until a clam appears. The clam is closed tightly, so the fish cannot eat it. But the tuskfish doesn't give up. It smashes the clam against a rock. In the end, the clam opens and dinner is served.

14 윗글의 괄호 안의 말 중 필요 없는 두 개를 빼고 바르게 배열하여 문장을 완성하시오.

     → _____

_____ to open them.

15 Why cannot be clams easily discovered? Answer in English.

→ _____

16 tuskfish가 조개를 여는 방법을 우리말로 설명하시오.

→ _____

고
/난도
17 다음 글의 내용과 일치하도록 아래 대화를 완성하시오.

You have probably seen a bird fly down to the sea to catch a fish. But have you ever seen a fish jump out of the water to catch a bird? Well, birds have to be careful when a giant trevally is around. This fish can grow up to 170cm and 80kg. But don't let its size fool you. This fish is quick and smart. It can spot a flying bird and calculate its speed and distance. When the bird flies nearby, the giant trevally jumps out of the water and catches it.

▼

A: Have you decided on a topic for the science report?
B: Yes. I will introduce a big fish, the giant trevally.
A: I've never heard of it. How big is it?
B: (1) _____
A: Oh, that's big for a fish. Why is it interesting?
B: It can catch a flying bird.
A: Wow! How does the fish catch the bird?
B: (2) _____

_____
A: That's amazing!

18 다음 글을 읽고, 주어진 질문에 완전한 영어 문장으로 답하시오.

Hello, I'm a beluga whale. I live in the Arctic Ocean. It's very cold. So my skin is very thick and about half of my body is fat. I also have a round head. When I'm hungry, I usually eat fish and clams. I'm white all over, so people also call me the white whale. When I was born, I was gray. But when I grew up, my body became white! I can make several sounds. I use these sounds to talk to other whales. Yes, we can communicate!

(1) Q: Where does the beluga whale live?
A: _____
(2) Q: What does the beluga whale usually eat?
A: _____
(3) Q: What color was the beluga whale when it was born?
A: _____
(4) Q: What do beluga whales use to communicate with each other?
A: _____

19 다음 글에서 어법상 틀린 부분을 모두 찾아 바르게 고쳐 쓰시오.

Arctic Ocean
This is the small of the five oceans. It is very cold. It surrounds by Europe, Asia and North America. Polar bears live around here!

(1) _____ → _____
(2) _____ → _____

01 다음 중 품사의 종류가 다른 하나는? [3점]

① shiny   ② friendly   ③ average

④ probably   ⑤ several

02 다음 중 영어 뜻풀이가 알맞지 않은 것은? [4점]

① smash: to break something into many pieces

② distance: the amount of space between two places or things

③ tool: a piece of equipment you use with your hands for a particular task

④ spot: to find a number, answer, etc. by using mathematical processes

⑤ wonder: a feeling of surprise and admiration for something very beautiful or new

03 다음 빈칸에 공통으로 들어갈 말로 알맞은 것은? [3점]

- The animal can eat _____ to 30 kilograms of leaves every day.
- I failed auditions many times but I didn't give _____ my dreams.

① at   ② up   ③ for

④ on   ⑤ with

04 다음 빈칸에 들어가지 않는 단어는? [4점]

- Are there any good restaurants _____?
- Let's _____ out all the candles on the cake.
- The sun began to _____ from behind the clouds.
- The train can run at a(n) _____ speed of 200 kilometers per hour.

① blow   ② dive   ③ appear

④ average   ⑤ nearby

05 다음 대화의 빈칸에 들어갈 말로 알맞은 것은? [4점]

A: We're finally here.

B: Yes, I'm so excited. Let's look around.

A: _____

B: It's next to the school.

A: You're right. Let's go.

① I wonder where the museum is.

② I'm curious about how old the school is.

③ I don't know when the museum is closed.

④ Can you tell me where the school is?

⑤ The article says the exhibition will be held in the museum next week.

[06-07] 다음 대화를 읽고, 물음에 답하시오.

A: Sally, look at the baby penguins on TV. They're so cute.

B: Yes, but they look very cold out there.

A: Yeah, the South Pole is the coldest place on Earth.

B: I wonder how cold it is there.

A: The average temperature is about -58℃ in July and -26℃ in December.

B: Oh, then, July _____ December there. Interesting!

A: Yes. Although it's very cold there, it doesn't snow much.

B: That's interesting, too!

서술형1

06 위 대화의 빈칸에 알맞은 말을 괄호 안의 단어를 이용하여 세 단어로 쓰시오. [4점]

→ _____ (cold)

07 위 대화의 내용과 일치하지 <u>않은</u> 것은? [4점]

① They are looking at the baby penguins on TV.

② The coldest place on Earth is the South Pole.

③ The average temperature in July in the South Pole is about -58℃.

④ Sally wonders how cold it is in the South Pole.

⑤ It snows a lot in the South Pole.

08 자연스러운 대화가 되도록 (A)~(E)를 순서대로 배열한 것은? [4점]

(A) Good idea. Can you check the weather?

(B) The weather is so nice outside.

(C) Oh, no! The weather forecast says it'll be rainy in the afternoon.

(D) Yeah. How about going on a picnic this afternoon?

(E) Let's go another time, then.

① (A)–(B)–(D)–(C)–(E)   ② (B)–(A)–(C)–(E)–(D)

③ (B)–(D)–(A)–(C)–(E)   ④ (E)–(A)–(C)–(B)–(D)

⑤ (E)–(C)–(A)–(D)–(B)

[09-11] 다음 대화를 읽고, 물음에 답하시오.

A: Sumin, what are you going to do on Sunday?

B: ①I'm going to go hiking. Do you want to join me?

A: ②I'd love to, but I can't. Where do you want to go?

B: ③I'm thinking of going to Namsan.

A: Oh, the scenery there is so beautiful this time of year.

B: Right. ④I heard that it's covered with red autumn leaves now.

A: Great. How long does the shortest hiking course take?

B: ⑤The Internet says it takes about two hours.

A: Okay, see you on Sunday!

09 위 대화의 밑줄 친 ①~⑤ 중 흐름상 <u>어색한</u> 것은? [4점]

①   ②   ③   ④   ⑤

서술형 2

10 다음 질문에 완전한 영어 문장으로 답하시오. [4점]

> When are they going to Namsan?

→ _____

11 위 대화를 통해 알 수 <u>없는</u> 것을 <u>모두</u> 고르면? [4점]

① 현재 계절

② 현재 남산의 경치

③ 남산의 등산 코스의 개수

④ 남산의 가장 짧은 등산 코스의 소요 시간

⑤ 인터넷에서 찾은 남산까지 가는 방법

12 다음 빈칸에 들어갈 말로 알맞은 것은? [3점]

> I'm looking for a rabbit _____ fur is white.

① that   ② who   ③ what

④ which   ⑤ whose

13 다음 중 문맥상 자연스럽지 <u>않은</u> 문장은? [4점]

① He doesn't speak while he has a meal.

② Steam the shrimps until they change color.

③ Don't forget to brush your teeth after you go to bed.

④ They have known each other since they were seven.

⑤ When I finished my homework, it was dark outside.

서술형 3

14 다음 우리말과 같도록 [조건]에 맞게 문장을 쓰시오. [각 3점]

> [조건]　1. 알맞은 관계대명사를 사용할 것
>
> 　　　　2. 괄호 안의 말을 이용할 것
>
> 　　　　3. 시제를 정확히 쓸 것

(1) 나는 취미가 사진을 찍는 것인 소년을 만났다.

→ _____

(a boy, hobby, taking pictures)

(2) 나는 주인이 캐나다인인 식당에서 점심을 먹었다.

→ _____

(have, owner, Canadian)

서술형 4

15 괄호 안의 접속사를 사용하여 두 문장을 한 문장으로 바꿔 쓰시오. [각 2점]

(1) She hurt her knee. She was playing baseball.
(while)

→ _____

(2) You should wash your hands. You have meals.
(before)

→ _____

(3) The clerk had to wait. The last customer left.
(until)

→ _____

[16-20] 다음 글을 읽고, 물음에 답하시오.

> Can you guess what these whales are doing in the picture? 그것들은 무리를 지어 서 있는 것처럼 보인다. But they are actually sleeping! Humpback whales stand on their tails _____(A)_____ they sleep. They sleep near the surface. _____(B)_____ they are not fish, they need to come up ⓐto breathe. Also, they don't fall asleep completely. _____(C)_____ they wake up, they come out of the water for a deep breath and dive back into the sea.

서술형 5

16 윗글의 밑줄 친 우리말을 괄호 안의 단어들을 바르게 배열하여 영어 문장으로 쓰시오. [4점]

→ _____

(it, up, looks, they, standing, like, are, a, in, group)

17 윗글의 빈칸 (A), (B), (C)에 알맞은 접속사가 순서대로 짝지어진 것은? [4점]

　　(A)　　(B)　　　(C)

① while – Since – Although

② after – If – When

③ while – Since – When

④ after – Since – Although

⑤ while – If – When

18 윗글의 밑줄 친 ⓐto breathe와 쓰임이 다른 것은? [3점]

① They did their best to win the prize.

② He went to the bakery to buy some bread.

③ Ann turned on the computer to check her email.

④ Our team practiced hard not to make any mistakes.

⑤ I need some help since there are many things to do.

서술형 6

19 다음 질문에 완전한 영어 문장으로 답하시오. [4점]

> Where do humpback whales sleep?

→ _____

20 윗글을 읽고 혹등고래에 대해 알 수 있는 것은? [3점]

① 몸 길이　　　　　　② 평균 수명

③ 수면 시간　　　　　④ 잠자는 모습

⑤ 주로 먹는 먹이

[21-22] 다음 글을 읽고, 물음에 답하시오.

If you think ⓐfish are not smart, take a look at the tuskfish. ⓑThis small fish whose favorite food is clams use a tool to open them. Clams usually hide under the sand, so they cannot be easily discovered. ⓒThe tuskfish blows on the sand until a clam appears. The clam is closed tightly, so ⓓthe fish cannot eat ⓔit. But the tuskfish doesn't give up. ⓕIt smashes the clam against a rock. In the end, the clam opens and dinner is served.

21 윗글의 밑줄 친 ⓐ~ⓕ 중 가리키는 대상이 같은 것끼리 짝 지어진 것은? [3점]

① ⓐ, ⓑ, ⓒ
② ⓐ, ⓒ, ⓓ, ⓕ
③ ⓑ, ⓒ, ⓓ, ⓕ
④ ⓑ, ⓒ, ⓔ
⑤ ⓑ, ⓓ, ⓔ, ⓕ

서술형 **7**

22 윗글에서 어법상 틀린 문장을 찾아 바르게 고쳐 쓰시오. [5점]

→ _____

_____

[23-24] 다음 글을 읽고, 물음에 답하시오.

You have probably seen a bird fly down to the sea to catch a fish. But have you ever seen a fish jump out of the water to catch a bird? Well, birds have to be ___ⓐ___ when a giant trevally is around. This fish can grow up to 170cm and 80kg. But don't let its size fool you. This fish is quick and ___ⓑ___. It can spot a flying bird and calculate its speed and distance. When the bird flies nearby, the giant trevally jumps out of the water and catches it.

23 윗글의 빈칸 ⓐ와 ⓑ에 알맞은 말이 순서대로 짝 지어진 것은? [4점]

① helpful – stupid
② careful – stupid
③ helpful – smart
④ careful – smart
⑤ harmful – smart

24 윗글의 giant trevally에 대한 내용과 일치하지 않는 것은? [4점]

① 새를 잡을 수 있다.
② 크기가 큰 물고기이다.
③ 새를 속여서 수면 가까이로 오게 만든다.
④ 움직이는 속도가 빠르다.
⑤ 물 밖으로 뛰어오를 수 있다.

서술형 **8**

25 다음 글을 읽고 답할 수 있는 질문을 골라 기호를 쓴 후, 완전한 영어 문장으로 답하시오. [5점]

My Fun Animal: Octopus

I will introduce the octopus. It lives on the ocean floor. It has no bones so it can move around easily in the ocean. It usually eats small fish. An interesting fact about the octopus is that it can change the color of its skin to hide from its enemies. When it meets an enemy, it shoots out dark black ink and swims away. I want to see this animal with my own eyes!

ⓐ How many arms does the octopus have?
ⓑ Why does the octopus eat small fish?
ⓒ What color is the octopus' blood?
ⓓ What does the octopus do to hide from its enemies?

(____) → _____

01 다음 영어 뜻풀이의 빈칸에 들어갈 말로 알맞은 것은? [4점]

> hide: to go to or stay at a place where _____ _____

① you can take a rest

② you can feel refreshed

③ you can buy what you want

④ you cannot be seen or found

⑤ you cannot talk about a particular subject

02 다음 빈칸에 공통으로 들어갈 말로 알맞은 것은? [4점]

> • Mina and David found a good _____ to plant the tree.
> • Can you _____ the difference between these two pictures?

① fool   ② spot   ③ land

④ book   ⑤ tear

03 다음 밑줄 친 부분의 우리말 뜻이 알맞지 않은 것은? [3점]

① Boston is so beautiful this time of year.
　　　　　　　　　　　　(이맘때쯤이면)

② Ms. Anderson decided to give up the new project.
　　　　　　　　　　　　(포기하다)

③ This tool is used by millions of people every day.
　　　　　　　　　　　　(수많은)

④ It is impossible for us to go without air.
　　　　　　　　　　　　(~ 없이 지내다)

⑤ Yesterday was the hottest day this year. The temperature went up to 43℃. (~ 이상으로)

서술형 1

04 다음 괄호 안의 말을 사용하여 대화의 빈칸에 알맞은 말을 쓰시오. [4점]

> A: We're almost at the top of the mountain.
> B: _____
> 　(wonder, this mountain)
> A: It's about 2,000m high.
> B: Wow! This is a really high mountain.

[05-06] 다음 대화를 읽고, 물음에 답하시오.

> A: Sumin, what are you going to do on Sunday?
> B: I'm going to go hiking. (①)
> A: I'd love to. Where do you want to go?
> B: I'm thinking of going to Namsan. (②)
> A: Oh, the scenery there is so beautiful this time of year. (③)
> B: Right. I heard that it's covered with red autumn leaves now. (④)
> A: Great. How long does the shortest hiking course take?
> B: The Internet says it takes about two hours. (⑤)
> A: Okay, see you on Sunday!

05 위 대화의 ①~⑤ 중 주어진 문장이 들어갈 알맞은 곳은? [4점]

> Do you want to join me?

①　　　②　　　③　　　④　　　⑤

06 위 대화를 읽고 답할 수 <u>없는</u> 질문은? [4점]

① What are they going to do on Sunday?

② How is the scenery in Namsan this time of year?

③ What season is it now?

④ Where can you enjoy the most beautiful scenery of Namsan?

⑤ How long does the shortest hiking course in Namsan take?

07 다음 중 짝 지어진 대화가 자연스럽지 <u>않은</u> 것은? [4점]

① A: Although it's very cold in the South Pole, it doesn't snow much.
　 B: That's interesting!

② A: How about going on a picnic this afternoon?
　 B: Good idea. Can you check the weather?

③ A: I wonder where the bus stop is.
　 B: You can take No. 1005 bus.

④ A: Which is the biggest planet in the solar system?
　 B: It is Jupiter.

⑤ A: Is there anything interesting in the newspaper?
　 B: This article says a whale family was seen in the East Sea.

서술형 2

08 다음 [조건]에 맞게 대화를 완성하시오. [4점]

[조건] ● 괄호 안의 단어 중 필요 없는 두 단어는 빼고 나머지 단어를 배열하여 문장을 쓸 것

A: I wonder how long the Amazon River is.
B: _____
(7,000km, the, Internet, is, about, long, hears, they, says, it,)

[09-10] 다음 대화를 읽고, 물음에 답하시오.

Suji: Check out this picture!
Tony: Wow! The camels are walking in a line in the desert.
Suji: Yeah. The desert looks very hot and dry.
Tony: I wonder how long camels can go without water in the desert.
Suji: _____
Tony: Okay. The Internet says they can go about two weeks without water.
Suji: Wow, that's amazing! Camels are really interesting animals.
Tony: I want to travel with them in the desert someday.

09 위 대화의 빈칸에 들어갈 말로 알맞은 것은? [4점]

① They are riding the camels.
② Let's find out on the Internet.
③ How about asking the science teacher about it?
④ Have you learned about it in the science class?
⑤ Why don't you borrow the book in the library?

서술형 3

10 위 대화의 내용과 일치하도록 다음 인터넷 Q&A를 완성하시오. [4점]

Interesting Facts about Camels
Q: How long can camels go without water in the desert?
A: _____
_____

11 다음 단어들을 자연스러운 문장이 되도록 배열할 때, 여섯 번째로 오는 단어는? [3점]

at, is, man, look, the, whose, blond, hair

① man ② is ③ hair
④ whose ⑤ blond

12 다음 우리말과 같도록 할 때 빈칸에 들어갈 말로 알맞은 것은? [4점]

내가 퇴근해서 집에 도착하면 네게 전화할게.
→ I'll call you _____.

① since I get home from work
② when I get home from work
③ until I get home from work
④ when I'll get home from work
⑤ until I'll get home from work

세로 왼쪽: 모의고사

서술형 4

13 다음 두 문장을 관계대명사를 사용하여 한 문장으로 연결하여 쓰시오. [각 3점]

(1) I have a cat. Its name is Dubu.

→ _____

(2) He's the writer. His new book became a bestseller.

→ _____

14 다음 중 어법상 옳은 것끼리 짝 지어진 것은? [4점]

> ⓐ I want to invent a robot whose can talk.
> ⓑ I'm going to buy a bike whose color is red.
> ⓒ Do you know the boy that name is Eric?
> ⓓ Before she goes to the movies, she will finish her work.

① ⓐ, ⓒ   ② ⓐ, ⓓ   ③ ⓑ, ⓒ
④ ⓑ, ⓓ   ⑤ ⓒ, ⓓ

서술형 5

15 다음 우리말과 같도록 [조건]에 맞게 문장을 쓰시오. [각 3점]

> [조건]   1. 알맞은 접속사를 사용할 것
>   2. 괄호 안의 말을 이용하고, 시제에 유의할 것

(1) 비가 멈출 때까지 안에서 놀자. (let's, the rain, stop)

→ _____

(2) 나는 저녁을 먹은 후에 음악을 들었다.
(listen, music, have)

→ _____

16 다음 두 문장에 대한 설명으로 틀린 것은? [4점]

> ⓐ I have liked her since we first met.
> ⓑ I have a friend whose uncle lives in London.

① ⓐ의 have liked는 '계속'의 의미를 나타내는 현재완료이다.
② ⓐ의 since는 because로 바꿔 쓸 수 있다.
③ ⓑ의 whose는 소유격 관계대명사이다.
④ ⓑ의 whose는 that으로 바꿔 쓸 수 없다.
⑤ ⓑ의 whose uncle lives in London이 앞의 a friend를 수식한다.

[17-18] 다음 글을 읽고, 물음에 답하시오.

> Can you guess what these whales are doing in the picture? It looks like they are standing ___ⓐ___ in a group. But they are actually sleeping! Humpback whales stand on their tails while they sleep. They sleep near the surface. Since they are not fish, they need to come up to breathe. Also, they don't fall asleep completely. When they wake ___ⓑ___, they come out of the water for a deep breath and dive back into the sea.

17 윗글의 빈칸 ⓐ와 ⓑ에 공통으로 알맞은 것은? [3점]

① by   ② up   ③ away
④ back   ⑤ down

서술형 6

18 윗글의 내용과 일치하지 않는 것을 모두 골라 기호를 쓴 후, 문장을 바르게 고쳐 쓰시오. [4점]

> ⓐ Humpback whales are playing in the picture.
> ⓑ Humpback whales sleep near the surface.
> ⓒ Humpback whales always fall asleep completely.
> ⓓ Humpback whales need to come out of the water to breathe.

(   ) → _____
(   ) → _____

[19-21] 다음 글을 읽고, 물음에 답하시오.

> If you think fish are not smart, take a look at the tuskfish. This small fish ___ⓐ___ favorite food is clams uses a tool to open them. Clams usually hide under the sand, so they _____ⓑ_____.
> The tuskfish blows on the sand until a clam appears. The clam is closed tightly, so the fish cannot eat it. But the tuskfish doesn't give up. It smashes the clam against a rock. In the end, the clam opens and dinner is served.

19 윗글의 빈칸 ⓐ에 알맞은 관계대명사는? [3점]

① what   ② who   ③ whose

④ which   ⑤ that

20 윗글의 빈칸 ⓑ에 들어갈 말로 알맞은 것은? [4점]

① can swim away very fast

② cannot move themselves

③ cannot be easily discovered

④ can get the food in the sand

⑤ cannot close their shells tightly

서술형7

21 윗글의 내용과 일치하도록 다음 글의 빈칸에 알맞은 말을 쓰시오. [5점]

> (1) _____, the tuskfish's favorite food, are closed tightly. But the tuskfish doesn't (2) _____. It uses (3) _____ to open the clam.

[22-24] 다음 글을 읽고, 물음에 답하시오.

> You have probably seen a bird fly down to the sea to catch a fish. 그러나 당신은 물고기가 새를 잡기 위해 물 밖으로 뛰어오르는 것을 본 적이 있는가? Well, birds have to be careful when ①a giant trevally is around. ②This fish can grow up to 170cm and 80kg. But don't let ③its size fool you. This fish is quick and smart. ④It can spot a flying bird and calculate ⑤its speed and distance. When the bird flies nearby, the giant trevally jumps out of the water and catches it.

서술형8

22 윗글의 밑줄 친 우리말을 [조건]에 맞게 영어 문장으로 쓰시오. [4점]

> [조건] 1. 주어진 단어를 바르게 배열할 것
>
> 2. 필요 없는 두 개를 뺄 것
>
> 3. 대소문자를 구별하고 문장 부호를 정확히 쓸 것

> have, out of, catch, but, you, a fish, ever, to, are, seen, the water, a bird, jump, from

→ _____

_____

23 윗글의 밑줄 친 ①~⑤ 중 가리키는 대상이 다른 것은? [3점]

①   ②   ③   ④   ⑤

24 윗글을 읽고 giant trevally에 대해 알 수 있는 것은? [4점]

① 크기   ② 이동 거리   ③ 천적

④ 수면 자세   ⑤ 평균 수명

25 다음 글의 빈칸 ①~⑤에 들어갈 말로 알맞지 않은 것은? [4점]

> Hello, I'm a beluga whale. I live in the Arctic Ocean. It's very cold. So my skin is very ___①___ and about half of my body is fat. I also have a round head. When I'm ___②___, I usually eat fish and clams. I'm ___③___ all over, so people also call me the white whale. When I was born, I was gray. But when I ___④___, my body became white! I can make several sounds. I use these sounds to talk to other whales. Yes, we can ___⑤___!

① thick   ② hungry   ③ gray

④ grew up   ⑤ communicate

01 주어진 단어의 영어 뜻풀이에 해당하지 <u>않는</u> 것은? [4점]

| smash | Arctic | forecast | calculate |

① the area around the North Pole
② to break something into many pieces
③ to find a number, answer, etc. by using mathematical processes
④ to see, find, or become aware of something for the first time
⑤ a statement about what you think is going to happen in the future

02 다음 빈칸에 알맞은 말이 순서대로 짝 지어진 것은? [3점]

- This machine can make up _____ three copies at one time.
- It was not easy for me to go _____ my smartphone for a week.

① to – for
② to – without
③ with – with
④ with – without
⑤ on – with

03 다음 중 밑줄 친 단어의 쓰임이 알맞지 <u>않은</u> 것은? [3점]

① John held the baby <u>tightly</u> in his arms.
② I turned my face away to <u>discover</u> my tears.
③ There were three <u>shiny</u> gold coins in the box.
④ Mars is the fourth <u>planet</u> from the Sun.
⑤ Let's <u>calculate</u> how much it will cost to give a party for grandma.

서술형 **1**

04 다음 대화의 빈칸에 알맞은 말을 쓰시오. [3점]

A: _____ how big Jupiter is.
B: It's over 11 times bigger than Earth.

서술형 **2**

05 다음 우리말과 같도록 괄호 안의 말을 이용하여 대화를 완성하시오. [각 3점]

A: The highest mountain in the world is Mt. Everest.
B: (1) 나는 그것이 얼마나 높은지 궁금해.
A: (2) 신문에 따르면 에베레스트산은 높이가 약 8,850미터야.
B: That's amazing!

(1) _____
　(wonder, how, high)
(2) _____

_____
　(the newspaper, say, high)

[06-08] 다음 대화를 읽고, 물음에 답하시오.

Tim: Look at the baby penguins on TV. They're ①<u>so cute</u>.
Mina: Yes, but they look very cold out there.
Tim: Yeah, the South Pole is the ②<u>coldest</u> place on Earth.
Mina: I wonder how cold it is there.
Tim: The average temperature is about -58℃ in July and -26℃ in December.
Mina: Oh, then, July is ③<u>warmer</u> than December there. Interesting!
Tim: Yes. ④<u>Although</u> it's very cold there, it doesn't snow much.
Mina: That's ⑤<u>interesting</u>, too!

06 위 대화의 밑줄 친 ①~⑤ 중 흐름상 어색한 것은? [4점]

①　　②　　③　　④　　⑤

서술형 **3**

07 위 대화의 내용과 일치하도록 빈칸에 알맞은 말을 쓰시오. [4점]

Mina wondered _____ it is in _____ and Tim gave her the answer.

08 위 대화를 읽고 답할 수 있는 질문은? [4점]

① What are the baby penguins doing on TV?

② Where is the coldest place on Earth?

③ How many species live in the South Pole?

④ What is the average temperature in March in the South Pole?

⑤ Why doesn't it snow much in the South Pole?

[09-10] 다음 대화를 읽고, 물음에 답하시오.

A: Sumin, what are you going to do on Sunday?

B: I'm going to go hiking. Do you want to join me?

A: _____ Where do you want to go?

B: I'm thinking of going to Namsan.

A: Oh, the scenery there is so beautiful this time of year.

B: Right. I heard that it's covered with red autumn leaves now.

A: Great. How long does the shortest hiking course take?

B: The Internet says it takes about two hours.

A: Okay, see you on Sunday!

09 위 대화의 빈칸에 들어갈 수 있는 것끼리 짝 지어진 것은? [4점]

@ I'd love to.	ⓑ I agree.
ⓒ I'm afraid I can't.	ⓓ Of course.
ⓔ No, thank you.	ⓕ I'd love to, but I can't.

① @, ⓑ   ② @, ⓓ   ③ ⓑ, ⓒ, ⓔ

④ ⓑ, ⓓ, ⓕ   ⑤ ⓒ, ⓓ, ⓕ

서술형 4

10 위 대화의 내용과 일치하도록 다음 글을 완성하시오. [5점]

They are going to (1) _____ to Namsan on Sunday. It is covered with (2) _____ now. The shortest hiking course in Namsan (3) _____ _____.

11 다음 빈칸에 공통으로 들어갈 말로 알맞은 것은? [3점]

- Austin was only 17 _____ he won the gold medal.
- Can you remember _____ you sent the package?

① after   ② until   ③ since

④ while   ⑤ when

12 다음 빈칸에 알맞은 말이 순서대로 짝 지어진 것은? [3점]

- The boy _____ bike was stolen was very upset.
- The police arrested the thief _____ stole the bike yesterday.

① that – who   ② who – what

③ whose – who   ④ who – whose

⑤ whose – which

13 다음 중 어법상 틀린 것은? [4점]

① I have a friend who favorite number is 1.

② She couldn't understand what the teacher was saying.

③ They stood in front of the door until I came out.

④ The jacket whose zipper was broken is not mine.

⑤ After I finish my homework, I will go shopping.

14 다음 우리말을 영어로 잘못 옮긴 것을 모두 고르면? [4점]

① 나는 어렸을 때 롤러코스터 타는 것을 좋아했다.

→ I liked to ride the roller coaster when I was young.

② 그는 대학을 떠난 이후로 축구를 하지 않았다.

→ He hasn't played soccer since he left university.

③ 내가 병원에 입원해 있는 동안 Simpson 선생님이 내 수업을 맡았다.

→ Ms. Simpson took my classes for me until I was in the hospital.

④ 나는 꼬리가 긴 개를 키우고 싶다.

→ I want to raise a dog whose tail is long.

⑤ 과학 캠프에 내가 모르는 학생들이 많이 있다.

→ There are many students whose I don't know in the science camp.

15 다음 중 빈칸에 whose가 들어갈 수 <u>없는</u> 것은? [3점]

① They have a cat _____ eyes are different colors.

② Can you tell me _____ painting was chosen for the prize?

③ I met a child _____ mom works in the bank.

④ Did you see the letter _____ came this morning?

⑤ The girl _____ name is Melisa is waiting for you.

서술형5

16 다음 [조건]에 맞게 각 문장을 완성하시오. [각 2점]

| [조건] | 1. 각 상자에서 알맞은 말을 하나씩 골라 쓸 것 |
| | 2. 중복하여 사용하지 말 것 |

until	spring comes
when	the snow melted
since	he came back from holiday

(1) I haven't met him _____.

(2) I stayed at home _____.

(3) _____, I will plant lots of trees and flowers.

[17-18] 다음 글을 읽고, 물음에 답하시오.

①Two-thirds of our planet is covered by oceans. They are full of wonder and are home to ②millions of species. Every day, we are learning new things about them. Let's find out about some interesting sea animals.

Can you guess what these whales are doing in the picture? It looks like they are standing up ③in a group. But they are actually sleeping! Humpback whales stand on their tails while they sleep. They sleep near the surface. ④Since they are not fish, they need to come up to breathe. Also, they ⑤don't fall asleep completely. When they wake up, they come out of the water for a deep breath and dive back into the sea.

17 윗글의 밑줄 친 ①~⑤의 우리말 뜻이 알맞지 <u>않은</u> 것은? [3점]

① 우리 행성의 3분의 2   ② 수많은 종들

③ 무리를 지어   ④ ~한 이후로

⑤ 완전히 잠들지 않는다

서술형6

18 다음 질문에 완전한 영어 문장으로 답하시오. [4점]

What do humpback whales do when they wake up?

→ _____
_____

[19-20] 다음 글을 읽고, 물음에 답하시오.

If you think fish are not smart, take a look at the tuskfish. This small fish whose favorite food is clams uses a tool to (A)[open / close] them. Clams usually hide under the sand, so they cannot be easily discovered. The tuskfish blows on the sand until a clam (B)[appears / disappears]. The clam is closed tightly, so the fish cannot eat it. But the tuskfish doesn't (C)[give up / succeed]. It smashes the clam against a rock. In the end, the clam opens and dinner is served.

19 윗글의 (A)~(C)에서 문맥상 알맞은 말이 바르게 짝 지어진 것은? [4점]

	(A)	(B)	(C)
①	open	– appears	– succeed
②	close	– disappears	– give up
③	open	– appears	– give up
④	close	– appears	– succeed
⑤	open	– disappears	– give up

20 윗글을 읽고 알 수 <u>없는</u> 것은? [4점]

① tuskfish는 크기가 작다.

② tuskfish는 조개를 먹기 위해 도구를 사용한다.

③ 조개는 대개 모래 아래에 숨어 있다.

④ tuskfish는 모래에 입김을 불어 조개를 찾는다.

⑤ tuskfish의 서식지는 바위 사이에 있다.

[21-23] 다음 글을 읽고, 물음에 답하시오.

> You have probably seen a bird fly down to the sea to catch a fish. But have you ever seen a fish jump out of the water to catch a bird? Well, birds have to be careful when a giant trevally is around. This fish can grow up to 170cm and 80kg. ⓐ<u>But don't let its size to fool you.</u> This fish is quick and smart. It can ⓑ<u>spot</u> a flying bird and calculate its speed and distance. When the bird flies nearby, the giant trevally jumps out of the water and catches it.

서술형**7**

21 윗글의 밑줄 친 문장 ⓐ를 어법상 바르게 고쳐 쓰시오. [4점]

→ _____

22 윗글의 밑줄 친 ⓑ<u>spot</u>의 영어 뜻풀이로 알맞은 것은?
[4점]

① a particular area or place

② to break something into many pieces

③ to go to or stay at a place where you cannot be seen or found

④ a small mark on something, especially one that is made by a liquid

⑤ to see or notice someone or something that is difficult to see or find

23 윗글의 giant trevally에 관한 내용과 일치하는 것은?
[4점]

① It doesn't eat any birds.

② It can be eaten by a flying bird.

③ It is very slow.

④ It is too big to jump out of the water.

⑤ It can catch a flying bird.

[24-25] 다음 글을 읽고, 물음에 답하시오.

> **My Fun Animal: Beluga whale**
> I will introduce the beluga whale. (①) It lives in the Arctic Ocean. (②) It has a round head. It usually eats fish and clams. (③) An interesting fact about the beluga whale is that it is white all over. (④) When it is born, it is gray. (⑤) But when it grows up, its body becomes white! I want to see this animal with my own eyes!

24 윗글의 ①~⑤ 중 주어진 문장이 들어갈 알맞은 곳은?
[4점]

> That's why people call it the white whale.

①   ②   ③   ④   ⑤

서술형**8**

25 윗글의 내용과 일치하도록 다음 대화를 완성하시오. [각 2점]

> A: I learned about the beluga whale today.
> B: Oh, it lives (1) _____, right?
> A: Right! It has a round head and usually eats (2) _____.
> B: I see. What else did you learn about it?
> A: When it is born, it is gray. But (3) _____ _____!
> B: That's interesting!

01 다음 영어 뜻풀이에 해당하는 단어가 쓰인 문장은? [4점]

> the amount of space between two places or things

① The sea turtle is an endangered species.
② We have to buy several tools to fix the bike.
③ What's the distance between Seoul and Busan?
④ The temperature dropped to -10℃ this morning.
⑤ Monica watched the fireworks with wonder and amazement.

02 다음 중 밑줄 친 단어가 같은 의미로 쓰인 것은? [4점]

① The project was a complete success.
Did you complete the work by yourself?
② Can you return the book I lent you last month?
She needs to book a ticket for Jeju-do right now.
③ The land is so dry that plants can't survive there.
Did you see the bird land on the river over there?
④ I felt like a fool when I realized my mistake.
The man tried to fool everyone about the accident.
⑤ How could you spot me from the distance?
If you spot any mistakes in the article, mark them with a pencil.

서술형**1**

03 다음 우리말과 같도록 빈칸에 알맞은 말을 쓰시오. [각 2점]

(1) 뒤뜰의 잔디가 내 무릎까지 자랐다.
→ The grass in the backyard grew _____ _____ my knee.
(2) 마침내, 정말 막상막하였음에도 불구하고 우리 팀이 경기에서 이겼다.
→ _____ _____ _____, our team won the game although it was really close.

서술형**2**

04 다음 정보를 보고, 아래 대화를 완성하시오. [4점]

> The blue whale is about 30m long.

A: The blue whale is the largest animal in the world.
B: I wonder how (1) _____.
A: The book (2) _____.

[05-07] 다음 대화를 읽고, 물음에 답하시오.

> A: Look at the baby penguins on TV. They're so cute.
> B: Yes, but they look very cold out there.
> A: Yeah, the South Pole is the coldest place on Earth.
> B: I wonder how cold it is there.
> A: The average temperature is about -58℃ in July and -26℃ in December.
> B: Oh, then, _____ there. Interesting!
> A: Yes. Although it's very cold there, it doesn't snow much.
> B: That's interesting, too!

05 위 대화의 빈칸에 들어갈 말로 알맞은 것은? [4점]

① July is warmer than December
② July is colder than December
③ December is as warm as July
④ July is not as cold as December
⑤ December is the coldest month

서술형**3**

06 위 대화의 내용과 일치하도록 다음 문장을 완성하시오. [4점]

> The South Pole is _____ on Earth, but it _____ much.

서술형**4**

07 다음 질문에 완전한 영어 문장으로 답하시오. [4점]

> How cold is it in the South Pole?

→ _____

[08-09] 다음 대화를 읽고, 물음에 답하시오.

> Suji: Check out this picture!
> Tony: Wow! The camels are walking in a line in the desert.
> Suji: Yeah. The desert looks very hot and dry.
> Tony: _____ in the desert.
> Suji: Let's find out on the Internet.
> Tony: Okay. The Internet says they can go about two weeks without water.
> Suji: Wow, that's amazing! Camels are really interesting animals.
> Tony: I want to travel with them in the desert someday.

서술형**5**

08 위 대화의 빈칸에 알맞은 말을 [조건]에 맞게 쓰시오. [4점]

> [조건] 1. 괄호 안의 단어들과 대화 속 표현을 사용할 것
>   2. 총 9단어로 쓸 것

→ _____

(wonder, how, long)

09 위 대화의 내용과 일치하는 문장의 개수는? [4점]

> ⓐ They look for the answer to their question in a book.
> ⓑ Camels can live for three weeks without water in the desert.
> ⓒ Suji thinks camels are really interesting animals.
> ⓓ Tony is traveling with camels in the desert now.

① 0개　② 1개　③ 2개　④ 3개　⑤ 4개

10 다음 빈칸에 알맞은 말이 순서대로 짝 지어진 것은? [4점]

> • Look at the mountain _____ top is covered with snow.
> • Most people _____ Emma invited to her house didn't show up.
> • Let me show you _____ I bought at the mall.

① whose – who – whose　② which – whose – which
③ whose – whom – what　④ which – whom – what
⑤ whose – whose – what

11 다음 중 밑줄 친 <u>whose</u>의 쓰임이 나머지와 <u>다른</u> 하나는? [3점]

① Tell me about the fairy <u>whose</u> wings are pink.
② Jack has a cousin <u>whose</u> hobby is to play soccer.
③ We found the architect <u>whose</u> garden is very large.
④ I don't know <u>whose</u> gloves are left on the desk.
⑤ What is the name of the girl <u>whose</u> bag is white?

12 각 문장에 대한 설명으로 알맞지 <u>않은</u> 것은? [3점]

① Ants are insects that live in large groups.
　→ that은 주격 관계대명사로 which로 바꿔 쓸 수 있다.
② He has lived in that house since he moved here.
　→ since는 '~한 이후로'라는 의미의 접속사이다.
③ We'll visit the museum after we will walk the dog.
　→ 시간의 부사절은 미래의 의미일지라도 현재시제로 나타내므로 will walk의 will을 삭제해야 한다.
④ The novelist whose stories are full of imagination is my favorite writer.
　→ whose는 '누구의'라는 의미의 의문사이다.
⑤ Look at the building whose rooftop has a beautiful garden.
　→ Look at the building.과 Its rooftop has a beautiful garden.의 두 문장을 관계대명사로 연결한 문장이다.

서술형**6**

13 자연스러운 문장이 되도록 빈칸에 알맞은 말을 자유롭게 쓰시오. [각 2점]

(1) While I listened to music, _____.
(2) _____ since I was ten.
(3) I have a friend whose _____.

서술형**7**

14 다음 중 밑줄 친 부분이 어법상 틀린 문장을 골라 바르게 고쳐 쓴 후, 그 이유를 우리말로 쓰시오. [4점]

> ⓐ I mopped the floor <u>during</u> David watered the plants.
> ⓑ We have to wait <u>until</u> he arrives.
> ⓒ <u>Before</u> you make a decision, think carefully.
> ⓓ Do you know the old man <u>whose</u> last name is Smith?

(　　) → _____

이유: _____

15 다음 밑줄 친 부분을 어법상 바르게 고친 것 중 <u>틀린</u> 것은? [4점]

> - Winter is the season ①<u>whose</u> comes after fall.
> - There are lots of people ②<u>who</u> houses were destroyed by the typhoon.
> - The man ③<u>whose</u> painting is in the museum is my neighbor.
> - I will take care of your cats until you ④<u>will get</u> back from holiday.
> - I ⑤<u>have played</u> the piano since I was ten.

① → which   ② → that
③ → 고칠 필요 없음   ④ → get
⑤ → 고칠 필요 없음

[16-18] 다음 글을 읽고, 물음에 답하시오.

> ⓐTwo-thirds of our planet are covered by oceans. ⓑThey are full of wonder and are home to millions of species. Every day, we are learning new things about them. Let's find out about some interesting sea animals.
>
> ⓒCan you guess that these whales are doing in the picture? ⓓIt looks like they are standing up in a group. But they are actually sleeping! Humpback whales stand on their tails while they sleep. They sleep near the surface. ⓔSince they are not fish, they need to come up to breathe. Also, they don't fall asleep completely. When they wake up, they come out of the water for a deep breath and dive back into the sea.

16 윗글의 밑줄 친 ⓐ~ⓔ 중 어법상 틀린 것끼리 짝 지어진 것은? [4점]

① ⓐ, ⓑ   ② ⓐ, ⓒ   ③ ⓑ, ⓒ
④ ⓒ, ⓓ   ⑤ ⓒ, ⓔ

서술형8

17 윗글에서 다음 영어 뜻풀이에 해당하는 단어를 찾아, 그 단어를 사용한 문장을 자유롭게 쓰시오. [4점]

> a set of animals or plants that have similar characteristics to each other

→ _____

18 윗글을 <u>잘못</u> 이해한 사람을 <u>모두</u> 고르면? [4점]

① **Ray:** Two-thirds of the Earth is covered by oceans.
② **Amy:** Oceans are home to millions of species.
③ **Taeho:** While humpback whales sleep, they stand on their heads.
④ **Jina:** Humpback whales sleep far from the surface.
⑤ **Joe:** When humpback whales wake up, they come out of the water to breathe.

[19-21] 다음 글을 읽고, 물음에 답하시오.

> If you think fish are not smart, take a look at the tuskfish. ①This small fish whose favorite food is clams uses a tool to open them. ②Clams usually hide under the sand, so they cannot be easily discovered. (A)tuskfish는 조개가 나타날 때까지 모래에 입김을 분다. ③The clam is closed tightly, so the fish cannot eat it. ④But the tuskfish doesn't give up. It smashes the clam against a rock. ⑤In the end, the clam opens and dinner is served.

19 윗글의 밑줄 친 문장 ①~⑤에 대한 설명으로 알맞지 <u>않은</u> 것은? [3점]

① whose를 다른 관계대명사로 바꿔 쓸 수 없다.
② so의 앞과 뒤의 절의 위치를 바꿔 쓸 수 있다.
③ it은 the clam을 가리킨다.
④ 이 문장은 tuskfish가 조개를 여는 것을 포기하지 않는다는 의미를 나타낸다.
⑤ dinner is served는 dinner is ready와 같은 의미를 나타낸다.

서술형 9

20 윗글의 밑줄 친 우리말 (A)와 같도록 [조건]에 맞게 영작하시오. [4점]

> [조건] 1. 알맞은 접속사를 사용할 것
> 2. 괄호 안의 말을 사용할 것
> 3. 총 10단어로 쓸 것

→ _____

(the tuskfish, on the sand, a clam)

21 윗글을 읽고 알 수 없는 것을 모두 고르면? [4점]

① what the tuskfish's favorite food is
② why clams are closed tightly
③ why clams cannot be discovered easily
④ how the tuskfish opens clams
⑤ how many clams the tuskfish can eat

[22-23] 다음 글을 읽고, 물음에 답하시오.

　You have probably seen a bird fly down to the sea to catch a fish.
(A) This fish can grow up to 170cm and 80kg.
(B) But have you ever seen a fish jump out of the water to catch a bird?
(C) But don't let its size fool you.
(D) Well, birds have to be careful when a giant trevally is around.
This fish is quick and smart. It can spot a flying bird and calculate its speed and distance. When the bird flies nearby, the giant trevally jumps out of the water and catches it.

22 자연스러운 글이 되도록 (A)~(D)를 순서대로 배열한 것은? [4점]

① (A) – (C) – (B) – (D)　　② (B) – (A) – (C) – (D)
③ (B) – (D) – (A) – (C)　　④ (D) – (A) – (B) – (C)
⑤ (D) – (B) – (C) – (A)

서술형 10

23 윗글을 읽고 답할 수 있는 질문을 모두 골라 기호를 쓴 후, 완전한 영어 문장으로 답하시오. [5점]

> ⓐ What is the giant trevally's favorite food?
> ⓑ What can the giant trevally calculate?
> ⓒ How big can the giant trevally grow?
> ⓓ How does the giant trevally catch a bird?
> ⓔ How high can the giant trevally jump out of the water?

(　　) → _____
(　　) → _____
(　　) → _____

[24-25] 다음 글을 읽고, 물음에 답하시오.

　Hello, I'm an octopus. I live on the ocean floor. I'm different from other ocean animals in many ways. I have no bones so I can move around easily in the ocean. I have eight arms. My favorite food is small fish. I can change the color of my skin to hide from my enemies. When I meet an enemy, I shoot out dark black ink and swim away. Oh, one more thing. The color of my blood is blue.

24 윗글의 밑줄 친 문장의 내용으로 언급되지 않은 것은? [3점]

① 뼈가 없어서 바다에서 쉽게 돌아다닐 수 있다.
② 팔에 있는 빨판은 사물에 쉽게 달라붙는다.
③ 적으로부터 숨기 위해 피부색을 바꿀 수 있다.
④ 적을 만나면 먹물을 쏘고 헤엄쳐 가 버린다.
⑤ 피 색깔은 파란색이다.

서술형 11

25 윗글의 내용과 일치하도록 [1]의 빈칸에 알맞은 말을 쓴 다음, [1]의 두 문장을 관계대명사를 사용하여 한 문장으로 바꿔 [2]에 쓰시오. [5점]

[1] The octopus lives on _____.
　Its favorite food is _____.

[2] _____

_____

● 틀린 문항을 표시해 보세요.

● 부족한 영역을 점검해 보고 어떻게 더 학습할지 학습 계획을 적어 보세요.

〈제1회〉대표 기출로 내신 적중 모의고사　　총점 ＿＿＿＿＿ / 100

문항	영역	문항	영역	문항	영역
01	p.156(W)	10	p.163(L&S)	19	pp.178-179(R)
02	p.158(W)	11	p.163(L&S)	20	pp.178-179(R)
03	p.156(W)	12	p.170(G)	21	pp.178-179(R)
04	p.156(W)	13	p.171(G)	22	pp.178-179(R)
05	p.162(L&S)	14	p.170(G)	23	pp.178-179(R)
06	p.162(L&S)	15	p.171(G)	24	pp.178-179(R)
07	p.162(L&S)	16	pp.178-179(R)	25	p.193(M)
08	p.162(L&S)	17	pp.178-179(R)		
09	p.163(L&S)	18	pp.178-179(R)		

오답 공략
부족한 영역
학습 계획

〈제2회〉대표 기출로 내신 적중 모의고사　　총점 ＿＿＿＿＿ / 100

문항	영역	문항	영역	문항	영역
01	p.158(W)	10	p.163(L&S)	19	pp.178-179(R)
02	p.158(W)	11	p.170(G)	20	pp.178-179(R)
03	p.156(W)	12	p.171(G)	21	pp.178-179(R)
04	p.162(L&S)	13	p.170(G)	22	pp.178-179(R)
05	p.163(L&S)	14	pp.170-171(G)	23	pp.178-179(R)
06	p.163(L&S)	15	p.171(G)	24	pp.178-179(R)
07	p.161(L&S)	16	pp.170-171(G)	25	p.192(M)
08	p.161(L&S)	17	pp.178-179(R)		
09	p.163(L&S)	18	pp.178-179(R)		

오답 공략
부족한 영역
학습 계획

〈제3회〉대표 기출로 내신 적중 모의고사　　총점 ＿＿＿＿＿ / 100

문항	영역	문항	영역	문항	영역
01	p.158(W)	10	p.163(L&S)	19	pp.178-179(R)
02	p.156(W)	11	p.171(G)	20	pp.178-179(R)
03	p.156(W)	12	p.170(G)	21	pp.178-179(R)
04	p.161(L&S)	13	pp.170-171(G)	22	pp.178-179(R)
05	p.161(L&S)	14	pp.170-171(G)	23	pp.178-179(R)
06	p.162(L&S)	15	p.170(G)	24	p.193(M)
07	p.162(L&S)	16	p.171(G)	25	p.193(M)
08	p.162(L&S)	17	pp.178-179(R)		
09	p.163(L&S)	18	pp.178-179(R)		

오답 공략
부족한 영역
학습 계획

〈제4회〉고난도로 내신 적중 모의고사　　총점 ＿＿＿＿＿ / 100

문항	영역	문항	영역	문항	영역
01	p.158(W)	10	p.170(G)	19	pp.178-179(R)
02	p.158(W)	11	p.170(G)	20	pp.178-179(R)
03	p.156(W)	12	pp.170-171(G)	21	pp.178-179(R)
04	p.161(L&S)	13	pp.170-171(G)	22	pp.178-179(R)
05	p.162(L&S)	14	pp.170-171(G)	23	pp.178-179(R)
06	p.162(L&S)	15	pp.170-171(G)	24	p.192(M)
07	p.162(L&S)	16	pp.178-179(R)	25	p.192(M)
08	p.163(L&S)	17	pp.178-179(R)		
09	p.163(L&S)	18	pp.178-179(R)		

오답 공략
부족한 영역
학습 계획

동아출판 영어 교재 가이드

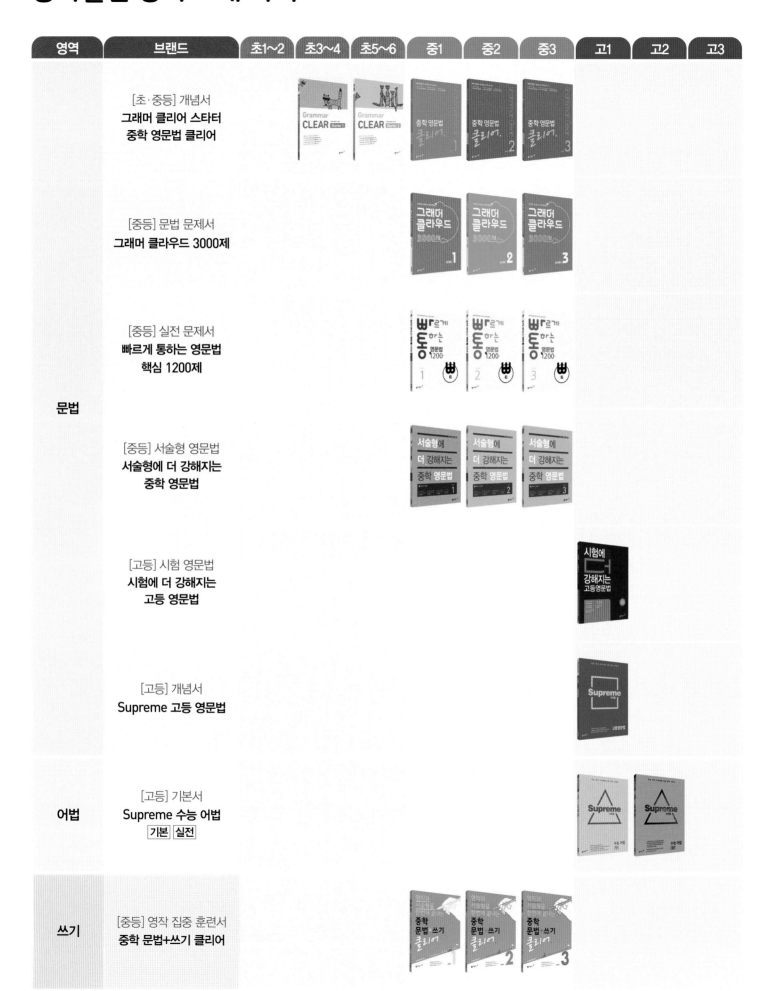

영역	브랜드	초1~2	초3~4	초5~6	중1	중2	중3	고1	고2	고3
문법	[초·중등] 개념서 그래머 클리어 스타터 중학 영문법 클리어		Grammar CLEAR Starter 1	Grammar CLEAR Starter 2	중학 영문법 클리어 1	중학 영문법 클리어 2	중학 영문법 클리어 3			
	[중등] 문법 문제서 그래머 클라우드 3000제				그래머 클라우드 3000제 1	그래머 클라우드 3000제 2	그래머 클라우드 3000제 3			
	[중등] 실전 문제서 빠르게 통하는 영문법 핵심 1200제				빠르게 통하는 영문법 1200 1	빠르게 통하는 영문법 1200 2	빠르게 통하는 영문법 1200 3			
	[중등] 서술형 영문법 서술형에 더 강해지는 중학 영문법				서술형에 더 강해지는 중학 영문법 1	서술형에 더 강해지는 중학 영문법 2	서술형에 더 강해지는 중학 영문법 3			
	[고등] 시험 영문법 시험에 더 강해지는 고등 영문법							시험에 더 강해지는 고등영문법		
	[고등] 개념서 Supreme 고등 영문법							Supreme 고등영문법		
어법	[고등] 기본서 Supreme 수능 어법 기본 실전							Supreme 수능 어법 기본	Supreme 수능 어법 실전	
쓰기	[중등] 영작 집중 훈련서 중학 문법+쓰기 클리어				중학 문법·쓰기 클리어 1	중학 문법·쓰기 클리어 2	중학 문법·쓰기 클리어 3			

동아출판이 만든 진짜 기출예상문제집

특급기출

중간고사

중학 영어 **3-2**

이병민

정답 및 해설

동아출판

Lesson 5

Believe in Yourself

STEP A

A 01 기대하다, 예상하다
02 여행, 여정
03 교육자
04 인내심
05 체육, 운동, 체육관
06 오케스트라, 관현악단
07 거대한
08 (미술·음악 등의) 작품
09 배우
10 응원하다
11 놀라운
12 해군 대장, 해군 장성
13 황홀해하는, 아주 신이 난
14 상
15 구르다, 굴러가다
16 대부분, 일반적으로
17 거대한
18 쓰레기 매립지
19 ~을 할 형편이 되다
20 공연, 연주회

B 21 environmental
22 trash
23 cheek
24 gather
25 situation
26 without
27 hurt
28 ocean
29 talented
30 appear
31 president
32 save
33 tear
34 parade
35 musical instrument
36 million
37 respect
38 stick
39 speech
40 battle

C 01 점차로
02 서로
03 그때부터 (쭉)
04 ~에게 큰 박수를 보내다
05 음이 맞지 않는
06 ~할 수 있다
07 ~을 실행에 옮기다
08 ~에 참가하다

W Words Plus 연습 문제   p.11

A 1 afford, ~을 할 형편이 되다
2 thrilled, 황홀해하는, 아주 신이 난 3 journey, 여행
4 roll, 구르다, 굴러가다 5 landfill, 쓰레기 매립지

---

6 musical instrument, 악기 7 educator, 교육자
8 patience, 인내심
B 1 environmental 2 huge 3 bored
C 1 journey 2 mostly 3 gather 4 respect
5 talented
D 1 Step by step 2 give, a big hand
3 put, into practice 4 take part in 5 from then on

01 ④ 02 ④ 03 ③ 04 ① 05 (1) scared (2) excited
06 ④ 07 give, big hand

01 ④는 부사이고, 나머지는 모두 명사이다.
|해석| ① 기쁨 ② 해군 대장, 해군 장성 ③ 여행, 여정
④ 대부분, 일반적으로 ⑤ 교육자
02 '생각보다는 행동'을 뜻하는 것은 practice(실행, 실천)이다.
03 '~을 할 형편이 되다'라는 의미의 동사는 afford이다.
04 ① out of tune은 '음이 맞지 않는'이라는 의미이다.
|해석| ① 그 기타는 음이 맞지 않았다.
② 겨울을 준비할 때이다.
③ 미나의 가족과 Alice는 서로 인사를 나누었다.
④ 연필을 꺼내서 시험을 시작하세요.
⑤ 그 회사는 새로운 아이디어들을 실행에 옮기기로 결정했다.
05 (1) 어둠 속에서 움직이는 무언가를 봐서 잠을 잘 수 없었다고 했으므
로, 빈칸에는 scared(무서워하는, 겁먹은)가 알맞다.
(2) 파리에 있는 가장 친한 친구를 방문할 예정이라고 했으므로, 빈칸에
는 excited(신이 난)가 알맞다.
|해석| (1) 나는 어둠 속에서 무언가가 움직이고 있는 것을 보았다. 나는
너무 무서워서 잠을 잘 수 없었다.
(2) 나는 파리에 있는 나의 가장 친한 친구를 방문할 예정이다. 나는 매
우 신이 난다.
06 ④ 바위가 언덕에서 굴러떨어지고 있다는 의미를 나타내는 문장이 되는
것이 자연스러우므로, gathering(gather: 모이다)이 아니라 rolling
(roll: 굴러가다)이 들어가는 것이 알맞다.
|해석| • 이 약은 매년 수천 명의 목숨을 구할 수 있다.
• 내 친구들과 나는 서서 우리 학교 축구팀을 응원했다.
• Mike는 재능 있는 배우이고, 많은 사람들이 그를 아주 좋아한다.
• 봐! 바위가 언덕에서 굴러떨어지고 있어.
• 그 거대한 나무는 거의 10미터 높이이다.
07 '~에게 큰 박수를 보내다'라는 뜻의 give ~ a big hand를 써 문장을
완성한다.

Listen & Speak 만점 노트　　pp. 14~15

Q1 보라는 록 밴드에서 기타를 연주한다.
Q2 나는 그것을 보는 게 정말 기대돼.
Q3 is going to travel to Jeju-do
Q4 소녀는 남동생을 돌봐야 하기 때문이다.
Q5 그는 3년 동안 기타를 쳤다.
Q6 He hurt his hand in gym class.
Q7 숙제를 해야 한다.
Q8 It's about a boy who became a famous dancer.
Q9 그녀는 이번 주말에 자원봉사 활동이 있기 때문이다.

 Listen & Speak 빈칸 채우기　　pp. 16~17

1 Welcome to, I'm looking forward to, We're excited
2 what are you reading, who was born, was made, to watching it, Can I join you
3 look happy today, I'm going to travel, riding a horse
4 Math is difficult, can you help me, but I can't, take care of
5 take part in, how to play the guitar, I'd love to, I'm sorry to hear that, to cheer
6 to ride my bike, have to do my homework, next time
7 watch the musical, who became a famous dancer, my favorite actor, want to join me, have volunteer work

 Listen & Speak 대화 순서 배열하기　　pp. 18~19

1 ⓒ-ⓓ-ⓑ-ⓐ
2 ⓐ-ⓕ-ⓒ-ⓔ-ⓘ-ⓑ-ⓗ-ⓓ-ⓖ
3 ⓑ-ⓒ-ⓐ-ⓓ
4 ⓓ-ⓐ-ⓒ-ⓔ-ⓑ
5 ⓒ-ⓓ-ⓖ-ⓐ-ⓕ-ⓑ-ⓗ-ⓔ
6 ⓐ-ⓓ-ⓒ-ⓑ
7 ⓓ-ⓘ-ⓑ-ⓖ-ⓔ-ⓐ-ⓕ-ⓒ-ⓙ-ⓗ

Listen & Speak 실전 TEST　　pp. 20~21

01 ④　02 ⑤　03 ④　04 ③　05 ②　06 ③　07 ⑤
08 ②　09 ④

[서술형]
10 I'm really looking forward to swimming in the ocean
11 (1) You know how to play the guitar, right?
　(2) Can you play the guitar while I sing in the contest?
　(3) I'm sorry to hear that.
12 He has played the guitar for 3 years.

01 I'm really looking forward to ~.는 '나는 ~하는 게 정말 기대돼.'라는 의미로 기대를 표현할 때 쓴다.
02 함께 축구를 하자는 A의 말에 B가 여동생을 돌봐야 한다고 말했으므로, 빈칸에는 거절하는 표현이 들어가는 것이 알맞다.
03 ④ 수학 숙제를 도와줄 수 있는지 묻는 말에 수락의 말(Of course.)을 한 후 봉사 활동을 해야 한다고 거절의 이유를 말하는 것은 어색하다.
　|해석| ① A: 너는 수학 숙제를 끝냈니?
　　B: 아직 끝내지 못했어. 수학은 어려워.
　② A: 나는 박물관을 방문할 거야. 나와 함께 가고 싶니?
　　B: 응, 가고 싶어.
　③ A: 너는 오늘 행복해 보여. 무슨 일이니?
　　B: 나는 매우 신이 나. 나는 드론을 날리는 것을 배울 거야.
　④ A: 네가 내 수학 숙제를 좀 도와줄래?
　　B: 물론이야. 나는 봉사 활동을 해야 해.
　⑤ A: 너는 축제에서 무엇을 할 거니?
　　B: 나는 퍼레이드를 볼 거야. 나는 그것을 보는 게 정말 기대돼.
04 우리 록 밴드에 온 걸 환영한다는 말(C)에 고맙다면서 함께 연주하는 공연이 기대된다는 말(A)이 이어진 후, 새로운 기타 연주자가 생겨서 신난다는 말(D)에, 금요일에 보자고 답하는(B) 흐름이 자연스럽다.
05 밑줄 친 우리말을 영어로 옮기면 I'm really looking forward to making it.이 되므로, 사용하지 않는 단어는 동사원형인 make이다.
06 그의 이야기가 영화로 만들어졌다는 내용의 주어진 문장은 영화에 대한 대화가 시작되는 부분인 ③에 와야 한다. ③ 다음 문장의 it이 주어진 문장의 영화를 가리킨다.
07 ⑤ 지호가 Ann에게 영화를 함께 봐도 되는지 묻자 Ann이 Sure.(물론이야.)라고 수락의 말을 했으므로, Ann은 토요일에 지호와 함께 영화를 볼 것이다.
08 ⓐ a boy를 선행사로 하는 주격 관계대명사 who가 와야 한다. who became a famous dancer가 a boy를 수식한다.
　ⓑ '누구'라는 의미의 의문사 Who가 와야 한다.
09 ④ Tony가 가장 좋아하는 배우는 언급되지 않아 알 수 없다.
10 기대를 나타내는 표현 I'm really looking forward to ~를 사용하여 문장을 완성한다.
11 (1) B가 기타를 3년 동안 쳤다고 답하는 것으로 보아, (1)에는 상대방이 기타를 치는 법을 알고 있음을 확인차 묻는 표현이 알맞다.
　(2) B가 A의 요청을 거절하면서 손을 다쳤다고 거절의 이유를 말하는 것으로 보아, (2)에는 기타를 쳐 줄 수 있는지 부탁하는 표현이 알맞다.

(3) 손을 다쳤다는 말에 유감을 나타내는 표현이 알맞다.

12 Alex는 3년 동안 기타를 쳤다고 했다.

G Grammar 핵심 노트 1 p. 22

QUICK CHECK

1 (1) were (2) would (3) were

2 (1) would (2) knew (3) 옳음

1 |해석| (1) John이 여기 있다면, 그는 그 일을 할 수 있을 텐데.
(2) 오늘이 토요일이라면, 나는 공원에 갈 텐데.
(3) 내가 충분히 크다면, 나는 롤러코스터를 탈 수 있을 텐데.

2 |해석| (1) 그녀가 시간이 더 있다면, 그녀는 그녀의 부모님을 찾아뵐 텐데.
(2) 그가 네 전화번호를 안다면, 그는 너에게 전화할 텐데.
(3) Bob이 피곤하지 않다면, 그는 그의 일을 끝낼 수 있을 텐데.

G Grammar 핵심 노트 2 p. 23

QUICK CHECK

1 (1) when to tell (2) where (3) what

2 (1) how to ride a bike (2) us when to arrive
(3) knows where to put

1 |해석| (1) 나는 언제 진실을 말해야 할지 몰랐다.
(2) 그는 그의 새 컴퓨터를 어디에 놓을지 결정했다.
(3) 나는 숙제가 많다. 나는 무엇을 먼저 해야 할지 모르겠다.

2 |해석| (1) 나는 자전거를 타는 법을 배웠다.
(2) Angela는 우리에게 언제 도착하는지 말하지 않았다.
(3) Tommy는 빈 병을 어디에 두는지 안다.

G Grammar 연습 문제 1 p. 24

A 1 would **2** lived **3** were **4** were **5** could

B 1 has → had **2** can → could
3 could fixed → could fix **4** have had → had

C 1 she could get a discount **2** If I had a million dollars
3 he would send me a letter

D 1 can't go shopping with Emma **2** had enough time
3 could go back in time

A |해석| 1. 내가 너라면, 나는 저 바지를 사지 않을 텐데.
2. 네가 여기 산다면, 나는 너를 매일 볼 수 있을 텐데.
3. 내가 새라면, 나는 구름으로 날아갈 텐데.
4. 그녀가 집에 있다면, 우리는 그녀를 방문할 수 있을 텐데.
5. 내게 충분한 우유가 있다면, 나는 남동생을 위해 쿠키를 좀 만들어 줄 수 있을 텐데.

B |해석| 1. 그녀가 날아다니는 신발을 가지고 있다면, 그녀는 하늘을 날 수 있을 텐데.
2. 일요일이라면, 우리는 캠핑을 갈 수 있을 텐데.
3. Robin이 여기 있다면, 그는 컴퓨터를 고칠 수 있을 텐데.
4. 내가 많은 돈을 가지고 있다면, 나는 그 건물을 살 수 있을 텐데.

D |해석| 1. 나는 피곤해서, Emma와 쇼핑을 갈 수 없다.
→ 내가 피곤하지 않다면, 나는 Emma와 쇼핑을 갈 수 있을 텐데.
2. 그들은 충분한 시간이 없어서, 방학 때 파리에 가지 않을 것이다.
→ 그들에게 충분한 시간이 있다면, 그들은 방학 때 파리에 갈 텐데.
3. 그녀는 타임머신이 없어서, 그녀는 과거로 돌아갈 수 없다.
→ 그녀에게 타임머신이 있다면, 그녀는 과거로 돌아갈 수 있을 텐데.

G Grammar 연습 문제 2 p. 25

A 1 to go **2** how **3** where **4** when **5** what

B 1 when to ask **2** where I should put

C 1 how to use this tool **2** where to buy apples
3 what to eat for lunch
4 when to bring the birthday cake

D 1 how to solve the problem **2** what to do today
3 when to turn right **4** where to stay this summer

A |해석| 1. 나는 방학 동안 어디에 갈지 결정하지 못했다.
2. 그는 나에게 토마토 스파게티를 요리하는 법을 가르쳐 주었다.
3. 나는 Laura를 만날 필요가 있다. 너는 그녀를 어디에서 찾을 수 있는지 아니?
4. 실례합니다. 저에게 언제 비행기에 탑승할지 말해 주실 수 있나요?
5. 도움이 필요한 아프리카의 아이들을 위해 무엇을 해야 할지 이야기해 보자.

B |해석| 1. 나는 내가 언제 그녀에게 그 질문을 해야 하는지 알고 싶다.
2. 나에게 이 탁자를 어디에 두어야 하는지 말해 주세요.

G Grammar 실전 TEST pp. 26~29

01 ③ **02** ③ **03** ② **04** ③ **05** ③ **06** ①, ④ **07** ③
08 ⑤ **09** can → could **10** ① **11** ② **12** ③ **13** ②

14 ⑤　15 ⑤　16 when she should take　17 ④　18 ③
19 ③　20 ③　21 ②　22 ③　23 ③

[서술형]
24 (1) how to fix this machine
　　너는 이 기계를 고치는 방법을(어떻게 고치는지) 아니?
　(2) where to go in New Zealand
　　뉴질랜드에서 어디에 갈지 결정하자.
　(3) the teacher what to do
　　나는 선생님께 다음에 무엇을 할지 물었다.
25 (1) If I were a super hero, I would(could) save people
　　and the world.
　(2) If it snowed a lot, I would(could) build a big
　　snowman.
　(3) If I understood French, I would(could) enjoy the
　　French movie.
26 The boy told me when to get off.
27 (1) had enough time, could eat breakfast
　(2) I were not tired, could play tennis with my dad
28 (1) He learned how to play the guitar.
　(2) If I had a spaceship, I would travel to Mars.
　(3) I don't know where to put this box.

01 현재 사실과 반대되는 상황을 가정하는 가정법 과거 문장으로 「If+주어(my uncle)+동사의 과거형(were) ~, 주어(I)+조동사의 과거형(would)+동사원형(be) ....」의 형태로 써야 하므로 빈칸에는 If가 알맞다.
　ㅣ해석ㅣ 나의 삼촌이 지금 나와 함께 있다면, 나는 행복할 텐데.
02 가정법 과거인 「If+주어+동사의 과거형 ~, 주어+조동사의 과거형+동사원형 ....」의 형태가 되어야 하므로, If I knew the answer가 알맞다.
　ㅣ해석ㅣ 내가 답을 안다면, 네게 말해 줄 텐데.
03 '~하는 방법'이나 '어떻게 ~할지'는 「how+to부정사」로 나타낸다.
　ㅣ해석ㅣ ・ 나에게 이 카메라를 어떻게 사용하는지 말해 줄래?
　　・ 너는 그곳에 어떻게 가야 하는지 아니?
04 가정법 과거인 「If+주어+동사의 과거형 ~, 주어+조동사의 과거형+동사원형 ....」의 형태가 되어야 하므로, if절의 동사는 과거형 had가 알맞다.
　ㅣ해석ㅣ 네가 더 좋은 카메라를 가지고 있다면, 너는 더 나은 사진을 찍을 수 있을 텐데.
05 주어진 우리말을 영어로 옮기면 Can you tell me where to go?이므로 여섯 번째로 오는 단어는 to이다.
06 If I were you로 보아 가정법 과거 문장이 되어야 하므로, 빈칸은 「주어+조동사의 과거형(would/could 등)+동사원형 ....」의 형태가 되어야 한다. 조동사 will이나 won't(= will not)는 쓰일 수 없다.
07 의문사 중에서 why는 「why+to부정사」 형태로 쓰지 않는다.
08 가정법 과거 문장은 「If+주어(I)+동사의 과거형(had) ~, 주어(I)+조동사의 과거형(could)+동사원형(be) ....」의 형태로 쓴다.
09 직설법 현재를 가정법 과거로 바꾼 문장으로, 가정법 과거는 「If+주어

+동사의 과거형 ~, 주어+조동사의 과거형+동사원형 ....」의 형태가 되어야 한다. 따라서 조동사 can은 과거형인 could로 고쳐 써야 한다.
　ㅣ해석ㅣ 나는 바쁘기 때문에 너와 점심을 먹을 수 없어.
　→ 내가 바쁘지 않다면, 너와 점심을 먹을 수 있을 텐데.
10 B가 기계를 사용하는 방법에 대해 설명하고 있으므로 빈칸에는 '어떻게 ~할지, ~하는 방법'이라는 의미의 「how+to부정사」가 알맞다.
　ㅣ해석ㅣ A: 너는 이 기계를 어떻게 사용하는지 아니?
　B: 응. 먼저, 빨간색 단추를 눌러.
11 B가 A에게 사야 할 물건에 대해 말해 주고 있으므로 빈칸에는 '무엇을 ~할지'라는 의미의 「what+to부정사」가 알맞다.
　ㅣ해석ㅣ A: 나에게 식료품 가게에서 무엇을 사야 할지 말해 줘.
　B: 너는 사과와 양파를 좀 사야 해.
12 직설법 현재를 가정법 과거로 바꾼 문장으로, 가정법 과거는 「If+주어+동사의 과거형 ~, 주어+조동사의 과거형+동사원형 ....」의 형태가 되어야 한다. 또한 가정법 과거는 현재 사실과 반대되는 상황을 가정하므로, 의미상 직설법 현재의 긍정은 부정으로, 부정은 긍정으로 바꿔 써야 한다.
　ㅣ해석ㅣ Chris는 독감에 걸려서 박물관에 갈 수 없어.
　→ Chris가 독감에 걸려 있지 않으면, 그는 박물관에 갈 수 있을 텐데.
13 가정법 과거는 「If+주어+동사의 과거형 ~, 주어+조동사의 과거형+동사원형 ....」의 형태로 쓰므로, ②는 조동사의 과거형인 would가 되어야 한다.
　ㅣ해석ㅣ 내가 너라면, 나는 내 생일 파티에 그를 초대할 텐데.
14 '언제 ~할지'라는 의미의 「when+to부정사」를 사용하여 when to start playing이 들어가는 것이 알맞다.
15 ⑤ 가정법 과거 문장이 되어야 하므로, 조동사 will을 과거형 would로 고쳐 써야 한다.
　ㅣ해석ㅣ ① 네가 여기에 산다면, 우리는 행복할 텐데.
　② 우리는 Paul을 위해 무엇을 살지 결정하지 못했다.
　③ Nicole에게 열쇠가 있다면, 그녀는 이 상자를 열 수 있을 텐데.
　④ 나에게 봉사 활동을 어떻게 하는지 말해 줄 수 있니?
　⑤ 내가 슈퍼맨이라면, 나는 위험에 처한 사람들을 구할 텐데.
16 「의문사+to부정사」는 「의문사+주어+should+동사원형」으로 바꿔 쓸 수 있다.
　ㅣ해석ㅣ 그녀는 약을 언제 복용해야 하는지 알지 못한다.
17 현재 사실의 반대를 나타내는 가정법 과거 문장이므로, 「If+주어(I)+동사의 과거형(had) ~, 주어(I)+조동사의 과거형(could)+동사원형(go) ....」의 형태가 되어야 한다.
　ㅣ해석ㅣ 나는 시간이 많지 않다. 내게 충분한 시간이 있다면, 나는 너와 함께 하이킹을 하러 갈 수 있을 텐데.
18 주어진 단어들을 배열하면 We haven't decided where to stay.가 된다. 「where+to부정사」가 haven't decided의 목적어로 쓰인 문장이다.
19 ③은 실제 일어날 수 있는 일을 나타내는 조건문으로, if절의 빈칸에는 현재시제인 be동사 are가 알맞다. 나머지는 현재 사실과 반대되거나 실제 일어날 가능성이 없는 것을 가정하는 가정법 과거 문장으로, 가정법 과거에서는 if절에 be동사가 쓰일 때 주로 were를 쓴다.

|해석| ① 내가 더 젊다면, 나는 해외에 갈 텐데.

② 내가 부자라면, 나는 우주를 여행할 텐데.

③ 네가 지금 바쁘다면, 나는 나중에 들를게.

④ 그녀가 바쁘지 않다면, 그녀는 나의 가족을 방문할 수 있을 텐데.

⑤ 그 컴퓨터가 더 싸다면, 나는 그것을 살 텐데.

20 첫 번째 문장: '~하는 방법'은 「how+to부정사」로 나타내므로 how to joining을 how to join으로 고쳐야 한다.

네 번째 문장: 가정법 과거는 「If+주어+동사의 과거형 ~, 주어+조동사의 과거형+동사원형 .....」의 형태로 나타내므로, 조동사 will을 과거형 would로 고쳐야 한다.

|해석| • 나는 노래 동아리에 가입하는 법을 알고 싶다.

• 우리는 그 소녀에게 지하철을 어디에서 타는지 물어보았다.

• 내게 시간이 더 있다면, 나는 숙제를 끝마칠 텐데.

• Peter가 피곤하지 않다면, 그는 그 모임에 올 텐데.

21 「If+주어(I)+동사의 과거형(were) ~, 주어(I)+조동사의 과거형(would)+동사원형(make) .....」의 형태로 이루어진 가정법 과거 문장이다.

|해석| 내가 발명가라면, 나는 요술 램프를 만들 텐데.

22 끓는 물에 넣어 요리하라는 말로 보아, 첫 번째 빈칸에는 달걀을 어떻게 요리하는지(how to cook) 말해 달라고 하는 것이 알맞다. 10분 후에 달걀을 꺼내라는 말로 보아, 두 번째 빈칸에는 달걀을 언제 꺼내는지(when to take out) 알려 달라고 하는 것이 알맞다.

|해석| A: 엄마, 저는 달걀을 요리할 거예요. 저에게 그것들을 <u>어떻게 요리하는지</u> 말해 주세요.

B: 달걀을 끓는 물에 넣어 요리하렴.

A: 알겠어요. 저에게 달걀을 <u>언제 꺼내는지</u> 알려 주세요.

B: 10분 후에 달걀을 꺼내렴.

A: 알겠어요. 고마워요, 엄마.

23 ③ 주절 「주어+조동사의 과거형(would)+동사원형(go)」의 형태로 보아 가정법 과거 문장이므로, if절은 「If+주어(it)+동사의 과거형(were)」이 되어야 한다. (→ were)

|해석| ① Aron은 어디로 여행을 갈지 결정할 수 없었다.

② 여행을 위해 무엇을 싸야 하는지 내게 알려 줘.

③ 날이 화창하면, 나는 낚시를 하러 갈 텐데.

④ 내게 시간이 있다면, 나는 너를 학교에 내려 줄 텐데.

⑤ 내가 왕이라면, 나는 내 나라를 더 아름답게 만들 텐데.

24 (1) how+to부정사: ~하는 방법, 어떻게 ~할지

(2) where+to부정사: 어디에 ~할지

(3) what+to부정사: 무엇을 ~할지

25 현재 사실과 반대되거나 실제 일어날 가능성이 없는 것을 가정하는 가정법 과거는 「If+주어+동사의 과거형 ~, 주어+조동사의 과거형(would/could)+동사원형 .....」의 형태로 쓴다.

26 「told+간접목적어(me)+직접목적어」 형태의 4형식 문장을 완성한다. '언제 ~할지'라는 의미의 「when+to부정사(to get off)」를 직접목적어로 쓴다.

27 직설법 현재의 문장을 가정법 과거 문장으로 바꿔 쓴다. 가정법 과거는 「If+주어+동사의 과거형 ~, 주어+조동사의 과거형(could)+동사원형 .....」의 형태로 쓴다.

|해석| (1) 나는 충분한 시간이 없어서 아침을 먹을 수 없다.

(2) 나는 피곤해서 아빠와 테니스를 칠 수 없다.

28 (1) '~하는 방법'을 뜻하는 「how+to부정사」를 문장의 목적어로 쓴다.

(2) 가정법 과거 문장은 「If+주어(I)+동사의 과거형(had) ~, 주어(I)+조동사의 과거형(would)+동사원형(travel) .....」의 형태로 쓴다.

(3) '어디에 ~할지'를 뜻하는 「where+to부정사」를 문장의 목적어로 쓴다.

Ⓡ Reading 빈칸 채우기   pp. 32~33

01 are rolling down   **02** happy and thrilled

03 I were, would fly   **04** look around   **05** one another

06 has just finished   **07** None of   **08** long journey

09 a violinist   **10** is it called   **11** from a landfill

12 known as   **13** Most of us   **14** a huge landfill

15 a giant landfill   **16** are poor

17 many hopes and dreams   **18** when we met

19 an environmental educator   **20** teach us music

21 a few musical instruments   **22** afford to buy

23 didn't give up   **24** make musical instruments

25 put this idea into practice   **26** made violins

27 turned, into   **28** another problem   **29** how to play

30 didn't even know   **31** with great patience

32 Step by step   **33** that we played

34 mostly out of tune   **35** the most beautiful music

36 in our hearts   **37** gathered to practice   **38** One day

39 have a concert   **40** in front of   **41** They love

42 send back music

Ⓡ Reading 바른 어휘·어법 고르기   pp. 34~35

01 are   **02** thrilled   **03** were   **04** look   **05** are

06 giving   **07** come   **08** has been   **09** and   **10** called

11 because   **12** known   **13** are   **14** is   **15** itself

16 Many   **17** weren't   **18** when   **19** an   **20** us music

21 a few   **22** to buy   **23** didn't give up   **24** from

25 into   **26** made   **27** into   **28** another

29 how to play   **30** how   **31** patience   **32** to make

33 that   **34** mostly   **35** to   **36** hearts   **37** to practice

38 us some great news   **39** have   **40** in front of

41 love   **42** trash, music

01 ×, are rolling up → are rolling down

02 ×, thrilling → thrilled　　03 ×, As → If　　04 ○　　05 ○

06 ×, giving a big hand us → giving us a big hand　　07 ○

08 ×, short → long　　09 ○　　10 ×, How → Why

11 ×, make of → are made of　　12 ×, what → why　　13 ○

14 ×, There are → There is　　15 ×, it → itself

16 ×, is → are　　17 ×, much → many　　18 ○

19 ×, environment → environmental

20 ×, wanted teaching → wanted to teach

21 ×, There was → There were　　22 ×, could → couldn't

23 ○　　24 ×, for objects → with objects

25 ×, put this idea into participation → put this idea into practice　　26 ×, into → from　　27 ○　　28 ○

29 ×, how to playing → how to play

30 ×, how reading → how to read　　31 ○

32 ×, Step to step → Step by step

33 ×, forget → remember

34 ×, most out of tune → mostly out of tune

35 ×, most beautiful → the most beautiful　　36 ○

37 ×, gathered practice → gathered to practice

38 ×, told some great news us → told us some great news　　39 ○　　40 ○　　41 ×, don't love → love

42 ×, sends trash us → sends us trash

01 ④　　02 (A) were　(B) giving　　03 ⑤　　04 ③　　05 ②

06 landfill　　07 ③　　08 ②　　09 ④　　10 ③　　11 ①

12 musical instruments　　13 ④　　14 ②　　15 ③　　16 ③

17 ①　　18 ⑤　　19 ③　　20 ④　　21 ①, ③

[서술형]

22 온 마을에 악기가 단지 몇 개뿐이었고 새 악기를 살 형편이 안 되었다는 것

23 A talented man named Nicholas was able to put this idea into practice.

24 (1) Andrea plays the violin (in the orchestra).

　　(2) Their musical instruments are made of objects from a landfill.

25 the first piece of music that we played

26 (1) No one knew how to play musical instruments.

　　(2) One day, Favio told us some great news. / One day, Favio told some great news to us.

27 We are going to have a concert, a real concert!

01 ④ 기쁨의 눈물을 흘리고 있고 사람들이 큰 박수를 보내고 있다고 한 것으로 보아, 글쓴이의 심정은 기쁘고 황홀할 것이다.

|해석| ① 피곤하고 축 쳐진　② 걱정스럽고 화가 난

③ 슬프고 겁먹은　④ 기쁘고 황홀한

⑤ 지루하고 졸린

02 (A) 실제 일어날 가능성이 없는 일을 가정하는 가정법 과거 문장이다. 가정법 과거에서 if절이 be동사일 경우 주어의 인칭과 수에 관계없이 주로 were를 쓴다.

(B) 등위접속사 and에 의해 is standing과 병렬을 이루고 있으므로 giving이 알맞다. 반복을 피하기 위해 is가 생략된 형태이다.

03 글의 흐름상 this day는 '연주회를 끝마치고 사람들(청중들)에게 큰 박수를 받는 날'을 의미한다.

04 ③은 앞 문장의 내용(Why is it called the Recycled Orchestra?)을 가리키고, 나머지는 the Recycled Orchestra를 가리킨다.

05 악기가 쓰레기 매립지에서 온 물건들로 만들어져 있다는 의미가 되도록 수동태(be동사+과거분사)가 알맞다. be made of는 '~로 만들어지다'라는 의미이다.

06 '땅속에 쓰레기가 묻힌 곳'은 landfill(쓰레기 매립지)을 의미한다.

07 ⓐ의 itself는 Cateura를 강조하는 강조 용법의 재귀대명사이다. 같은 용법으로 쓰인 것은 ⓑ와 ⓒ이다. ⓐ와 ⓓ는 목적어로 쓰인 재귀 용법의 재귀대명사이다.

|해석| ⓐ 우리는 우리 자신들을 거울 속에서 보았다.

ⓑ 나의 아버지께서 직접 이 피자를 만드셨다.

ⓒ 지난밤에 내 눈으로 직접 유령을 보았다.

ⓓ 그녀는 "나는 무엇을 해야 할까?"라고 그녀 자신에게 물었다.

08 ⓑ가 포함된 문장 앞에서 카테우라 마을에 꿈과 희망이 많지 않았던 상황을 설명하고 있다. ⓑ가 포함된 문장에서는 Favio Chávez를 만났을 때 모든 것이 바뀌기 시작했다고 했으므로, 빈칸에는 앞 내용에 반대되는 역접을 나타내는 말이 알맞다.

09 ④ 카테우라에는 희망이 많지 않았다고 했다.

10 온 마을에 악기가 단지 몇 개뿐이고 새 악기를 살 형편이 안 되었다는 문제가 있음에도 Favio 선생님이 포기하지 않았다는 흐름이 되는 것이 자연스러우므로 주어진 문장은 ③에 들어가는 것이 알맞다. 또한 ③ 다음에 문제점의 해결 방안이 제시되고 있다.

11 「teach+간접목적어(us)+직접목적어(music)」는 '~에게 …을 가르치다'라는 의미로, 「teach+직접목적어(music)+to+간접목적어(us)」로 표현할 수도 있다.

12 ones는 앞 문장의 musical instruments를 가리킨다.

13 ⓒ put ~ into practice: ~을 실행에 옮기다

ⓓ turn A into B: A를 B로 바꾸다

14 ② 마을에 악기는 몇 개밖에 없었다고 했다.

15 악기를 연주하는 법도 악보를 읽을 줄도 몰랐던 우리를 Favio 선생님이 인내심을 가지고 가르쳐서(B), 점차 우리는 악기로 소리를 만들어 내기 시작했고(D), 연주했던 첫 곡을 아직도 기억한다는 말(C)이 이어진 후, 그 곡은 매우 짧고 대부분이 음이 맞지 않았다는(A) 흐름이 되는 것이 자연스럽다.

16 ③ step by step: 점차로

17 연주했던 첫 곡이 매우 짧고 대부분 음이 맞지 않았지만 우리에게는 가장 아름다운 곡이었고 그때부터 매일 연습하러 모였다는 내용으로 보아, '새로운 희망'을 느꼈다는 내용이 되는 것이 알맞다.

|해석| ① 새로운 희망　② 갑작스러운 고통

　③ 깊은 슬픔　④ 상실감　⑤ 큰 실망

18 ⓑ와 ⑤는 '~하기 위해서'라는 의미의 목적을 나타내는 부사적 용법의 to부정사이다.

　① 목적어로 쓰인 명사적 용법의 to부정사

　② pen을 수식하는 형용사적 용법의 to부정사

　③ 보어로 쓰인 명사적 용법의 to부정사

　④ 감정의 원인을 나타내는 부사적 용법의 to부정사

　|해석| ① 그들은 일찍 떠나기로 결정했다.

　② Amy는 쓸 펜이 없다.

　③ 그의 꿈은 영화배우가 되는 것이다.

　④ 나는 너를 다시 보게 되어 매우 기뻐.

　⑤ Harry는 뉴스를 보기 위해 텔레비전을 켰다.

19 (A) 주어인 it이 Recycled Orchestra로 불리는 것으로 수동태(be동사+과거분사)가 되어야 하므로 과거분사 called가 알맞다.

　(B) Most of us가 주어인데, of 뒤에 복수 대명사 us가 왔으므로 복수 동사 are가 알맞다.

　(C) 뒤에 단수 명사(구) a huge landfill이 왔으므로 단수 동사 is가 알맞다. there is 뒤에는 단수 명사가 오고, there are 뒤에는 복수 명사가 온다.

20 ④ 카테우라 자체가 거대한 쓰레기 매립지라고 할 수 있다고 했고, 마을에 꿈과 희망이 많지 않았다고 했으므로, 글의 흐름상 카테우라 마을의 많은 사람들이 부유한(rich) 것이 아니라 가난하다고(poor) 하는 것이 자연스럽다.

21 Andrea는 바이올린 연주자라고 했으며, 파라과이의 카테우라 출신이라고 했다.

22 a big problem이 무엇인지 바로 뒤에서 설명하고 있다.

23 named Nicholas가 주어인 A talented man을 뒤에서 수식하고, '~할 수 있었다'라는 뜻의 was able to 뒤에는 동사원형을 쓴다. '~을 실행에 옮기다'라는 뜻의 put ~ into practice를 사용하여 문장을 완성한다.

24 (1) Andrea는 바이올린 연주자라고 했다.

　(2) 그들의 악기는 쓰레기 매립지에서 나온 물건들로 만들어져 있다고 했다.

　|해석| (1) Andrea는 오케스트라에서 어떤 악기를 연주하는가?

　(2) 그들의 악기는 무엇으로 만들어져 있는가?

25 It은 앞 문장에 나온 the first piece of music that we played(우리가 연주했던 첫 곡)를 가리킨다.

26 (1) '~하는 방법'은 「how+to부정사」로 나타내므로 how to playing을 how to play로 고쳐 써야 한다.

　(2) 「told+간접목적어(us)+직접목적어(some great news)」의 어순이 되어야 하므로 to를 삭제한다. 또는 「told+직접목적어(some great news)+to+간접목적어(us)」의 어순으로 쓸 수도 있다.

27 Favio 선생님이 전한 엄청난 소식은 공연을 하게 될 것이라는 것이다.

|해석| A(Favio): 안녕하세요, 여러분! 여러분에게 말할 좋은 소식이 있어요.

B: 그 소식이 뭔데요?

A: 우리는 공연을, 진짜 공연을 하게 될 거예요!

C: 정말요? 믿을 수가 없어요!

 기타 지문 실전 TEST p.45

01 ③　**02** ②　**03** ①　**04** ③　**05** If I had a time machine, I would go to meet you!　**06** ①

01 Andrea가 기분이 황홀하다고 답하고 있으므로 빈칸에는 기분을 묻는 표현이 알맞다.

|해석| ① 당신은 왜 그것을 좋아하나요?

② 어떻게 지냈나요?

③ 지금 기분이 어때요?

④ 제가 무엇을 도와드릴까요?

⑤ 당신은 내가 무엇을 하길 원하나요?

02 ② 주어인 the orchestra가 the Recycled Orchestra로 불리는 것이므로 수동태(be동사+과거분사)가 되도록 과거분사 called로 써야 한다.

③ 문맥상 '그것은 ~이기 때문이다.'라는 의미를 나타내는 That's because ~.가 되는 것이 알맞다. That's why ~.는 '그것은 ~한 이유이다.'라는 의미이다.

03 ① Andrea는 방금 연주회를 끝냈다고 했으므로, 연주회 후에 인터뷰를 하고 있음을 알 수 있다.

04 ③ 이 편지글에서의 saved는 '구했다'라는 의미로 쓰였다.

05 가정법 과거 문장이므로 「If+주어+동사의 과거형 ~, 주어+조동사의 과거형+동사원형 .....」의 형태가 되도록 영작한다.

06 이 글은 병 셰이커를 만드는 방법을 설명하는 글이다.

|해석| ① 병 셰이커를 만드는 방법

② 왜 우리는 병을 재활용해야 하는가

③ 병을 사용하는 독특한 예술 작품들

④ 다른 종류의 병 셰이커들

⑤ 병 셰이커를 장식하는 방법들

STEP B

Words 고득점 맞기 pp.46~47

01 ② 02 ② 03 ③ 04 save 05 piece 06 ⑤
07 out of tune 08 ⑤ 09 ④ 10 ① 11 (1) surprised
(2) boring (3) excited (4) worried 12 (1) educator (2)
performance (3) environmental 13 ⑤ 14 ②

01 joy와 pleasure가 '기쁨'이라는 의미의 유의어 관계이므로, '거대한'이
라는 의미의 유의어 관계인 ②가 알맞다.

02 landfill(쓰레기 매립지)은 '땅속에 쓰레기(waste)가 묻힌 곳'을 의미
한다.

03 일요일에 집에 있지 않고 일반적으로(mostly) 나가서 논다는 의미가
되는 것이 알맞다.

|해석| 수미는 일요일에 집에 머무르는 것을 좋아하지 않는다. 그녀는
일요일에 일반적으로 나가서 논다.

04 빈칸에 '구하다, (시간을) 절약하다, 저축하다'라는 의미가 순서대로 필
요하므로 save가 공통으로 들어가는 것이 알맞다.

|해석| • 우리는 위험에 처한 동물들을 구해야 한다.

• 당신이 이 길로 간다면 두 시간 정도를 절약할 거예요.

• 나는 새 스마트폰을 사기 위해 내 용돈을 저축하려고 계획한다.

05 빈칸에 '(미술·음악 등의) 작품, 조각'이라는 의미가 순서대로 필요하므
로 piece가 공통으로 들어가는 것이 알맞다.

|해석| • 이 음악 작품에는 강렬한 첼로 소리가 있다.

• 나는 케이크를 한 조각 더 먹을 거야.

06 ⑤ 문맥상 '~할 수 있었다'의 의미가 되도록 was able to를 써야 한다.

① give ~ a big hand: ~에게 큰 박수를 보내다

② take care of: ~을 돌보다

③ turn off: ~을 끄다

④ step by step: 점차로

|해석| ① 이 위대한 과학자에게 큰 박수를 보내 줍시다.

② Kevin은 방과 후에 그의 아픈 남동생을 돌봤다.

③ 방을 나갈 때 불을 꺼라.

④ 점차로, 우리 밴드는 아름다운 소리를 만들어 내기 시작했다.

07 out of tune: 음이 맞지 않는

08 첫 번째 빈칸에는 educator(교육자)가 들어가고, 두 번째 빈칸에는
respect(존경하다)가 들어간다. 세 번째 빈칸에는 stick(붙이다)이 들
어가고, 네 번째 빈칸에는 gathered(모였다)가 들어간다.

|해석| • Anne Sullivan은 훌륭한 교육자였다.

• 우리 동아리 부원들은 Kelly를 동아리 회장으로서 존경한다.

• 우리는 생일 풍선을 벽에 붙이기 위해 테이프를 사용했다.

• 나의 학급 친구들은 지난주 일요일에 공원을 청소하기 위해 모였다.

09 ④ practice는 '실행, 실천'이라는 뜻으로, '불평 없이 침착을 유지하고
지연이나 고통을 받아들이는 능력'은 patience(인내심)에 대한 뜻풀
이다.

|해석| ① ~할 형편이 되다: 무언가에 대한 값을 지불할 수 있다

② 뺨: 눈 아래쪽 얼굴의 양옆

③ 무인 항공기, 드론: 조종사 없이 지상의 누군가에 의해 조종되는 항
공기

⑤ 환경의: 사람과 동물, 식물이 살고 있는 자연적인 환경과 관련이 있는

10 Brian이 결석한 이유를 물었으므로 그가 무거운 상자를 옮기다가 등
을 다쳤다(hurt)고 말하는 흐름이 자연스럽다.

|해석| A: Brian이 오늘 학교를 결석했어. 너는 그 이유를 아니?

B: 응. 그는 무거운 상자를 옮기다가 등을 다쳤어.

A: 오, 그 말을 들어서 유감이야.

11 (1), (3), (4) 감정을 느끼는 주체(I)가 주어이므로 과거분사형 형용사를
쓴다.

(2) 감정을 느끼게 하는 상황(His speech)이 주어이므로 현재분사형
형용사(boring)를 쓴다.

|해석| (1) 나는 누군가 문을 세게 두드렸을 때 정말 놀랐다.

(2) 그의 연설이 너무 지루해서 나는 거의 잠들 뻔했다.

(3) 나는 이번 주말에 놀이공원에 갈 것이다. 나는 새로운 롤러코스터를
탈 거라 신이 난다.

(4) 내 남동생의 팔이 부러져서 나는 그가 걱정된다.

12 (1) 「동사 – 명사(행위자)」의 관계이다.

(2) 「동사 – 명사」의 관계이다.

(3) 「명사 – 형용사」의 관계이다.

13 put ~ into practice: ~을 실행에 옮기다

from then on: 그때부터 (쭉)

take part in: ~에 참가하다

|해석| • 나는 네가 네 계획을 실행에 옮기는 것을 도와줄 것이다.

• Andy는 또 거짓말을 했다. 그때부터 우리는 더이상 그를 신뢰하지
않는다.

• 200명 이상의 학생들이 그 마라톤에 참가할 것이다.

14 '다양한 종류의 많은 악기를 연주하는 음악가들의 그룹'은 orchestra
(오케스트라, 관현악단)에 대한 설명이다.

|해석| ① 이 음악 작품을 잘 들어 보세요.

② 내 여동생은 학교 오케스트라에서 플루트를 연주한다.

③ 너는 기호가 결승 골을 넣었을 때 기쁨의 눈물을 봤니?

④ 그 팀이 금메달을 딴 후에, 그 도시는 그들을 위한 퍼레이드를 했다.

⑤ 나의 동아리 부원들은 봉사 활동을 위해 매달 아동 병원에 간다.

Listen & Speak 고득점 맞기 pp. 50~51

01 ②, ⑤ 02 ③ 03 ⓐ was made ⓑ watching 04 ④
05 ② 06 ①, ⑤

[서술형]

07 (1) Not yet.
   (2) I'd love to, but I can't.
08 It's about a boy who became a famous dancer.
09 musical, this weekend, favorite actor, has volunteer work this weekend
10 We're excited to have a new guitar player.
11 (1) I'm going to play a water balloon game
   (2) to playing it
   (3) I'm going to have the longest hot dog

01 방과 후에 박물관에 같이 가고 싶은지 묻는 A의 제안에 B가 숙제를 해야 한다고 말하고 있으므로, 빈칸에는 거절하는 표현이 들어가야 한다.
02 ③ Jim Abbott은 오른손 없이 태어났다고 했다.
   |해석| ① A: 지호는 무엇을 읽고 있니?
   B: 그는 Jim Abbott에 관한 책을 읽고 있어.
   ② A: Jim Abbott은 야구 선수니?
   B: 응, 맞아.
   ③ A: Jim Abbott은 오른손 없이 태어났니?
   B: 아니, 그는 사고 때문에 오른손을 잃었어.
   ④ A: Jim Abbott에 관한 영화의 제목이 무엇이니?
   B: 그것은 "우리의 영웅"이야.
   ⑤ A: 지호는 이번 주 토요일에 무엇을 할 예정이니?
   B: 그는 Ann과 함께 영화를 볼 예정이야.
03 ⓐ 주어인 그의 이야기(His story)가 영화로 만들어진 것이므로 수동태(be동사+과거분사)로 써야 한다.
   ⓑ 기대를 나타내는 표현인 I'm really looking forward to ~.에서 to는 전치사이므로 to 뒤에 동사가 올 경우 동명사 형태로 쓴다.
04 ④ B가 어제 체육 수업 중에 손을 다쳤다고 했는데, A가 그 말을 들어서 기쁘다고 말하는 것은 어색하다. 유감을 표현하는 I'm sorry to hear that. 등으로 말하는 것이 자연스럽다.
05 '~하는 동안'이라는 의미를 나타내는 접속사 while이 들어가야 한다.
06 ② Alex는 기타 치는 법을 안다.
   ③ Alex는 어제 체육 수업 중에 손을 다쳤다.
   ④ 노래 대회에서 자신이 노래하는 동안 기타를 연주해 달라는 수민이의 부탁에, Alex는 손을 다쳐서 안 된다고 거절했다.
07 (1) 수학 숙제를 끝냈냐는 물음에 대한 답으로 수학이 어렵다고 했고, 뒤에 상대방에게 숙제를 도와달라고 했으므로 아직 다 못했다는 말이 오는 것이 자연스럽다.
   (2) 수학 숙제를 도와달라는 말에 남동생을 돌봐야 한다고 했으므로, 빈칸에는 거절의 말이 들어가야 한다.
08 a boy는 사람을 나타내므로, 선행사가 사물일 때 쓰이는 관계대명사 which는 알맞지 않다. 사람을 선행사로 하는 주격 관계대명사 who로 고쳐야 한다.

09 Tony는 이번 주말에 뮤지컬 "빌리 엘리어트"를 볼 것이며, 이 뮤지컬의 주연 배우는 Linda가 가장 좋아하는 배우인 Jason Kim이다. Linda는 이번 주말에 자원봉사 활동이 있어서 Tony와 뮤지컬을 볼 수 없다.
   |해석| Tony는 <u>이번 주말에</u> <u>뮤지컬</u> "빌리 엘리어트"를 볼 것이다. "빌리 엘리어트"의 주연 배우는 Jason Kim이다. 그는 Linda가 가장 좋아하는 배우이다. Linda는 <u>이번 주말에 자원봉사 활동이 있어서</u> Tony와 함께 갈 수 없다.
10 We're가 주어와 동사이고, 주어인 We가 신나는 감정을 느끼는 주체이므로 excited를 쓴다. 그 뒤에는 감정의 원인을 나타내는 to부정사구를 쓴다.
11 (1) James는 10시 30분에 물 풍선 게임을 할 것이다.
   (2) 기대를 나타내는 표현인 I'm really looking forward to ~.에서 to는 전치사이므로 뒤에는 동명사 형태로 쓴다.
   (3) 미나는 10시 30분에 가장 긴 핫도그를 먹을 것이다.

Grammar 고득점 맞기 pp. 52~54

01 ⑤ 02 ⑤ 03 ② 04 ④ 05 ③ 06 ④ 07 ④, ⑤
08 ③ 09 ② 10 ④ 11 ③ 12 ④

[서술형]

13 (1) He asked me when to have dinner.
   (2) I know where to find the map.
   (3) If he were here, he could fix the computer.
14 (모범답) I would send Daisy a letter
15 ⓑ , If my uncle were here, he would help me.
16 (1) I were rich, I could travel all around the world
   (2) she helped me, I could make a robot
   (3) he didn't play mobile games so much, he could read more books
17 (1) where to go
   (2) what to do
   (3) how to ride
   (4) when to leave

01 풍선을 문에 붙이라는 답으로 보아 빈칸에는 '어디에 붙일지'를 뜻하는 where to stick이 알맞다.
   |해석| A: 나에게 파티를 위한 풍선들을 <u>어디에 붙여야 할지</u> 말해 줘.
   B: 문에 붙여.
02 if절의 동사(were)로 보아 현재 사실과 반대되는 상황을 가정하는 가정법 과거의 문장이 되어야 한다. 가정법 과거의 주절의 동사는 「조동사의 과거형+동사원형」이 되어야 한다.
   |해석| A: 네가 백만장자라면 너는 무엇을 할 거니?
   B: 나는 아프리카에 병원을 지을 거야.
03 첫 번째 문장은 실제로 일어날 수 있는 일을 나타내는 조건문으로, 미

래를 나타낼 때 if절의 동사는 현재형(fails)으로 쓴다. 두 번째 문장은 가정법 과거로 if절의 동사는 과거형(had)으로 쓴다.

|해석| • 그녀가 시험에 실패한다면, 그녀의 삶은 많이 바뀔 것이다.
• 내가 노트북 컴퓨터를 가지고 있다면, 나는 도서관에 가지 않을 텐데.

04 '무엇을 먹을지'를 뜻할 때 「의문사+to부정사」를 사용하여 what to eat으로 쓴다.

|해석| 나는 점심으로 무엇을 먹을지 모르겠다.

05 '~하는 방법'은 「how+to부정사」로 나타내므로 ③에는 how가 들어가야 한다.

06 ④ 가정법 과거 문장이므로 if절의 동사는 과거형이 되어야 한다. 따라서 knew로 고쳐야 한다.

|해석| • 그 운전자는 나에게 어디에서 멈출지 물었다.
• 내가 너라면, 나는 빈 병을 버리지 않을 텐데.
• 나에게 이 앱을 사용하는 법을 알려 줄 수 있니?
• 그녀가 내 주소를 안다면, 그녀는 나에게 편지를 쓸 텐데.
• Austin의 키가 더 크다면, 그는 꼭대기 선반에 손이 닿을 수 있을 텐데.

07 ④ '무엇을 ~할지'는 「what+to부정사」로 나타내므로 what to 뒤에는 동사원형이 와야 한다. (sold → sell)
⑤ '어디서 ~할지'는 「where+to부정사」로 나타내므로 where to 뒤에는 동사원형이 와야 한다. (buying → buy)

08 ⓑ 의문사 why는 「의문사+to부정사」로 사용하지 않는다.
ⓓ 가정법 과거 문장이므로 주절에 조동사의 과거형이 와야 한다. (will → would)

|해석| ⓐ 누군가가 네 비밀을 안다면, 너는 화가 날 텐데.
ⓑ 나는 여러분에게 어려움에 처한 사람들을 왜 돕는지 말해 드리고 싶습니다.
ⓒ 그는 다음에 무엇을 말해야 할지 몰랐다.
ⓓ 내게 타임머신이 있다면, 나는 과거로 돌아가 세종대왕을 만날 텐데.

09 직설법 현재를 가정법 과거 문장으로 바꿀 때, 내용상 긍정은 부정으로, 부정은 긍정으로 바꿔야 한다는 점에 유의한다. 가정법 과거는 「If+주어+동사의 과거형 ~, 주어+조동사의 과거형+동사원형 .....」의 형태로 쓴다.

|해석| 내게 날아다니는 양탄자가 없어서 나는 전 세계를 여행할 수 없다.

10 ④ 앞의 if절의 동사가 과거형 were인 것으로 보아 가정법 과거 문장이 되어야 하므로, 주절에 쓰인 조동사 can을 과거형 could로 고쳐 써야 한다.

|해석| A: 나는 지금 배가 고파.
B: 나도 그래. 나는 토마토 스파게티가 먹고 싶어.
A: 너는 토마토 스파게티를 요리하는 법을 아니?
B: 아니, 몰라. 내가 훌륭한 요리사라면, 나는 맛있는 토마토 스파게티를 만들 수 있을 텐데.
A: 우리는 인터넷에서 조리법을 찾을 수 있어.
B: 네 말이 맞아. 지금 당장 인터넷에서 찾아보자.

11 ⓐ Mary의 생일 선물로 스마트폰 케이스를 사 줄 것이라고 했으므로, '무엇을 ~할지'를 뜻하는 「what+to부정사」가 들어간다.
ⓑ 뒤에서 Great 쇼핑몰에 괜찮은 가게가 있다고 했으므로, '어디서 ~

할지'를 뜻하는 「where+to부정사」가 들어간다.
ⓒ 뒤에서 쇼핑몰에 함께 가자고 했으므로, '어떻게 ~할지'를 뜻하는 「how+to부정사」가 들어가는 것이 알맞다.

|해석| A: 나는 Mary의 생일을 위해 무엇을 살지 결정하지 못했어. 너는 어때?
B: 나는 그녀에게 스마트폰 케이스를 사 줄 거야.
A: 그거 좋은 생각이구나.
B: 하지만 나는 그것을 사기 위해 어디로 가야 할지 모르겠어.
A: Great 쇼핑몰에 괜찮은 가게가 있어.
B: 정말? 그곳에 어떻게 가는지 나에게 말해 줄 수 있니?
A: 음, 우리 함께 가는 게 어떨까? 나도 그 몰을 둘러보고 싶어.
B: 좋아.

12 ④ 가정법 과거가 아닌 조건문으로 쓰인 문장이다. 가정법 과거는 현재 사실과 반대되는 상황을 가정하여 말하는 것으로, 「If+주어+동사의 과거형 ~, 주어+조동사의 과거형+동사원형 .....」의 형태로 쓴다.

|해석| ① 우리 비행편을 언제 예약할지 내게 말해 주세요.
② 그 이야기가 사실이라면, 사람들은 놀랄 텐데.
③ 나는 이 코트를 어디에 놓아야 할지 모르겠다.
④ 네가 먼저 그에게 사과한다면, 그는 너를 용서해 줄 거야.
⑤ 그는 파티에 무엇을 입어야 할지 결정하지 못했다.

13 (1) 「의문사(when)+to부정사(to have)」가 asked의 직접목적어가 되도록 문장을 배열한다.
(2) 「의문사(where)+to부정사(to find)」가 know의 목적어가 되도록 문장을 배열한다.
(3) 가정법 과거인 「If+주어(he)+동사의 과거형(were) ~, 주어(he)+조동사의 과거형(could)+동사원형(fix) .....」의 형태가 되도록 문장을 배열한다.

14 자신이 Mary라고 가정하고 가정법 과거 「If+주어+동사의 과거형 ~, 주어+조동사의 과거형+동사원형 .....」의 형태인 문장을 자유롭게 완성한다.

|해석| Mary는 요즘 걱정스럽다. 그녀의 가장 친한 친구인 Daisy가 그녀에게 말을 하지 않는다. Daisy는 심지어 그녀에게 인사도 하지 않는다. Mary는 무엇을 해야 할지 모르겠다. 당신이 Mary라면 어떻게 하겠는가?

15 ⓑ if절의 were로 보아 가정법 과거 문장이 되어야 하므로 조동사 will은 과거형 would로 고쳐 써야 한다.

|해석| ⓐ 그 안내문은 내 차를 어디에 주차해야 하는지 알려 주었다.
ⓑ 삼촌이 여기 계신다면, 나를 도와주실 텐데.
ⓒ 내가 돈이 많다면, 나는 이곳에 머물지 않을 텐데.
ⓓ 내 친구들과 나는 우리가 다음 날 무엇을 해야 하는지에 대해 이야기를 나누었다.

16 직설법 현재를 가정법 과거로 바꿔 쓸 때, 내용상 긍정은 부정으로, 부정은 긍정으로 바꿔 쓴다. 가정법 과거는 「If+주어+동사의 과거형 ~, 주어+조동사의 과거형+동사원형 .....」의 형태로 쓴다.

|해석| (1) 나는 부자가 아니라서 전 세계를 여행할 수 없다.
(2) 그녀가 나를 도와주지 않아서 나는 로봇을 만들 수 없다.
(3) 그는 모바일 게임을 너무 많이 해서 더 많은 책을 읽을 수 없다.

17 (1) 문맥상 '어디로 갈지'를 뜻하는 where to go가 알맞다.

(2) 문맥상 '무엇을 할지'를 뜻하는 what to do가 알맞다.

(3) 문맥상 '타는 방법, 어떻게 타는지'를 뜻하는 how to ride가 알맞다.

(4) 문맥상 '언제 떠날지'를 뜻하는 when to leave가 알맞다.

|해석| A: 너는 휴가 때 어디로 갈지 결정했니?

B: 응. 나는 제주도에 갈 거야. 하지만 나는 그곳에서 무엇을 할지 결정하지 못했어.

A: 나는 말을 타는 것이 매우 신이 난다고 들었어.

B: 정말? 그거 좋은 것 같은데, 나는 말을 타는 법을 몰라.

A: 그것에 관해서는 걱정하지 마. 직원이 도와줄 거야.

B: 네 말이 맞아. 너는 어때? 휴가 때 무엇을 할 거니?

A: 나는 부산을 방문하는 것을 생각 중이야.

B: 그거 좋겠다. 너는 언제 떠날 거니?

A: 나는 언제 떠날지 결정하지 못했어. 나는 먼저 프로젝트를 끝내야 해.

ⓡ Reading 고득점 맞기   pp.57~59

01 ① 02 ⑤ 03 ② 04 ② 05 ⑤ 06 ① 07 ③
08 ③ 09 ② 10 ② 11 ⑤

[서술형]

12 (1) will fly → would fly

(2) is hugging → are hugging

(3) given → giving

13 music, only a few musical instruments,
musical instruments with objects from the landfill,
into practice

14 Why is it called the Recycled Orchestra?

15 아무도 악기를 연주하는 법을 몰랐고, 악보를 읽는 법도 알지 못했다.

16 (1) It was very short and mostly out of tune.

(2) They felt a new hope (in their hearts).

(3) They gathered to practice every day.

---

01 ① 주어인 I가 감정을 느끼는 주체이므로 thrilling은 과거분사 형태의 형용사인 thrilled가 되어야 한다.

02 ⑤ 글쓴이는 자신들 중 누구도 이런 날이 올 거라고 예상하지 못했다고 했다.

03 첫 번째 단락은 Recycled Orchestra에 대해 설명하는 글인데 '오케스트라에는 여러 종류의 악기가 있다.'라는 ②는 글의 흐름과 관계없는 문장이다.

04 ⓐ be known as: ~로 알려지다

ⓑ 국가 앞에는 전치사 in을 쓴다.

05 ⑤ Andrea가 Favio Chávez 선생님을 언제 처음 만났는지는 글에 나와 있지 않다.

|해석| ① Andrea는 오케스트라에서 어떤 악기를 연주하는가?

② 그들의 악기는 무엇으로 만들어져 있는가?

③ Andrea는 어디 출신인가?

④ 몇몇 사람들이 카테우라에 대해 심지어 뭐라고 말하는가?

⑤ Andrea는 Favio Chávez를 언제 처음 만났는가?

06 Favio 선생님이 쓰레기 매립지에서 나온 물건들로 악기를 만들려고 한 것으로 보아 빈칸에는 그가 음악을 가르치고 싶어 했다는 내용이 들어가는 것이 알맞다.

|해석| ① 우리에게 음악을 가르치다 ② 우리에게 콘서트를 보여 주다

③ 우리를 위해 음악을 연주하다 ④ 우리를 위해 노래를 작곡하다

⑤ 악기를 만들다

07 (A) '약간, 몇 개의'라는 의미로 셀 수 있는 명사(musical instruments) 앞에 오는 수량형용사는 a few이다. a little은 셀 수 없는 명사 앞에 쓴다.

(B) afford는 to부정사를 목적어로 취하는 동사이다.

(C) name이 동사로 '이름을 지어 주다'이므로 'Nicholas라는 이름의 남자'라는 의미가 되려면 과거분사를 쓰는 것이 알맞다.

08 ①은 practice의 영어 뜻풀이고, ②는 afford, ③은 journey, ④는 landfill, ⑤는 environmental의 영어 뜻풀이다. 이 중 journey는 글에 쓰이지 않았다.

09 글의 흐름상 악기를 연주하는 방법과 악보를 읽는 방법을 모른다는 내용이 되는 것이 자연스러우므로, '~하는 방법'이라는 의미의 「how+to부정사」가 되도록 how to가 들어가는 것이 알맞다.

10 ② that은 목적격 관계대명사이므로 생략할 수 있다.

11 ⑤ 그들은 첫 곡을 연주한 이후에 매일 모여서 연습했다고 했다.

① 그들은 악기를 연주하는 법과 심지어 악보를 읽는 법도 몰랐으며, Favio 선생님이 엄청난 인내심을 가지고 가르쳤다고 했다.

② 그들은 악보를 읽는 방법, 악기를 연주하는 방법도 몰랐다고 했다.

③ 그들이 연주한 첫 곡은 음이 맞지 않았다고 했다.

④ 글쓴이는 그들이 연주한 첫 곡이 가장 아름다운 곡이었다고 했다.

|해석| ① Favio는 그들을 가르치는 데 아무 문제점이 없었다.

② 그들은 악보를 읽지 못했지만, 악기를 연주할 수는 있었다.

③ 그들이 연주했던 첫 곡은 짧았지만 완벽했다.

④ 글쓴이는 그들이 연주했던 첫 곡이 마음에 들지 않았다.

⑤ 그들은 첫 곡을 연주한 후에 매일 연습했다.

12 (1) 내가 새가 될 수는 없으므로, 일어날 가능성이 없는 일을 가정하여 말하는 가정법 과거인 「If+주어+동사의 과거형 ~, 주어+조동사의 과거형(would)+동사원형 ...」으로 써야 한다.

(2) 주어가 The other members로 복수형이므로 복수 동사 are로 고쳐야 한다.

(3) 등위접속사 and에 의해 is standing과 병렬 구조를 이루고 있으므로 giving으로 고쳐야 한다. is가 생략된 형태이다.

13 Favio 선생님은 음악을 가르치고 싶어 했지만 온 마을에 악기가 몇 개뿐이어서 쓰레기 매립지에서 나온 물건들로 악기를 만들어 보자는 생각을 떠올렸고, Nicholas 아저씨가 이 생각을 실행에 옮겼다.

|해석| Favio는 우리에게 음악을 가르치고 싶었지만, 온 마을에 단지 몇 개의 악기만 있었다. Favio에게 생각이 떠올랐다. 그 생각은 쓰레기

매립지에서 나온 물건들로 악기를 만드는 것이었다. Nicholas가 이 생각을 실행에 옮겼고, 그것은 성공적이었다.

14 주어인 it이 불리는 것이므로 수동태로 나타내야 한다. 따라서 「의문사(Why)+be동사(is)+주어(it)+과거분사(called) ~?」 형태의 수동태가 포함된 의문문 형태로 쓴다.

15 두 번째 문장(No one knew how to play musical instruments.)과 세 번째 문장(We didn't even know how to read music.)에서 문제가 무엇인지 설명하고 있다.

16 (1) 그들이 연주했던 첫 곡은 매우 짧고 대부분은 음이 맞지 않았다고 했다.

(2) 그들은 첫 곡을 연주하고는 마음속에 새로운 희망을 느꼈다고 했다.

(3) 그들은 첫 곡을 연주한 후 매일 연습을 하기 위해 모였다고 했다.

|해석| A: 그들이 연주했던 첫 곡은 어땠니?

B: 그것은 매우 짧고 대부분은 음이 맞지 않았어.

A: 그들은 그 곡을 연주했을 때 마음속에 무엇을 느꼈니?

B: 그들은 (마음속에) 새로운 희망을 느꼈어.

A: 그 후 그들은 무엇을 했니?

B: 그들은 매일 연습하기 위해 모였어.

서술형 100% TEST

pp. 60~63

01 patience

02 (1) take part in (2) out of tune (3) is able to

03 I'd love to, but I can't. I have to visit my grandparents.

04 I'm really looking forward to watching it.

05 book, right hand, baseball player, movie, this Saturday

06 (1) know how to play the guitar

(2) play the guitar while I sing in the contest

(3) I'm sorry to hear that

07 (1) He thinks (that) math(it) is difficult.

(2) Because she has to take care of her brother.

08 (1) I don't have the book, I can't lend it to you

(2) he lived in Seoul, I could see him every day

09 (1) She told him when to feed the cat.

(2) Let me know what to prepare for the race.

(3) Brian found out where to buy the tickets.

10 (1) how to use (2) what to do (3) when to arrive

11 (1) If I had a million dollars, I could travel all over the world.

(2) If I knew his address, I would send him a gift.

12 were not too busy, could go on a picnic

13 ⓐ → His history class is not boring.

ⓑ → Please tell me where to go after school.

14 (1) where to stick

(2) when to bring

(3) how to make

15 (1) [모범답] I could travel all over the world

(2) [모범답] I could buy a big house with a garden

(3) [모범답] I would travel to Jupiter

16 (1) He wanted to teach us music

(2) We couldn't afford to buy new ones.

(3) was able to put this idea into practice

17 It was that they could make musical instruments with objects from the landfill. / It was to make musical instruments with objects from the landfill.

18 (1) How do you feel now?

(2) Why is the orchestra called the Recycled Orchestra?

(3) That is a wonderful story.

19 (1) It's because our musical instruments are made of objects from a landfill.

(2) Some people even say that Cateura itself is a giant landfill.

20 (1) Because he never gave up in difficult situations.

(2) He saved the country and the people.

(3) He won the battle with only 12 ships.

(4) I'd like to ask him how to make geobukseon.

01 '인내심'이라는 뜻의 명사 patience가 알맞다.

02 문맥상 (1)에는 '~에 참가하다'를 뜻하는 take part in이 알맞고, (2)에는 '음이 맞지 않는'을 뜻하는 out of tune이 알맞으며, (3)에는 '~할 수 있다'를 뜻하는 is able to가 알맞다.

|해석| A: 나는 내일 장기 자랑에 참가할 거야.

B: 잘됐구나!

A: 응, 하지만 문제가 있어.

B: 뭔데?

A: 나는 기타를 연주할 건데, 내 기타가 음이 맞지 않아. 소리가 이상해.

B: 내 생각에 나의 삼촌이 너를 도와줄 수 있을 것 같아.

A: 정말? 정말 고마워.

03 토요일에 조부모님을 찾아뵈어야 해서 축구를 함께 하자는 친구의 제안을 거절해야 하는 상황이다. 거절할 때 사용하는 표현인 I'd love to, but I can't. 뒤에 거절하는 이유를 덧붙인다.

|해석| 너는 집에 가는 길에 친구를 만난다. 친구는 너에게 이번 주 토요일에 함께 축구를 하자고 청한다. 너는 조부모님을 찾아뵈어야 해서 그날 축구를 할 수 없다. 이러한 상황에서, 너는 친구에게 뭐라 말할 것인가?

04 '나는 ~하는 것이 정말 기대돼.'라는 표현은 I'm really looking forward to ~.를 사용하며, to는 전치사이므로 뒤에 동사가 오는 경우 동명사 형태로 쓴다.

05 지호는 Jim Abbott에 관한 책을 읽고 있는데, Jim Abbott은 오른손이 없는 야구 선수이다. Ann은 그의 이야기가 "우리의 영웅"이라는 영

화로 만들어졌다고 말한다. 두 사람은 이번 주 토요일에 함께 그 영화를 보러 가기로 했다.

|해석| 지호는 Jim Abbott에 관한 책을 읽고 있다. Jim Abbott은 오른손이 없다. 하지만 그는 정말 열심히 노력해서 훌륭한 야구 선수가 되었다. Ann은 그의 이야기가 영화 "우리의 영웅"으로 만들어졌다고 말한다. Ann과 지호는 이번 주 토요일에 함께 그것을 볼 것이다.

06 (1) 기타를 치는 방법을 아는지 묻는 말이 되도록 '~하는 방법'이라는 의미를 나타내는 「how+to부정사」를 사용하여 배열한다.

(2) 대회에서 노래하는 동안 기타를 쳐 줄 수 있는지 묻는 질문이 되도록 배열한다.

(3) 손을 다쳤다는 말을 들었으므로 유감을 나타내는 표현이 되도록 배열한다.

07 (1) 민호는 수학이 어렵다고 말했다.

(2) Sally는 남동생을 돌봐야 해서 민호의 숙제를 도와줄 수 없다고 거절했다.

|해석| (1) 민호는 수학에 대해 어떻게 생각하는가?

(2) Sally는 왜 민호의 수학 숙제를 도와줄 수 없는가?

08 직설법 현재를 가정법 과거로 바꾸거나 가정법 과거를 직설법 현재로 바꿀 때 의미상 긍정은 부정으로, 부정은 긍정으로 바꿔 쓰는 것에 유의한다. 가정법 과거는 「If+주어+동사의 과거형 ~, 주어+조동사의 과거형+동사원형 .....」의 형태로 쓴다.

|해석| (1) 내게 그 책이 있다면, 네게 빌려 줄 수 있을 텐데.

(2) 그가 서울에서 살지 않아서 나는 그를 매일 볼 수 없다.

09 (1) when+to부정사: 언제 ~할지

(2) what+to부정사: 무엇을 ~할지

(3) where+to부정사: 어디에서 ~할지

10 (1) 문맥상 '~하는 방법, 어떻게 ~할지'를 뜻하는 「how+to부정사」를 사용하여 문장을 완성한다.

(2) 문맥상 '무엇을 ~할지'를 뜻하는 「what+to부정사」를 사용하여 문장을 완성한다.

(3) 문맥상 '언제 ~하는지'를 뜻하는 「when+to부정사」를 사용하여 문장을 완성한다.

|해석| (1) 그 책임자는 커피 기계를 사용하는 법을 설명했다.

(2) 우리는 다음에 무엇을 해야 하나요? 우리에게 무엇을 할지 말해 주세요.

(3) 나는 우리가 언제 공항에 도착해야 하는지 잊어버렸어. 너는 언제 도착하는지 아니?

11 가정법 과거는 「If+주어+동사의 과거형 ~, 주어+조동사의 과거형+동사원형 .....」의 형태로 쓴다.

12 가정법 과거는 「If+주어+동사의 과거형 ~, 주어+조동사의 과거형+동사원형 .....」의 형태로 쓴다.

|해석| Mark: 오늘 화창하다! 우리 소풍 가자, Laura!

Laura: 미안하지만, 안 되겠어. 나는 너무 바빠.

13 ⓐ 주어인 His history class가 지루한 것이므로 bored를 현재분사 형태의 형용사인 boring으로 고쳐 써야 한다.

ⓑ '어디로 ~할지'는 「where+to부정사」로 나타내므로, going을 go로 고쳐 써야 한다.

|해석| ⓐ 그의 역사 수업은 지루하지 않다.

ⓑ 나에게 방과 후에 어디로 갈지 말해 주세요.

ⓒ 내가 농장에서 산다면, 나는 이 말을 기를 수 있을 텐데.

ⓓ 나는 그 시간에 페이스 페인팅을 받을 것이다.

14 (1) 문맥상 '어디에 ~할지'를 뜻하는 「where+to부정사」를 사용한다.

(2) 문맥상 '언제 ~할지'를 뜻하는 「when+to부정사」를 사용한다.

(3) 문맥상 '~하는 방법, 어떻게 ~할지'를 뜻하는 「how+to부정사」를 사용한다.

|해석| A: 엄마의 생일 파티를 준비하자.

B: 좋아. 나에게 풍선을 어디에 붙여야 하는지 말해 줘.

A: 벽에 붙여. 나는 생일 케이크를 안으로 언제 가져와야 하는지 모르겠어.

B: 불이 꺼졌을 때 안으로 가져와.

A: 알겠어. 나는 쿠키를 좀 만들 거야. 너는 그것을 만드는 법을 아니?

B: 물론이야. 같이 만들자.

15 「If+주어+동사의 과거형 ~, 주어+조동사의 과거형+동사원형 .....」 형태의 가정법 과거 문장을 자유롭게 완성한다.

16 (1) 동사 want는 목적어로 to부정사(to teach)가 오며, 「teach+간접목적어(us)+직접목적어(music)」의 순서로 배열한다.

(2) '~을 할 형편이 안 되었다'라는 의미의 couldn't afford to 뒤에는 동사원형(buy)이 온다.

(3) was able to(~할 수 있었다) 뒤에는 동사원형(put)이 오며, put ~ into practice는 '~을 실행에 옮기다'라는 뜻을 나타낸다.

17 Favio 선생님의 생각은 쓰레기 매립지에서 나온 물건들로 악기를 만들 수 있다는 것이었다.

|해석| 악기에 관한 Favio의 생각은 무엇이었는가?

19 (1) It's because of ~. 뒤에는 명사(구)가 오고, It's because ~. 뒤에는 「주어+동사 ~」로 이루어진 절이 오는데, 뒤에 절이 이어지므로 It's because of가 아니라 It's because로 써야 한다.

(2) Cateura를 지칭하는 재귀대명사가 필요하므로 themselves가 아니라 itself로 고쳐 써야 한다.

20 (1) 수민이가 이순신 장군을 존경하는 이유는 어려운 상황에서 결코 포기하지 않았기 때문이라고 했다.

(2), (3) 이순신 장군은 나라와 백성을 구했고, 단지 12척의 배로 전투에서 이겼다고 했다.

(4) 수민이는 이순신 장군을 만나면 거북선을 어떻게 만드는지를 묻고 싶다고 했다.

|해석| A: 수민아, 네가 가장 존경하는 사람이 누구니?

B: 이순신 장군이야.

A: 너는 그를 왜 존경하니?

B: 그는 어려운 상황에서 결코 포기하지 않았기 때문이야.

A: 그가 무슨 일을 했는데?

B: 그는 나라와 백성을 구했어. 그는 단지 12척의 배로 전투에서 이겼어.

A: 그를 만난다면 너는 그에게 무엇을 물어보고 싶니?

B: 나는 그에게 거북선을 어떻게 만드는지 물어보고 싶어.

01 ③　**02** ①　**03** ③　**04** ③, ④　**05** ⑤　**06** ⑤
07 모범답 I'd love to, but I can't. / I'm sorry, but I can't.
08 ④　**09** ⑤　**10** without a right hand, baseball player
11 ②　**12** ①　**13** (1) I had enough eggs, I could bake bread for you　(2) I were a super hero, I could help people in need　**14** Let's decide where to go this Sunday. 해석: 이번 주 일요일에 어디에 갈지 결정하자.　**15** ④　**16** (1) where to stick the balloons　(2) when to bring the birthday cake in　**17** ③　**18** If I were a bird, I would fly.　**19** ④　**20** ⑤
21 It is also known as the Landfill Harmonic Orchestra.
22 ③　**23** (1) 아무도 악기를 연주하는 법을 몰랐다.　(2) 우리는 심지어 악보를 읽는 법도 알지 못했다.　(3) 세상은 우리에게 쓰레기를 보내지만, 우리는 음악을 돌려보낸다!　**24** ⑤　**25** ②

01 ③은 '거대한'이라는 뜻의 유의어 관계이고, 나머지는 반의어 관계이다.

02 ① '무언가에 대한 값을 지불할 수 있다'는 afford(~할 형편이 되다)의 영어 뜻풀이다. expect는 '예상하다, 기대하다'라는 뜻의 단어이다.

03 take out: 꺼내다
take care of: ~을 돌보다
|해석| • 여러분의 책을 꺼내서 10쪽을 펴세요.
• 네가 없는 동안 누가 네 개를 돌볼 거니?

04 ③ 첫 번째 문장의 gym은 '체육'이라는 뜻을 나타내고, 두 번째 문장의 gym은 '체육관'이라는 뜻을 나타낸다.
④ 첫 번째 문장의 save는 '절약하다'라는 뜻을 나타내고, 두 번째 문장의 save는 '구하다'라는 뜻을 나타낸다.
|해석| ① 치즈가 작은 조각들로 잘렸다.
　두 조각의 퍼즐이 남았다.
② 그 밴드는 비틀즈 노래를 연주했다.
　보라는 록 밴드에서 드럼을 연주한다.
③ Kevin은 체육 수업에서 다리를 다쳤다.
　비가 올 때 우리는 체육관에서 농구를 한다.
④ 우리 시간을 절약하기 위해 택시를 타는 게 어떨까?
　그는 나라와 국민을 구하려고 노력했다.
⑤ 나는 이 영화 포스터를 벽에 붙일 것이다.
　그녀는 편지 위에 붙이기 위해 우표 두 장을 샀다.

05 ⑤ B는 해변에 가게 되어 신이 나 있으므로 빈칸에는 I'm really looking forward to ~.를 사용하여 바다에서 수영하는 것에 대해 기대를 표현하는 말이 알맞다.

06 ⑤ 축구를 같이 하겠냐는 제안에 Sure, I'd love to.라고 수락의 말을 한 다음 몸이 좋지 않다며 거절의 이유를 덧붙이는 것은 어색하다.
|해석| ① A: 너는 내일 무엇을 할 거니?
　B: 나는 자전거를 탈 거야.

② A: 나는 어제 체육 수업에서 손을 다쳤어.
　B: 오! 그 말을 들어서 유감이야.
③ A: 너는 기타를 연주하는 법을 알지, 그렇지?
　B: 응, 나는 기타를 3년 동안 연주했어.
④ A: 얘, 보라야. 우리 록 밴드에 온 걸 환영해.
　B: 고마워. 나는 공연에서 너희들과 함께 연주하는 게 기대돼.
⑤ A: 나는 방과 후에 축구를 할 거야. 나와 함께 하고 싶니?
　B: 응, 그러고 싶어. 나는 오늘 몸이 좋지 않아.

07 빈칸 다음에 숙제를 해야 한다고 말하는 것으로 보아, 함께 영화 보러 가자는 제안을 거절하는 말이 들어가는 것이 알맞다.

08 (A) '~라는 이름의, ~라고 이름 지어진'이라는 수동의 의미의 과거분사가 알맞다.
(B) 선행사 the man이 사람이고, 관계대명사가 이끄는 절에서 관계대명사가 주어 역할을 하므로 주격 관계대명사인 who가 알맞다.
(C) 주어인 His story(그의 이야기)가 영화로 만들어진 것이므로 수동태(be동사+과거분사)가 알맞다.

09 ⑤ 지호가 Jim Abbott에 관한 책을 읽고 있다고 했지만, 그것이 Jim Abbott이 쓴 자서전인지는 대화를 통해 알 수 없다.

10 Jim Abbott은 오른손이 없이 태어났지만, 열심히 노력해서 최우수 선수 상까지 받는 야구 선수가 되었다.
|해석| Jim Abbott은 오른손 없이 태어났다. 그는 정말 열심히 노력했고 훌륭한 야구 선수가 되었다.

11 ② 주어진 문장은 '수학은 어려워.'라는 의미로, 수학 숙제를 아직 끝내지 못했다는 말 뒤에 이어지는 것이 자연스럽다. 또한 ② 다음의 Yes, but it's interesting, too.의 it은 math(수학)를 가리킨다.

12 B가 소파 옆에 탁자를 놓으라고 답한 것으로 보아, A는 소파 옆에 '무엇을 놓을지' 알려달라고 말하는 것이 알맞다. '무엇을 ~할지'는 「what+to부정사」로 표현한다.
|해석| A: 소파 옆에 무엇을 둘 지 알려줘.
B: 음, 소파 옆에 탁자를 놓아줘.

13 직설법 현재를 가정법 과거로 바꾸는 문제이다. 가정법 과거는 「If+주어+동사의 과거형 ~, 주어+조동사의 과거형+동사원형 .....」의 형태로 쓴다.
|해석| (1) 나는 달걀이 충분히 없어서, 너에게 빵을 구워 줄 수 없어.
(2) 나는 슈퍼히어로가 아니어서, 도움이 필요한 사람들을 도울 수 없어.

14 Let's는 '~하자'라는 의미로 뒤에 동사원형(decide)이 오고, 동사 decide의 목적어로 '어디에 갈지'라는 의미를 나타내는 where to go 를 쓴다.

15 ④ 주절이 wouldn't wear인 것으로 보아, 가정법 과거인 「If+주어+동사의 과거형 ~, 주어+조동사의 과거형+동사원형 .....」의 형태가 되어야 한다. 가정법 과거의 if절에 be동사가 쓰일 경우 주로 were를 쓴다. (am → were)
|해석| ① 나는 그에게 저녁을 언제 먹는지 물어보았다.
② 그 야구 모자가 더 저렴하다면, 나는 그것을 살 텐데.
③ 나는 Nick이 나에게 그 일을 어떻게 하는지 말해 주지 않아서 화가 났다.
④ 내가 너라면, 나는 빨간 코트를 입지 않을 텐데.

⑤ 그녀가 충분한 돈을 가지고 있다면, 그녀는 새 집을 살 수 있을 텐데.

16 (1) A가 벽에 풍선을 붙이라고 말하는 것으로 보아, '어디에 ~할지'라는 의미의 「where+to부정사(to stick)」를 사용하여 문장을 완성한다.

(2) B가 언제 생일 케이크를 안으로 가져오는지 알려 주고 있는 것으로 보아, '언제 ~할지'라는 의미의 「when+to부정사(to bring)」를 사용하여 문장을 완성한다.

17 ③ one another: 서로

18 가정법 과거는 현재 사실과 반대되거나 실제 일어날 가능성이 없는 것을 가정할 때 사용하며, 「If+주어+동사의 과거형 ~, 주어+조동사의 과거형+동사원형 ....」의 형태로 쓴다. 가정법 과거의 if절에 be동사가 쓰일 경우 주어의 인칭과 수에 관계없이 주로 were를 쓴다.

19 ④ Cateura를 가리키는 재귀대명사이므로 단수형 재귀대명사인 itself로 고쳐야 한다.

20 ⑤ 카테우라의 많은 사람들이 가난하고, 마을에는 희망이 많지 않았다고 했다.

|해석| ① Andrea는 재활용 오케스트라에서 바이올린을 연주한다.

② 재활용 오케스트라의 악기들은 쓰레기 매립지에서 나온 물건들로 만들어져 있다.

③ 카테우라는 파라과이에 위치해 있다.

④ Andrea의 마을에 거대한 쓰레기 매립지가 있다.

⑤ 카테우라의 많은 사람들은 부유하고 그들에게는 희망이 많다.

21 That's why it's also known as the Landfill Harmonic Orchestra.를 통해 Recycled Orchestra가 Landfill Harmonic Orchestra로도 알려졌음을 알 수 있다.

|해석| Q: 재활용 오케스트라는 또한 무엇으로도 알려져 있나요?

22 ③ 온 마을에 악기가 몇 개뿐이고 새 악기를 살 형편도 되지 않았지만 Favio 선생님의 아이디어로 쓰레기 매립지에서 나온 물건들로 악기를 만들었다고 했으므로, Favio 선생님이 포기했다는 내용의 ③은 글의 흐름상 어색하다. 포기하지 않았다는 뜻의 But Favio didn't give up.이 되어야 한다.

23 (1), (2) 「how+to부정사」는 '~하는 방법, 어떻게 ~할지'라는 의미를 나타낸다.

(3) send A(us) B(trash)는 'A에게 B를 보내다'라는 뜻을 나타내고, send back은 '(되)돌려보내다'라는 뜻을 나타낸다.

24 ⓐ와 ⑤는 목적격 관계대명사이다.

① It ~ that ... 강조구문에 쓰인 that이다.

② '저것'을 뜻하는 지시대명사이다.

③ 목적어 역할을 하는 명사절을 이끄는 접속사이다.

④ '저'를 뜻하며 뒤의 명사를 수식하는 지시형용사이다.

|해석| ① 창문을 깬 것은 바로 새였다.

② 이것은 나의 배낭이고 저것은 너의 것이다.

③ 나는 Clare가 음악에 관심이 있다고 생각한다.

④ 너는 노란 재킷을 입은 저 소녀가 누구인지 아니?

⑤ 네가 내게 보여 준 그림들은 아름다웠다.

25 ⓑ 뒤에 나오는 We were going to have a concert, a real concert!의 내용을 의미한다.

제 **2** 회 대표 기출로 내신 **적중** 모의고사　　pp. 68~71

01 ② **02** (1) worried (2) bored (3) scared **03** ⑤ **04** I'm looking forward to playing in a concert with you. **05** ②
06 ③ **07** ④ **08** ⓐ → She is going to take part in a singing contest. ⓑ → He has played the guitar for 3 years. **09** ②
10 ④, ⑤ **11** ③ **12** ⓒ → when to take ⓓ → had a flying carpet **13** ② **14** ③ **15** If I had a pet **16** ② **17** (A) are made (B) are (C) itself **18** (1) I play the violin (in the orchestra). (2) I'm from Cateura, a small town in Paraguay.
19 ③ **20** ④ **21** 쓰레기 매립지에서 나온 물건들로 악기를 만드는 것 **22** ④ **23** ② **24** It was very short and mostly out of tune. **25** (1) It was amazing that you won the battle with only 12 ships. (2) I'd like to ask you how to make geobukseon.

01 '조각, 일부분'이라는 뜻과 '(글, 미술, 음악 등의) 작품'이라는 뜻을 나타내는 piece가 알맞다.

|해석| • 그는 나에게 치즈 케이크 한 조각을 주었다.

• 그 피아노 연주자는 최근에 새로운 곡을 연주했다.

02 (1) 문맥상 '걱정하는'을 뜻하는 worried가 알맞다.

(2) 문맥상 '지루한'을 뜻하는 bored가 알맞다.

(3) 문맥상 '무서워하는'을 뜻하는 scared가 알맞다.

|해석| (1) 나는 내 개가 걱정돼. 그는 지금 아파.

(2) 그의 연설은 매우 길었다. 우리는 그 연설이 정말 지루했다.

(3) Aron은 어둠 속에서 이상한 소리를 들었을 때 매우 무서웠다.

03 ⑤ give ~ a big hand: ~에게 큰 박수를 보내다

|해석| ① 나는 음악 소리 때문에 공부에 집중할 수 없었다.

② 힘든 시기였지만 나는 결코 포기하지 않았다.

③ 그들은 서로를 바라보고 웃었다.

④ 점차로, 나는 두려움을 극복하고 수영하는 것을 배웠다.

⑤ 우리의 발표 후, 선생님들은 우리에게 큰 박수를 보냈다.

04 '나는 ~하는 것이 기대돼.'라고 기대를 나타낼 때는 I'm looking forward to ~.를 사용한다. 이때 to는 전치사이므로 뒤에 동명사 형태로 써야 한다.

05 박물관에 같이 가겠냐는 A의 제안에 B가 숙제를 해야 한다고 말하고 있으므로, 빈칸에는 A의 제안을 거절하는 말이 들어가야 한다. ⓑ와 ⓒ는 제안을 수락할 때 쓰는 표현이고, ⓓ는 상대방의 말에 동의할 때 쓰는 표현이다.

06 ⓐ how+to부정사(to play): 연주하는 법, 어떻게 연주하는지

ⓑ '~하는 동안'이라는 의미를 나타내는 접속사 while이 들어가야 한다.

07 노래 대회에서 기타를 연주해 달라는 부탁에 I'd love to, but I can't.라고 거절의 응답을 하였으므로, 빈칸에는 거절의 이유에 해당하는 말이 들어가는 것이 알맞다.

|해석| ① 나는 너를 도울 수 있어서 기뻐.

② 나는 무대에서 기타를 치는 것을 좋아해.

③ 나는 노래 대회를 열 거야.

④ 나는 어제 체육 시간에 손을 다쳤어.

⑤ 나도 대회에 참가할 거야.

08 ⓒ 수민이가 대회에서 무슨 노래를 부를지는 대화에 나와 있지 않다.

ⓓ 두 사람이 대화 후에 무엇을 할지는 언급되어 있지 않다.

|해석| ⓐ 수민이는 다음 주 월요일에 무엇을 할 예정인가?

ⓑ Alex는 얼마 동안 기타를 쳐 왔는가?

ⓒ 수민이는 대회에서 무슨 노래를 부를 예정인가?

ⓓ 그들은 대화 후 무엇을 할 것인가?

09 빈칸 순서대로 ⑤, ①, ③, ④가 들어간다.

10 ④ Linda는 작년에 Jason Kim의 뮤지컬을 봤다고 했다.

⑤ Tony는 주말에 뮤지컬을 볼 것이고, Linda는 자원봉사 활동을 할 것이다.

|해석| ① "빌리 엘리어트"는 유명한 무용수에 관한 뮤지컬이다.

② Tony는 뮤지컬 "빌리 엘리어트"를 어서 보고 싶어 한다.

③ Jason Kim은 Linda가 가장 좋아하는 배우이다.

④ Linda는 전에 Jason Kim의 뮤지컬을 본 적이 없다.

⑤ Tony와 Linda는 이번 주말에 뮤지컬을 볼 것이다.

11 자연스러운 문장으로 단어들을 배열하면 I didn't know where to put the book.이 된다.

12 ⓒ 「where+to부정사」가 되어야 하므로 to 다음에 동사원형(take)이 와야 한다.

ⓓ 주절이 could travel인 것으로 보아 가정법 과거 문장이 되어야 하므로, if절의 동사는 과거형(had)이 되어야 한다.

|해석| ⓐ 나는 그에게 컴퓨터를 어떻게 고치는지 물어보았다.

ⓑ 내가 피곤하지 않다면, 나는 Sam과 하이킹을 갈 텐데.

ⓒ 언제 약을 먹어야 하는지 내게 말해 줄래요?

ⓓ 그녀에게 날아다니는 양탄자가 있다면, 그녀는 전 세계를 여행할 수 있을 텐데.

13 주절이 could open인 것으로 보아 가정법 과거 문장이 되어야 한다. 가정법 과거는 「If+주어(he)+동사의 과거형(won) ~, 주어+조동사의 과거형+동사원형 ....」의 형태로 쓴다.

|해석| 그가 복권에 당첨된다면, 그는 자신의 음식점을 개업할 수 있을 텐데.

14 A가 B에게 코트를 놓을 곳을 알려 주고 있으므로 첫 번째 빈칸에는 코트를 어디에 둘지 묻는 것이 자연스럽다. 따라서 「where+to부정사 (to put)」가 알맞다. A가 애플파이를 만드는 조리법을 적어 주겠다고 했으므로 두 번째 빈칸에는 애플파이를 만드는 방법을 묻는 것이 자연스럽다. 따라서 「how+to부정사(to make)」가 알맞다.

|해석| A: 나의 새 집에 온 걸 환영해.

B: 나를 초대해 줘서 고마워. 내 코트를 어디에 두어야 할지 말해 줘.

A: 벽에 걸면 돼.

B: 알겠어. 와! 네가 이 애플파이를 만들었니?

A: 당연하지.

B: 맛있어 보여. 그것을 어떻게 만드는지 나에게 말해 줘.

A: 내가 내 비밀 조리법을 적어 줄게.

15 '만약 ~라면, …할 텐데.'라는 뜻의 가정법 과거 문장이므로, 「If+주어+동사의 과거형 ~, 주어+조동사의 과거형+동사원형 ....」의 형태로

써야 한다.

16 '무엇을 ~할지'는 「what+to부정사」로 나타내며, to 다음에는 동사원형이 온다.

17 (A) 악기는 만들어지는 것이므로 수동태(be동사+과거분사)가 알맞다.

(B) 주어가 Most of us로 of 다음에 복수 대명사 us가 왔으므로 복수 동사 are가 알맞다.

(C) Cateura를 강조하는 재귀대명사는 itself가 알맞다.

18 (1) Andrea는 바이올린 연주자이다.

(2) Andrea는 파라과이의 작은 마을인 카테우라 출신이다.

|해석| A: Andrea, 오케스트라에서 어떤 악기를 연주하나요?

B: 저는 (오케스트라에서) 바이올린을 연주해요.

A: 당신은 어디 출신인가요?

B: 저는 파라과이에 있는 작은 마을인 카테우라 출신이에요.

19 ③ Recycled Orchestra는 Landfill Harmonic Orchestra라고도 알려졌다고 했으므로 둘은 같은 오케스트라이다.

20 Favio 선생님은 우리에게 음악을 가르치고 싶어 했지만 문제가 있었다 (C)는 내용 다음에는 그 문제에 대해 설명하는 (B)와 (D)가 이어진다. (D)의 ones가 (B)의 musical instruments를 가리키므로 (B) 다음에 온다. 그 뒤로 이런 문제가 있음에도 Favio 선생님은 포기하지 않았다(A)는 흐름이 되는 것이 자연스럽다.

21 this idea는 앞 문장에 나온 '쓰레기 매립지에서 나온 물건들로 악기를 만드는 것'을 의미한다.

22 ④ 얼마나 많은 악기를 필요로 했는지는 글에 나와 있지 않아 알 수 없다.

|해석| ① Favio의 직업은 무엇인가요?

② Favio는 무엇을 가르치고 싶어 했나요?

③ 큰 문제점은 무엇이었나요?

④ 그들은 얼마나 많은 악기들이 필요했나요?

⑤ 악기에 관한 Favio의 생각은 무엇이었나요?

23 ② 아무도 악기를 연주하는 방법과 악보를 읽는 방법을 알지 못했다는 문제가 있었다는 내용 뒤에 'Favio 선생님은 엄청난 인내심을 가지고 우리를 가르쳤다.'라는 주어진 문장이 오는 것이 자연스럽다. ② 뒤에서는 Favio 선생님의 노력의 결과가 나온다.

24 '음이 맞지 않는'이라는 뜻을 나타내는 out of tune을 사용하여 문장을 완성한다.

25 (1) It은 가주어, that이 이끄는 절(that you won the battle with only 12 ships)이 진주어인 문장이다. 진주어가 감정을 느끼는 주체가 아니므로 현재분사형 형용사(amazing)가 되어야 한다.

(2) 동사 ask의 직접목적어 역할을 하는 「의문사+to부정사」 형태(how to make)가 되어야 한다.

01 ② **02** (1) get ready for (2) out of tune **03** ③ **04** ④
05 (D) − (E) − (B) − (C) − (A) **06** I'm reading a book about
a baseball player named Jim Abbott. **07** ⑤ **08** ⓓ a
book → a movie ⓔ this Sunday → this Saturday **09** ②
10 If he knew her phone number, he could call her.
11 (1) where to park (2) what to buy **12** ⑤ **13** ①
14 ② **15** ③ **16** It's because our musical instruments
are made of objects from a landfill. **17** ④ **18** ③ **19** ②
20 ② → There were only a few musical instruments 틀린
이유: There was 뒤에는 단수 명사(구)가 오고, There were 뒤에
는 복수 명사(구)가 오는데, a few musical instruments는 복수
명사구이므로 앞에 There were를 써야 한다. **21** It was that
they could make musical instruments with objects from
the landfill. / It was to make musical instruments with
objects from the landfill. **22** No one knew how to play
musical instruments. **23** ② **24** ①, ⑤ **25** ①

01 ② '한 장소에서 다른 장소까지 이동하는 행위'는 journey(여행)의 영
어 뜻풀이다.
　|해석| ① 그 거대한 공룡은 키가 6미터였다.
　② White 씨는 스페인으로 긴 여행을 시작했다.
　③ Dean은 새 운동화 한 켤레를 살 형편이 안 된다.
　④ 우리는 환경 문제에 큰 관심을 가지고 있다.
　⑤ 우리가 재활용을 더 한다면, 우리는 더 적은 쓰레기를 쓰레기 매립
지로 보낼 것이다.

02 (1) '~을 준비하다'를 뜻하는 get ready for가 들어가는 것이 알맞다.
　(2) '음이 맞지 않는'을 뜻하는 out of tune이 들어가는 것이 알맞다.
　|해석| (1) A: Sophie의 생일 파티를 준비하자.
　　B: 좋아. 나는 방을 장식하고 케이크를 구울게.
　(2) A: Paul은 노래를 정말 못 불러.
　　B: 맞아. 그의 노래는 항상 음이 맞지 않아.

03 ③ huge는 '거대한'이라는 뜻으로, '이 공이 너무 거대해서 나는 한 손
으로 잡을 수 있다.'라는 뜻의 문장은 어색하다. huge 대신 small(작
은) 등으로 바꿔야 한다.
　|해석| ① 나의 볼이 눈물로 젖었다.
　② 올빼미는 주로 밤에 활동적이다.
　③ 이 공은 너무 거대해서(→ 작아서) 내가 한 손으로 잡을 수 있다.
　④ 나는 이 시스템이 우리의 삶을 더 편리하게 만들 거라고 기대한다.
　⑤ 한 나이 든 여성이 그 건물로 가는 길을 설명해 주어서, 우리는 어려
움 없이 그것을 찾을 수 있었다.

04 I'd love to, but I can't.는 상대방의 제안을 거절할 때 쓰는 표현으로
I'm sorry, but I can't. 또는 I'm afraid I can't.로 바꿔 쓸 수 있다.

05 수학 숙제를 끝냈는지 묻는 말(D)에 아직 못 끝냈다면서 수학이 어렵다
고 말하면(E), 그렇지만 수학은 재미있다는 말(B)이 이어진 후, 그럼 자
신의 수학 숙제를 도와줄 수 있는지 묻고(C) 자원봉사 활동을 해야 해

서 안 된다고 거절하는(A) 흐름이 자연스럽다.

06 무엇을 읽고 있는지 묻는 말에 대한 답으로 I'm reading a book을
쓰고, 그 뒤에 about ~을 붙여 책에 관한 내용을 쓴다. named Jim
Abbott이 a baseball player를 뒤에서 수식하여 'Jim Abbott이라
는 이름의 야구 선수'라는 뜻을 나타낸다.

07 ⑤는 '나와 함께 영화를 보고 싶니?'라는 의미로, 상대방에게 함께 하고
싶은지 제안할 때 쓰는 표현이다. 대화에서 영화를 보러 간다고 말한 사
람은 A이므로, ⑤는 B가 아니라 A가 할 말로 알맞다. B는 Can I join
you?(나도 너와 함께 해도 될까?) 등으로 말하는 것이 자연스럽다.

08 ⓓ "우리의 영웅"은 책이 아니라 영화 제목이다.
　ⓔ 두 사람은 이번 주 토요일에 영화를 보러 갈 예정이다.
　|해석| ⓐ Jim Abbott은 오른손이 없다.
　ⓑ Jim Abbott은 야구 선수이다. 그는 최우수 선수 상을 받았다.
　ⓒ Jim Abbott의 이야기가 영화로 만들어졌다.
　ⓓ "우리의 영웅"은 Jim Abbott에 관한 책(→ 영화)이다.
　ⓔ 그들은 이번 주 일요일(→ 토요일)에 영화를 볼 것이다.

09 ② A가 화가 나 보인다고 말하며 무슨 일인지 묻고 있는데, 매우 신이
난다고 말하며 제주도로 여행을 갈 거라고 답하는 것은 어색하다.
　|해석| ① A: 나는 축구를 할 거야. 함께 하자.
　　B: 난 안 되겠어. 나는 할머니를 찾아뵈어야 해.
　② A: 너는 오늘 화가 나 보여. 무슨 일 있니?
　　B: 나는 너무 신이 나. 나는 제주도로 여행을 갈 거야.
　③ A: 나는 자전거를 탈 거야. 나와 함께 타고 싶니?
　　B: 응, 타고 싶어.
　④ A: 내가 대회에서 노래를 부르는 동안 네가 기타를 연주해 줄 수 있니?
　　B: 그러고 싶지만, 안 돼. 나는 어제 손을 다쳤어.
　⑤ A: 나는 축제에서 물 풍선 게임을 할 거야. 나는 그것을 하는 게 너
　　무 기대돼.
　　B: 재미있겠다.

10 가정법 과거인 「If+주어+동사의 과거형 ~, 주어+조동사의 과거형+
동사원형 .....」의 형태가 되어야 하므로, if절의 동사를 과거형인 knew
로 고쳐야 한다.

11 「의문사+to부정사」를 사용하여 문장을 완성한다.
　(1) 문맥상 '어디에 주차할지'를 뜻하는 where to park가 알맞다.
　(2) 문맥상 '무엇을 사야 할지'를 뜻하는 what to buy가 알맞다.
　|해석| (1) A: 실례합니다. 여기에 주차하실 수 없어요. 저쪽에 있는 표
　　지판을 보세요.
　　B: 오, 죄송해요. 몰랐습니다. 어디에 주차해야 하는지 제게 말해 주
　　시겠어요?
　(2) A: 이 상점에는 티셔츠가 많이 있어.
　　B: 응. 나는 무엇을 사야 할지 모르겠어.

12 ⑤ 가정법 과거는 현재 사실에 대한 반대의 의미이므로 직설법으로 바
꿀 때는 현재시제를 써야 한다. 따라서 위 문장을 직설법으로 바꾸면
As I don't have time to relax, I can't enjoy taking a walk.가
된다.

13 모두 옳은 문장이다.
　ⓐ, ⓓ 가정법 과거 문장은 「If+주어+동사의 과거형 ~, 주어+조동사

의 과거형+동사원형 .....」의 형태로 쓴다.

ⓑ 「when+주어(I)+should+동사원형(feed)」은 「when+to부정사」와 같은 의미를 나타낸다.

ⓒ how+to부정사: ~하는 방법, 어떻게 ~할지

| 해석 | ⓐ 내가 영화감독이라면, 나는 공포 영화를 만들 텐데.

ⓑ 언제 개에게 먹이를 주어야 하는지 저에게 말해 주세요.

ⓒ 그녀는 나에게 그 수학 문제를 푸는 법을 가르쳐 주었다.

ⓓ 그에게 요술 램프가 있다면, 그는 세 가지 소원을 빌 텐데.

14 ② if절의 주어 I 뒤에 were가 쓰인 것으로 보아 가정법 과거 문장임을 알 수 있다. 가정법 과거 문장은 「If+주어+동사의 과거형 ~, 주어+조동사의 과거형+동사원형 .....」의 형태로 쓰므로, 조동사는 will이 아니라 과거형인 would가 들어가야 한다.

15 ③ 모든 사람들이 일어서서 큰 박수를 보내고 있다고 했다.

16 괄호 안의 단어들 중 why를 제외한 나머지 단어들을 배열하여 문장을 완성한다. 앞에 나온 질문(Why is it called the Recycled Orchestra?)에 대한 답에 해당하므로 '그것은 ~이기 때문이다.'라는 의미의 It's because ~.를 사용하여 문장을 완성한다.

17 ⓑ와 ④는 '~할 때'라는 의미의 접속사로 쓰였다. 나머지는 '언제'라는 의미의 의문사로 쓰였다.

| 해석 | ① 내가 너에게 언제 멈출지 말할게.

② 너는 언제 그녀를 만나기로 약속했니?

③ 우리는 언제 우리의 시험 결과를 알게 될까?

④ 나는 중학생이었을 때 역사를 정말 좋아했다.

⑤ 경찰관이 내가 언제 그녀를 마지막으로 보았는지 나에게 물어보았다.

18 ③ 카테우라에는 이미 커다란 쓰레기 매립지가 있다.

19 ② 그들에게 음악을 가르치고 싶어 했던 Favio는 온 마을에 악기가 몇 개뿐이고 새 악기를 살 형편이 안 되는 상황에서도 포기하지 않았다고 했다.

| 해석 | ① Favio는 악기를 잘 만들었다.

② Favio는 그들에게 음악을 가르치는 것을 포기하지 않았다.

③ 마을 전체에 많은 악기가 있었다.

④ Favio는 새 악기를 사기로 결정했다.

⑤ Nicholas는 수도관으로 바이올린을 만들었다.

21 악기가 온 마을에 몇 개뿐이고 새 악기를 살 형편도 안 되는 상황에서 Favio 선생님은 쓰레기 매립지에서 나온 물건들로 악기를 만들 수 있다고 했다.

| 해석 | 악기에 관한 Favio의 생각은 무엇이었는가?

22 '아무도 몰랐다'는 No one knew로 쓰고, '연주하는 법'은 how to play로 쓴다.

23 ② Favio 선생님이 엄청난 인내심을 가지고 가르쳐서 점차로 곡을 연주할 수 있게 되었다는 내용의 글이므로, '인내심은 사람들이 필요로 하는 가장 중요한 자질 중 하나이다.'라는 문장은 글의 흐름과 관계없다.

24 ① '대부분, 일반적으로'는 mostly에 대한 영어 뜻풀이다.

⑤ '불평 없이 침착함을 유지하고 지연이나 고통을 받아들이는 능력'은 patience(인내심)에 대한 영어 뜻풀이다.

25 병 셰이커를 만드는 방법을 설명하는 글이다.

01 ②   **02** ③   **03** ④   **04** ③   **05** [1] Yes, I've played the guitar for 3 years.   [2] I'd love to, but I can't.   [3] I'm sorry to hear that.   **06** ②   **07** new guitar player, is looking forward to playing in a concert   **08** ⓐ What ⓑ What ⓒ who ⓓ Who   **09** ③, ⑤   **10** [1] He is going to watch the musical, *Billy Elliot*.   [2] Because she has volunteer work this weekend.   **11** [1] I'm going to watch a parade   [2] [모범답] looking forward to watching it   [3] [모범답] I'd love to, but I can't.   [4] make a mask   **12** ⑤   **13** ⑤   **14** ②   **15** ③   **16** ②   **17** ⓐ → Andrea plays the violin (in the orchestra).   ⓑ → They(Their musical instruments) are made of objects from a landfill.   **18** ②   **19** He made violins from oil drums. He turned water pipes into flutes.   **20** [모범답] I can't afford to buy a new smartphone.   **21** ③   **22** ③   **23** Why is the orchestra called the Recycled Orchestra?   **24** ④   **25** [1] [모범답] I could buy a new car for my family   [2] [모범답] I would create flying shoes

01 ②는 cheek(볼, 뺨)의 영어 뜻풀이다.

① thrilled(황홀해하는, 아주 신이 난)의 영어 뜻풀이다.

③ roll(구르다, 굴러가다)의 영어 뜻풀이다.

④ drone(무인 항공기, 드론)의 영어 뜻풀이다.

⑤ landfill(쓰레기 매립지)의 영어 뜻풀이다.

02 ⓐ stick(붙이다)이 들어간다.

ⓑ scared(무서워하는, 겁먹은)가 들어간다.

ⓒ patience(인내심)가 들어간다.

ⓓ gather(모이다)이 들어간다.

| 해석 | ⓐ Amy가 이 메모를 게시판에 붙였니?

ⓑ 나는 유령이 화면에 나타났을 때 무서웠다.

ⓒ 결국 나는 인내심을 잃고 David에게 소리쳤다.

ⓓ 선수들이 코치의 계획을 듣기 위해 모이기 시작했다.

03 ④ 달걀을 끓는 물에서 '꺼내다'라는 뜻이 되어야 하므로, Take care of(~을 돌보다)가 아니라 Take out(꺼내다)이 되어야 한다.

| 해석 | ① 점차로, 그 남자는 숲에서 사는 법을 배웠다.

② Smith 박사는 희망을 포기하지 않았고 아이들을 돕기 위해 노력했다.

③ 우리는 현재 소셜 미디어를 통해 서로 의사소통을 할 수 있다.

④ 10분 뒤에 끓는 물에서 달걀을 돌봐라(→ 빼라).

⑤ 나는 지난달에 차 사고가 났고 그때부터 목 통증으로 고통받고 있다.

04 '(미술·음악 등의) 작품'을 뜻하는 piece가 들어가는 것이 알맞다.

| 해석 | 이것은 연주하기 매우 어려운 곡이다.

05 [1] 기타 치는 방법을 아는지 묻는 질문에 대한 답이므로 그렇다고 하면서 3년 동안 기타를 쳤다고 말하는 것이 자연스럽다.

[2] 노래 대회에서 자신이 노래를 부르는 동안 기타를 쳐 줄 수 있는지 묻는 질문에 대한 답이 들어가야 하는데, 빈칸 뒤에 손을 다쳤다고 한

것으로 보아 거절의 표현이 들어가는 것이 알맞다.

(3) 체육 수업 중에 손을 다쳤다는 말에 유감을 표현하는 것이 알맞다.

06 대화의 내용과 일치하는 것은 ⓐ와 ⓒ이다.

ⓑ, ⓓ, ⓔ Alex는 기타 치는 법을 알지만, 어제 체육 수업 중에 손을 다쳐서 수민이가 노래를 부르는 동안 기타를 쳐 줄 수 없다.

|해석| ⓐ 수민이는 다음 주 월요일에 대회에서 노래를 부를 것이다.

ⓑ Alex는 기타 치는 법을 모른다.

ⓒ 수민이는 그녀를 위해 기타를 연주해 줄 누군가를 찾고 있다.

ⓓ Alex는 수민이와 대회에 참가할 것이다.

ⓔ Alex는 어제 체육 수업 중에 다리를 다쳤다.

07 보라는 Tom의 록 밴드의 새 기타 연주자이고, 공연에서 함께 연주하는 게 기대된다고 했다.

08 ⓐ, ⓑ '무엇'이라는 뜻의 의문사 What이 알맞다.

ⓒ a boy를 선행사로 하는 주격 관계대명사 who가 알맞다.

ⓓ '누구'를 뜻하는 의문사 Who가 알맞다.

09 ③ Jason Kim은 Tony가 아니라 Linda가 가장 좋아하는 배우이다.

⑤ Jason Kim이 어렸을 때부터 배우로 활동했는지는 대화에 나와 있지 않다.

10 (1) Tony는 이번 주말에 뮤지컬 "빌리 엘리어트"를 보러 갈 것이다.

(2) Linda는 자원봉사 활동이 있어서 뮤지컬을 함께 보러 가겠냐는 Tony의 제안을 거절했다.

|해석| (1) Tony는 이번 주말에 무엇을 할 것인가?

(2) Linda는 왜 Tony와 함께 갈 수 없는가?

11 (1) Olivia는 11시 30분에 퍼레이드를 볼 계획이다.

(2) 기대를 나타내는 표현인 I'm really looking forward to ~.를 사용한다.

(3) 표를 보면 Leo는 11시 30분에 가면을 만들 예정이므로 Olivia와 퍼레이드를 함께 볼 수 없다. 따라서 거절하는 표현이 들어가야 한다.

(4) Leo는 11시 30분에 가면을 만들 예정이다.

12 ⑤ 주절이 could help인 것으로 보아 가정법 과거 문장이 되어야 하므로, 「If+주어+동사의 과거형 ~, 주어+조동사의 과거형+동사원형 .....」의 형태가 되도록 has를 과거형 had로 고쳐야 한다.

|해석| • 그녀는 그 앱을 사용하는 법을 설명해 주었다.

• 내가 피곤하지 않다면, 나는 영화를 보러 갈 텐데.

• 만약 내일 날씨가 화창하다면, 우리는 현장 학습을 갈 것이다.

• 어디에서 왼쪽으로 돌아야 하는지 나에게 알려 줘.

• Brian에게 돈이 더 많다면, 그는 병원에 있는 아이들을 도울 수 있을 텐데.

13 주어진 우리말을 영작하면 Do you know how to use this washing machine?이므로 네 번째로 오는 단어는 how이다.

14 ⓐ 주어인 I가 황홀한 감정을 느끼는 주체이므로 thrilling을 thrilled로 고쳐야 한다.

ⓒ 주어가 The other members로 복수형이므로 단수 동사 is를 복수 동사 are로 고쳐야 한다.

15 ③ 글쓴이는 오케스트라의 단원 중 한 명이다.

① 기쁨의 눈물이 흐르고 있다고 했다.

② 큰 박수를 받고 있는 것으로 보아 연주회는 성공적으로 끝났음을 알 수 있다.

④ 모두가 일어서서 큰 박수를 보내고 있다고 했다.

⑤ 글쓴이를 포함한 단원 중 누구도 이런 날이 올 것이라고 예상하지 못했다고 했다.

|해석| ① 글쓴이는 슬픔을 느꼈고 울었다.

② 연주회는 청중을 실망시켰다.

③ 글쓴이는 오케스트라 단원 중 한 명이다.

④ 대부분의 청중이 즉시 자리를 떠났다.

⑤ 글쓴이는 이 상황을 예상했다.

16 ⓐ의 itself는 Cateura를 강조하는 강조 용법의 재귀대명사이며, 쓰임이 같은 것은 ②이다. 나머지는 목적어로 쓰인 재귀 용법의 재귀대명사이다.

|해석| ① 그녀는 자신에게 화가 났다.

② Eric은 직접 자신의 차를 고칠 수 있다.

③ 나는 거울 속의 나 자신을 바라보았다.

④ 고양이들은 먼지를 제거하기 위해 스스로를 청소한다.

⑤ 그 남자는 손님들에게 자신을 소개했다.

17 ⓐ Andrea는 바이올린 연주자이다.

ⓑ 그들의 악기는 쓰레기 매립지에서 나온 물건들로 만들어진다.

|해석| ⓐ Andrea는 오케스트라에서 어떤 악기를 연주하는가?

ⓑ 그들의 악기는 무엇으로 만들어져 있는가?

ⓒ 카테우라의 대부분의 사람들은 왜 가난한가?

ⓓ Andrea는 언제 Favio Chávez를 처음으로 만났는가?

18 ② 「teach+간접목적어(us)+직접목적어(music)」는 「teach+직접목적어+to+간접목적어」로 바꿔 쓸 수 있다. 따라서 teach music us가 아니라, teach music to us로 바꿔 쓸 수 있다.

19 Nicholas는 쓰레기 매립지에서 나오는 물건들로 악기를 만들 수 있다는 Favio 선생님의 생각을 실행에 옮겨, 기름통으로 바이올린을 만들고 수도관을 플루트로 바꾸었다.

|해석| Nicholas는 어떻게 Favio의 생각을 실행에 옮겼는가?

20 '어떤 것을 지불할 수 있다'에 해당하는 단어는 afford(~을 할 형편이 되다)이다. 이 단어를 포함하는 문장을 자유롭게 완성한다.

21 ⓒ the first piece of music을 뒤의 what we played가 수식해야 하는 구조인데, what은 선행사가 앞에 있는 경우 함께 쓸 수 없으므로 what을 목적격 관계대명사 that으로 고쳐 써야 한다.

22 주어진 문장의 it은 그들이 연주했던 첫 곡을 가리키는데 문장이 But으로 시작하고 있으므로, 연주했던 첫 곡이 매우 짧고 대부분은 음이 맞지 않았지만 그들에게는 가장 아름다운 곡이었다는 흐름이 되는 것이 자연스럽다.

23 That's because our musical instruments are made of objects from a landfill.(그것은 우리의 악기가 쓰레기 매립지에서 나온 물건들로 만들어져 있기 때문이다.)가 바로 앞 문장의 답에 해당하므로, What이 아니라 이유를 묻는 의문사 Why를 써야 한다.

24 ④ Andrea가 None of us knew how to play musical instruments (우리 중 누구도 악기를 연주하는 법을 알지 못했다)라고 했으므로, Andrea도 악기를 연주하는 법을 알지 못했음을 알 수 있다.

|해석| ① 민기: Andrea는 인터뷰를 하고 있다.

② 나리: Andrea는 재활용 오케스트라의 단원이다.

③ 진수: 재활용 오케스트라의 악기들은 쓰레기 매립지에서 나온 물건들로 만들어져 있다.

④ 지민: 재활용 오케스트라에서 오직 Andrea만이 처음에 악기를 연주하는 법을 알았다.

⑤ 유나: Favio는 재활용 오케스트라의 단원들을 엄청난 인내심을 가지고 가르쳤다.

25 가정법 과거는 '만약 ~라면, …할 텐데.'라는 뜻으로, 「If+주어+동사의 과거형 ~, 주어+조동사의 과거형+동사원형 ….」의 형태로 쓴다.

Lesson 6
Make the World Beautiful

STEP A

W Words 연습 문제   p.83

A 01 존재하다
02 허락하다, 허용하다
03 건축가, 설계자
04 영감을 주다
05 기본적인
06 곡선 모양의, 굽은
07 비추다
08 부서지기 쉬운, 섬세한
09 실내로, 실내에
10 외국인
11 분명한, 명백한
12 예시, 사례, 보기
13 담아내다, 표현하다, 포착하다
14 표지판
15 지붕
16 미술품, 예술품
17 파도, 물결
18 즐거운, 기분 좋은
19 상기시키다, 생각나게 하다
20 추가하다

B 21 book
22 inspiration
23 exhibit
24 beauty
25 expression
26 total
27 wet
28 lend
29 pick
30 column
31 nature
32 touch
33 shelf
34 spaceship
35 imagination
36 imitate
37 contents
38 peel
39 lift
40 story

C 01 통과하다
03 ~에게 구경시켜 주다
05 관광 명소
07 ~ 덕분에
02 판매 중인
04 그때부터
06 건강을 유지하다
08 민속 마을, 민속촌

W Words Plus 연습 문제   p.85

A 1 delicate, 부서지기 쉬운, 섬세한   2 exist, 존재하다
3 imagination, 상상력   4 exhibit, 전시하다

5 inspiration, 영감   6 allow, 허락하다, 허용하다

7 architect, 건축가, 설계자   8 spaceship, 우주선

B 1 obvious   2 indoors   3 imitate   4 expression

5 inspire

C 1 obvious   2 contents   3 remind   4 imitate

5 capture

D 1 go through   2 stay healthy   3 on sale   4 Thanks to

5 show, around

Words 실전 TEST

p. 86

01 ①   02 ②   03 sign   04 ②   05 ③   06 ①   07 ④

01 ①은 '실내로, 실내에'라는 뜻의 부사이고, 나머지는 모두 명사이다.

02 '미래에 대비하여 예약을 하다'라는 의미의 단어는 book(예약하다, 예매하다)이다.

03 첫 번째 문장의 빈칸에는 '표지판'이라는 뜻의 명사 sign이 들어가고, 두 번째 문장의 빈칸에는 '서명하다'라는 뜻의 동사 sign이 들어간다.

|해석| • 제과점의 문에 '닫힘' 표지판이 있었다.

• 문서에 당신의 이름을 서명하는 것을 잊지 마세요.

04 ② show ~ around는 '~에게 구경시켜 주다'라는 의미를 나타낸다.

|해석| ① Alice는 빗속을 걸어다니는 것을 좋아한다.

② 너는 내게 너의 새 사무실을 구경시켜 줄 수 있니?

③ 그 가족 뮤지컬의 표는 5월 3일부터 판매 중이다.

④ 열심히 일한 덕분에, 그 회의는 성공적이었다.

⑤ 버킹엄 궁전은 런던의 인기 있는 관광 명소이다.

05 '모방하다'라는 의미를 나타내는 단어는 imitate이다.

06 ① '존재하다'를 뜻하는 exist 대신에 '상기시키다'를 뜻하는 remind가 들어가는 것이 알맞다.

|해석| • 만약 네가 Helen에게 상기시켜 주지 않는다면, 그녀는 의사에게 전화하는 것을 잊을 것이다.

• 그 미술관은 다음 달부터 피카소의 그림 몇 점을 전시할 예정이다.

• 나의 모둠이 그린 그 벽화는 보기에 매우 좋다.

• 바나나 껍질에 미끄러져 넘어지지 않도록 조심하세요.

• Ben은 책상 위에 그의 가방 안의 내용물을 꺼내 놓았다.

07 조동사(can't) 뒤에는 동사(동사원형)가 오고, 소유격(her) 뒤에는 명사가 오는 것에 유의하여 문맥상 의미가 가장 자연스러운 단어를 찾는다.

|해석| • 나는 공기와 물이 없는 세상은 상상할 수 없다.

• 그 예술가는 자연에서 영감을 얻었다.

Listen & Speak 만점 노트

pp. 88~89

Q1 It is Lisa's birthday.

Q2 It is leaving in five minutes.

Q3 Daniel은 민속촌이 가장 좋았다.

Q4 책을 빌려준 것을 고마워한다.

Q5 (밖에 있는) 우산꽂이에 두어야 한다.

Q6 They are going to go to the World Music Concert.

Q7 They booked three tickets.

Q8 B는 새들에게 먹이를 주고 있었다.

Q9 The museum opened in 1995.

Q10 우리가 관람을 시작하기 전에, 여러분에게 기본 규칙을 상기시켜 드리겠습니다.

Listen & Speak 빈칸 채우기

pp. 90~91

1 Thank you for inviting me, My pleasure, Happy birthday

2 in five minutes, Which place did you like most,

the most popular place, looked really cool,

for showing me around

3 for lending me the book, You're welcome

4 not allowed to bring, an umbrella stand

5 on sale, book the tickets online, do you mind if I,

you are not allowed to bring, I can't wait

6 feed the birds, check the sign

7 Thank you for visiting, has exhibited,

let me remind you, you're not allowed to touch

Listen & Speak 대화 순서 배열하기

pp. 92~93

1 ⓑ-ⓒ-ⓓ-ⓐ

2 ⓒ-ⓕ-ⓐ-ⓓ-ⓑ-ⓘ-ⓖ-ⓔ-ⓙ-ⓗ

3 ⓑ-ⓐ-ⓒ

4 ⓐ-ⓒ-ⓑ-ⓓ

5 ⓓ-ⓗ-ⓑ-ⓐ-ⓔ-ⓖ-ⓒ-ⓕ-ⓙ-ⓘ

6 ⓑ-ⓓ-ⓒ-ⓐ

7 ⓒ-ⓕ-ⓑ-ⓔ-ⓖ-ⓐ-ⓓ-ⓗ

Listen & Speak 실전 TEST pp. 94~95

01 ② **02** ②, ⑤ **03** ③ **04** ② **05** ① **06** ④ **07** ③
08 ④ **09** ④
[서술형]
10 작품의 사진을 찍을 수는 있지만 만지는 것은 허용되지 않는다는 규칙
11 It takes place at an art museum.
12 (1) You're not allowed to use a flash here.
　　(2) Thank you for understanding.

01 상대방에게 고마움을 나타낼 때는 Thank you for ~. 뒤에 고마운 이유를 말한다.
02 B가 사과의 말을 하며 몰랐다고 말하는 것으로 보아 빈칸에는 You shouldn't ~.나 You're not allowed to ~.와 같은 금지하는 말이 들어가는 것이 자연스럽다.
03 생일 파티에 초대해 줘서 고맙다는 말(C)에 와 줘서 기쁘다고 답한(A) 후, 선물로 꽃을 주며 생일을 축하하고(D) 이에 답하는(B) 흐름이 되는 것이 자연스럽다.
04 ② B가 우산을 어디에 두어야 하는지 묻는 것으로 보아, A는 우산을 안으로 가져오면 안 된다고 금지의 말을 하는 것이 흐름상 자연스럽다.
(→ You're not allowed to bring your umbrella inside.)
05 대화의 빈칸에는 고마움을 표현하는 말(Thank you for showing me around.)이 들어가는 것이 알맞다. 이때 다섯 번째로 오는 단어는 me이다.
06 ④ 대화에서의 cool은 '멋진'이라는 뜻으로, Daniel은 한복을 입은 자신이 정말 멋져 보였다고 했다.
07 ③ Do you mind if I ~?는 상대방의 허락을 구할 때 사용하는 표현이다. 이때 mind는 '언짢아하다, 꺼리다'라는 의미로 '제가 ~하면 언짢을까요?'의 의미를 가진다고 볼 수 있으므로, 허락할 때는 부정의 의미를 포함하여 Not at all. / Of course not. 등으로 말해야 한다.
08 ④ what이 아니라 동사 says의 목적어 역할을 하는 명사절을 이끄는 접속사 that이 쓰여야 한다.
09 ④ 소미의 남동생은 10살이라고 했다.
|해석| ① 그들은 '세계 음악 콘서트'의 표 3장을 예매하고 있다.
② 그들은 11월 5일에 콘서트에 갈 것이다.
③ 소미는 그녀의 남동생을 콘서트에 데려갈 것이다.
④ 소미의 남동생은 8세 미만이다.
⑤ Joe는 콘서트를 보는 게 기대된다.
10 바로 뒤에 제시되는 내용(You can take pictures of the artworks, but you're not allowed to touch them.)을 가리킨다.
11 Thank you for visiting our art museum.이라고 말하는 것으로 보아, 미술관에서 말하고 있음을 알 수 있다.
|해석| 이 말을 어디에서 하고 있나요?
12 (1) 플래시를 사용해도 되는지 묻는 말에 Sorry.라고 답했으므로, 빈칸에는 플래시를 사용하는 것이 허용되지 않는다는 말이 들어가는 것이 알맞다.
(2) 이해해 줘서 고맙다는 말이 들어가는 것이 알맞다.

Grammar 핵심 노트 1 p. 96

QUICK CHECK
1 (1) that (2) in order to (3) so that
2 (1) ⓑ (2) ⓐ (3) ⓒ

1 |해석| (1) White 씨는 건강을 유지할 수 있도록 매일 아침 조깅을 한다.
(2) 나는 새 자전거를 사기 위해 돈을 모았다.
(3) Ann은 환경을 보호할 수 있도록 절대 비닐봉지를 사용하지 않는다.
2 |해석| (1) 나는 제시간에 도착할 수 있도록 학교로 달려갔다.
(2) Tom이 칠 수 있도록 그 공을 천천히 던져라.
(3) 나는 우리 축구팀이 경기를 이길 수 있도록 최선을 다해야 한다.

Grammar 핵심 노트 2 p. 97

QUICK CHECK
1 (1) enough (2) enough (3) brave enough
2 (1) diligent enough (2) to move (3) to fit

1 |해석| (1) Helen은 학교에 가기에 충분한 나이이다.
(2) 내 가방은 10권의 책을 담을 만큼 충분히 크다.
(3) Thomas는 그 도둑을 쫓을 만큼 충분히 용감했다.
2 |해석| (1) 그는 매일 일기를 쓸 만큼 충분히 부지런하다.
(2) 내 여동생은 이 상자들을 옮길 만큼 충분히 힘이 세다.
(3) 이 장난감 차는 내 주머니에 들어갈 만큼 충분히 작다.

Grammar 연습 문제 1 p. 98

A 1 that 2 so 3 so 4 so that
B 1 so that he could catch the first bus
　2 so that he could bake a cake
　3 so that he could understand them
C 1 so that she can stay healthy
　2 so that we could see the sunrise
　3 so as to get there on time
　4 so that she could find the way
　5 in order to feel the fresh air
D 1 Emily는 잠을 잘 잘 수 있도록 따뜻한 우유를 마신다.
　2 호수는 친구들과 여행을 갈 수 있도록 돈을 모았다.
　3 Bill은 모든 사람들이 들을 수 있도록 큰 소리로 말했다.

A |해석| 1. 내가 책을 읽을 수 있도록 조용히 해 주세요.

   2. Henry는 Jane이 들을 수 없도록 그의 목소리를 낮추었다.

   3. 내가 나의 안경을 가져가는 것을 기억할 수 있도록 나에게 메모를 남겨 줘.

   4. 너는 서두를 필요가 없도록 일찍 시작하는 게 어떠니?

B |해석| 1. Jack은 첫 버스를 탈 수 있도록 빨리 달렸다.

   2. Peter는 케이크를 구울 수 있도록 제빵 수업을 들었다.

   3. 나는 학급 규칙을 그가 이해할 수 있도록 그에게 명확히 설명했다.

Ⓖ Grammar 연습 문제 2
p.99

A 1 big enough to have

  2 brave enough to speak

  3 old enough to look after

  4 smart enough to understand

  5 not old enough to ride

B 1 My dog was fast enough to catch the ball.

  2 Judy is wise enough to give advice to her friends.

  3 The rope is strong enough to hold my weight.

  4 Robin was not rich enough to lend his friend the money.

C 1 I was hungry enough to eat a whole pizza.

  2 The string is long enough to go around the house.

  3 He was lucky enough to get the job.

D 1 Amy is smart enough to speak three languages.

  2 Bora's English is good enough to talk with a foreigner.

  3 The coat is big enough for her to wear.

A |해석| 1. 이 교실은 안에 50명의 학생들을 수용할 만큼 충분히 크다.

  2. Sam은 대중 앞에서 연설할 만큼 충분히 용감했다.

  3. 그들은 스스로를 돌볼 만큼 충분히 나이가 많다.

  4. 유나는 그 영어 책을 이해할 만큼 충분히 똑똑하다.

  5. Terry는 그 롤러코스터를 탈 만큼 충분히 나이가 있지 않다.

B |해석| 1. 내 개는 그 공을 잡을 만큼 충분히 빨랐다.

  2. Judy는 그녀의 친구들에게 조언을 해 줄 만큼 충분히 현명하다.

  3. 그 줄은 나의 무게를 견딜 만큼 충분히 튼튼하다.

  4. Robin은 그의 친구에게 돈을 빌려줄 만큼 충분히 부유하지 않았다.

C |해석| 1. 나는 매우 배가 고파서 피자 한 판을 먹을 수 있었다.

  2. 그 끈은 매우 길어서 집을 두를 수 있다.

  3. 그는 매우 운이 좋아서 그 직장을 얻을 수 있었다.

Ⓖ Grammar 실전 TEST
pp. 100~103

01 ③	02 ⑤	03 ⑤	04 ⑤	05 ⑤	06 ③	07 ③
08 ④	09 ①	10 ④	11 ②	12 ①	13 ①	14 ⑤
15 ③, ④	16 ⑤	17 ②	18 ③	19 ③	20 ⑤	

[서술형]

21 (1) strong enough to lift the box

  (2) small enough to go through the hole

22 (1) so that she could feel the fresh air

  (2) so that everyone could hear her speech

  (3) so that she could donate them

23 (1) The ladder is long enough to reach the ceiling.

  (2) This bag is not big enough to carry two basketballs.

  (3) The smartphone is easy enough for my grandmother to use.

24 (1) Tony는 건강을 유지할 수 있도록 매일 아침 수영을 한다.

  (2) Julie는 어려운 퍼즐들을 풀 만큼 충분히 똑똑하다.

  (3) 그 영화가 너무 재미있어서 나는 그것을 두 번 보았다.

25 (1) Mary is wise enough to advise her older sister.

  (2) The old man was rich enough to buy several cars.

  (3) It was windy enough for us to fly a kite.

26 (1) so that he could travel with his friends

  (2) not tall enough to reach the bookshelf

  (3) long enough for her to wear

01 '∼하도록, ∼하기 위해(서)'라는 뜻으로 목적을 나타내는 절을 이끄는 so that이 알맞다.

  |해석| John은 일찍 일어날 수 있도록 일찍 잠자리에 들었다.

02 '∼할 만큼(∼하기에) 충분히 …한'은 「형용사+enough to+동사원형」으로 쓴다.

  |해석| Jessica는 어려운 수학 문제들을 풀 만큼 충분히 똑똑하다.

03 목적을 나타내는 so that이 이끄는 절은 「so that+주어+동사 ∼」의 어순으로 쓴다.

  |해석| 찬 바람이 들어올 수 없도록 창문이 닫혀 있었다.

04 「so+형용사+that+주어+can+동사원형」은 '너무(매우) ∼해서 …할 수 있다'라는 뜻으로, 「형용사+enough to+동사원형」으로 바꿔 쓸 수 있다.

  |해석| 그 농구 선수는 매우 키가 커서 천장에 닿을 수 있다.

05 '∼하도록, ∼하기 위해(서)'라는 뜻으로 목적을 나타내는 절을 이끄는 so that이 알맞다.

  |해석| 그녀는 좋은 성적을 받기 위해 과학을 열심히 공부했다.

06 첫 번째 빈칸에는 '∼할 만큼(∼하기에) 충분히 …하게'라는 뜻의 「부사+enough to+동사원형」의 enough가 들어가야 한다.

  두 번째 빈칸에는 「so+형용사+that+주어+can+동사원형」의 so가 들어가야 한다.

  |해석| • 나는 Sara를 따라잡을 만큼 충분히 빨리 달릴 수 없었다.

    • Andrew는 매우 재능이 많아서 장기 자랑에서 우승할 수 있다.

07 완전한 문장은 Tom takes yoga classes so that he can relieve

his stress.이다.

08 완전한 문장은 She is strong enough to win the boxing match. 이다.

09 ① 목적을 나타내는 so that 뒤에는 「주어+동사 ~」 형태의 절이 와야 하므로 so that 뒤에 주어인 he를 써야 한다.

|해석| ① 그는 늦지 않도록 서둘렀다.

② 그녀는 경기를 이기기 위해 열심히 연습했다.

③ Robert는 옷을 좀 사기 위해 인터넷을 검색했다.

④ 내 남동생은 우유를 사기 위해 슈퍼마켓에 갔다.

⑤ Julia는 그녀가 가장 좋아하는 프로그램을 들을 수 있도록 7시 정각에 라디오를 켠다.

10 ④ '~할 만큼〔~하기에〕충분히 …한'은 「형용사+enough to+동사원형」의 형태로 쓰므로, to donate로 고쳐야 한다.

|해석| ① 그녀는 스스로 결정을 내릴 만큼 충분히 나이가 있다.

② 지호는 경주를 이길 만큼 충분히 빨리 달렸다.

③ Nick은 틀린 것을 고칠 만큼 충분히 똑똑했다.

④ 그들은 많은 돈을 기부할 만큼 충분히 부유하다.

⑤ 그 소파는 우리가 앉을 만큼 충분히 튼튼하지 않았다.

11 '~하도록, ~하기 위해(서)'라는 뜻으로 목적을 나타내는 「in order to+동사원형」은 「so that+주어+동사 ~」의 절로 바꿔 쓸 수 있다.

|해석| 나의 아버지께서는 푹 주무시기 위해 텔레비전을 끄셨다.

12 ①의 빈칸에는 because 등과 같이 이유를 나타내는 절을 이끄는 접속사가 들어가고, 나머지 빈칸에는 모두 so가 들어간다.

|해석| ① Joan은 매우 아팠기 때문에 어제 학교에 결석했다.

② Amy는 시험에 통과할 수 있도록 열심히 공부했다.

③ Simon은 Judy의 생일 선물을 사기 위해 돈을 모았다.

④ 나는 매우 피곤해서 뒤뜰을 청소할 수 없었다.

⑤ 우리는 그곳에 제시간에 도착할 수 있도록 택시를 탔다.

13 「so+형용사+that+주어+can+동사원형」은 '너무〔매우〕~해서 …할 수 있다'라는 뜻으로, 「형용사+enough to+동사원형」으로 바꿔 쓸 수 있다.

|해석| 유미는 매우 부자라서 그 집을 살 수 있다.

14 자연스러운 문장으로 배열하면 Minho collected used clothes so that he could donate them.이므로 여섯 번째로 오는 단어는 that 이다.

15 「형용사+enough to+동사원형」은 '~할 만큼〔~하기에〕충분히 …한' 이라는 의미를 나타낸다. 형용사와 enough의 위치는 서로 바꿔 쓸 수 없으며, 「too+형용사+to+동사원형」은 '너무 ~해서 …할 수 없다'라는 의미이므로 서로 다른 의미를 나타낸다.

16 '~하도록, ~하기 위해(서)'라는 뜻으로 목적을 나타내는 「so that+주어+동사」를 이용한 문장을 찾는다.

17 '~할 만큼 충분히 …한'은 「형용사+enough to+동사원형」으로 쓸 수 있다.

18 「형용사+enough to+동사원형」의 어순으로 써야 하므로 enough는 형용사(warm)와 to 사이인 ③에 오는 것이 알맞다.

|해석| 짧은 소매를 입을 만큼 충분히 따뜻하다.

19 ⓐ 목적을 나타내는 so that 뒤에는 「주어+동사 ~」로 이루어진 절이 온다.

ⓑ와 ⓒ는 옳은 문장이다.

ⓓ 「형용사(tall)+enough to」 뒤에는 동사원형이 와야 한다.

|해석| ⓐ 나는 그가 길을 잃지 않도록 그에게 지도를 주었다.

ⓑ 나는 네가 그 책들을 쉽게 찾을 수 있도록 알파벳 순서로 놓을게.

ⓒ 나는 너무 피곤해서 회의에서 거의 잠들었다.

ⓓ 그 소녀는 맨 위 선반에 닿을 만큼 충분히 키가 크지 않다.

20 문장은 My younger sister is old enough to go to college.로 완성해야 하므로, 추가해야 하는 단어는 enough이다.

21 「형용사+enough to+동사원형」은 '~할 만큼 충분히 …한'의 의미를 나타낸다.

22 「so that+주어+동사 ~」는 '~하도록'이라는 뜻으로 목적을 나타낸다.

|해석| (1) Lucy는 신선한 공기를 느낄 수 있도록 창문을 열었다.

(2) Lucy는 모든 사람이 자신의 연설을 들을 수 있도록 크게 말했다.

(3) Lucy는 기부할 수 있도록 오래된 물품들을 모았다.

23 「형용사+enough to+동사원형」은 '~할 만큼 충분히 …한'의 의미를 나타낸다.

24 (1) so that이 이끄는 절은 목적을 나타내어 '~하도록, ~하기 위해 (서)'라는 의미를 나타낸다.

(2) 「형용사+enough to+동사원형」은 '~할 만큼〔~하기에〕충분히 …한'이라는 의미를 나타낸다.

(3) so ~ that은 '너무〔매우〕~해서 …하다'라는 의미를 나타낸다.

25 「so+형용사+that+주어+can/could+동사원형」은 '너무〔매우〕~해서 …할 수 있다〔있었다〕'라는 뜻으로, 「형용사+enough to+동사원형」으로 바꿔 쓸 수 있다. to부정사의 의미상의 주어가 문장의 주어와 다를 경우, to부정사 앞에 「for+목적격」을 써서 나타낸다.

|해석| (1) Mary는 매우 현명해서 그녀의 언니에게 조언을 해 줄 수 있다.

(2) 그 노인은 매우 부자라서 여러 대의 차를 살 수 있었다.

(3) 바람이 매우 불어서 우리가 연을 날릴 수 있었다.

26 (1) 목적을 나타내는 so that이 이끄는 절은 「so that+주어+동사 ~」의 어순으로 쓴다.

(2), (3) '~할 만큼〔~하기에〕충분히 …한'의 의미의 「형용사+enough to+동사원형」을 쓸 때, to부정사의 의미상의 주어(for+목적격)는 to부정사 앞에 쓴다.

|해석| (1) Fred는 그의 친구들과 여행할 수 있도록 돈을 모았다.

(2) 그 소년은 책장에 닿을 만큼 충분히 키가 크지 않다.

(3) 그 바지는 그녀가 입을 만큼 충분히 길다.

01 Have you heard **02** their ideas and inspirations
03 This is because **04** The shapes in nature
05 For example **06** Isn't it beautiful
07 strong enough to protect **08** looks like
09 actually exists in **10** has inspired **11** in Spain
12 the most famous churches **13** beautiful tall columns
14 don't they **15** the shape of trees
16 the beauty of nature **17** what inspired the architect
18 not so obvious **19** added his imagination
20 Can you guess **21** a sailing boat **22** came from
23 closely **24** the peels **25** more clearly
26 What about **27** Have you ever been to
28 a giant spaceship **29** took the curved lines
30 a popular tourist attraction **31** try to capture
32 perfect examples **33** what would you choose

R **Reading 바른 어휘·어법 고르기** pp. 108~109

01 heard **02** get **03** because **04** are
05 For example **06** beautiful **07** to protect **08** that
09 exists **10** many **11** This is **12** churches
13 inside **14** don't **15** in **16** how **17** easily
18 obvious **19** added **20** what **21** that
22 interestingly **23** closely **24** orange **25** more
26 about **27** to **28** looks like **29** so that
30 Thanks to **31** to capture **32** Nature **33** were

R **Reading 틀린 문장 고치기** pp. 110~111

01 ×, hear → heard **02** ×, it → them **03** ×, are → is
04 ×, pleased → pleasing **05** ○ **06** ○
07 ×, enough strong → strong enough
08 ×, look → looks **09** ×, exist → exists **10** ○
11 ×, to → in **12** ×, more → most **13** ○
14 ×, for → like **15** ○ **16** ○ **17** ○ **18** ○
19 ×, architecture → architect
20 ×, what inspired to him → what inspired him
21 ×, but → or **22** ×, inspire → inspiration **23** ○
24 ○ **25** ×, more clear → more clearly
26 ×, What of → What about **27** ○
28 ×, which → that **29** ×, such that → so that **30** ○
31 ×, While → As **32** ○ **33** ×, will → would

R **Reading 실전 TEST** pp. 114~117

01 ③ **02** ③ **03** ④ **04** ② **05** ⑤ **06** architect
07 ④ **08** ⑤ **09** ⑤ **10** ④ **11** ② **12** ④ **13** ④
14 ④ **15** ② **16** ④ **17** ② **18** ③ **19** ①

[서술형]

20 It is round and delicate, yet strong enough to protect its contents.
21 nature, their ideas and inspirations, beautiful place, egg
22 ⓒ → It is one of the most famous churches in the world.
　　ⓓ → They look like trees, don't they?
23 shape of trees, columns, beauty of nature, indoors
24 ⓐ 하지만 건축가인 Zaha Hadid는 도시 사람들이 즐길 수 있도록 자연에서 곡선을 가져왔다.
　　ⓑ 그것의 특별한 디자인 덕분에, 그것은 서울의 인기 있는 관광 명소가 되었다.

01 예술가들이 자연에서 영감을 얻는다는 내용의 글이므로, ③ '예술이 자연을 모방한다'라는 말이 들어가는 것이 가장 알맞다.
　|해석| ① 예술이 자연에게 영감을 준다
　② 위대한 예술은 바로 우리의 인생이다
　④ 자연이 진정한 법이다
　⑤ 자연이 예술가처럼 보인다
02 (A) '이것은 ~이기 때문이다.'라는 의미의 This is because ~.가 알맞다.
　(B) 주어가 The shapes이므로 복수 동사 are가 알맞다.
　(C) '~할 만큼 충분히 …한'은 「형용사(strong)+enough to+동사원형」의 형태로 쓴다.
03 ④ Isn't it beautiful?에서 it은 '달걀'을 가리킨다.
04 성당 안의 아름다운 높은 기둥을 보라고(B) 한 후 기둥이 나무처럼 보인다며 동의를 구하고(A), Antoni Gaudi가 성당에 나무의 형태를 사용했고(D), 그것이 그가 자연의 아름다움을 실내로 가져온 방법임을 설명하는(C) 흐름이 되는 것이 자연스럽다.
05 has inspired는 과거부터 현재까지 계속 영감을 주어 왔다는 '계속'의 의미를 나타내는 현재완료이다.
　⑤ 계속 ①, ②, ④ 경험 ③ 완료
　|해석| ① 나는 프랑스 음식을 먹어 본 적이 전혀 없다.
　② 지민이는 전에 캐나다에 간 적이 있다.
　③ Anna는 그녀의 숙제를 막 끝마쳤다.
　④ Tom은 유명한 영화배우를 본 적이 있다.
　⑤ 나는 내가 어린아이였을 때부터 Judy를 알아 왔다.
06 '건물을 설계하는 사람'은 architect(건축가, 설계자)의 영어 뜻풀이다.
07 ④ 사그라다 파밀리아 성당의 기둥이 무엇으로 만들어졌는지는 글에 제시되어 있지 않다.
　|해석| ① 무엇이 많은 건축가들에게 영감을 주어 왔는가?
　② 사그라다 파밀리아 성당은 어디에 위치해 있는가?

③ 사그라다 파밀리아 성당 내부의 기둥은 무엇처럼 보이는가?

④ 사그라다 파밀리아 성당 내부의 기둥은 무엇으로 만들어졌는가?

⑤ Antoni Gaudi는 사그라다 파밀리아 성당에 무슨 형태를 사용했는가?

08 첫 번째 문장 '앞의 두 예시에서 우리는 무엇이 건축가에게 영감을 주었는지 쉽게 알 수 있다.'를 통해 ⑤의 내용이 나왔을 거라고 유추할 수 있다.

09 앞의 두 예시에서는 쉽게 알 수 있다고 했으므로, But으로 시작한 문장에서는 '그다지 명확하지(obvious) 않다'고 하는 것이 자연스럽다.

10 take A from B: B에서 A를 가져오다

11 주어진 문장은 많은 사람들이 시드니 오페라 하우스를 보고 건축가에게 영감을 주었다고 생각하는 것에 관한 내용이므로, ②에 들어가서 실제로 건축가에게 영감을 준 것은 '오렌지'라는 것을 알려주는 순서로 이어지는 것이 자연스럽다.

12 ④ 시드니 오페라 하우스의 건축가는 오렌지에서 영감을 받았다고 했다.

13 ④ '〜하도록, 〜하기 위해(서)'라는 뜻으로 목적을 나타내는 절을 이끄는 so that이 되어야 한다. so as to 뒤에는 동사원형이 온다.

14 ⓐ와 ④의 that은 목적어 역할을 하는 절을 이끄는 접속사이다.

① 지시 형용사

②, ③ 지시 대명사

⑤ 주격 관계대명사

|해석| ① 너는 이 가방을 원하니 아니면 저 가방을 원하니?

② 저쪽에 계신 분이 너의 할아버지시니?

③ 나는 네가 그런 말을 하지 않았으면 좋겠다.

④ Julia는 나에게 그녀가 오늘 아침에 통학 버스를 놓쳤다고 말했다.

⑤ 이것은 나의 삼촌이 그린 그림이다.

15 it은 Dongdaemun Design Plaza를 가리킨다.

16 ④ Zaha Hadid는 도시 사람들이 즐길 수 있도록 자연에서 곡선의 형태를 가져와 동대문 디자인 플라자를 건축했다고 했고, 재료에 관해서는 언급되지 않았다.

17 글의 밑줄 친 As와 ⓒ의 As는 접속사로 '〜다시피, 〜듯이'의 뜻으로 쓰였다.

ⓐ 〜로(서) 〈전치사〉

ⓑ 〜하면서 〈접속사〉

ⓓ 〜이기 때문에, 〜이므로 〈접속사〉

|해석| ⓐ 나의 삼촌은 여행 가이드로 일한다.

ⓑ Jenny는 일어나면서 물을 엎질렀다.

ⓒ 네가 알다시피, David는 곧 캘리포니아로 이사 간다.

ⓓ 나는 피곤함을 느꼈기 때문에 집으로 걸어가는 대신 택시를 탔다.

18 앞에서 많은 건물들이 디자인에 자연의 아름다움을 담아내려고 한다고 했으므로, 만약 당신이 건축가라면 '자연(nature)'에서 무엇을 선택할지 물어보는 것이 자연스럽다.

19 첫 번째 문장을 통해 ①을 추론할 수 있다.

20 '〜할 만큼 충분히 …한'은 「형용사+enough to+동사원형」의 어순으로 쓴다. yet은 접속사로 '그렇지만, 그럼에도'라는 뜻으로 쓰인다.

21 '예술은 자연(nature)을 모방한다'라는 표현이 있듯이 많은 예술가들이 아이디어와 영감을 그들 주변의 세상에서 얻는다. 이는 자연계가 아름다운 곳(beautiful place)이기 때문이며, 예시로 런던에 있는 달걀

(egg)처럼 생긴 건물을 언급하고 있다.

|해석| "예술이 자연을 모방한다"

· 요지: 많은 예술가들이 그들의 아이디어와 영감을 그들 주변의 세상에서 얻는다.

· 이유: 자연계는 아름다운 곳이다.

· 예: 런던에 있는 한 건물은 달걀처럼 생겼다.

22 ⓒ '가장 〜한 … 중의 하나'라는 뜻은 「one of the+최상급+복수 명사」로 써야 하므로 church를 복수 명사인 churches로 고쳐 써야 한다.

ⓓ 부가의문문은 앞에 일반동사가 쓰인 경우 do/does의 긍정이나 부정 형태로 써야 하므로 aren't를 don't로 고쳐 써야 한다.

23 Antoni Gaudi는 사그라다 파밀리아 성당의 기둥에 나무의 형태를 사용했고, 이것이 그가 자연의 아름다움을 실내로 가져온 방법이라고 했다.

|해석| Antoni Gaudi는 사그라다 파밀리아 성당 내부의 기둥을 지을 때 자연에서 나무의 형태를 가져왔다. 이런 방법으로, 자연의 아름다움이 그에 의해 실내로 가져와졌다.

24 ⓐ so that은 '〜하도록'의 의미를 나타낸다.

ⓑ Thanks to: 〜 덕분에

tourist attraction: 관광 명소

 기타 지문 실전 TEST p.119

01 ④ 02 ③ 03 We grow some vegetables there so that we can have fresh food. 04 ③ 05 ④

01 (A) look like: 〜처럼 보이다

(B) 「be동사+과거분사」의 수동태 문장에서 행위자는 by와 함께 쓴다.

(C) take A from B: B에서 A를 가져오다

02 ③ 시드니 오페라 하우스의 외관의 색은 알 수 없다.

03 「so that+주어+동사 〜」가 목적을 나타내는 절이 되도록 문장을 완성한다.

04 ③ 정원은 학교 건물의 옥상에 있다고 했다.

05 빈칸에는 looks, that, time, around의 순서로 들어가는 것이 알맞다.

STEP B

01 ④   02 ⑤   03 ①   04 ③   05 book   06 ②   07 ⑤
08 on sale   09 ④   10 ③   11 (1) attraction
(2) expression (3) attract   12 ④   13 ④   14 ⑤

01 helpful과 useful은 '유용한'이라는 의미의 유의어 관계이고, indoors (실내로, 실내에)와 outdoors(야외로, 야외에)는 반의어 관계이다.

02 actually(실제로, 정말로)는 부사이고, 나머지는 모두 형용사이다.

03 architect는 '건축가, 설계자'라는 뜻으로 '건물들을 설계하는 사람'이라는 뜻풀이가 자연스러우므로 빈칸에는 buildings(건물들)가 알맞다.

04 thanks to: ~ 덕분에

show ~ around: ~에게 구경시켜 주다

|해석| • Richard 덕분에, 나는 이 훌륭한 서점을 발견했다.

• 내가 네 고향을 방문하면 네가 나를 구경시켜 줄 수 있니?

05 첫 번째 문장의 빈칸에는 '예약하다, 예매하다'라는 뜻의 동사 book이 들어가고, 두 번째 문장의 빈칸에는 '책'이라는 뜻의 명사 book이 들어간다.

|해석| • 축제 표를 얻기 위해서 당신은 미리 예매해야 합니다.

• 나는 이 책을 7월 6일까지 학교 도서관에 반납해야 한다.

06 산과 해변은 자연(nature)의 일부분이다.

|해석| 나는 산과 해변과 같은 자연을 사진 찍는 것을 아주 좋아한다.

07 ⑤ peel((과일·채소의) 껍질)의 영어 뜻풀이는 the skin of a fruit이다.

|해석| ① 그들은 상자의 내용물을 점검하고 있다.

② 그 바늘은 끝이 약간 구부러져 있었다.

③ 아기들은 매우 연약한 피부를 가지고 있으니 조심해.

④ Joe는 유령이 정말로 존재한다고 믿는다.

⑤ 올리브유에 레몬 껍질을 추가하고 2분 동안 끓이세요.

08 '판매 중인'이라는 뜻을 나타낼 때는 on sale을 쓴다.

09 ⓐ '일몰의 아름다움'이라는 의미가 자연스러우므로 beauty(아름다움)가 들어간다.

ⓑ '총 인구'라는 의미가 되도록 total(총, 전체의)이 들어간다.

ⓒ 'Paul에게 상기시켜 주다'라는 의미가 자연스러우므로 remind(상기시키다)가 들어간다.

ⓓ '어떤 소리도 모방하다'라는 의미가 자연스러우므로 imitate(모방하다)가 들어간다.

|해석| ⓐ 우리는 일몰의 아름다움을 감탄하며 바라보았다.

ⓑ 그 나라는 총 인구가 대략 1억 명 정도이다.

ⓒ 네가 Paul에게 금요일 저녁 식사에 관해 상기시켜 줄 수 있니?

ⓓ 그는 그가 듣는 어떤 소리도 모방하는 독특한 능력이 있다.

10 '어떤 것을 말이나 그림을 이용하여 매우 정확하게 표현하거나 묘사하다'라는 의미의 단어는 capture(담아내다, 표현하다)이다.

|해석| ① 그 조각상을 만지지 말아 주세요.

② 그는 자신이 옳다는 것을 보여 주기 위해 몇 가지 예를 들었다.

③ 그녀의 아름다움을 그림 속에 담아내는 것은 불가능하다.

④ 실내에서 사진을 찍을 때 플래시를 사용하세요.

⑤ 그 사원의 지붕은 일렬로 늘어선 두꺼운 돌기둥에 의해 떠받쳐져 있었다.

11 (1) '관광 명소'라는 의미가 자연스러우므로 attraction(명소)이 들어간다.

(2) '표현'을 아는지 물어보는 것이 자연스러우므로 expression(표현)이 들어간다.

(3) '많은 사람들을 끌어모은다'라는 의미가 자연스러우므로 attract(마음을 끌다, 끌어모으다)가 들어간다.

|해석| (1) 남산 서울 타워는 서울의 인기 있는 관광 명소이다.

(2) 너는 "I have butterflies in my stomach"라는 표현을 아니?

(3) 그 상점들은 흥미로운 물건들이 많이 있어서 많은 사람들을 끌어모은다.

12 ⓑ, ⓓ, ⓕ는 「동사 – 명사」의 관계이다.

ⓐ, ⓒ는 「형용사 – 부사」의 관계이고, ⓔ는 「동사 – 형용사」의 관계이다.

13 ④ '영감'이라는 뜻의 명사 대신에 '영감을 주었다'라는 뜻의 동사가 쓰여야 하므로 inspired가 되어야 한다.

|해석| ① 거대한 파도가 해안가에 부딪쳐 부서지고 있었다.

② 너는 나에게 네 펜을 빌려줄 수 있니?

③ Lucy는 다른 사람들을 돕는 것에서 기쁨을 얻는다.

④ 그의 어린 시절이 그가 첫 소설을 쓰도록 영감을 주었다.

⑤ 나는 곧장 문으로 가서 크게 문을 두드렸다.

14 ⑤ foreigner는 '외국인'이라는 뜻이다.

① (꽃을) 꺾다 / 고르다, 뽑다

② 체육 / 체육관

③ 이야기 / (건물의) 층

④ 건네주다 / 통과하다, 합격하다

|해석| ① 공원에서 꽃을 꺾어서는 안 됩니다.

1부터 10까지 수 중 네가 가장 좋아하는 수를 골라라.

② David는 체육 수업에서 손을 다쳤다.

비가 올 때는 체육관에서 놀자.

③ 그 영화는 실제 이야기를 바탕으로 했다.

그 건물은 20층 높이다.

④ 제게 후추를 건네주시겠어요?

유진이는 댄스 오디션에 통과하기 위해 매일 연습했다.

⑤ 학교에 가는 길에 두 명의 외국인들이 나에게 시청으로 가는 길을 물었다.

약 4,000만 명의 외국인들이 작년에 미국을 방문했다.

01 ③ 02 ⑤ 03 ③ 04 ⑤ 05 ④ 06 ⑤

[서술형]

07 Thank you for helping me make a cake.

08 The tickets for the World Music Concert are on sale now.

09 They are not allowed to bring children under 8 (to the concert).

10 the tickets, November, bring her little brother

11 (1) Can I ask you a question?

　(2) You're not allowed to eat snacks here.

　(3) Thank you for understanding.

01 ③ You're not allowed to ~.로 상대방의 행동을 금지하는 말을 했는데, '이해해 주셔서 감사합니다.'로 답하는 것은 어색하다.

　|해석| ① A: 실례합니다. 여기서 드론을 날리면 안 됩니다.

　　B: 네, 알겠습니다.

　② A: 이 꽃들은 너를 위한 거야. 생일 축하해!

　　B: 아름답구나. 고마워.

　③ A: 여기서 음료를 드시면 안 됩니다.

　　B: 이해해 주셔서 감사합니다.

　④ A: 제가 플래시를 사용해도 되나요?

　　B: 죄송합니다. 여기서 플래시를 사용해서는 안 됩니다.

　⑤ A: 네 생일 파티에 나를 초대해 줘서 고마워.

　　B: 천만에. 나는 네가 와서 기뻐.

02 You're not allowed to ~.는 상대방에게 하지 말아야 할 행동을 말할 때 사용하는 표현이다.

　|해석| ① 의견 말하기

　② 다른 사람의 의견에 동의하기

　③ 누군가에게 조언 요청하기

　④ 누군가에게 무언가를 하는 방법 말하기

　⑤ 누군가에게 무언가를 하지 말라고 말하기

03 You're welcome. It was my pleasure.는 고마움에 답하는 표현이므로 빈칸에는 고마움을 나타내는 표현이 들어가야 한다.

04 ⑤ Thank you for ~.로 고마움을 표현하는 말에 '네 말에 동의해.'라고 답하는 것은 어색하다.

05 ④ Daniel은 민속촌이 가장 좋았다고 했다.

　|해석| ① Daniel은 며칠을 여행했는가?

　② Daniel은 수민이의 마을에서 무엇을 먹었는가?

　③ 수민이는 Daniel의 마을을 언제 방문할 것인가?

　④ Daniel은 수민이의 마을에서 어떤 장소가 가장 좋았는가?

　⑤ 기차로 Daniel의 마을에 가는 데 얼마나 걸리는가?

06 빈칸 앞에 할 수 있는 행동을 말했으므로, 역접의 접속사 but으로 이어지는 빈칸에는 하지 말아야 할 행동을 금지하는 말이 들어가는 것이 알맞다.

07 A가 '천만에.'라고 고마움에 답하는 말을 하는 것으로 보아 빈칸에는 고마움을 나타내는 표현이 들어가는 것이 알맞다. 고마움을 나타낼 때는 Thank you for ~.를 사용하며, 전치사 for 뒤에 동사가 올 경우에

는 동명사 형태로 쓴다.

08 '세계 음악 콘서트' 표가 지금 판매 중이다.

　|해석| 지금 어떤 표가 판매 중인가?

09 8세 미만의 어린이들은 데려오지 못한다고 했다.

　|해석| 소미와 Joe는 어떤 아이들을 콘서트에 데려가는 게 허용되지 않는가?

10 두 사람은 11월 5일 '세계 음악 콘서트'에 가는데, 소미는 10살인 남동생을 데려갈 예정이다.

　|해석| 소미와 Joe는 11월 5일에 하는 '세계 음악 콘서트' 표를 예매 중이다. 소미는 그녀의 남동생을 데려갈 것이다. 그는 다행히 열 살이기 때문에 그 콘서트에 갈 수 있다.

11 (1) 문맥상 질문을 해도 되는지 묻는 말이 알맞다.

　(2) A가 과자를 먹는 것이 허용되는지 묻자 B가 Sorry.라고 답하는 것으로 보아, 빈칸에는 허용되지 않는다는 말이 들어가는 것이 알맞다.

　(3) 이해해 줘서 고맙다고 말하는 것이 알맞다.

G **Grammar 고득점 맞기** pp. 126~128

01 ③ 02 ⑤ 03 ② 04 ④ 05 ② 06 ③ 07 ②

08 ④ 09 ⑤ 10 ②, ③, ④ 11 (1) ⓒ (2) ⓑ (3) ⓐ 12 ②

[서술형]

13 (1) 모범답 so that she could buy a new bicycle

　(2) 모범답 so that he could donate it to the poor

14 (1) The stadium is large enough to hold 3,000 people.

　(2) Sora is brave enough to go into the Ghost House.

　(3) The skirt was cheap enough for Amy to buy.

15 (1) in order to pass the final exam,

　　so that he could pass the final exam

　(2) so as to catch the last bus,

　　so that she could catch the last bus

16 (1) The basket is big enough to hold all the balls.

　(2) John is strong enough to lift the rock.

　(3) This book is easy enough for my brother to understand.

17 (1) 모범답 I jumped rope every day so that I could lose weight.

　(2) 모범답 I read English books so that I could develop my English.

01 우리말을 영어로 옮기면 He practices playing the violin very hard so that he can be a violinist.이다.

02 「형용사(small)+enough to+동사원형(fit)」의 어순으로 쓰므로 문장은 The kitten is small enough to fit in my hand.가 된다.

03 ② 콤마(,) 다음에 오는 so는 콤마 앞에 오는 절의 결과를 나타내어 '그래서'로 해석한다. (→ 그녀는 따뜻한 우유를 마셔서 잠을 잘 잤다.)

04 ⓑ, ⓒ, ⓓ가 옳은 문장이다.

ⓐ 「형용사+enough to+동사원형」의 어순으로 써야 하므로 enough old를 old enough로 고쳐 써야 한다.

ⓔ 목적을 나타내는 so that 뒤에는 「주어+동사 ~」로 이루어진 절이 와야 하므로 stays 앞에 주어(it)가 추가되어야 한다.

|해석| ⓐ 그는 자신을 돌볼 만큼 충분히 나이가 많지 않다.

ⓑ 그녀는 스트레스를 풀 수 있도록 웹툰을 읽는다.

ⓒ 그 난방기는 화상을 일으킬 만큼 충분히 뜨거우니 조심하세요.

ⓓ 그 호수의 물은 우리가 마실 만큼 충분히 깨끗했다.

ⓔ 너는 우유가 신선하게 유지되도록 냉장고에 넣어 두어야 한다.

05 첫 번째 문장의 빈칸에는 '~하도록'의 뜻을 나타내는 so that이 되도록 so가 와야 하고, 두 번째 문장의 빈칸에는 '그래서'의 뜻으로 쓰이는 접속사 so가 와야 한다.

|해석| · 좋은 자리를 얻을 수 있도록 그곳에 일찍 가자.

· 의자가 더 없어서 우리는 서야 할 것이다.

06 「형용사+enough to+동사원형」의 어순으로 써야 하므로 comfortable을 enough 앞에 써야 한다.

07 첫 번째 빈칸에는 목적을 나타내는 절을 이끄는 so that이 알맞다. 두 번째 빈칸에는 '~하기에〔~할 만큼〕 충분히 …한'의 의미를 나타내는 「형용사+enough to+동사원형」이 되도록 enough to가 와야 한다.

|해석| 세미는 건강을 유지할 수 있도록 매일 수영을 한다. 그녀는 무거운 상자들을 들어올릴 만큼 충분히 힘이 세다.

08 주어진 문장의 to catch the first train과 ④의 so that I could catch the first train은 집을 일찍 나온 목적을 나타낸다.

|해석| 나는 첫 기차를 타기 위해 집을 일찍 나왔다.

09 ⑤ 첫 번째 문장은 'Kate의 아들은 유치원에 갈 만큼 충분히 나이가 있다.'라는 뜻을 나타내고, 두 번째 문장은 'Kate의 아들은 너무 나이가 많아서 유치원에 갈 수 없다.'라는 뜻을 나타낸다.

|해석| ① Rick은 꼭대기 선반에 닿을 만큼 충분히 키가 크다.

Rick은 매우 키가 커서 꼭대기 선반에 닿을 수 있다.

② 나의 할머니께서는 매우 약하셔서 그녀의 정원에서 일하실 수 없다.

③ Linda는 그 의자들을 옮길 만큼 충분히 힘이 세다.

Linda는 매우 힘이 세서 그 의자들을 옮길 수 있다.

④ 그 소년은 여행 가이드가 될 수 있도록 여러 언어를 공부한다.

그 소년은 여행 가이드가 되기 위해 여러 언어를 공부한다.

⑤ Kate의 아들은 유치원에 갈 만큼 충분히 나이가 있다.

Kate의 아들은 너무 나이가 많아서 유치원에 갈 수 없다.

10 ② so that은 '목적'을 나타내는 절을 이끈다.

③, ④ 목적을 나타내는 so that이 이끄는 절은 '~하도록, ~하기 위해(서)'라는 의미를 나타낸다. too ~ to...는 '너무 ~해서 …할 수 없다'라는 의미를 나타내고, so ~ that은 '너무〔매우〕 ~해서 …한'이라는 의미를 나타낸다. 이때 so 뒤에 동사(climbed)는 오지 않는다.

|해석| ① 그 피자는 네 사람이 먹을 만큼 충분히 컸다.

② 내가 책에 집중할 수 있도록 조용히 해 주세요.

③ 나는 Kevin이 나의 한국어를 이해할 수 있도록 천천히 말했다.

④ 그 원숭이는 바나나를 먹을 수 있도록 바나나 나무를 올라갔다.

⑤ 이 여행 가방은 비행기 안에 들고 갈 만큼 충분히 작다.

11 so that이 이끄는 절의 내용이 so that 앞의 내용의 목적에 해당하는

것을 찾아 기호를 쓴다.

|해석| (1) 문을 닫아라.

(2) 그는 차를 그늘에 주차했다.

(3) Brown 씨는 창가 자리를 예매했다.

ⓐ 그는 멋진 풍경을 볼 수 있었다.

ⓑ 그것은 너무 뜨거워지지 않을 것이었다.

ⓒ 찬 공기가 안으로 들어오지 않는다.

12 완전한 문장은 This table is small enough for me to carry.이다.

13 목적을 나타내는 so that 뒤에 그림의 내용을 「주어+동사 ~」 형태의 절로 써서 문장을 완성한다.

14 「so+형용사+that+주어+can/could+동사원형」은 '너무〔매우〕 ~해서 …할 수 있다〔있었다〕'라는 뜻으로, 「형용사+enough to+동사원형」으로 바꿔 쓸 수 있다.

|해석| (1) 그 경기장은 매우 넓어서 3,000명의 사람들을 수용할 수 있다.

(2) 소라는 매우 용감해서 '유령의 집'에 들어갈 수 있다.

(3) 그 치마는 매우 싸서 Amy는 그것을 살 수 있었다.

15 주어진 문장의 to부정사는 목적을 나타내며, 「so that+주어+동사 ~」, 「in order to+동사원형」, 「so as to+동사원형」도 목적을 나타낸다.

|해석| (1) Lucas는 기말고사를 통과하기 위해 열심히 공부했다.

(2) 보라는 마지막 버스를 타기 위해 빨리 달렸다.

16 '~할 만큼 충분히 …한'은 「형용사+enough to+동사원형」으로 쓴다.

17 so that이 이끄는 절의 내용이 이루고자 했던 목적에 해당한다.

Ⓡ Reading 고득점 맞기   pp.131~133

01 ④   **02** ②, ③   **03** ⑤   **04** ④   **05** ①   **06** ④   **07** ⑤

08 ②, ③   **09** ④   **10** ③   **11** As you can see   **12** ⑤

[서술형]

13 많은 예술가들이 그들의 아이디어와 영감을 그들 주변의 세상에서 얻는다.

14 (1) The shapes in nature are very pleasing to the eye.

(2) Can you imagine a building that(which) looks like an egg?

15 Can you guess what inspired him?

16 the waves in the ocean or a sailing boat, an orange

17 (1) Many people think that it looks like a giant spaceship.

(2) Zaha Hadid took the curved lines from nature so that city people could enjoy them.

01 ④ 달걀은 둥글고 부서지기 쉽다고 말한 뒤 yet(그렇지만, 그럼에도)으로 문장을 이어가고 있으므로, weak이 아니라 strong이 나오는 것이 자연스럽다.

02 빈칸에는 a building을 선행사로 하는 주격 관계대명사가 와야 하므로 that 또는 which가 들어갈 수 있다.

03 ⑤ allow(허락하다, 허용하다)의 영어 뜻풀이로, allow는 글에 나오지 않는 단어이다.

① exist(존재하다)의 영어 뜻풀이다.

② delicate(부서지기 쉬운, 섬세한)의 영어 뜻풀이다.

③ imitate(모방하다)의 영어 뜻풀이다.

④ contents(내용물, 안에 든 것)의 영어 뜻풀이다.

04 ⓐ 앞 문장의 '사그라다 파밀리아 성당'을 가리킨다.

ⓑ 앞 문장의 '아름다운 높은 기둥들'을 가리킨다.

05 앞에 Antoni Gaudi가 성당에 나무의 형태를 사용했다는 내용이 나오므로, That's how ~.로 시작하는 문장이 이어져서 '그것이 ~한 방법이다, 그런 식으로 ~하는 것이다'라는 뜻이 되는 것이 자연스럽다.

06 ④ 성당 안에 있는 기둥이 나무처럼 보인다고 했다.

|해석| ① 많은 건축가들이 자연에서 영감을 받아왔다.

② 사그라다 파밀리아 성당은 스페인에 있다.

③ 사그라다 파밀리아 성당은 세계적으로 유명하다.

④ 사그라다 파밀리아 성당 밖의 기둥들은 나무처럼 보인다.

⑤ Antoni Gaudi는 사그라다 파밀리아 성당의 기둥을 지을 때 나무에서 영감을 받았다.

07 (A) 뒤에 이어지는 문장이 But으로 시작하며 다음의 예시에서는 명확히 알 수 없다고 했으므로, 빈칸에는 easily(쉽게)가 들어가는 것이 알맞다.

(B) think의 목적어 역할을 하는 명사절을 이끄는 접속사 that이 알맞다.

(C) 문맥상 imagination(상상력)이 아니라 inspiration(영감)이 알맞다.

08 ② 등위접속사 and에 의해 동사 took과 add가 연결되어 있으므로 add를 과거형인 added로 고쳐 써야 한다.

③ what은 '무엇'이라는 뜻의 의문대명사로 명사절 안에서 주어 역할을 하므로 it을 삭제해야 한다.

09 ④ 시드니 오페라 하우스의 높이는 글을 통해서는 알 수 없다.

|해석| ① 시드니 오페라 하우스의 건축가는 누구였는가?

② 시드니 오페라 하우스의 건축가는 무엇에서 영감을 받았는가?

③ 많은 사람들은 시드니 오페라 하우스의 건축가가 무엇에서 영감을 받았다고 생각하는가?

④ 시드니 오페라 하우스는 얼마나 높은가?

⑤ 언제 시드니 오페라 하우스의 오렌지 껍질 형태를 더 명확하게 볼 수 있는가?

10 (A) Have you ever been to ~?로 '너는 ~에 가 본 적이 있니?'라는 뜻의 '경험'을 나타내는 현재완료 시제가 쓰여야 알맞다.

(B) '~하도록, ~하기 위해(서)'라는 뜻의 목적을 나타내며 「주어+동사 ~」로 이루어진 절을 이끌어야 하므로 so that이 알맞다. in order to 뒤에는 동사원형이 온다.

(C) if절의 동사가 were인 것으로 보아 가정법 과거 문장이므로, 조동사는 과거형 would를 써야 한다.

11 첫 번째 단락은 한국에 있는 동대문 디자인 플라자가 무엇에서 영감을 얻어서 만들어진 것인지를 설명하고 있고, 두 번째 단락은 많은 건물들이 디자인에 자연의 아름다움을 담아내려 한다며 글을 마무리하고 있다.

12 ⑤ 동대문 디자인 플라자가 무엇에 사용되는지는 글에 제시되어 있지 않다.

14 (1) 문장의 주어 The shapes가 복수형이므로 is를 복수 동사 are로 고쳐 써야 한다.

(2) 주격 관계대명사가 이끄는 절이 선행사 a building을 수식해야 하므로 what을 주격 관계대명사 that(which)으로 고쳐 써야 한다.

15 의문사 what이 이끄는 절(what inspired him)이 문장의 목적어 역할을 하도록 문장을 완성한다.

16 |해석| 많은 사람들은 시드니 오페라 하우스가 <u>바다의 파도</u>나 돛단배에서 영감을 받았다고 생각한다. 하지만 시드니 오페라 하우스의 건축가에게 영감을 준 것은 <u>오렌지</u>였다.

17 (1) 많은 사람들은 동대문 디자인 플라자가 거대한 우주선처럼 보인다고 생각한다고 했다.

(2) Zaha Hadid는 도시 사람들이 즐길 수 있도록 자연에서 곡선을 가져왔다고 했다.

|해석| (1) 많은 사람들은 동대문 디자인 플라자가 무엇처럼 보인다고 생각하는가?

(2) Zaha Hadid는 왜 자연에서 곡선을 가져왔는가?

서술형 100% TEST

01 book

02 (1) imitate (2) expression (3) inspiration

03 You're not allowed to fish here.

04 Thank you for lending me the book.

05 (1) 작품의 사진을 찍는 것 (2) 작품을 만지는 것

06 Thank you for helping me plant some flowers in my garden.

07 You're not allowed to eat snacks here.

08 (1) I liked the folk village most.

(2) I really liked walking around in hanbok.

(3) Thank you for showing me around.

09 ⓒ → It was warm enough to eat out this evening.

ⓓ → David practices playing the guitar very hard (in order) to win the contest.

10 (1) Ben studies hard so that he can pass the exam.

(2) Amy went to bed early so that she could catch the first train.

11 (1) to got → to get (2) bravery → brave

12 (1) (모범답) baking classes so that you can make a cake (for your mother's birthday)

(2) (모범답) the volume down so that I can concentrate on my book

13 (1) Peter is smart enough to solve the difficult quiz.

(2) Amy is not strong enough to lift the box.

14 (1) 모범답 so that we can stay healthy

    (2) 모범답 so that you can remember your past

    (3) 모범답 so that you can get some fresh air

15 그것은 둥글고 부서지기 쉽지만, 내용물을 보호할 만큼 충분히 튼튼하다.

16 (1) It's because the natural world is a beautiful place.

    (2) We can find the building in London. / The building that looks like an egg is in London.

17 Nature has inspired many architects around the world.

18 (1) the shape of trees

    (2) the beautiful tall columns inside the church

19 what inspired the architect

20 architect, an orange

21 (1) Many people think that the building looks like a giant spaceship.

    (2) Thanks to its special design, it has become a popular tourist attraction in Seoul.

22 the curved lines from nature, city people could enjoy

23 (1) My school has a 4-story building, a large playground, a gym and a small garden.

    (2) The garden is on top of the school building.

    (3) My favorite place is the bench under the big tree.

01 '표지 안에 함께 묶여진 인쇄된 종이의 한 세트'와 '미래에 대비하여 예약을 하다'를 뜻하는 단어는 book(책, 예약하다)이다.

02 (1) 조동사(can) 뒤에는 동사원형이 오며, '(목소리를) 모방하다(imitate)'가 알맞다.

    (2), (3) 정관사(the)나 소유격(her) 뒤에는 명사가 온다. (2)는 '표현 (expression)'을 아는지 묻는 것이 알맞다. (3)은 '영감(inspiration)'을 얻었다는 것이 알맞다.

    I해석I (1) 그 앵무새는 나의 목소리를 모방할 수 있다.

    (2) 너는 "시간은 돈이다"라는 표현을 아니?

    (3) 그 예술가는 그녀 주변의 세상에서 영감을 얻었다.

03 금지를 나타내는 표현인 You're not allowed to ~.를 사용하여 낚시를 하면 안 된다는 금지의 말을 완성한다.

04 A가 고마움에 답하는 말을 하는 것으로 보아 빈칸에는 고마움을 표현하는 말이 오는 것이 알맞다. 고마움을 나타낼 때는 Thank you for ~.를 쓰고 for 뒤에 동사가 올 때는 동명사 형태로 써야 한다.

05 You can take pictures of the artworks, but you're not allowed to touch them.에 허용되는 것과 허용되지 않는 것이 나와 있다.

06 고마움을 나타내는 표현인 Thank you for ~.를 사용한다.

    I해석I 당신의 친구가 당신이 정원에 꽃을 심는 것을 도와주었다. 당신은 친구에게 뭐라고 말할 것인가?

07 금지를 나타내는 표현인 You're not allowed to ~.를 사용한다.

    I해석I 당신은 도서관에서 사서로 일한다. 당신은 한 소년이 과자를 먹고 있는 것을 본다. 당신은 그에게 과자를 먹지 말라고 말해야 한다. 당

신은 그에게 뭐라고 말할 것인가?

08 (1) 민속촌이 가장 좋았다고 했다.

    (2) 한복을 입고 돌아다니는 게 정말 좋았다고 했다.

    (3) 수민이에게 여기저기 구경시켜 줘서 고맙다고 감사의 말을 했다.

    I해석I 8월 20일

    나는 오늘 집에 돌아왔다. 멋진 여행이었다. 나는 민속촌이 가장 좋았다. 나는 한복을 입고 돌아다니는 게 정말 좋았다. 내가 정말 멋져 보였다. 나는 수민이에게 나에게 구경시켜 줘서 고맙다고 말했다.

09 ⓒ 「형용사+enough to+동사원형」의 어순으로 써야 하므로, enough warm을 warm enough로 고쳐야 한다.

    ⓓ 목적을 나타낼 때 in order that 뒤에는 「주어+동사 ~」로 이루어진 절이 오므로, in order that을 (in order) to 등으로 고쳐야 한다.

    I해석I ⓐ 그의 그림은 팔 만큼 충분히 좋다.

    ⓑ 너는 동아리 모임에 늦지 않도록 서둘러야 한다.

    ⓒ 오늘 저녁은 외식할 만큼 충분히 따뜻했다.

    ⓓ David는 경연 대회에서 우승할 수 있도록 기타를 연주하는 것을 매우 열심히 연습한다.

    ⓔ 나는 기부하기 위해 중고 서적을 모았다.

10 「so that+주어+동사 ~」는 '~하도록, ~하기 위해(서)'라는 뜻으로 목적을 나타낸다.

11 「형용사+enough to+동사원형」의 형태로 써야 한다. bravery는 '용기'라는 뜻의 명사이다.

12 「so that+주어+동사 ~」는 '~하도록'이라는 목적의 의미를 나타낸다.

    I해석I (1) 보라는 그녀의 어머니의 생일을 위한 케이크를 만들고 싶어한다. 당신은 제빵 수업을 듣는 것이 좋은 생각인 것 같다.

    (2) 당신은 책을 읽고 있고 남동생 기호는 거실에서 텔레비전을 보고 있다. 그가 음량을 높이고 당신은 책에 집중할 수 없다.

13 '~할 만큼 충분히 …한'의 뜻이 되도록 「형용사+enough to+동사원형」의 어순으로 문장을 완성한다.

14 so that이 이끄는 절의 내용이 앞에 주어진 말과 의미가 통하도록 문장을 완성한다. so that 뒤에 오는 내용이 앞의 내용의 '목적'이 되어야 한다.

15 「형용사(strong)+enough to+동사원형(protect)」은 '~할 만큼 충분히 …한'으로 해석한다. yet은 접속사로 '그렇지만, 그럼에도'라는 뜻을 나타낸다.

16 (1) 많은 예술가들이 아이디어와 영감을 그들 주변의 세상에서 얻는데, 이는 자연계가 아름다운 곳이기 때문이라고 했다.

    (2) 달걀처럼 생긴 건물이 런던에 실제로 존재한다고 했다.

    I해석I (1) 많은 예술가들은 왜 그들의 아이디어와 영감을 그들 주변의 세상에서 얻는가?

    (2) 어느 도시에서 달걀처럼 생긴 건물을 발견할 수 있는가?

17 현재완료 시제는 「have/has+과거분사(inspired)」로 쓰고, 이 문장에서는 계속의 의미를 나타낸다.

18 Antoni Gaudi는 사그라다 파밀리아 성당 안의 기둥에 나무의 형태를 사용하여 자연의 아름다움을 실내로 가져왔다.

    I해석I 기자: 당신은 어떻게 자연의 아름다움을 실내로 가져왔나요?

    Antoni Gaudi: 저는 사그라다 파밀리아 성당에 나무의 형태를 사용했어요.

기자: 어디에 그 형태를 적용했나요?

Antoni Gaudi: 성당 안에 있는 아름답고 높은 기둥들을 보세요.

기자: 오, 기둥들이 나무처럼 보이네요!

19 this는 앞 문장의 what inspired the architect를 가리킨다.

20 Jørn Utzon은 시드니 오페라 하우스의 건축가이고, 그는 오렌지에서 영감을 받았다고 했다.

|해석| 시드니 오페라 하우스의 <u>건축가</u>인 Jørn Utzon은 오렌지에서 영감을 받았다.

21 (1) '~처럼 보이다'는 「look like+명사(구)」로 쓴다.

(2) '~ 덕분에'는 thanks to로 쓴다.

22 Zaha Hadid는 도시 사람들이 즐길 수 있도록 자연에서 곡선을 가져왔다고 했다.

|해석| Zaha Hadid는 도시 사람들이 즐길 수 있도록 <u>자연에서 곡선</u>을 가져와서 동대문 디자인 플라자에 사용했다.

23 |해석| (1) 너희 학교에는 무엇이 있니?

(2) 정원은 어디에 있니?

(3) 네가 가장 좋아하는 장소는 어디니?

모의고사

제 **1** 회   대표 기출로 내신 **적중** 모의고사   pp. 138~141

01 ②   **02** ②   **03** ③   **04** ③   **05** ②   **06** ③   **07** ③
08 Thank you for inviting me to your birthday party.
09 ③   **10** one child ticket, November 5th   **11** ③   **12** ⑤
13 ⑤   **14** (1) He was kind enough to show me around the town. (2) She is strong enough to lift the heavy box.
15 많은 예술가들이 그들의 아이디어와 영감을 그들 주변의 세상에서 얻는 것   **16** ⑤   **17** (A) It is round and delicate, yet strong enough to protect its contents. (B) Can you imagine a building that looks like an egg?   **18** ④   **19** ②   **20** ①, ④
21 ①   **22** the waves in the ocean or a sailing boat, an orange   **23** ⓑ → We can see it in Australia.   **24** ②
25 (1) looks like a tree (2) get fresh air and sunshine all the time (3) move around

01 [보기]는 '허락하다, 허용하다', ②는 '분명한, 명백한'의 의미로 유의어 관계이고, 나머지는 반의어 관계이다.

02 ② delicate(부서지기 쉬운, 섬세한)의 영어 뜻풀이는 easily broken or damaged(쉽게 깨지거나 손상을 입는)이다.

03 첫 번째 빈칸에는 '예약하다, 예매하다'를 뜻하는 동사 book이 들어가고, 두 번째 빈칸에는 '책'을 뜻하는 명사 book이 들어가는 것이 알맞다.

|해석| • 만약 당신이 지금 박물관 표를 예매하면 할인을 받을 수 있습니다.

• '톰 소여의 모험'은 Mark Twain이 쓴 <u>책</u>이다.

04 ⓐ '전시하다'를 뜻하는 exhibit이 들어간다.

ⓑ '기본적인'을 뜻하는 basic이 들어간다.

ⓒ '영감'을 뜻하는 inspiration이 들어간다.

ⓓ '표현하다'를 뜻하는 express가 들어간다.

|해석| ⓐ 그 미술관은 다음 달부터 반 고흐의 그림을 <u>전시할</u> 것이다.

ⓑ Lucy는 나에게 춤의 <u>기본적인</u> 스텝을 몇 가지 가르쳐 주었다.

ⓒ 그 예술가는 대개 자연에서 <u>영감</u>을 얻는다.

ⓓ Bill은 자신의 감정을 다른 사람들에게 <u>표현하지</u> 않는다.

05 상대방에게 고마움을 표현할 때는 Thank you for 뒤에 고마운 이유를 말한다.

06 미술관에서 보게 될 것을 말한(B) 후, 관람을 시작하기 전에 기본 규칙을 상기시켜 주며(C) 구체적으로 규칙을 언급하고(A) 관람을 시작하자고 하는(D) 흐름이 되는 것이 자연스럽다.

07 ③ 미술관에서 전시하고 있는 작품의 수는 알 수 없다.

08 Thank you for ~.를 사용하여 고마움을 나타내는 표현을 쓴다. for 뒤에 동사가 오는 경우 동명사 형태로 쓰는 것에 유의한다.

09 ③ 대화의 흐름상 '8세 미만의 어린이들은 데려오지 못한다고 쓰여 있다(But it says that you are not allowed to bring children under 8.)'고 해야 자연스럽다.

10 두 사람은 '세계 음악 콘서트'의 11월 5일 표를 학생용 두 장과 어린이용 한 장을 예매했다.

|해석| 그들은 <u>11월 5일</u>에 '세계 음악 콘서트'의 학생 표 두 장과 어린이 표 <u>한 장</u>을 예매했다.

11 '~하도록, ~하기 위해(서)'라는 의미로 목적을 나타내는 절을 이끄는 so that이 알맞다. in order to 또한 목적을 나타내지만 뒤에 동사원형이 와야 한다.

|해석| Anna는 코미디 쇼를 볼 수 있도록 텔레비전을 켰다.

12 '~할 만큼 충분히 …한'의 의미를 나타내는 「형용사(smart)+enough to+동사원형」 구문이 되도록 enough가 알맞다.

|해석| William은 어려운 퍼즐을 풀 만큼 충분히 똑똑하다.

13 ⑤ so that 다음에는 「주어+동사 ~」 형태의 절이 와야 하므로 so that 뒤에 주어 she를 추가해야 한다.

|해석| ① 나는 가난한 사람들에게 기부할 수 있도록 돈을 모으고 있다.

② 나는 테니스 시합에서 우승하기 위해 테니스 치는 것을 매우 열심히 연습한다.

③ Jason은 첫 기차를 타기 위해 일찍 일어났다.

④ 나는 미술 숙제를 끝내기 위해 집에 머물렀다.

⑤ Amy는 잘 잘 수 있도록 따뜻한 우유를 마셨다.

14 '~할 만큼 충분히 …한'은 「형용사+enough to+동사원형」으로 쓴다.

15 This는 바로 앞 문장(Many artists get their ideas and inspirations from the world around them.)의 내용을 가리킨다.

16 달걀을 예로 들고 있으므로 '예를 들어'라는 뜻으로 예시를 나타내는 For example이 알맞다.

17 (A) '~할 만큼 충분히 …한'은 「형용사(strong)+enough to+동사원

형(protect)」의 형태로 쓰므로 strong enough protect를 strong enough to protect로 고쳐 써야 한다.

(B) that은 주격 관계대명사이고, 주격 관계대명사가 이끄는 절의 동사는 선행사의 수에 일치시키는데, 선행사 a building이 단수형이므로 동사도 단수 동사인 looks로 고쳐 써야 한다.

18 (A) 자연이 세계의 많은 건축가들에게 '영감을 주어 왔다'고 하는 것이 알맞다. capture는 '담아내다, 표현하다, 포착하다'라는 뜻이다.

(B) 기둥이 나무처럼 보인다고 했으므로, Antoni Gaudi가 '나무'의 형태를 사용했다고 하는 것이 알맞다.

(C) 앞에서 성당 안에 있는 기둥을 예로 설명하고 있으므로, 자연의 아름다움을 '실내로' 가져왔다고 해야 자연스럽다. outdoors는 '야외로, 야외에서'라는 뜻이다.

19 ⓐ와 ②의 like는 '~처럼'이라는 뜻의 전치사로 쓰였다.

①, ③, ⑤ '좋아하다'라는 뜻의 동사

④ I'd like to: ~하고 싶다

|해석| ① 나는 야구를 좋아하지만, 내 여동생은 농구를 정말 좋아한다.

② 그 소년은 어린아이처럼 행동하고 있었다.

③ Judy는 텔레비전 앞에서 그녀의 저녁 시간을 보내는 것을 좋아하지 않는다.

④ 나는 그 주제에 관한 네 의견을 듣고 싶다.

⑤ 너는 어떤 종류의 동아리 활동을 가장 좋아하니?

20 ①, ④ 사그라다 파밀리아 성당은 스페인에 있고, Antoni Gaudi가 기둥을 만들 때 영감을 받은 것은 나무의 형태라고 했다.

21 ⓐ what이 이끄는 절은 see의 목적어 역할을 하는 명사절이다. what(무엇)은 명사절 안에서 주어 역할을 하고 있으며, 동사는 '영감을 주었다'라는 능동의 의미가 되도록 inspired가 알맞다.

ⓑ 건축가가 자신의 상상력을 '더했다'라는 능동의 의미가 되도록 added가 알맞다.

ⓒ 문장 전체를 수식하는 부사가 와야 한다.

22 |해석| 많은 사람들은 바다의 파도나 돛단배가 시드니 오페라 하우스의 건축가에게 영감을 주었다고 생각한다. 하지만 그가 실제로 영감을 받은 것은 오렌지였다.

23 ⓑ But in the next example from Australia ~.에서 뒤에 제시되고 있는 시드니 오페라 하우스가 '호주'에 위치해 있음을 알 수 있다.

|해석| ⓐ 앞의 두 예시에서 건축가는 무엇에서 영감을 받았는가?

ⓑ 어느 나라에서 시드니 오페라 하우스를 볼 수 있는가?

ⓒ 시드니 오페라 하우스의 건축가는 왜 자연에서 형태를 가져왔는가?

ⓓ 시드니 오페라 하우스의 건축가는 왜 자신의 상상력을 더했는가?

24 ② '그 나무는 오랜 세월을 살아남았다.'는 문장은 나무처럼 생긴 모양의 집을 설명하는 전체 글의 흐름과 관계없다.

25 지호가 자신의 집을 소개하는 글로, 지호의 집은 나무처럼 보이며, 항상 선선한 공기를 얻고 햇빛을 받을 수 있도록 지붕이 열리고, 집이 움직일 수 있다고 했다.

|해석| 지호: 우리 집에 온 걸 환영해.

Ella: 와, 집이 멋지구나!

지호: 고마워. 집이 무엇처럼 보이니?

Ella: 음, 나무처럼 보여.

지호: 맞아. 지붕을 봐. 항상 신선한 공기를 얻고 햇빛을 받기 위해 지붕이 열려.

Ella: 그거 좋구나! 네 집은 그 밖에 어떤 점이 특별하니?

지호: 우리 집은 움직일 수 있어.

제2회 대표 기출로 내신 **적중** 모의고사 pp. 142~145

01 ② **02** ④ **03** ③ **04** ⑤ **05** ④ **06** ⑤ **07** folk village, walking around, hanbok **08** art museum **09** ③, ④ **10** ② **11** (1) Sue turned on the TV so that she could watch the baseball game. (2) This book is easy enough for me to read. **12** ③, ④ **13** ② **14** The dog was small enough to go through the hole. **15** ③ **16** It is one of the most famous churches in the world. **17** shape of trees, columns inside, beauty of nature **18** ④ **19** architect, orange, his imagination **20** ④ **21** ② **22** ③ **23** ⑤ **24** ① **25** a 4-story building, a large playground, a gym, a small garden, we can have fresh food

01 ②는 '지역의 – 장소'의 의미로 「형용사 – 명사」의 관계이고, 나머지는 모두 「동사 – 명사」의 관계이다.

02 ④ go through는 '통과하다'라는 뜻을 나타낸다.

|해석| ① 나는 건강을 유지하기 위해 요가 수업을 듣는다.

② 내가 너에게 이 마을을 구경시켜 줄게.

③ 지도 덕분에, 우리는 길을 쉽게 찾을 수 있었다.

④ 그 공은 구멍을 통과하기에 너무 크다.

⑤ 이 탑은 나의 고향에서 유명한 관광 명소가 되었다.

03 ③ 주어(Liszt's music)가 감정을 느끼게 하는 대상이므로 pleased가 아닌 현재분사 형태의 형용사인 pleasing(즐거운, 기분 좋은)을 써야 한다.

|해석| ① 나에게 이 편지를 부치라고 상기시켜 줘.

② 그 소년은 그의 손 위에 있는 애벌레를 만졌다.

③ 리스트의 음악은 듣기에 매우 좋다.

④ 나는 그 풍경의 아름다움에 감동했다.

⑤ 이 유리는 매우 깨지기 쉬우니 조심하세요.

04 ⑤ 상대방에게 하지 말아야 할 행동을 말할 때는 You're not allowed to ~.를 사용한다.

05 ④ 꽃을 주며 생일을 축하해 주는 말에 유감을 표현하는 말(I'm sorry to hear that.)로 답하는 것은 어색하다.

|해석| ① A: 당신은 여기서 새에게 먹이를 주면 안 됩니다.

B: 죄송합니다. 몰랐어요.

② A: 너의 엄마의 생일 파티는 어땠니?

B: 좋았어. 내가 케이크를 만드는 것을 도와줘서 고마워.

③ A: 실례합니다. 제가 질문을 해도 될까요?

B: 물론이에요. 무엇인가요?

④ A: 이 꽃들은 너를 위한 거야. 생일 축하해!
　　B: 꽃들이 아름답구나. 그 말을 들어서 유감이야.
⑤ A: 제가 애완동물을 데려와도 될까요?
　　B: 죄송합니다. 여기에 애완동물을 데려오면 안 됩니다.

06 ⑤ Thank you for ~.는 상대방에게 고마움을 나타낼 때 사용하는 표현으로, 이에 대한 응답은 It was my pleasure. 또는 You're welcome. 등으로 말해야 한다.

07 Daniel은 민속촌이 가장 좋았고, 한복을 입고 돌아다니는 게 정말 좋았다고 했다.
|해석| Daniel은 수민이의 동네를 여행했다. 그는 민속촌이 가장 좋았다. 그는 한복을 입고 돌아다니는 게 정말 좋았다.

08 Thank you for visiting our art museum.이라고 말하는 것으로 보아, 미술관에서 말하고 있음을 알 수 있다.

09 ③ you will see some famous artworks from the art books에서 미술 책에 실린 유명한 작품들이 전시되고 있음을 알 수 있다.
④ You can take pictures of the artworks에서 작품의 사진을 찍을 수 있다는 것을 알 수 있다.

10 첫 번째 빈칸에는 '목적'을 나타내는 절을 이끄는 so that의 that이 알맞다. 두 번째 빈칸에는 「형용사(old)+enough to+동사원형」 구문의 enough가 알맞다.
|해석| • 나는 Mike가 공원에서 탈 수 있도록 내 자전거를 빌려주었다.
• Tim은 그 롤러코스터를 탈 만큼 충분히 나이가 있다.

11 (1) '~하도록, ~하기 위해(서)'라는 의미로 목적을 나타낼 때는 「so that+주어+동사 ~」를 쓴다.
(2) '~할 만큼 충분히 …한'은 「형용사+enough to+동사원형」을 쓰고, to부정사의 의미상의 주어는 to부정사 앞에 「for+목적격(me)」으로 쓴다.

12 ③ 「형용사(tall)+enough to+동사원형(touch)」의 어순이 되어야 하므로 tall enough to touch로 고쳐 써야 한다.
④ everybody could understand his speech는 주어와 동사가 모두 있는 절이므로, 목적을 나타내려면 so as to 대신에 so that이 절을 이끌어야 한다.
|해석| ① 나는 스트레스를 풀기 위해 피아노 음악을 듣는다.
② 우리는 전기를 절약하기 위해 전등을 꺼야 한다.
③ Rachel은 선반에 닿을 만큼 충분히 키가 크지 않다.
④ Johns 씨는 모든 사람이 그의 연설을 이해할 수 있도록 명확하게 말했다.
⑤ 그 치즈케이크는 다섯 사람이 먹을 만큼 충분히 크다.

13 ⓐ와 ⓒ에는 so가 들어가고, ⓑ와 ⓓ에는 to가 들어간다.
|해석| ⓐ Amy는 그녀의 조카를 위한 선물을 살 수 있도록 돈을 모았다.
ⓑ 너는 햇빛에 타지 않도록 자외선 차단제를 발라야 한다.
ⓒ 나는 가족과 함께 저녁을 먹기 위해 집에 일찍 왔다.
ⓓ 깨끗하게 만들기 위해 당신의 운동화를 이 비누로 세탁하세요.

14 '~할 만큼 충분히 …한'은 「형용사(small)+enough to+동사원형 (go)」으로 쓰고, '통과하다'는 go through로 쓴다.

15 ③ 앞 문장의 동사가 일반동사(look)의 현재형이므로, 부가의문문은 don't they?로 써야 한다.

16 '가장 ~한 … 중의 하나'라는 뜻은 「one of the+최상급(most famous) +복수 명사(churches)」로 쓴다.

17 Antoni Gaudi는 사그라다 파밀리아 성당의 기둥에 나무의 형태를 사용했고, 이것이 그가 자연의 아름다움을 실내로 가져온 방법이라고 했다.
|해석| Antoni Gaudi는 사그라다 파밀리아 성당 안에 기둥을 건축할 때 자연에서 나무의 형태를 가져왔다. 이러한 방식으로, 자연의 아름다움이 그에 의해 실내로 옮겨졌다.

18 ⓐ에는 easily(쉽게), ⓑ에는 interestingly(흥미롭게도), ⓒ에는 closely(자세히), ⓓ에는 clearly(명확하게)가 들어간다. hardly는 '거의 ~ 않다'라는 뜻의 부사이다.

19 |해석| 시드니 오페라 하우스의 건축가는 오렌지에서 영감을 받아 그의 상상력을 더했다.

20 ④ 많은 사람들이 시드니 오페라 하우스의 건축가에게 영감을 준 것이 바다의 파도나 돛단배라고 생각한다고 했다.

21 주어진 문장은 많은 사람들이 동대문 디자인 플라자를 보고 떠올리는 것에 관한 내용이므로, But으로 시작하는 문장 앞인 ②에 들어가서 실제로 건축가가 건물에 담고 싶었던 것을 언급하는 순서로 이어지는 것이 자연스럽다.

22 (A) '~하도록, ~하기 위해(서)'라는 의미로 목적을 나타내는 절을 이끄는 so that이 알맞다.
(B) '~다시피'라는 뜻으로 쓰이는 As가 알맞다.
(C) 가정법 과거 문장의 종속절을 이끄는 If가 알맞다.

23 다니는 학교의 이름을 말한 후(E) 학교에 있는 것을 말하고(B) also를 이용해 학교에 있는 다른 것들을 말한다(A). 그 중 정원의 위치를 언급한 후(D) 정원에서 무엇을 기르는지 말하는(C) 흐름이 되는 것이 자연스럽다.

24 학교의 특징과 학교에서 자신이 좋아하는 장소 등 자신이 다니는 학교를 소개하고 있다.

25 보람중학교에는 4층짜리 건물, 넓은 운동장, 체육관, 작은 정원이 있으며, 신선한 음식을 먹을 수 있도록 정원에서 채소를 기른다고 했다.
|해석| Mike: 너희 학교에는 무엇이 있니?
보라: 우리 학교에는 4층짜리 건물이 있어. 또한 넓은 운동장, 체육관, 작은 정원이 있어.
Mike: 작은 정원? 그곳에서 무엇을 기르니?
보라: 우리는 신선한 음식을 먹을 수 있도록 채소를 길러.
Mike: 좋구나!

01 ③   02 ②   03 (1) come from (2) on sale   04 ④   05 ②
06 November, 2, 1, 25 dollars   07 ⑤   08 ④   09 ③
10 ⑤   11 (1) tall enough to get (2) brave enough to go
(3) good enough to talk   12 (1) Ms. Brown went to the
train station so that she could pick up her sister. (2) I was
tired enough to fall asleep at the dinner table.   13 ①
14 ①   15 ②   16 Can you imagine a building that looks
like an egg   17 ②   18 ⓐ → Many architects around the
world have been inspired by nature. ⓒ → They look like
trees.   19 ②   20 ①   21 Australia, Architect, orange
22 ③   23 the architect, Zaha Hadid, took the curved
lines from nature so that city people could enjoy them
24 ④, ⑤   25 The roof opens so that I can get fresh air and
sunshine all the time.

01 '실내에, 실내로'를 뜻하는 indoors의 영어 뜻풀이다.
   I해석I ① 네 감정을 표현하는 것이 좋다.
   ② 내 몸의 움직임을 모방하지 마라.
   ③ 실내로 들어가서 뭐 좀 먹자.
   ④ 벽의 표지판은 '손을 씻어라'라고 쓰여 있었다.
   ⑤ 그 책들을 두 번째 칸으로 옮겨 주세요.

02 ⓐ '들어 올리다'를 뜻하는 lift가 들어간다.
   ⓑ '(시험에) 통과하다, 합격하다'를 뜻하는 pass가 들어간다
   ⓒ '내용물, 안에 든 것'을 뜻하는 contents가 들어간다.
   ⓓ '기둥'을 뜻하는 column의 복수형 columns가 들어간다.
   I해석I ⓐ 나는 등을 다쳐서 당분간 어떤 것도 들지 못한다.
   ⓑ Tom은 시험에 통과하기 위해 정말 열심히 공부했다.
   ⓒ 그들은 가방의 내용물을 점검하고 있다.
   ⓓ 이 건물의 기둥들은 돌로 만들어져 있다.

03 (1) come from: ~에서 비롯되다(나오다)
   (2) on sale: 판매 중인

04 You're welcome.은 '천만에.'라는 뜻으로 감사하는 말에 대한 응답
   의 표현이다. 따라서 빈칸에는 Thank you for ~.와 같은 감사하는
   말이 들어가는 것이 알맞다.
   I해석I ① 나는 너를 위해 이 케이크를 만들었어.
   ② 나는 네가 파티를 즐겼기를 바라.
   ③ 나는 그를 위해 파티를 열고 싶었어.
   ④ 내가 케이크를 만드는 것을 도와줘서 고마워.
   ⑤ 나는 너를 그의 생일 파티에 초대하고 싶었어.

05 B가 8세 미만의 어린이들은 데려오지 못한다고 쓰여 있다고 했는데
   빈칸 뒤에 동생은 10살이라고 답하고 있으므로, 빈칸에는 '문제없어.
   (No problem.)'라는 말이 들어가는 것이 알맞다.

06 두 사람은 11월 5일 날짜로 '세계 음악 콘서트'의 학생 표 두 장과 어
   린이 표 한 장을 예매했다. 표 구입의 총액은 25달러이다.

07 You're not allowed to ~.는 금지하는 말이므로 허락을 묻는 Am I

allowed to use a flash?에 대한 답으로 오는 것이 알맞다.

08 플래시를 사용하는 것이 허용되지 않는다는 말에 알겠다고 답했으므
   로, 빈칸에는 이해해 줘서 고맙다는 말이 들어가는 것이 알맞다.
   I해석I ① 당신은 사진을 찍는 것을 좋아하잖아요.
   ② 상황이 곧 나아질 거예요.
   ③ 제 사진을 찍어 주세요.
   ④ 이해해 줘서 고마워요.
   ⑤ 저는 플래시를 사용하는 게 걱정돼요.

09 ③ you will see some famous artworks from the art books
   에서 미술관의 작품 몇 점이 미술 책에 실려 있음을 알 수 있다.

10 ① to that → so that
   ② in order → in order to
   ③ to getting → to get
   ④ so to → so as to
   I해석I ① Andy는 환경을 보호할 수 있도록 절대 플라스틱 병을 사용
   하지 않는다.
   ② Rosa는 유진이의 생일 선물을 사기 위해 돈을 모았다.
   ③ Wendy는 더 좋은 성적을 받기 위해 매우 열심히 공부한다.
   ④ 나의 아버지는 건강을 유지하기 위해 매일 아침 수영을 하신다.
   ⑤ 나는 다음 날 아침에 일찍 일어날 수 있도록 일찍 잠자리에 들었다.

11 「형용사+enough to+동사원형」의 형태를 이용하여 빈칸을 채운다.

12 (1) so that은 '~하도록, ~하기 위해(서)'라는 뜻으로 목적을 나타내
   는 절을 이끈다.
   (2) 「형용사+enough to+동사원형」의 형태로 문장을 바꿔 쓴다.
   I해석I (1) Brown 씨는 여동생을 태우기 위해 기차역에 갔다.
   (2) 나는 매우 피곤해서 저녁 식탁에서 잠이 들었다.

13 모두 옳은 문장이다.
   I해석I ⓐ 나는 Helen에게 주기 위해 샌드위치를 좀 만들었다.
   ⓑ 그 리본은 선물을 휘감을 만큼 충분히 길다.
   ⓒ 우리는 기부할 수 있도록 헌 옷을 모았다.
   ⓓ 그 보트는 우리 모두를 태울 만큼 충분히 크지 않다.

14 주어진 문장은 많은 예술가들이 아이디어와 영감을 그들의 주변의 세상
   에서 얻는다는 내용이므로, ①에 들어가서 그 이유를 설명하는 This is
   because ~. 문장이 이어지는 것이 자연스럽다.

15 ⓐ에는 '~할 만큼 충분히 …한'의 뜻을 나타낼 수 있도록 enough가
   들어가는 것이 알맞다. enough가 사용된 문장은 ②이다.
   I해석I ① 너는 원숭이를 모방할 수 있니?
   ② Lukas는 일을 하고 돈을 벌 만큼 충분히 나이가 많다.
   ③ Julian은 학교에서 최고의 축구 선수이다.
   ④ 우리는 더 잘 보기 위해 일어섰다.
   ⑤ 해야 할 일이 너무 많아서 나는 네 도움이 필요하다.

16 선행사 a building을 주격 관계대명사 that이 이끄는 관계대명사절
   (that looks like an egg)이 수식하는 구조로 단어를 배열한다.

17 자연이 건축가들에게 영감을 준 것에 관한 글이므로, 빈칸에는 nature
   (자연)가 알맞다.

18 ⓐ 세계의 많은 건축가들에게 영감을 주어 온 것은 자연이라고 했다.
   ⓒ 성당 안에 있는 기둥들은 나무처럼 보인다고 했다.

|해석| ⓐ 세계의 많은 건축가들은 무엇에 영감을 받아 왔는가?

ⓑ 사그라다 파밀리아 성당 안의 기둥들은 얼마나 높은가?

ⓒ 사그라다 파밀리아 성당 안의 기둥들은 무엇처럼 보이는가?

ⓓ Antoni Gaudi는 왜 사그라다 파밀리아 성당을 지었는가?

19 빈칸 ⓐ에는 '(보고) 알다'의 의미를 나타내는 see가 들어가고, 빈칸 ⓑ에는 '(눈으로) 보다'라는 의미를 나타내는 see가 들어간다.

20 ① 역접의 접속사 But으로 이어지는 문장이므로, this is not so obvious (이것이 그다지 명확하지 않다)라고 해야 글의 흐름이 자연스럽다.

21 시드니 오페라 하우스는 호주에 있으며, 건축가 Jørn Utzon은 오렌지에서 영감을 받았다.

22 빈칸에는 차례로 to, like, in, of가 들어간다.

23 the architect와 건축가의 이름 Zaha Hadid를 콤마로 연결하여 동격 관계를 나타내고, so that을 이용하여 목적을 나타내는 절을 쓴다.

24 ④는 spaceship(우주선)의 영어 뜻풀이고, ⑤는 capture(담아내다, 표현하다, 포착하다)의 영어 뜻풀이다.

①은 obvious(분명한, 명백한), ②는 delicate(부서지기 쉬운, 섬세한), ③은 imitate(모방하다)의 영어 뜻풀이다.

25 too와 as를 제외한 나머지 단어들을 이용한다. 목적을 나타내는 so that 뒤에는 「주어+동사 ～」의 절이 이어진다.

제 **4** 회 고난도로 내신 **적중** 모의고사   pp. 150~153

01 ②   **02** (1) attract (2) imagination (3) express   **03** ⑤
04 ①   **05** ③   **06** (1) You're not allowed to fly a drone here. (2) check the sign over there   **07** ④   **08** ④   **09** ①
→ I hope you enjoyed your trip, Daniel.   **10** ⑤   **11** ②
12 ⑤   **13** (1) I turned off the TV so that I could concentrate on studying math. (2) My (little) brother saved money so that he could buy a new bike.   **14** (1) [모범답] My backpack is big enough to put a basketball in it. (2) [모범답] The movie is interesting enough to watch again.   **15** ④   **16** ②
17 They get their ideas and inspirations from the world around them.   **18** ②   **19** [모범답] 각 건축물의 건축가는 자연에서 영감을 받았다.   **20** architect, the shape of trees, the beautiful tall columns, an orange   **21** ③   **22** ③   **23** you were an architect, what would you choose from nature
24 so what → so that   **25** ③

01 ①은 exist(존재하다), ③은 inspiration(영감), ④는 exhibit(전시하다), ⑤는 wave(파도, 물결)의 영어 뜻풀이다. 제시되지 않은 단어는 ② contents(내용물, 안에 든 것)이다.

02 (1) '나비들을 끌어모으기 위해'라고 해야 자연스러우므로 attract(끌어모으다)가 알맞다.

(2) '작가의 상상력'이라고 해야 자연스러우므로 imagine(상상하다)의 명사형인 imagination(상상력)이 알맞다.

(3) '고마움을 표현하고 싶다'고 해야 자연스러우므로 express(표현하다)가 알맞다.

|해석| (1) 이 꽃들은 나비들을 끌어모으기 위해 화려한 빛깔이다.

(2) 그 판타지 소설은 미래 세계에 관한 작가의 상상력에서 비롯되었다.

(3) 나는 네 친절에 고마움을 표현하고 싶다.

03 ⑤ book은 '예매하다, 예약하다'라는 뜻이다.

① 껍질을 벗기다 / 껍질   ② 서명하다 / 표지판

③ 고르다 / (꽃을) 꺾다   ④ 이야기 / (건물의) 층

|해석| ① 감자의 껍질을 벗길래?

바나나의 껍질을 벗겨라.

② 당신의 이름을 여기에 서명해 주세요.

문 위의 표지판에 "출입 금지"라고 쓰여 있었다.

③ 나는 무슨 색을 고를지 모르겠다.

공원에서 장미를 꺾지 마세요.

④ 그 연극은 실제 이야기를 바탕으로 한다.

그녀의 새 집은 다락을 포함하여 4층이다.

⑤ 부산행 표 세 장을 예매하고 싶어요.

내가 그 음악 축제의 좌석을 예매하는 것은 불가능했다.

04 ① '판매 중인'이라는 뜻은 on sale로 나타낸다.

|해석| ① 아기 신발이 저 상점에서 판매 중이다.

② 나에게 네 새 집을 구경시켜 줄 수 있니?

③ 너는 밤에 혼자 걸어다니지 않는 것이 좋다.

④ 네 덕분에, 나는 내 과학 프로젝트를 시간에 맞춰 끝낼 수 있었다.

⑤ 이 문을 통과해라, 그러면 너는 부엌이 보일 것이다.

05 Thank you for ~.는 상대방에게 고마움을 나타낼 때 쓰는 표현이다.

|해석| ① 누군가에게 인사하기

② 걱정 표현하기

③ 감사 표현하기

④ 당부의 말 하기

⑤ 좋은 소식이나 나쁜 소식에 응답하기

06 (1) 금지를 나타내는 표현인 You're not allowed to ~.를 사용하여 드론을 날리면 안 된다는 말을 완성한다.

(2) '저쪽에 있는 표지판을 확인해 주세요.'라는 말이 되도록 단어를 배열한다.

07 ④ 작품을 만져도 되는지 물었는데 Sorry.라고 답한 후 만져도 된다고 말하는 것은 어색하다. 금지하는 말은 You're not allowed to ~.로 해야 한다.

|해석| ① A: 네 생일 파티에 나를 초대해 줘서 고마워.

B: 천만에. 나는 네가 와서 기뻐.

② A: 내가 콘서트에 여동생을 데려가도 될까?

B: 물론이지.

③ A: 실례합니다. 여기서 탄산음료를 드시면 안 됩니다.

B: 네, 알겠습니다.

④ A: 제가 작품을 만져도 되나요?

B: 죄송합니다. 여기서 작품을 만지는 것이 허용됩니다.

⑤ A: 내가 책을 책장에 정리하는 것을 도와줘서 고마워.

B: 천만에. 별거 아니야.

08 우산을 안으로 가져오면 안 된다는 말(C)에 우산을 어디에 두어야 하는지 물으면(B), 밖에 우산꽂이가 있다고 알려 주고(D) 이에 답하는(A) 흐름이 되는 것이 자연스럽다.

09 ① 대화의 흐름상 '나는 네가 ~했기를 바란다'는 의미가 되도록 you 뒤의 동사는 과거형 enjoyed로 써야 한다.

10 ⑤ Daniel이 입은 한복의 색은 대화를 통해서는 알 수 없다.

|해석| ① Daniel의 기차가 언제 떠나는지

② Daniel이 가장 좋아했던 장소

③ 수민이의 동네에서 가장 유명한 곳

④ Daniel이 정말 좋아했던 것

⑤ Daniel이 입었던 한복의 색

11 ⑥ '~하기 위해(서)'라는 뜻의 in order that이 되도록 order를 써야 한다.

ⓓ '~하기 위해(서)'라는 뜻의 so as to가 되도록 to를 써야 한다.

|해석| ⓐ White 씨는 아기의 소리를 들을 수 있도록 문을 열어 두었다.

ⓑ Joe는 잊어버리지 않도록 Fred의 생일을 자신의 수첩에 적어 놓았다.

ⓒ 내 앞의 남성이 매우 키가 커서 나는 영화를 볼 수 없었다.

ⓓ 나리는 충분한 잠을 자기 위해 일찍 잠자리에 든다.

12 「형용사+enough to+동사원형」은 '~할 만큼 충분히 …한'의 뜻을 나타내며, too ~ to...는 '너무 ~해서 …할 수 없다'라는 뜻을 나타내므로 바꿔 쓸 수 없다.

|해석| 이 책은 우리가 이해할 만큼 충분히 쉽다.

13 「so that+주어+동사 ~」의 절이 '목적'을 나타내도록 문장을 쓴다.

14 「형용사(big, interesting)+enough to+동사원형」을 사용하여 문장을 완성해 본다.

15 ⓐ expression(표현)이 들어간다.

ⓑ shape(형태)의 복수형 shapes가 들어간다.

ⓒ like(~처럼)가 들어간다.

ⓓ actually(실제로, 정말로)가 들어간다.

16 (A) 뒤에 앞 문장의 '이유'에 해당하는 내용이 이어지므로 because가 알맞다. This is because ~.는 '이것은 ~이기 때문이다.'라는 뜻이다.

(B) 뒤에 예시가 이어지고 있으므로 For example(예를 들면)이 알맞다.

(C) delicate와 strong은 의미상 반대를 나타내므로, 역접의 의미를 가진 접속사 yet이 알맞다.

17 예술가들은 아이디어와 영감을 그들 주변에서 얻는다고 했다.

|해석| 많은 예술가들은 그들의 아이디어와 영감을 어디에서 얻는가?

18 ① '가장 ~한 … 중 하나'는 「one of the+최상급(most famous)+복수 명사」로 나타내므로, church를 복수 명사 churches로 고쳐 써야 한다.

19 건축가인 Antoni Gaudi는 사그라다 파밀리아 성당에 나무의 형태를 사용했고, 시드니 오페라 하우스의 건축가는 오렌지에서 영감을 받았다.

20 |해석| A: 무엇이 각 건축가에게 영감을 주었니?

B: Antoni Gaudi는 사그라다 파밀리아 성당에 나무의 형태를 사용했어. 너는 성당 안에 있는 아름답고 높은 기둥들에서 그 형태를 볼 수 있어.

A: 오, 알겠어. 시드니 오페라 하우스는 어때?

B: Jørn Utzon은 오렌지에서 영감을 받았어.

A: 흥미롭구나!

21 ③ 시드니 오페라 하우스는 무엇이 건축가에게 영감을 주었는시 그나지 명확하지 않다고 했다.

22 ③ 이 디자인 덕분에 동대문 디자인 플라자가 인기 있는 관광 명소가 되었다고 했으므로, ordinary(평범한)가 아니라 special(특별한)을 쓰는 것이 자연스럽다.

23 「If+주어+동사의 과거형 ~, 주어+조동사의 과거형+동사원형 ....」형태의 가정법 과거 문장에서 주절이 의문문이 되도록 문장을 완성한다.

24 '~하도록, ~하기 위해(서)'라는 뜻으로 목적을 나타낼 때는 「so that+주어+동사 ~」를 쓴다.

25 ③ 학생들은 학교 건물 옥상에 있는 작은 정원에서 채소를 기른다고 했다.

|해석| ① 수원에 있다.

② 학교 건물 옥상에 정원이 있다.

③ 학생들은 넓은 운동장에서 채소를 기른다.

④ 미나는 커다란 나무 아래에 있는 벤치를 가장 좋아한다.

⑤ 미나는 그녀의 학교를 아주 좋아한다.

5 smash, 때려 부수다, 깨뜨리다   6 clam, 조개

7 dive, 뛰어들다, 다이빙하다   8 forecast, 예측, 예보

B 1 probably   2 appear   3 completely   4 friendly

C 1 spot   2 breath   3 average   4 surface   5 wonder

D 1 up to   2 give up   3 this time of year   4 go without

5 Take a look at

STEP A

Words 연습 문제   p.157

A 01 단단히, 꽉
02 경치, 풍경
03 완전히
04 대걸레로 닦다
05 숨, 호흡
06 진공청소기로 청소하다
07 몇몇의
08 북극 (지방)
09 가까이에, 근처에
10 발견하다, 찾아내다
11 도구
12 친절한, 상냥한
13 속이다, 기만하다
14 발견하다
15 조개
16 (동물의) 꼬리
17 궁금하다, 궁금해하다,
경이, 경탄, 놀라움
18 나타나다
19 아마도
20 때려 부수다, 깨뜨리다

B 21 blow
22 planet
23 average
24 species
25 hide
26 surface
27 breathe
28 serve
29 enemy
30 distance
31 deep
32 calculate
33 temperature
34 abroad
35 surround
36 someday
37 whale
38 round
39 weather forecast
40 the South Pole

C 01 수많은
02 ~까지
03 마침내, 결국
04 ~을 (한번) 보다
05 ~ 없이 지내다
06 포기하다
07 ~으로 덮여 있다
08 이맘때는, 이맘때쯤이면

Words Plus 연습 문제   p.159

A 1 tightly, 단단히, 꽉   2 distance, 거리
3 serve, (음식을) 제공하다, 차려 주다   4 tool, 도구

Words 실전 TEST   p.160

01 ②   02 ①   03 ④   04 ①   05 ②   06 ②   07 ⑤
08 up to

01 ② breathe는 '숨을 쉬다'라는 뜻의 동사이고, 나머지는 모두 명사이다.

02 '보이거나 발견될 수 없는 장소에 가거나 머물다'라는 의미의 단어는 hide(숨다)이다.

03 첫 번째 문장의 빈칸에는 '바보'라는 뜻의 명사 fool이 들어가고, 두 번째 문장의 빈칸에는 '속이다'라는 뜻의 동사 fool이 들어가는 것이 알맞다.
|해석| • 경험은 바보조차 현명하게 만든다.
• 그의 친절한 미소에 속지 마라.

04 ① take a look at: ~을 (한번) 보다
|해석| ① 내가 네 옛 사진들을 한번 봐도 될까?
② Luke의 소설은 수많은 독자들에게 즐거움을 주었다.
③ 만약 네가 네 목표를 이루고 싶다면, 계속 하고 포기하지 마라.
④ 결국, 그들은 집에서 크리스마스를 보내기로 결정했다.
⑤ 사람이 40일 동안 음식과 물 없이 지내는 것은 불가능하다.

05 '표면, 수면'이라는 뜻의 단어는 surface이다

06 주어진 문장과 ②의 spot은 '장소, 위치'라는 뜻의 명사로 쓰였다.
①, ④ 얼룩 〈명사〉
③, ⑤ 발견하다, 찾아내다 〈동사〉
|해석| 이곳은 사진 찍기에 가장 좋은 장소이다.
① Olivia는 치마에 잉크 얼룩이 있다.
② 그는 차를 주차할 좋은 장소를 알고 있다.
③ 나는 숲에서 사슴을 발견하길 기대했다.
④ 네 흰 블라우스에 묻은 얼룩을 지워라.
⑤ 여러분은 빛 축제에서 알록달록한 등불들을 쉽게 발견할 수 있다.

07 대화의 흐름상 휴가에 필요한 돈이 얼마인지 '계산해 본다(calculate)' 고 하는 것이 자연스럽다.
|해석| A: 너는 무엇을 하고 있니?
B: 나는 휴가에 내가 얼마의 돈이 필요할지 계산해 보고 있어.

08 '~까지'는 up to로 나타낸다.

Listen & Speak 만점 노트 pp. 162~163

Q1 소녀는 오르고 있는 산의 높이를 궁금해한다.

Q2 7월이 12월보다 더 춥다.

Q3 비록 그곳은 매우 춥지만 눈은 많이 내리지 않는다.

Q4 It's in front of the police station.

Q5 날씨가 아주 좋다.

Q6 약 두 시간 걸린다.

Q7 on Sunday

Q8 과학자들이 새로운 행성을 발견했다는 내용이다.

Q9 They are walking in a line in the desert.

Q10 낙타들이 사막에서 물 없이 얼마나 오래 지낼 수 있는지에 관해 찾아보았다.

 Listen & Speak 빈칸 채우기 pp. 164~165

1 at the top, I wonder how high, keep going

2 look very cold, the coldest place, how cold it is, is colder than, Although it's very cold

3 look around, where the bus stop is, in front of

4 How about going, Can you check, The weather forecast says

5 I'm going to go hiking, I'd love to, thinking of going to, it's covered with, The Internet says

6 What are you doing, anything interesting, have discovered a new planet

7 are walking in a line, very hot and dry, how long camels can go, The Internet says, want to travel

 Listen & Speak 대화 순서 배열하기 pp. 166~167

1 ⓑ-ⓔ-ⓒ-ⓓ-ⓐ

2 ⓐ-ⓔ-ⓒ-ⓑ-ⓕ-ⓖ-ⓓ-ⓗ

3 ⓒ-ⓐ-ⓔ-ⓓ-ⓑ

4 ⓔ-ⓑ-ⓓ-ⓒ-ⓐ

5 ⓒ-ⓖ-ⓐ-ⓕ-ⓓ-ⓔ-ⓘ-ⓑ-ⓗ

6 ⓑ-ⓒ-ⓓ-ⓐ

7 ⓓ-ⓔ-ⓗ-ⓐ-ⓑ-ⓕ-ⓒ-ⓖ

 Listen & Speak 실전 TEST pp. 168~169

01 ① **02** ② **03** ① **04** ⑤ **05** ④ **06** ② **07** ⑤

08 ⑤ **09** ②

[서술형]

10 I wonder how big Jupiter is.

11 (1) Do you want to join me?

(2) I heard that it's covered with red autumn leaves now.

(3) The Internet says it takes about two hours.

12 They are going to go hiking to Namsan (on Sunday).

01 B가 높이가 2,000미터 정도라고 답하는 것으로 보아, 빈칸에는 높이를 궁금해하는 말이 오는 것이 알맞다.

02 무엇을 하고 있는지 묻자(A) 신문을 읽고 있다고 답한(D) 후, 신문에 재미있는 내용이 있는지 묻고(B) 신문에 난 기사를 알려주는(C) 흐름이 되는 것이 자연스럽다.

03 I wonder ~.는 '나는 ~이 궁금하다.'라는 뜻으로, I wonder 뒤에는 「의문사+주어+동사」로 이루어진 의문사절이 올 수 있다. 이에 따라 우리말을 영어로 옮기면 I wonder where the library is.가 된다.

04 일기 예보에서 오후의 날씨를 확인한 후 Oh, no!라고 하고, 다음에 소풍을 가자고 하는 말이 이어지는 것으로 보아, 오후의 날씨가 소풍 가기에 적합하지 않음을 알 수 있다. 따라서 일기 예보에 따르면 오후에 맑을 거라는 ⑤가 대화의 흐름상 어색하다.

05 ④ I wonder 뒤에 의문사가 이끄는 절이 올 때 「의문사+형용사+주어+동사」의 어순으로 쓰므로, I wonder how cold it is로 써야 한다.

06 7월 평균 기온은 약 섭씨 영하 58도이고, 12월 평균 기온은 약 섭씨 영하 26도이므로, 7월이 12월보다 더 춥다.

07 ⑤ 남극에 왜 눈이 많이 내리지 않는지는 대화를 통해 알 수 없다.

|해석| ① 그들은 텔레비전에서 무엇을 보고 있는가?

② 지구상에서 가장 추운 곳은 어디인가?

③ Sally는 무엇이 궁금한가?

④ 남극에서 12월의 평균 기온은 얼마인가?

⑤ 남극에는 왜 눈이 많이 내리지 않는가?

08 인터넷에서 찾은 정보가 낙타가 물 없이 2주 정도를 지낼 수 있다는 내용이므로, Tony가 궁금해한 것은 낙타가 사막에서 물 없이 얼마나 오래(how long) 지낼 수 있는지에 대한 것임을 알 수 있다.

09 ② The Internet says ~. 문장을 통해 두 사람은 궁금한 점을 인터넷에서 찾아보았음을 알 수 있다.

10 I wonder ~.는 '나는 ~이 궁금하다.'라는 뜻으로 I wonder 뒤에는 의문사절이 「의문사+형용사+주어+동사」의 어순으로 이어진다.

11 (1) B의 말에 A가 I'd love to.(그러고 싶어.)라고 답했으므로, 빈칸에는 B가 등산을 같이 가자고 제안하는 것이 알맞다.

(2) 남산의 경치가 이맘때쯤에 아주 아름답다는 A의 말에 동의하면서 그에 대해 부연 설명하는 것이 알맞다.

(3) 가장 짧은 등산 코스가 얼마나 걸리는지 물었으므로, 그 답으로 인터넷에서 찾은 정보를 말해 주는 것이 알맞다.

12 두 사람은 일요일에 남산으로 등산을 갈 예정이다.

Grammar 핵심 노트 1
p.170

QUICK CHECK

1 (1) whose (2) whom (3) whose

2 (1) ⓑ (2) ⓒ (3) ⓐ

1 |해석| (1) 팔이 부러진 소녀는 Olivia이다.

(2) Brown 선생님은 내가 가장 존경하는 선생님이다.

(3) 나는 주인이 프랑스인인 식당에서 저녁을 먹었다.

2 |해석| (1) 나는 머리카락이 회색인 한 노인을 만났다.

(2) 그 가족은 이름이 Max인 개가 한 마리 있다.

(3) 직업이 유명한 사람들의 사진을 찍는 것인 그 여성은 나의 이웃이다.

Grammar 핵심 노트 2
p.171

QUICK CHECK

1 (1) when (2) After (3) since

2 (1) until the snow stops, 눈이 그칠 때까지

(2) Before I left the room, 나는 방을 나가기 전에

(3) when I passed the audition, 나는 오디션에 통과했을 때

1 |해석| (1) 내 스웨터는 내가 그것을 뜨거운 물에 세탁했을 때 작아졌다.

(2) 그는 짐을 싼 후에 출장을 떠났다.

(3) 나의 아빠는 내가 어렸을 때부터 은행에서 일하신다.

2 |해석| (1) 눈이 그칠 때까지 기다리자.

(2) 나는 방을 나가기 전에 전등을 껐다.

(3) 나는 오디션에 통과했을 때 정말 기뻤다.

Grammar 연습 문제 1
p.172

A 1 whose 2 which 3 whose 4 who 5 whose

B 1 whose 2 who(that) 3 whose 4 옳음

5 which(that)

C 1 whose bike was stolen called the police

2 whose head is round

3 the student whose name is Paul Anderson

D 1 a woman whose car broke down

2 a friend whose favorite subject is Math

3 beautiful princess whose hair is very long

A |해석| 1. 나는 꿈이 유명한 무용수가 되는 것인 한 소녀를 안다.

2. Joan이 길에서 발견한 그 지갑은 나의 것이 아니다.

3. 나는 할아버지가 과학 선생님인 한 아이를 만났다.

4. 나는 다른 사람들에게 친절한 사람들을 좋아한다.

5. Bill은 색이 빨간 뱀을 보았다.

B |해석| 1. Mary는 눈이 파란색인 고양이가 있다.

2. 나는 자신의 개들을 산책시키고 있던 소년을 발견했다.

3. 우리는 아들이 테니스 선수인 남자에 대해 이야기했다.

4. 이름이 Emma인 소녀가 벤치에 앉아 있다.

5. 내 남동생이 잡은 물고기는 매우 컸다.

C |해석| 1. 그 여자는 경찰을 불렀다. 그녀의 자전거를 도난당했다.

→ 자전거를 도난당한 그 여자는 경찰을 불렀다.

2. 문어를 봐. 그것의 머리는 둥글다.

→ 머리가 둥근 문어를 봐.

3. 너는 그 학생을 아니? 그의 이름은 Paul Anderson이다.

→ 너는 이름이 Paul Anderson인 학생을 아니?

Grammar 연습 문제 2
p.173

A 1 since 2 while 3 After 4 until

B 1 before 2 until 3 while

C 1 will come → comes 2 During → While

3 up to → until

D 1 When Kevin called me

2 has been busy since he came back

3 before we went to the amusement park

4 cleaned the windows while her sister vacuumed the living room

B |해석| 1. 잠자리에 들기 전에 양치질을 해라.

2. 나는 누군가가 나올 때까지 문 앞에서 기다렸다.

3. 그녀는 차로 출근하는 동안 음악을 듣고 있었다.

C |해석| 1. 그녀가 집에 오면 거실을 청소할 것이다.

2. 그가 런던에 살았던 동안 많은 친구들이 그를 방문했다.

3. 내 여동생과 나는 반짝거려 보일 때까지 대걸레로 바닥을 닦았다.

Grammar 실전 TEST
pp.174~177

01 ② **02** ④ **03** ⑤ **04** ③ **05** ④ **06** ④ **07** ⑤
08 ① **09** ④ **10** ④ **11** ③ **12** ② **13** whom → whose **14** ⑤ **15** ① **16** ① **17** ⑤ **18** ③ **19** ①
20 ③ **21** ② **22** ④

[서술형]

23 (1) They played basketball until it got dark.

해석: 어두워질 때까지 그들은 농구를 했다.

(2) She read a newspaper while the baby was sleeping.

해석: 아기가 자는 동안에 그녀는 신문을 읽었다.

(3) You have to eat something before you take this medicine.

해석: 너는 이 약을 먹기 전에 뭔가를 먹어야 한다.

24 (1) has a dog whose ears are very long

(2) whose name is Melisa is flying a drone

25 (1) When Amy visited me

(2) after she worked out

(3) before she goes to bed

26 (1) The girl whose hair is long and curly is Kate.

(2) I want to have a robot which(that) can cook for me.

(3) Look at the parrot whose feathers are orange.

27 (1) while, vacuumed the living room

(2) until, looked very shiny

(3) After, finished cleaning

01 '~할 때까지'라는 의미의 접속사는 until이다.

02 '나는 기차를 기다리는 동안 Terry를 보았다.'라는 의미가 자연스러우므로 접속사 while(~하는 동안에)이 알맞다.

|해석| 나는 기차를 기다리는 <u>동안</u> Terry를 보았다.

03 빈칸을 포함하는 절은 바로 앞의 선행사 a friend를 수식하는 관계대명사절로, 빈칸에는 소유격 대명사를 대신하는 소유격 관계대명사 whose가 알맞다.

|해석| 나는 할머니가 유명한 화가인 친구가 한 명 있다.

04 첫 번째 빈칸에는 '신호등이 빨간색일 때 너는 인도에서 기다려야 한다.'는 의미가 자연스러우므로 접속사 when(~할 때)이 알맞다.

두 번째 빈칸에는 '먹기 전에 채소를 주의 깊게 씻어라.'는 의미가 자연스러우므로 접속사 before(~하기 전에)가 알맞다.

|해석| • 신호등이 빨간색일 <u>때</u> 너는 인도에서 기다려야 한다.

• 먹기 전에 채소를 주의 깊게 씻어라.

05 첫 번째 빈칸에는 선행사(two books)가 사물이고 주어를 대신해야 하므로, 주격 관계대명사 which가 알맞다.

두 번째 빈칸에는 선행사가 a woman이고 소유격 대명사를 대신해야 하므로, 소유격 관계대명사 whose가 알맞다.

|해석| • 나는 Roald Dahl에 의해 쓰인 책이 두 권 있다.

• 나는 자신의 개가 20살이 넘는 여성을 인터뷰했다.

06 '~한 이후로'라는 의미의 접속사는 since이다.

07 선행사인 a man 뒤에 선행사를 수식하는 관계대명사절이 이어져야 하는데, '그 남자의(그의) 별명'이라는 의미로 소유격 대명사 his를 대신하는 소유격 관계대명사 whose가 와야 한다.

08 ①의 when은 '언제'라는 의미의 의문사로 when이 이끄는 절이 목적어로 쓰인 간접의문문이다. 나머지 When(when)은 '~할 때'라는 의미의 접속사로 쓰였다.

|해석| ① 나는 우리가 언제 그녀를 방문할 수 있는지 모른다.

② 내가 어렸을 때, 나는 스페인어를 배웠다.

③ Brian은 태어났을 때 아주 작았다.

④ 나는 스마트폰을 사용할 때 눈이 건조함을 느낀다.

⑤ 어두워지면 너는 별이 빛나는 것을 볼 수 있다.

09 두 문장에서 the tiger와 Its가 공통된 부분이므로 소유격 대명사 Its를 대신하는 소유격 관계대명사 whose를 사용하여 문장을 연결한다. 이때 관계대명사가 대신한 Its는 삭제해야 한다.

10 ④ 시간을 나타내는 접속사가 이끄는 부사절은 미래의 의미일지라도 현재시제로 쓰므로 finish로 고쳐 써야 한다.

11 문장을 완성하면 The vet healed my dog whose leg was broken. 이다.

12 after는 '~한 후에'라는 의미의 접속사로 아침을 먹은 후에 산책을 하는 순서를 나타낸다. 따라서 '~하기 전에'라는 의미의 접속사 before 를 사용하여 '산책을 하기 전에 아침을 먹는다'라고 할 수 있다.

|해석| David는 아침을 먹은 후에 산책을 한다.

13 '그 여자의(그녀의) 가방'이라는 의미로 소유격 대명사 her를 대신해야 하므로, whom을 소유격 관계대명사 whose로 고쳐 써야 한다.

|해석| 가방을 도난당한 그 여자는 경찰서에 갔다.

14 ⑤의 빈칸에는 목적격 관계대명사가 들어가야 하는데, 선행사(this desk)가 사물이므로 which나 that이 알맞다. 나머지는 소유격 관계대명사 whose가 알맞다.

|해석| ① 나는 코가 아주 납작한 고양이를 보았다.

② 나는 머리카락이 갈색인 그 여자를 안다.

③ 그는 자신의 책이 흥행한 영화가 된 저자이다.

④ 여기 털이 매우 비싼 양들이 있다.

⑤ 나는 삼촌이 내게 만들어 준 이 책상이 마음에 든다.

15 ① '~하는 동안에'라는 의미의 접속사 while이 와야 한다. before는 '~하기 전에'라는 의미의 접속사이다.

16 '~한 이후로'라는 의미의 시간을 나타내는 접속사와 '~이기 때문에'라는 의미의 이유를 나타내는 접속사로 쓰일 수 있는 것은 since이다.

|해석| • Jason은 10살 때부터 이 마을에 살고 있다.

• 나는 아기를 깨우고 싶지 않았기 때문에 방에 조용히 들어왔다.

17 '누구의'라는 의미의 의문사와 소유격 관계대명사로 쓰일 수 있는 것은 whose이다.

|해석| • 그들은 누구의 이름이 목록에 있는지 말하지 않을 것이다.

• 삼촌이 유명한 발명가인 Daisy는 나의 가장 친한 친구이다.

18 ③ during은 전치사로 뒤에 명사(구)가 오는데 「주어+동사」의 절이 이어지고 있으므로, '~하는 동안에'라는 의미의 접속사 while로 고쳐 써야 한다.

|해석| ① Jessie는 파리로 이사 간 후에 프랑스어를 배웠다.

② 우리는 날씨가 좋을 때 캠핑을 갈 것이다.

③ 운전하는 동안 스마트폰을 사용하지 마라.

④ 숨겨진 보물을 발견할 때까지 계속 걸어가자.

⑤ 나는 지난주 토요일에 그와 점심을 먹은 이후로 그를 보지 못했다.

19 ① '그 소녀의(그녀의) 이름'이라는 의미로 소유격을 대신하므로 소유격 관계대명사 whose로 고쳐 써야 한다.

|해석| ① 나는 이름이 Anna인 한 소녀를 만났다.

② 털이 두꺼운 토끼를 찾자.

③ 거북이는 딱딱한 껍데기를 가진 동물이다.

④ 그녀가 하고 있는 목걸이는 금으로 만들어졌다.

⑤ 기자는 금메달을 딴 수영 선수를 인터뷰했다.

20 ⓐ, ⓓ '누구의'라는 의미의 의문사이다.

ⓑ, ⓒ a boy와 an animal을 선행사로 하는 소유격 관계대명사이다.

|해석| ⓐ 너는 저것이 누구의 노트북인지 아니?

ⓑ 나는 꿈이 유명한 발레 무용수가 되는 것인 한 소년을 안다.

ⓒ 순록은 뿔이 나뭇가지처럼 생긴 동물이다.

ⓓ 나는 누구의 이야기가 학교 연극에 채택되었는지 궁금하다.

21 ② 소유격 관계대명사 whose는 that으로 바꿔 쓸 수 없다.

Ⅰ해석Ⅰ ⓐ Paul은 팔이 부러진 한 남자를 도와주었다.

ⓑ 내가 집에 도착하면 내 개는 항상 문 앞에 앉아 있다.

22 ⓑ, ⓒ, ⓔ가 옳은 문장이다.

ⓐ until이 '~할 때까지'라는 의미의 접속사로 쓰였으므로 「주어+동사 ~」로 이루어진 절이 와야 한다. 따라서 주어(it)가 필요하다.

ⓓ whose 뒤의 절에 목적어가 없으므로 whose를 목적격 관계대명사 which나 that으로 고쳐 써야 한다.

Ⅰ해석Ⅰ ⓐ 버터가 갈색으로 변할 때까지 열을 가해라.

ⓑ 그는 운동을 끝낸 후에 샤워를 했다.

ⓒ 피노키오는 소년이 되는 것이 바람인 귀여운 인형이다.

ⓓ Clark 씨가 나에게 보여 준 그림들은 아름다웠다.

ⓔ 방을 나가기 전에 창문을 닫아라.

23 시간 접속사 until(~할 때까지), while(~하는 동안에), before(~하기 전에) 다음에 「주어+동사 ~」의 순서로 절을 완성한다.

24 소유격 대명사(Its, Her)를 대신하는 소유격 관계대명사 whose를 사용하여 문장을 연결한다. 이때 소유격 관계대명사가 대신한 Its나 Her는 삭제해야 한다.

Ⅰ해석Ⅰ (1) Ted는 개가 한 마리 있다. 그것의 귀는 매우 길다.

→ Ted는 귀가 매우 긴 개가 한 마리 있다.

(2) 한 소녀가 드론을 날리고 있다. 그녀의 이름은 Melisa이다.

→ 이름이 Melisa인 소녀가 드론을 날리고 있다.

25 접속사 when(~할 때), after(~한 후에), before(~하기 전에)가 이끄는 부사절을 써서 문장을 완성한다.

26 (1) 선행사는 The girl이고, '그 소녀의(그녀의) 머리카락'이라는 의미로 쓰이는 소유격 대명사 her를 대신하는 소유격 관계대명사 whose를 사용하여 문장을 완성한다.

(2) a robot을 선행사로 하는 주격 관계대명사 which나 that을 사용하여 문장을 완성한다.

(3) the parrot을 선행사로 하는 소유격 관계대명사 whose를 사용하여 문장을 완성한다.

27 (1) '아빠가 거실을 진공청소기로 청소하는 동안 지호는 창문을 닦았다.'는 말이 되는 것이 알맞다.

(2) '바닥이 매우 반짝여 보일 때까지 그(지호)의 여동생이 바닥을 대걸레로 닦았다.'는 말이 되는 것이 알맞다.

(3) '그들이 청소하는 것을 끝낸 후에, 엄마가 탁자 위에 꽃을 놓았다.'는 말이 되는 것이 알맞다.

 Reading 빈칸 채우기 pp. 180~181

01 is covered by 02 millions of 03 are learning

04 Let's find out 05 Dreams 06 Can you guess

07 in a group 08 are actually sleeping

09 stand on their tails 10 near the surface

11 to breathe 12 don't fall asleep completely

13 come out of the water 14 Enjoy 15 take a look at

16 whose favorite food is clams

17 cannot be easily discovered 18 until a clam appears

19 is closed tightly 20 doesn't give up

21 smashes, against 22 In the end 23 Jump

24 to catch a fish 25 have you ever seen

26 have to be careful 27 grow up to 28 let its size fool

29 quick and smart 30 its speed and distance

31 When the bird flies nearby

Reading 바른 어휘 · 어법 고르기 pp. 182~183

01 Two-thirds 02 full 03 them 04 about 05 Dreams

06 what 07 like 08 sleeping 09 while 10 near

11 Since 12 asleep 13 wake up 14 Enjoy 15 If

16 whose 17 cannot 18 until 19 it

20 doesn't give up 21 smashes 22 is served 23 Jump

24 fly 25 seen 26 careful 27 up to 28 fool 29 quick

30 its 31 catches

Reading 틀린 문장 고치기 pp. 184~185

01 ×, covered → is covered 02 ×, is → are 03 ○

04 ×, finding out → find out 05 ○ 06 ×, is → are

07 ×, looks → looks like 08 ○ 09 ×, back → tails

10 ○ 11 ×, Although → Since

12 ×, complete → completely 13 ×, Before → When

14 ×, Enjoys → Enjoy 15 ×, As → If 16 ○

17 ×, cannot be easily discover → cannot be easily discovered

18 ×, disappears → appears 19 ×, open → closed

20 ○ 21 ○ 22 ×, serves → is served 23 ○

24 ×, catch → to catch 25 ×, jumps → jump 26 ○

27 ×, grows → grow 28 ×, fooling → fool 29 ○

30 ×, calculates → calculate 31 ○

01 (A) is (B) learning 02 ③ 03 ② 04 ② 05 ③
06 ⑤ 07 ⑤ 08 ③ 09 ④ 10 ① 11 ③ 12 ②
13 ① 14 ① 15 calculate 16 ⑤ 17 ③ 18 ③
19 ⑤ 20 ② 21 ③
[서술형]
22 혹등고래는 잠을 자는 동안 꼬리로 서 있다.
23 This small fish whose favorite food is clams uses a tool to open them.
24 (1) They usually hide under the sand.
   (2) It smashes the clam against a rock.
25 But have you ever seen a fish jump out of the water to catch a bird?
26 (모범답) big/large, quick and smart
27 When the bird flies nearby, the giant trevally jumps out of the water and catches it.

01 (A) 주어가 「분수(Two-thirds)+of+명사(our planet)」일 때 of 다음의 명사의 수에 동사의 수를 일치시킨다. 따라서 단수 동사 is가 알맞다.
(B) 문맥상 능동의 의미가 되어야 하고 앞에 be동사 are가 있으므로 현재진행형 시제가 되도록 learning이 알맞다.
02 ⓐ be full of: ~으로 가득 차다
ⓑ millions of: 수많은
03 마지막 문장에서 '몇몇 흥미로운 바다 동물들을 알아보자.'라고 했으므로 이어질 내용으로 가장 알맞은 것은 ②이다.
04 주어진 문장은 '그러나 그것들은 실제로는 잠을 자고 있다!'라는 내용이므로 글의 흐름상 '그것들은 무리를 지어 서 있는 것처럼 보인다.'는 문장 뒤에 오는 것이 자연스럽다.
05 '그들은 물고기가 아니기 때문에 숨을 쉬기 위해 위로 나올 필요가 있다.'라는 의미가 되어야 하므로, 이유를 나타내는 접속사 Since가 알맞다.
06 ⑤ 혹등고래는 잠에서 깨면 심호흡을 하러 물 밖으로 나왔다가 바다로 다시 뛰어든다고 했다.
07 '이 작은 물고기의(그것의)'라는 의미로 소유격 대명사 its를 대신하는 소유격 관계대명사 whose가 알맞다.
08 (A) 조개는 대개 모래 아래에 숨어 있다고 했으므로 '쉽게 발견될(discovered) 수 없다'고 하는 것이 자연스럽다.
(B) 모래 아래에 숨어 있는 조개가 '나타날(appears)' 때까지 모래에 입김을 분다고 하는 것이 자연스럽다.
(C) 단단히 닫혀 있는 조개를 바위에 내리친다고 했고 뒤에 식사가 준비된다는 말이 이어지는 것으로 보아, 마침내 조개가 '열린다(opens)'고 하는 것이 자연스럽다.
09 it은 앞에 나온 the clam을 가리킨다.
10 ① 앞에서 조개가 단단히 닫혀 있어서 열 수 없다고 했고 뒤에서는 조개를 바위에 내리쳐서 연다고 했으므로, 조개를 여는 것을 포기하지 않는다고 하는 것이 자연스럽다.
|해석| ① 포기하지 않는다
② 모래를 깐다

③ 도구를 사용하지 않는다
④ 그것을 먹고 싶어 하지 않는다
⑤ 조개를 숨기려고 한다
11 ③ 조개를 열기 위해 바위에 내리친다고 했으므로 이용하는 도구가 바위임을 알 수 있다.
12 ② 「지각동사(see)+목적어(a fish)+목적격보어」 구문에서 목적격보어로 to부정사는 쓸 수 없고 동사원형이나 현재분사를 쓴다.
13 ① giant trevally가 새를 잡는다는 내용의 글이므로, giant trevally가 주변에 있을 때 '새들은 조심해야 한다'는 내용이 되는 것이 알맞다.
|해석| ① 조심해야 한다
② 흥미로운 도구를 사용한다
③ 물고기를 쉽게 잡을 수 있다
④ 천적이 없다
⑤ 서로 의사소통을 해야 한다
14 ⓐ, ⓑ는 giant trevally를 가리키고, ⓒ, ⓓ는 a flying bird를 가리킨다.
15 '수학적인 방법을 사용해서 수, 답 등을 찾다'는 calculate(계산하다)의 영어 뜻풀이다.
16 ⑤ giant trevally는 날고 있는 새의 속도와 거리를 계산해서 물 밖으로 뛰어올라서 새를 잡는다고 했다. 새를 유인해서 잡는다는 내용은 없다.
17 ③ take a look at: ~을 (한번) 보다
18 (A) 잠자는 동안의 모습을 설명하고 있으므로 '~하는 동안'을 뜻하는 접속사 while이 들어가는 것이 알맞다.
(B) 조개가 보통 모래 아래에 숨어 있어 쉽게 찾을 수 없다고 했으므로, '조개가 나타날 때까지 모래에 입김을 분다'는 내용이 되는 것이 자연스럽다. 따라서 접속사 until(~할 때까지)이 알맞다.
19 ⓐ와 ⑤는 '~하기 위해서'라는 의미의 목적을 나타내는 부사적 용법의 to부정사로 쓰였다.
① 앞의 명사 수식 (형용사적 용법)
② 진주어 (명사적 용법)
③ 보어 역할 (명사적 용법)
④ 목적어 역할 (명사적 용법)
|해석| ① 그녀는 먹을 빵을 좀 원한다.
② 자연을 보호하는 것이 중요하다.
③ 지나의 꿈은 조종사가 되는 것이다.
④ 그들은 모두 해변에 가는 것에 동의했다.
⑤ 나는 책을 반납하기 위해 도서관에 갔다.
20 ② 주어는 3인칭 단수 형태인 This small fish이고 whose favorite food is clams는 This small fish를 수식하는 관계대명사절이다. 따라서 동사도 단수 형태인 uses가 되어야 한다. 또한 이 작은 물고기가 도구를 사용한다는 능동태가 되어야 하므로 수동태로 쓰지 않는다.
21 ③ 혹등고래가 하루에 몇 시간을 자는지는 글을 통해 알 수 없다.
|해석| ① 혹등고래는 어디에서 자는가?
② 혹등고래는 왜 물 밖으로 나오는가?
③ 혹등고래는 하루에 몇 시간을 자는가?
④ 조개는 주로 어디에 숨어 있는가?
⑤ tuskfish는 어떻게 조개를 여는가?

22 Humpback whales stand on their tails while they sleep.에서 혹등고래가 자는 모습을 알 수 있다.

23 This small fish가 문장의 주어이자 관계대명사절의 수식을 받는 선행사가 되고, '이 작은 물고기의(그것의) 가장 좋아하는 먹이'라는 뜻이 되어야 하므로 소유격 관계대명사 whose를 사용하여 관계대명사절을 쓴다. 동사는 주어인 This small fish에 맞춰 단수형인 uses를 쓴다.

24 (1) 조개는 대개 모래 아래에 숨어 있다고 했다.

(2) tuskfish는 조개를 바위에 내리쳐서 연다고 했다.

|해석| (1) 조개는 주로 어디에 숨어 있는가?

(2) tuskfish는 어떻게 조개를 여는가?

25 「Have you ever+과거분사(지각동사)+목적어+목적격보어 ~?」의 어순이 되도록 단어를 배열한다. 또한 '~하기 위해서'라는 의미로 목적을 나타내는 to부정사를 사용한다.

26 물고기가 170cm 길이에 80kg의 무게까지 자랄 수 있다면서 그 크기에 속지 말라는 말은 '물고기가 매우 크지만' 빠르고 영리하다는 말과 의미가 통한다.

27 giant trevally는 새가 가까이 날고 있을 때, 물 밖으로 뛰어올라 새를 잡는다고 했다.

|해석| giant trevally는 어떻게 날고 있는 새를 잡나요? 영어로 답하시오.

Ⓜ 기타 지문 실전 TEST   pp.194~195

01 Two-thirds of our planet is covered   **02** ⑤   **03** ⑤
04 ②   **05** ⑤   **06** ⑤   **07** I have no bones so I can move around easily   **08** ②   **09** ④   **10** ②   **11** ④   **12** It shoots out dark black ink and swims away.   **13** (A) smallest (B) is surrounded   **14** ④

---

01 분수를 쓸 때 분자는 기수로, 분모는 서수로 표현하며, 분자가 2 이상일 때는 분모를 나타내는 서수에 -s를 붙인다. 또한 주어가 「분수+of+명사」일 때 of 다음의 명사에 동사의 수를 일치시킨다.

02 바다 동물들에 관한 재미있는 사실이 많이 있다는 문장 뒤에 그 예로 혹등고래에 대해 설명하고 있으므로, '예를 들어'라는 의미의 For example이 알맞다.

03 주어진 문장이 '하지만 자라자 제 몸은 흰색이 되었어요!'라는 의미를 나타내므로, 태어났을 때 회색이었다는 문장 다음에 오는 것이 자연스럽다.

04 몇몇 소리를 낼 수 있는데 이러한 소리들을 다른 고래들과 이야기할 때 사용한다고 했다. 이는 곧 의사소통을 할 수 있음을 의미한다.

|해석| ① 높이 뛰다

② 의사소통을 하다

③ 물고기를 쉽게 잡다

④ 사람들과 친구가 되다

⑤ 하루에 130킬로미터까지 이동하다

05 ⑤ 태어났을 때는 몸이 회색이었다고 했다.

06 ⓐ be different from: ~과 다르다

ⓑ from my enemies: 나의 적으로부터

07 뼈가 없어서 쉽게 돌아다닐 수 있다는 내용이 되도록 배열한다. so는 '그래서'라는 의미의 접속사이다.

08 ② 문어의 평균 수명은 글에 나와 있지 않다.

09 ④ That's because ~.는 '그것은 ~이기 때문이다.'라는 의미이고, That's why ~.는 '그것이 ~한 이유이다.'라는 의미이다. Beluga 고래의 온몸이 하얀 것이 사람들이 Beluga 고래를 흰고래라고 부르는 이유이므로 That's why ~.가 되어야 한다.

10 '~할 때'라는 의미의 시간의 접속사 When(when)이 알맞다.

11 글 속 about과 ⓑ, ⓓ의 about은 '~에 관한'이라는 의미의 전치사이다. ⓐ와 ⓒ의 about은 '약, 대략'이라는 의미의 부사이다.

|해석| ⓐ 나의 자전거의 수리는 대략 50달러가 들 것이다.

ⓑ 나는 기후 변화에 관한 책을 찾고 있다.

ⓒ 양파와 마늘을 약 2분 동안 볶으세요.

ⓓ 너는 한글에 관한 역사 프로젝트를 언제 시작할 예정이니?

12 문어는 적을 만나면 먹물을 내뿜고 헤엄쳐 가 버린다고 했다.

|해석| 문어는 적을 만나면 무엇을 하나요? 영어로 답하시오.

13 (A) 앞에 the가 쓰였고 '다섯 개의 대양 중에서'라는 범위를 한정하는 표현이 뒤에 있으므로, 최상급으로 쓰는 것이 알맞다.

(B) 그것(북극해)이 유럽, 아시아, 북아메리카에 둘러싸여 있는 것이므로 수동태(be동사+과거분사)로 쓰는 것이 알맞다.

14 ④ 북극해 주변에 북극곰이 산다고 했다.

|해석| ① 북극해는 얼마나 큰가?

② 북극해는 얼마나 깊은가?

③ 북극해에 사람들이 사는가?

④ 북극해 근처에 어떤 동물들이 사는가?

⑤ 북극해에서 몇 개의 섬이 발견되었는가?

Words 고득점 맞기 pp. 196~197

01 ④　**02** ①　**03** ②　**04** ①　**05** ④　**06** (f)ool　**07** ②
08 go without　　**09** ⑤　　**10** ①　　**11** ③　　**12** ④
13 (1) distance　(2) species　(3) wonder　　**14** ②

01 [보기]는 「형용사(쉬운)-부사(쉽게)」의 관계이다. ④는 「명사(친구)-형용사(친절한, 상냥한)」의 관계이고, 나머지는 「형용사-부사」의 관계이다.

02 blow((입으로) 불다)는 '입으로부터 공기(air)를 내보내다'를 의미한다.

03 '특정 지역이나 장소'라는 의미와 '보거나 발견하기 어려운 누군가나 무언가를 보거나 알아차리다'라는 의미를 모두 가진 단어는 spot(장소, 위치 / 발견하다, 찾아내다)이다.

04 ① '그 배는 10톤까지 운반할 수 있다.'라는 의미가 되는 것이 자연스러우므로 '~까지'라는 뜻의 up to를 쓰는 것이 알맞다.
　② this time of year: 이맘때는, 이맘때쯤이면
　③ take a look at: ~을 (한번) 보다
　④ millions of: 수많은
　⑤ give up: 포기하다
　|해석| ① 그 배는 10톤까지 운반할 수 있다.
　② 날씨는 이맘때쯤 매우 춥다.
　③ 정글에 사는 몇몇 야생 동물들을 한번 보자.
　④ 그 슈퍼스타는 매달 수많은 팬레터를 받는다.
　⑤ Clare는 자신의 꿈을 포기하지 않고 매일 피아노를 치는 것을 연습했다.

05 순서대로 vacuumed(진공청소기로 청소했다), smashed(때려 부수었다, 깨뜨렸다), breathed(숨을 쉬었다), discovered(발견했다)가 들어가는 것이 알맞다.
　|해석| ・내가 거실을 진공청소기로 청소한 후에, 내 여동생이 바닥을 대걸레로 닦았다.
　・그 장인은 하나를 제외하고 모든 꽃병을 망치로 깨뜨렸다.
　・Dean은 다시 말을 시작하기 전에 깊게 숨을 쉬었다.
　・그 과학자들은 지진을 예측하는 방법을 발견했다.

06 첫 번째와 세 번째 빈칸에는 '바보'라는 의미의 명사 fool이 들어가고, 두 번째 빈칸에는 '속이다'라는 뜻의 동사 fool이 들어가는 것이 알맞다.
　|해석| ・바보같이 굴지 마!
　・그 소년은 자신의 나이에 관해 다른 사람들을 속이려고 한다.
　・바보처럼, 나는 모두에게 내 비밀을 말했다.

07 B가 그녀가 만든 지도를 찾으면 보물을 찾을 수 있다고 하는 것으로 보아, A는 그녀가 보물을 어디에 '숨겼는지' 묻는 것이 자연스럽다. 따라서 빈칸에는 hide(숨기다)의 과거형인 hid가 들어가는 것이 알맞다.
　|해석| A: 너는 그녀가 그 보물을 어디에 숨겼는지 아니?
　B: 아니, 하지만 나는 그녀가 지도를 만들었다고 들었어. 만약 우리가 그 지도를 찾는다면, 우리는 그 보물을 찾을 수 있어.

08 go without: ~ 없이 지내다

09 completely와 totally는 '완전히'라는 뜻을 나타낸다.
　|해석| 나는 오늘이 Sam의 생일이라는 것을 완전히 잊었다.

10 ⓐ 걸어갈 수 있는 거리에 주차되어 있다고 했으므로 차가 '근처에 (nearby)' 있다고 하는 것이 알맞다.
　ⓑ 디저트가 '제공된다'고 하는 것이 자연스러우므로 '(음식을) 제공하다'라는 뜻의 serve의 과거분사형인 served가 알맞다.
　ⓒ 컴퓨터가 총액을 우리보다 훨씬 더 빨리 '계산한다(calculate)'는 것이 자연스럽다.
　|해석| ⓐ 내 차가 근처에 주차되어 있어서 우리는 그곳에 걸어갈 수 있다.
　ⓑ 디저트는 식사를 마친 후에 제공될 것입니다.
　ⓒ 컴퓨터는 총액을 우리가 할 수 있는 것보다 훨씬 더 빨리 계산할 수 있다.

11 ⓐ up to: ~까지
　ⓑ take a look at: ~을 (한번) 보다
　ⓒ look around: 둘러보다
　|해석| ⓐ 이 지역은 7월에 기온이 섭씨 42도까지 올라간다.
　ⓑ 이 그림을 자세히 한번 봐.
　ⓒ Ann은 마을을 둘러보는 데 오후를 보냈다.

12 ④는 dive((물속으로) 뛰어들다)의 영어 뜻풀이고, smash(때려 부수다, 깨뜨리다)의 영어 뜻풀이는 to break something into many pieces(무언가를 여러 조각으로 부수다)이다.

13 |해석| (1) 두 지점 사이의 거리를 재라.
　(2) 일부 식물과 동물의 종은 아마존 열대 우림에서만 발견된다.
　(3) 그녀가 그랜드 캐니언을 보았을 때, 그녀의 눈은 경이로움으로 커졌다.

14 '특정한 일을 위해 손으로 사용하는 장비'는 tool(도구)의 영어 뜻풀이다.
　|해석| ① 섭씨 230도의 온도까지 오븐을 예열해라.
　② 이 도구는 다양한 방식으로 사용될 수 있다.
　③ Brown 씨의 바람은 자신의 식당을 운영하는 것이다.
　④ 모두가 우리 행성을 보호하는 데 참여해야 한다.
　⑤ 그 연못의 수면은 빨간 단풍잎으로 덮여 있었다.

Listen & Speak 고득점 맞기 pp. 200~201

01 ②　**02** ③　**03** ①　**04** ④　**05** ③
[서술형]
06 (1) The weather is so nice outside.
　(2) Good idea.
　(3) The weather forecast says it'll be rainy in the afternoon.
07 I wonder how high Mt. Everest is.
08 (1) the largest animal in the world
　(2) how large
　(3) it is about 30m long
09 They are walking in a line in the desert.
10 (1) the Internet
　(2) can go about two weeks without water
　(3) travel with camels in the desert someday

01 A가 남극이 지구상에서 가장 추운 곳이라고 했고 빈칸 다음에 남극의 평균 기온에 대해 말하고 있으므로, 빈칸에는 남극이 얼마나 추운지 궁금하다는 말인 ②가 알맞다.

02 ⓐ 두 사람은 텔레비전에 나온 아기 펭귄들을 보고 있다.

ⓑ 남극에서는 7월이 12월보다 더 춥다고 했으므로 12월은 가장 추운 달이 아니다.

ⓒ 남극은 매우 춥지만 눈은 많이 내리지 않는다고 했다.

ⓓ A는 남극이 지구상에서 가장 추운 곳이라고 말했다.

|해석| ⓐ 그들은 텔레비전을 보고 있다.

ⓑ 12월은 남극에서 가장 추운 달이다.

ⓒ 남극에는 눈이 많이 내린다.

ⓓ 그들은 세계에서 가장 추운 곳이 어디인지 모른다.

03 주어진 문장은 어디로 가고 싶은지 묻고 있으므로 남산에 가려고 생각 중이라는 문장 앞인 ①에 오는 것이 자연스럽다.

04 ④ Brian은 매년 이맘때 남산의 경치가 아주 아름답다고 말했다.

05 ③ 버스 정류장이 어디에 있는지 궁금하다는 말에 1005번 버스를 탈 수 있다고 답하는 것은 어색하다.

|해석| ① A: 나는 세상에서 가장 작은 나라가 무엇인지 궁금해.

B: 인터넷에서 찾아보자.

② A: 이 산은 높이가 약 2,000미터야.

B: 와! 정말 높은 산이구나.

③ A: 나는 버스 정류장이 어디에 있는지 궁금해.

B: 너는 1005번 버스를 탈 수 있어.

④ A: 세상에서 가장 긴 강은 무엇이니?

B: 나는 아마존강이라고 생각해.

⑤ A: 신문에 재미있는 내용이 있니?

B: 이 기사에 따르면 과학자들이 새로운 행성을 발견했대.

06 (1) Yeah.라고 답하면서 오늘 오후에 소풍을 가자고 제안하는 것으로 보아 날씨가 아주 좋다는 말이 알맞다.

(2) 오후에 소풍 가자는 제안에 날씨를 확인해 달라고 요청하는 것으로 보아 제안에 동의하는 말이 알맞다.

(3) 날씨를 확인한 후 다음에 가자고 하는 것으로 보아 오후 날씨가 소풍 가기에 적합하지 않음을 알 수 있다.

07 I wonder 뒤에 「의문사(how)+형용사(high)+주어(Mt. Everest)+동사(is)」의 어순으로 배열하여 문장을 완성한다.

08 대왕고래는 세상에서 가장 큰 동물이며, 기사에 따르면 길이가 약 30미터 정도이다.

|해석| A: 세상에서 가장 큰 동물은 뭐니?

B: 대왕고래야.

A: 나는 그것이 얼마나 큰지 궁금해.

B: 기사에 따르면 그것은 길이가 약 30미터야.

A: 놀랍구나!

09 사진 속 낙타들은 사막에서 한 줄로 걸어가고 있다고 했다.

|해석| Q: 사진 속 낙타들이 무엇을 하고 있는가?

10 |해석| Tony는 낙타들이 사막에서 물 없이 얼마나 오래 지낼 수 있는지 궁금해한다. 인터넷에 따르면 낙타들은 물 없이 2주 정도 지낼 수 있다. Tony는 언젠가 사막에서 낙타와 여행하고 싶어 한다.

---

01 ④	02 ④	03 ①	04 ④	05 ③, ⑤	06 ①, ③, ⑤
07 ⑤	08 ④	09 ②	10 ④	11 ②	12 ②	13 ①, ④

[서술형]

14 (1) I met a boy whose dream is to be a scientist.

(2) Can you see the man whose arm is broken?

(3) I'm looking for a book which(that) I borrowed from Bill yesterday.

(4) Look at the spiders whose shapes are all similar.

15 (1) Keep going until I tell you to stop.

(2) She changed her name after she left Spain. / After she left Spain, she changed her name.

(3) I have lived in Seoul since I was born.

(4) I washed the dishes when Lucas watered the flowers in the garden. / When Lucas watered the flowers in the garden, I washed the dishes.

16 ⓑ → I want to visit the British Museum while I am in London.

ⓔ → The present (which/that) my aunt sent to me hasn't arrived yet.

17 (1) While you were sleeping

(2) I saw a dog whose legs were very short

(3) I'll have lunch after I take a shower

---

01 a pianist를 선행사로 하는 소유격 관계대명사 whose가 쓰인 문장이다. 따라서 관계대명사가 소유격 대명사를 대신하는 경우만 빈칸에 들어갈 수 있다. ④와 같이 소유격 대명사(her)는 소유격 관계대명사와 함께 쓸 수 없다.

02 첫 번째 빈칸에는 빈칸 뒤의 절에 목적어가 없고 선행사(The novels)가 사물이므로 목적격 관계대명사 which나 that이 알맞다.

두 번째 빈칸에는 빈칸 뒤의 절에 주어가 없고 선행사(students)가 사람이므로 주격 관계대명사 who나 that이 알맞다.

세 번째 빈칸에는 소유격 대명사 her를 대신하는 소유격 관계대명사 whose가 알맞다.

|해석| • J. K. Rowling이 쓴 소설들은 많은 나라에서 읽힌다.

• 우리는 일요일에 봉사 활동을 할 수 있는 학생들을 찾고 있다.

• Helen은 운동화가 빨간색과 흰색인 소녀이다.

03 순서대로 '~하는 동안'이라는 의미의 접속사 while, '~할 때까지'라는 의미의 접속사 until, '~하기 전에'라는 의미의 접속사 before가 알맞다.

|해석| • 네가 나가 있는 동안, 누군가 문을 두드렸다.

• 음식이 모두에게 나올 때까지 먹기 시작하지 마세요.

• 우리는 너무 늦기 전에 우리의 행성을 보호해야 한다.

04 두 문장에서 my neighbor와 His가 공통 대상이므로 소유격 대명사 His를 대신하는 소유격 관계대명사 whose를 사용하여 문장을 연결한다. 이때 관계대명사가 대신한 His는 삭제해야 한다.

05 '~한 후에'를 뜻하는 접속사 after를 사용하여 부사절을 완성한다. 시

간을 나타내는 접속사가 이끄는 부사절은 미래의 의미일지라도 현재시제로 쓰므로 will은 부사절에 필요하지 않다. 문장을 완성하면 After I buy a pair of roller skates, Joan will show me how to ride them.이 된다.

06 ① 소유격 관계대명사 whose와 ③ 선행사를 포함하는 관계대명사 what, ⑤ 주격 관계대명사 who는 생략할 수 없다.

|해석| ① 머리카락이 금발인 그 소년을 봐.

② Mary는 그녀의 엄마가 만든 모자를 쓰고 있다.

③ 너는 저녁으로 네가 먹은 것을 기억하니?

④ 네가 보고 있는 사진은 내가 가장 좋아하는 것이다.

⑤ 이 마을에 사는 사람들은 매우 친절하다.

07 [보기]와 ⑤의 when은 '~할 때'라는 의미의 접속사이고, 나머지 when (When)은 '언제'라는 의미의 의문사이다.

|해석| [보기] 내가 라디오를 켰을 때 벨이 울렸다.

① 너는 나에게 언제 도착하는지 말해 줄 수 있니?

② 당신의 신곡은 언제 나오나요?

③ 나는 그 다리가 언제 지어졌는지 알고 싶다.

④ 그는 나에게 여름 방학이 언제 시작했는지 물었다.

⑤ 나는 대중 앞에서 이야기할 때 목소리가 매우 낮아진다.

08 ① 소유격 관계대명사 whose로 고쳐야 한다.

② 선행사를 포함하는 관계대명사 what으로 고쳐야 한다.

③ 목적격 관계대명사 which나 that으로 고쳐야 한다.

⑤ 주격 관계대명사 who나 that으로 고쳐야 한다.

|해석| ① 나는 어머니가 유명한 과학자인 한 소녀를 안다.

② 오늘 할 수 있는 일을 내일로 미루지 마라.

③ 내가 지난주에 산 자전거는 이미 고장이 났다.

④ 코가 하얀 그 말은 Moore 씨의 소유이다.

⑤ 너는 이 사진의 사람처럼 생긴 남자를 본 적이 있니?

09 ② 둘 다 '~할 때까지'라는 의미를 나타내는 접속사로 쓰였다.

① ~하는 동안 〈접속사〉 / ~하는 반면에 〈접속사〉

③ ~한 이후로 〈접속사〉 / ~이기 때문에 〈접속사〉

④ ~인지 아닌지 〈접속사〉 / 만약 ~라면 〈접속사〉

⑤ 언제 〈의문사〉 / ~할 때 〈접속사〉

|해석| ① 그는 해외에 있는 동안 많은 외국인들을 만났다.

Kelly는 외향적인 반면에 그녀의 쌍둥이 여동생은 부끄러움을 많이 탄다.

② 그 아기는 엄마가 올 때까지 계속 울었다.

비가 그칠 때까지 건물 안에서 기다리자.

③ 그들은 12살 때부터 친구로 지내 왔다.

Peter가 독감에 걸렸기 때문에 우리는 소풍을 취소했다.

④ 나는 Robert가 그 사실을 아는지 궁금하다.

문의 사항이 있으시다면, 우리에게 언제든지 연락 주세요.

⑤ 너는 그 차 사고가 언제 났는지 기억하니?

나는 눈이 피로할 때 잠시 동안 눈을 감는다.

10 ④ '그 파란 배낭의(그것의) 주머니'라는 의미로 소유격 대명사 its를 대신하는 소유격 관계대명사 whose로 고쳐 써야 한다.

|해석| A: 너는 Green 공원에서 열린 벼룩시장에 갔었니?

B: 응, 갔었어. 거의 새것인 유용한 물건들이 많았어.

A: 좋구나. 너는 벼룩시장에서 무언가 샀니?

B: 응, 샀지. 나는 주머니가 아주 큰 파란색 배낭을 샀어. 너는?

A: 음, 나는 거기에 가고 싶었지만 가지 못했어. 나는 남동생을 돌봐야 했거든.

11 ② 빈칸 뒤의 절에 주어가 없고 선행사(the car)가 사물이므로 주격 관계대명사 which나 that이 들어가야 한다.

① '누구의'라는 의미의 의문사 whose가 들어간다.

③, ④, ⑤ 소유격 관계대명사 whose가 들어간다.

|해석| ① 너는 그것이 누구의 스마트폰인지 아니?

② 먼지로 덮인 차를 봐.

③ Shrek은 몸이 녹색인 다정한 괴물이다.

④ 눈이 녹색인 그 소년은 Jane의 사촌이다.

⑤ 저에게 소매가 짧은 셔츠를 보여 주시겠어요?

12 ⓑ whose 뒤의 절에 주어가 없고 선행사(a person)가 사람이므로 whose를 주격 관계대명사 who나 that으로 고쳐 써야 한다.

ⓒ during은 전치사로 뒤에 명사(구)가 오는데, 뒤에 「주어+동사 ~」로 이루어진 절이 있으므로 during을 접속사 while로 고쳐 써야 한다.

|해석| ⓐ 우리는 버스 체계가 편리한 마을에 갔다.

ⓑ 좀도둑은 가게에서 물건을 훔치는 사람이다.

ⓒ 내가 병원에 있는 동안 네가 내 고양이들을 돌봐 줄 수 있니?

ⓓ Rosa는 그 판타지 소설을 읽은 후에 Colin에게 빌려주었다.

13 ① '그 원숭이의(그것의) 꼬리'라는 의미로 소유격 대명사를 대신하는 소유격 관계대명사 whose의 쓰임은 옳다.

④ Since는 '~이기 때문에'라는 의미의 이유를 나타내는 접속사로 쓰였으므로, 시간을 나타내는 접속사인 When으로 바꿔 쓸 수 없다.

|해석| ① 꼬리가 13센티미터 길이인 원숭이를 봐.

② 나는 그들이 일을 마친 후에 그들에게 그 소식을 말할 것이다.

③ Emma는 백화점이 문을 열 때까지 밖에서 기다렸다.

④ 이번 주 화요일은 휴일이기 때문에 우리는 학교에 갈 필요가 없다.

⑤ 이 기부금은 폭풍에 집이 부서진 가족들을 위해 사용될 것이다.

14 (1), (2), (4) 관계대명사가 소유격 대명사(His, His, Their)를 대신하므로 소유격 관계대명사 whose를 사용하여 두 문장을 연결한다. 이때 관계대명사가 대신한 소유격 대명사는 삭제해야 한다.

(3) 관계대명사가 목적어 it을 대신하고 선행사(a book)가 사물이므로 목적격 관계대명사 which나 that을 사용하여 두 문장을 연결한다. 이때 관계대명사가 대신한 목적어 it은 삭제해야 한다.

|해석| (1) 나는 한 소년을 만났다. 그의 꿈은 과학자가 되는 것이다.

(2) 너는 그 남자가 보이니? 그의 팔이 부러졌다.

(3) 나는 책을 한 권 찾고 있다. 나는 그것을 어제 Bill에게 빌렸다.

(4) 거미들을 봐. 그들의 모양이 모두 비슷하다.

15 (1)은 until(~할 때까지), (2)는 after(~한 후에), (3)은 since(~한 이후로), (4)는 when(~할 때)을 사용하여 문장을 완성한다.

16 ⓑ 시간을 나타내는 접속사(while)가 이끄는 부사절은 미래의 의미를 나타내도 현재시제로 쓰므로 will be는 am으로 고쳐 써야 한다.

ⓔ 관계대명사가 이끄는 절에 목적어가 없고 선행사(The present)가 사물이므로, whose를 목적격 관계대명사 which나 that으로 고쳐 쓰

거나 생략할 수 있다.

|해석| ⓐ 우리가 어제 만난 여자는 변호사다.

ⓑ 내가 런던에 있는 동안 나는 대영 박물관을 방문하고 싶다.

ⓒ 우리 축구팀은 Jacob이 팀에 합류한 후로 모든 경기를 이겼다.

ⓓ Charlotte은 가장 친한 친구가 Wilbur인 현명한 거미이다.

ⓔ 이모가 나에게 보낸 선물은 아직 도착하지 않았다.

17 (1) '~하는 동안'이라는 의미의 접속사 while 뒤에 「주어+동사 ~」의 절이 되도록 배열한다.

(2) 소유격 관계대명사 whose가 이끄는 관계대명사절이 선행사 a dog를 수식하도록 배열한다.

(3) 대화의 흐름상 샤워를 한 후에(after) 점심을 먹겠다는 의미가 자연스럽다.

|해석| A: 저 집에 왔어요, 엄마.

B: 오, Mike. 내가 잠시 잠이 들었구나. Lucky와 나갔었니?

A: 네, 엄마. 엄마가 주무시는 동안 저는 공원 주변에서 Lucky를 산책시켰어요.

B: 잘했구나! 착한 아이구나.

A: 공원에서, 저는 다리가 매우 짧은 개를 보았어요. 정말 귀여웠어요.

B: 그랬구나. 지금 점심을 먹을래?

A: 음, 저는 샤워를 한 후에 점심을 먹을게요.

ⓡ Reading 고득점 맞기 · pp. 207~209

01 ② **02** ③ **03** ③ **04** ②, ④ **05** ③ **06** ④ **07** ②
08 ③ **09** ⑤ **10** ③ **11** ⑤ **12** ③

[서술형]

13 Can you guess what these whales are doing

14 They come out of the water for a deep breath. /
They come out of the water to breathe.

15 (1) This small fish whose favorite food is clams uses a tool to open them.

(2) Clams usually hide under the sand, so they cannot be easily discovered.

16 (1) Its favorite food

(2) blows on the sand until a clam appears

(3) smashes the clam against a rock

17 (1) grow up to 170cm and 80kg

(2) calculate its speed and distance

(3) When the bird flies nearby, the giant trevally jumps out of the water and catches it.

---

01 그림 속 고래들이 무리를 지어 서 있는 것처럼 보이지만 실제로는 잠을 자고 있다는 내용이 되어야 하므로 sleeping이 알맞다.

02 (A) 문맥상 '잠을 자는 동안(while) 꼬리로 서 있는다'는 말이 되는 것이 알맞다.

(B) 문맥상 '물고기가 아니기 때문에(since) 숨을 쉬기 위해 위로 나올 필요가 있다'는 말이 되는 것이 알맞다.

(C) '잠에서 깰 때(when) 심호흡을 하러 물 밖으로 나왔다가 바다로 다시 뛰어든다'는 말이 되는 것이 알맞다.

03 ① 주어가 「분수(Two-thirds)+of+명사(our planet)」일 경우 동사는 of 뒤의 명사(our planet)의 수에 일치시키므로 are를 단수 동사 is로 고쳐야 한다.

④ looks likely를 '~처럼 보이다'라는 뜻을 나타내는 looks like로 고쳐야 한다.

04 ① 우리 행성(지구)의 3분의 2가 대양들로 덮여 있다고 했다.

③ 혹등고래는 잠을 자는 동안 꼬리로 서 있다고 했다.

⑤ 혹등고래는 잠에서 깨면 심호흡을 하러 물 밖으로 나온다고 했다.

05 ③ 문장의 주어는 This small fish(단수형)이므로 단수 동사 uses의 쓰임은 옳다.

06 ⓐ와 ④는 '~하기 위해서'라는 의미의 목적을 나타내는 부사적 용법의 to부정사이다.

① 목적어 역할 (명사적 용법) ② 앞의 대명사 수식 (형용사적 용법)

③ 진주어 (명사적 용법) ⑤ 목적어 역할 (명사적 용법)

|해석| ① Kevin은 언젠가 자신의 꿈이 실현되기를 바란다.

② 나는 학교 축제에 관해 너에게 말할 것이 있다.

③ 나는 일요일에 일찍 일어나는 것이 어렵다.

④ 그 배드민턴 선수는 경기에서 이기기 위해 매우 열심히 연습했다.

⑤ 나의 동아리 부원들은 봉사 활동으로 벽화 그리기를 하기로 결정했다.

07 조개는 대개 모래 아래에 숨어 있어서 쉽게 발견될 수 없다고 했으므로, tuskfish는 조개가 나타날 때까지 모래에 입김을 분다는 내용이 되는 것이 알맞다.

|해석| ① 조개가 움직이는 동안

② 조개가 나타날 때까지

③ 조개가 사라진 후에

④ 만약 조개가 지나가지 않는다면

⑤ 조개가 딱딱한 껍데기를 가지고 있기 때문에

08 ③ '땅이나 물의 면적의 상층'을 뜻하는 surface(표면, 수면)의 영어 뜻풀이로, 글에서는 surface가 쓰이지 않았다.

① blow의 영어 뜻풀이다.

② smash의 영어 뜻풀이다.

④ discover의 영어 뜻풀이다.

⑤ tool의 영어 뜻풀이다.

09 ① This small fish가 tuskfish를 가리키므로 거대한 물고기는 아님을 알 수 있다.

② tuskfish가 가장 좋아하는 먹이는 조개라고 했다.

③ 조개는 보통 모래 아래에 숨어 있다고 했다.

④ tuskfish는 모래에 입김을 불어서 모래 아래에 숨어 있는 조개를 찾는다고 했다.

|해석| ① tuskfish는 거대한 물고기이다.

② tuskfish는 조개를 먹는 것을 좋아하지 않는다.

③ 조개는 대개 바위 사이에서 발견된다.

④ tuskfish가 조개를 발견하는 것은 불가능하다.

⑤ tuskfish는 조개를 열기 위해 바위를 사용한다.

10 주어진 문장은 But으로 시작하면서 그것의 크기에 속지 말라는 내용이므로, 170센티미터에 80킬로그램까지 자랄 수 있다는 내용 다음에 오는 것이 알맞다.

11 밑줄 친 spot은 '발견하다'라는 의미의 동사로 쓰였다.

①, ③ 얼룩 〈명사〉 ②, ④ 장소 〈명사〉 ⑤ 발견하다 〈동사〉

|해석| ① 커튼에 큰 얼룩이 있었다.

② 우리는 소풍을 위한 좋은 장소를 찾고 있다.

③ 너는 티셔츠의 얼룩을 씻어 내야 한다.

④ 나는 이곳이 벼룩시장을 열기에 가장 좋은 장소라고 생각한다.

⑤ 네가 큰 모자를 쓰고 있었기 때문에 나는 관중석에서 너를 쉽게 발견할 수 있었다.

12 ③ giant trevally가 가장 좋아하는 음식이 무엇인지는 글에 나와 있지 않다.

|해석| ① giant trevally는 얼마나 크게 자랄 수 있는가?

② giant trevally는 무엇을 계산할 수 있는가?

③ giant trevally가 가장 좋아하는 먹이는 무엇인가?

④ giant trevally는 어떻게 새를 잡는가?

⑤ giant trevally가 주변에 있을 때 새는 왜 조심해야 하는가?

13 의문사가 이끄는 절(의문사(what)+주어(these whales)+동사(are doing))이 동사 guess의 목적어로 쓰인 문장을 완성한다.

14 혹등고래는 잠에서 깨면 심호흡을 하러 물 밖으로 나온다고 했다.

|해석| Q: 혹등고래는 잠에서 깨어났을 때 왜 물 밖으로 나오는가?

15 (1) which를 '이 작은 물고기의(그것의)'라는 의미로 소유격 대명사를 대신하는 소유격 관계대명사 whose로 고쳐야 한다.

(2) 주어인 they는 조개를 가리키므로, 조개는 모래 아래에 숨어서 쉽게 발견될 수 없다는 의미의 조동사가 있는 수동태 「조동사(cannot)+be+과거분사(discovered)」가 되어야 한다.

16 (1) tuskfish가 가장 좋아하는 먹이는 조개라고 했다.

(2) tuskfish는 모래 속에 숨어 있는 조개가 나타날 때까지 모래에 입김을 분다고 했다.

(3) 찾은 조개가 단단히 닫혀 있어서 조개를 바위에 내리친다고 했다.

|해석| A: 너는 tuskfish에 대해 들어 본 적이 있니?

B: 아니, 없어. 그것에 관해 나에게 말해 주겠니?

A: 물론이야. 그것이 가장 좋아하는 먹이는 조개야.

B: 조개? 음, 조개는 대개 모래 아래에 숨어 있잖아. tuskfish가 조개를 어떻게 발견하니?

A: 이 물고기는 조개가 나타날 때까지 모래에 입김을 불어.

B: 흥미롭구나!

A: 응. 하지만 조개는 단단히 닫혀 있어서 그 물고기는 조개를 바위에 내리쳐.

B: 오, tuskfish는 매우 똑똑하구나!

17 (1) giant trevally는 170센티미터에 80킬로그램까지 자랄 수 있다.

(2) 빠르고 똑똑해서 날고 있는 새를 발견하고 그 새의 속도와 거리를 계산할 수 있다.

(3) 새가 가까이에 날고 있을 때 물 밖으로 뛰어올라 새를 잡는다.

서술형 100% TEST

pp. 210~213

01 breathe

02 [모범답] Did you spot some mistakes in my writing?

03 (1) go without

해석: 인간은 얼마나 오래 음식 없이 지낼 수 있을까?

(2) up to

해석: 그 나무들은 30미터까지 자랄 수 있다.

(3) millions of

해석: 이 약은 수많은 생명을 구할 수 있다.

04 I wonder where the museum is.

05 (1) How about going on a picnic this afternoon?

(2) The weather forecast says it'll be rainy in the afternoon.

06 (1) the South Pole

(2) in July

(3) in December

(4) colder than

(5) it doesn't snow much

07 (1) The camels are walking in a line in the desert.

(2) I wonder how long camels can go without water in the desert.

08 (1) how big it(Jupiter) is

(2) says it(Jupiter) is over 11 times bigger than Earth

09 (1) Dean is the student whose nickname is Smile Prince.

(2) I want to ride a horse whose tail is black.

(3) We're looking for the girl who(that) is wearing a blue hat.

10 (1) [모범답] I didn't eat carrots

(2) [모범답] I took a walk with Sam

(3) [모범답] I will watch my favorite TV show

11 (1) whose hobby is rock-climbing

(2) what I do in my free time

(3) whose top is covered with snow

(4) which(that) was written by Shakespeare

12 (1) Genie whose body is blue lives in a magic lamp.

(2) The student whose smartphone was stolen called the police.

(3) I will play tennis with Bill after I finish my homework. / After I finish my homework, I will play tennis with Bill.

(4) We haven't heard from him since he went to Italy.

13 (1) stand on their tails while they sleep

(2) Since they are not fish, need to come up to breathe

14 This small fish whose favorite food is clams uses a tool

15 Because they usually hide under the sand.

16 조개를 바위에 내리쳐서 연다.

17 (1) It can grow up to 170cm and 80kg.

(2) When the bird flies nearby, the giant trevally jumps out of the water and catches it.

18 (1) It lives in the Arctic Ocean.

(2) It usually eats fish and clams.

(3) It was gray (when it was born).

(4) They use several sounds (to communicate with each other).

19 (1) small → smallest

(2) surrounds → is surrounded

01 '공기를 폐 안팎으로 움직이게 하다'라는 뜻을 나타내는 동사 breathe(숨을 쉬다)가 알맞다.

|해석| 당신은 입을 통해서가 아니라 코를 통해서 숨을 쉴 필요가 있다.

02 주어진 문장의 spot은 '발견하다, 찾아내다'라는 의미의 동사로 쓰였다.

|해석| 도시에서 밤에 별을 발견하는 것은 쉽지 않다.

03 (1) go without: ~ 없이 지내다

(2) up to: ~까지

(3) millions of: 수많은

04 지도에서 카페와 제과점 사이에 있는 것은 박물관이므로 빈칸에는 박물관의 위치를 궁금해하는 말이 들어가는 것이 알맞다. I wonder 뒤에는 「의문사(where)+주어(the museum)+동사(is)」의 어순으로 쓴다.

05 (1) How about ~?을 사용하여 제안하는 표현을 쓴다. about 뒤에 동사가 올 경우 동명사 형태로 쓰는 것에 유의한다.

(2) 일기 예보의 내용을 보고할 때 The weather forecast says ~.로 표현할 수 있다.

06 (1) 남극이 지구상에서 가장 추운 곳이라고 했다.

(2), (3), (4) 남극은 평균 기온이 7월에는 약 섭씨 영하 58도이고, 12월에는 약 섭씨 영하 26도로, 7월이 12월보다 더 춥다고 했다.

(5) 남극은 매우 춥지만 눈은 많이 내리지 않는다고 했다.

|해석| 지구상에서 가장 추운 곳은 남극이다. 평균 기온이 7월에는 약 섭씨 영하 58도이고, 12월에는 약 섭씨 영하 26도이다. 흥미로운 점은 그곳은 7월이 12월보다 더 춥다는 것이다. 또한, 그곳은 매우 춥지만 눈은 많이 내리지 않는다.

07 (1) 주어(The camels) 다음에 현재진행형(are walking)이 오고, '한 줄로'라는 뜻의 in a line과 '사막에서'라는 뜻의 in the desert가 이어진다.

(2) 궁금함을 표현하는 I wonder 뒤에 「의문사(how)+형용사(long)+주어(camels)+동사(can go) ~」의 어순으로 배열한다.

08 (1) 목성이 얼마나 큰지 궁금하다는 말이 알맞다. I wonder 뒤에 「의문사(how)+형용사(big)+주어(it/Jupiter)+동사(is)」의 어순으로 쓴다.

(2) 주어진 인터넷 정보에 따르면 목성은 지구보다 11배 이상 더 크다. 인터넷 정보를 전달할 때 The Internet says ~.로 표현한다.

|해석| 여러분은 태양계에서 어느 행성이 가장 큰지 아나요? 정답은 목성입니다. 그것은 지구보다 11배 이상 더 큽니다. 얼마나 놀라운가요!

09 (1) who를 소유격 대명사(his)를 대신하는 소유격 관계대명사 whose로 고쳐야 한다.

(2) a horse 뒤에 a horse를 선행사로 하는 소유격 관계대명사 whose를 써야 한다.

(3) 관계대명사가 주어 역할을 해야 하고 선행사(the girl)가 사람이므로 whose를 주격 관계대명사 who나 that으로 고쳐야 한다.

|해석| (1) Dean은 별명이 '미소 왕자'인 학생이다.

(2) 나는 꼬리가 검은 말을 타고 싶다.

(3) 우리는 파란색 모자를 쓰고 있는 소녀를 찾고 있다.

10 접속사 when(~할 때), until(~할 때까지), after(~한 후에)의 의미에 맞게 문장을 완성한다.

11 (1) '그 여자의(그녀의) 취미'라는 의미가 되도록 소유격 관계대명사 whose를 사용한다.

(2) 선행사를 포함하는 관계대명사 what을 사용한다.

(3) '그 산의(그것의) 꼭대기'라는 의미가 되도록 소유격 관계대명사 whose를 사용한다.

(4) 주격 관계대명사 which나 that을 사용한다.

|해석| (1) 나는 취미가 암벽 등반인 한 여성을 만났다.

(2) 그림 그리기는 내가 여가 시간에 하는 것이다.

(3) 꼭대기가 눈으로 덮여 있는 산을 봐.

(4) 그는 셰익스피어가 쓴 책을 한 권 샀다.

12 (1), (2) 'Genie의(그의) 몸'과 '그 학생의 스마트폰'이라는 의미가 되도록 소유격 관계대명사 whose를 사용하여 문장을 영작한다.

(3) '~한 후에'라는 의미의 접속사 after를 사용하여 문장을 영작한다.

(4) '~한 이후로'라는 의미의 접속사 since를 사용하여 문장을 영작한다.

13 (1) '~하는 동안'이라는 의미의 접속사 while을 사용한다.

(2) '~이기 때문에'라는 의미의 이유를 나타내는 접속사 since를 사용한다.

14 '가장 좋아하는 먹이가 조개인 이 작은 물고기는 조개를 열기 위해 도구를 사용한다.'라는 의미가 되도록 문장을 배열한다. 소유격 관계대명사 whose가 이끄는 절(whose favorite food is clams)이 주어이자 선행사인 This small fish를 수식하는 구조가 되도록 문장을 완성한다.

15 조개는 대개 모래 아래에 숨어 있어서 쉽게 발견될 수 없다고 했다.

|해석| 왜 조개가 쉽게 발견될 수 없나요? 영어로 답하시오.

16 It smashes the clam against a rock.에서 tuskfish가 조개를 여는 방법을 알 수 있다.

17 (1) giant trevally는 170센티미터에 80킬로그램까지 자랄 수 있다고 했다.

(2) giant trevally는 새가 가까이에 날고 있을 때 물 밖으로 뛰어올라 새를 잡는다고 했다.

|해석| A: 너는 과학 리포트의 주제를 정했니?

B: 응. 나는 큰 물고기인 giant trevally를 소개할 거야.

A: 나는 그것에 대해 들어 본 적이 전혀 없어. 그것은 얼마나 크니?

B: 그것은 170센티미터에 80킬로그램까지 자랄 수 있어.

A: 오, 물고기치고는 크구나. 그것이 왜 흥미롭니?

B: 그것은 날고 있는 새를 잡을 수 있어.

A: 왜! 그 물고기가 어떻게 새를 잡니?

B: 새가 가까이에 날고 있을 때, giant trevally는 물 밖으로 뛰어올라 새를 잡아.

A: 그거 놀랍구나!

18 (1) Beluga 고래는 북극해에 산다고 했다.

(2) Beluga 고래는 주로 물고기와 조개를 먹는다고 했다.

(3) Beluga 고래는 태어났을 때 회색이었다고 했다.

(4) Beluga 고래는 소리를 사용해 의사소통을 한다고 했다.

|해석| (1) beluga 고래는 어디에 사는가?

(2) beluga 고래는 주로 무엇을 먹는가?

(3) beluga 고래는 태어났을 때 무슨 색이었는가?

(4) beluga 고래는 서로 의사소통을 하기 위해 무엇을 사용하는가?

19 (1) 앞에 the가 쓰였고, '다섯 개의 대양 중에서'라고 범위를 한정하고 있으므로, 형용사 small을 '가장 작은'이라는 의미의 최상급으로 고쳐야 한다.

(2) 그것(북극해)은 유럽, 아시아, 북아메리카에 '둘러싸여 있는' 것이므로 수동태(be동사+과거분사)로 고쳐야 한다.

모의고사

01 ④ **02** ④ **03** ② **04** ② **05** ① **06** is colder than **07** ⑤ **08** ③ **09** ② **10** They are going to Namsan on Sunday. **11** ③, ⑤ **12** ⑤ **13** ③ **14** (1) I met a boy whose hobby is taking pictures. (2) I had lunch at the restaurant whose owner is Canadian. **15** (1) She hurt her knee while she was playing baseball. / While she was playing baseball, she hurt her knee. (2) You should wash your hands before you have meals. / Before you have meals, you should wash your hands. (3) The clerk had to wait until the last customer left. **16** It looks like they are standing up in a group. **17** ③ **18** ⑤ **19** They sleep near the surface. **20** ④ **21** ③ **22** This small fish whose favorite food is clams uses a tool to open them. **23** ④ **24** ③ **25** ⓓ → It can change the color of its skin.

01 probably는 '아마도'를 뜻하는 부사이고, 나머지는 모두 형용사이다.

02 ④ '수학적인 방법을 사용해서 수, 답 등을 찾다'는 calculate(계산하다)의 영어 뜻풀이다.

03 up to: ~까지 / give up: 포기하다

|해석| · 그 동물은 매일 나뭇잎을 30킬로그램까지 먹을 수 있다.

· 나는 오디션에 여러 번 떨어졌지만 내 꿈을 포기하지 않았다.

04 문맥상 순서대로 nearby(가까이에, 근처에), blow(불다), appear(나타나다), average(평균의)가 들어가는 것이 알맞다.

|해석| · 근처에 괜찮은 식당이 있니?

· 케이크에 있는 촛불을 모두 불어서 끄자.

· 태양이 구름 뒤에서 나타나기 시작했다.

· 그 기차는 평균 시속 200킬로미터로 달릴 수 있다.

05 ① B가 학교 옆에 있다며 위치를 말하고 있으므로 빈칸에는 박물관의 위치를 궁금해하는 말이 들어가는 것이 알맞다.

|해석| ① 나는 박물관이 어디에 있는지 궁금해.

② 나는 학교가 얼마나 오래되었는지 궁금해.

③ 나는 박물관이 언제 문을 닫는지 몰라.

④ 너는 나에게 학교가 어디에 있는지 말해 줄 수 있니?

⑤ 기사에 따르면 전시회가 다음 주에 박물관에서 열린대.

06 평균 기온이 7월에는 약 섭씨 영하 58도이고, 12월에는 약 섭씨 영하 26도라고 했으므로 7월이 12월보다 더 춥다고 하는 것이 알맞다.

07 ⑤ 남극은 매우 춥지만 눈이 많이 내리지 않는다고 했다.

|해석| ① 그들은 텔레비전에 나온 아기 펭귄들을 보고 있다.

② 지구상에서 가장 추운 곳은 남극이다.

③ 남극의 7월의 평균 기온은 약 섭씨 영하 58도이다.

④ Sally는 남극이 얼마나 추운지 궁금해한다.

⑤ 남극에는 눈이 많이 내린다.

08 밖의 날씨가 아주 좋아서(B) 오늘 오후에 소풍을 가자고 제안하고(D), 좋은 생각이라며 날씨를 확인해 달라고 한(A) 후, 일기 예보에서 오후에 비가 올 거라고 전하자(C) 소풍은 다음에 가자고 말하는(E) 흐름이 되는 것이 자연스럽다.

09 ② 대화의 맨 마지막에 A가 일요일에 보자고 말하는 것으로 보아 A는 일요일에 등산을 같이 가자는 수민이의 제안을 수락했음을 알 수 있다. 따라서 ②는 거절이 아닌 수락하는 표현(I'd love to.)이 되어야 한다.

10 두 사람은 일요일에 남산에 갈 예정이다.

|해석| 그들은 언제 남산에 갈 예정인가?

11 남산의 등산 코스의 개수와 남산까지 가는 방법에 대해서는 대화에 나와 있지 않다.

① 단풍잎을 언급하는 것으로 보아 현재 계절은 가을이다.

② 현재 남산은 빨간 단풍잎으로 덮여 있다고 했다.

④ 남산의 가장 짧은 등산 코스가 두 시간 정도 걸린다고 했다.

12 빈칸을 포함하는 절이 바로 앞의 선행사 a rabbit을 수식하는 역할을 하는 관계대명사절로, 빈칸에는 소유격 대명사를 대신하는 소유격 관계대명사 whose가 알맞다.

13 ③ 잠자리에 든 후에 양치질하는 것을 잊지 말라는 것은 어색하므로 접속사 after(~한 후에)를 before(~하기 전에)로 바꾸어야 자연스럽다.

|해석| ① 그는 식사를 하는 동안 말을 하지 않는다.

② 색이 변할 때까지 새우를 쪄라.

③ 잠자리에 든 후에(→ 들기 전에) 양치질하는 것을 잊지 마.

④ 그들은 일곱 살 때부터 서로 알아 왔다.

⑤ 내가 숙제를 끝냈을 때 밖은 어두웠다.

14 (1) 선행사는 a boy이고 '그 소년(그)의 취미'라는 의미로 소유격 대명사 his를 대신하는 소유격 관계대명사 whose를 사용하여 문장을 쓴다.

(2) 선행사는 the restaurant이고 '그 식당(그곳)의 주인'이라는 의미로 소유격 대명사 its를 대신하는 소유격 관계대명사 whose를 사용하여 문장을 쓴다.

15 (1) 접속사 while은 '~하는 동안'이라는 의미를 나타낸다.

(2) 접속사 before는 '~하기 전에'라는 의미를 나타낸다.

(3) 접속사 until은 '~할 때까지'라는 의미를 나타낸다.

|해석| (1) 그녀는 무릎을 다쳤다. 그녀는 야구를 하고 있었다.

(2) 너는 손을 씻어야 한다. 너는 식사를 한다.

(3) 점원은 기다려야 했다. 마지막 손님이 나갔다.

16 It looks like 뒤에 「주어+동사 ~」로 이루어진 절이 이어지는 문장을 쓴다.

17 (A) '~하는 동안'이라는 의미의 접속사 while이 알맞다.

(B) '~이기 때문에'라는 의미의 이유를 나타내는 접속사 Since가 알맞다.

(C) '~할 때'라는 의미의 접속사 When이 알맞다.

18 ⑤는 명사구 many things를 꾸며 주는 형용사적 용법의 to부정사이고, ⓐ와 나머지는 모두 '~하기 위해서'라는 의미의 목적을 나타내는 부사적 용법의 to부정사이다.

|해석| ① 그들은 상을 타기 위해 최선을 다했다.

② 그는 빵을 좀 사기 위해 제과점에 갔다.

③ Ann은 이메일을 확인하기 위해 컴퓨터를 켰다.

④ 우리 팀은 실수를 하지 않기 위해 열심히 연습했다.

⑤ 해야 할 많은 일들이 있기 때문에 나는 도움이 필요하다.

19 혹등고래는 수면 근처에서 잠을 잔다고 했다.

|해석| 혹등고래는 어디서 자는가?

20 Humpback whales stand on their tails while they sleep.을 통해 잠자는 모습을 알 수 있다. 나머지는 글에 나와 있지 않다.

21 ⓐ는 일반적인 물고기를 가리키고, ⓔ는 the clam을 가리킨다. 나머지는 the tuskfish를 가리킨다.

22 주어가 This small fish이고 소유격 관계대명사가 이끄는 절인 whose favorite food is clams가 주어를 수식하는 구조의 문장이다. 따라서 문장의 동사는 주어에 맞춰 3인칭 단수 동사인 uses로 고쳐 써야 한다.

23 ⓐ giant trevally가 새를 잡는다고 했으므로 새는 giant trevally가 근처에 있으면 '조심해야' 한다는 말이 되는 것이 자연스럽다.

ⓑ giant trevally가 날고 있는 새를 발견하고 그 새의 속도와 거리를 계산할 수 있다고 했으므로 '똑똑하다'고 하는 것이 자연스럽다.

24 ③ giant trevally는 새가 가까이에 날고 있을 때 물 밖으로 뛰어올라 새를 잡는다고 했다.

25 ⓓ 문어는 적으로부터 숨기 위해 피부색을 바꿀 수 있다고 했다.

|해석| ⓐ 문어는 몇 개의 팔이 있는가?

ⓑ 문어는 왜 작은 물고기를 먹는가?

ⓒ 문어의 피는 무슨 색인가?

ⓓ 문어는 적으로부터 숨기 위해 무엇을 하는가?

제 2 회 대표 기출로 내신 **적중** 모의고사 pp.218~221

01 ④ **02** ② **03** ⑤ **04** I wonder how high this mountain is. **05** ① **06** ④ **07** ③ **08** The Internet says it is about 7,000km long. **09** ② **10** They(Camels) can go about two weeks without water. **11** ③ **12** ② **13** (1) I have a cat whose name is Dubu. (2) He's the writer whose new book became a bestseller. **14** ④ **15** (1) Let's play inside until the rain stops. (2) I listened to music after I had dinner. / After I had dinner, I listened to music. **16** ② **17** ② **18** ⓐ → Humpback whales are sleeping in the picture. ⓒ → Humpback whales don't fall asleep completely. **19** ③ **20** ③ **21** (1) Clams (2) give up (3) a rock **22** But have you ever seen a fish jump out of the water to catch a bird? **23** ⑤ **24** ① **25** ③

01 ④ hide(숨다)의 영어 뜻풀이로 '보이거나 발견될 수 없는 장소에 가거나 머물다'가 알맞다.

02 첫 번째 문장의 빈칸에는 '장소'라는 뜻을 나타내는 명사 spot이 들어가고, 두 번째 문장의 빈칸에는 '발견하다, 찾아내다'라는 뜻을 나타내는 동사 spot이 들어가는 것이 알맞다.

|해석| • 미나와 David는 그 나무를 심기에 좋은 장소를 찾았다.

• 너는 이 두 그림 사이의 차이점을 찾아낼 수 있니?

03 ⑤ up to: ~까지

|해석| ① 보스턴은 이맘때쯤이면 무척 아름답다.

② Anderson 씨는 새 프로젝트를 포기하기로 결정했다.

③ 이 도구는 매일 수많은 사람들에 의해 사용된다.

④ 우리가 공기 없이 지내는 것은 불가능하다.

⑤ 어제는 올해 가장 무더운 날이었다. 기온이 섭씨 43도까지 올라갔다.

04 빈칸 다음에 A가 오르고 있는 산의 높이를 말해 주고 있으므로, 빈칸에는 산이 얼마나 높은지 궁금하다는 말이 오는 것이 알맞다. I wonder 뒤에는 「의문사(how)+형용사(high)+주어(this mountain)+동사(is)」의 어순으로 쓴다.

05 주어진 문장은 함께 가자고 제안하는 내용이므로 이에 대한 수락의 답을 하는 I'd love to. 앞에 오는 것이 알맞다.

06 ④ 남산의 가장 아름다운 풍경을 어디에서 볼 수 있는지에 관해서는 언급되지 않았다.

|해석| ① 그들은 일요일에 무엇을 할 것인가?

② 이맘때 남산의 경치는 어떤가?

③ 지금은 어느 계절인가?

④ 어디에서 남산의 가장 아름다운 경치를 즐길 수 있는가?

⑤ 남산에서 가장 짧은 등산 코스는 얼마나 걸리는가?

07 ③ 버스 정류장이 어디에 있는지 궁금하다는 말에 1005번 버스를 타면 된다고 답하는 것은 어색하다.

|해석| ① A: 남극은 매우 춥지만 눈은 많이 내리지 않아.

B: 흥미롭구나!

② A: 오늘 오후에 소풍 가는 게 어때?

B: 좋은 생각이야. 날씨를 확인해 줄래?

③ A: 나는 버스 정류장이 어디에 있는지 궁금해.

B: 1005번 버스를 타면 돼.

④ A: 태양계에서 가장 큰 행성이 무엇이니?

B: 목성이야.

⑤ A: 신문에 재미있는 내용이 있니?

B: 이 기사에 따르면 고래 가족이 동해에서 발견되었대.

08 인터넷의 정보를 보고하거나 전달할 때 The Internet says ~.(인터넷에 따르면 ~.)라고 표현한다.

09 빈칸 앞에서 낙타들이 사막에서 물 없이 얼마나 오래 지낼 수 있는지 궁금하다고 했고, 빈칸 다음에 인터넷에서 찾은 정보를 말하고 있으므로, 빈칸에는 인터넷에서 정보를 찾아보자는 말이 들어가는 것이 자연스럽다.

|해석| ① 그들은 낙타를 타고 있어.

② 인터넷에서 찾아보자.

③ 그것에 관해 과학 선생님께 물어보는 게 어떠니?

④ 너는 그것에 관해 과학 수업에서 배운 적이 있니?

⑤ 너는 도서관에서 그 책을 빌리는 게 어떠니?

10 낙타들은 사막에서 물 없이 2주 정도 지낼 수 있다고 했다.

|해석| 낙타에 관한 흥미로운 사실

Q: 낙타들은 사막에서 물 없이 얼마나 오래 지낼 수 있는가?

11 자연스러운 문장으로 배열하면 Look at the man whose hair is blond.가 된다.

12 '~할 때'라는 의미의 시간의 접속사 when을 사용하며, 시간을 나타내는 접속사가 이끄는 부사절은 미래의 의미일지라도 현재시제로 쓴다.

13 각각 소유격 대명사 Its와 His를 대신하는 소유격 관계대명사 whose를 사용하여 두 문장을 연결하며, whose가 대신한 소유격 대명사는 삭제한다.

|해석| (1) 나는 고양이가 있다. 그것의 이름은 두부이다.

(2) 그는 작가이다. 그의 새 책이 베스트셀러가 되었다.

14 ⓐ 관계대명사가 이끄는 절에 주어가 없고 선행사(a robot)가 사물이므로 whose를 주격 관계대명사 which나 that으로 고쳐 써야 한다.

ⓒ '그 소년(그)의 이름'이라는 의미가 되어야 하므로 that을 소유격 대명사를 대신하는 소유격 관계대명사 whose로 고쳐 써야 한다.

|해석| ⓐ 나는 말할 수 있는 로봇을 발명하고 싶다.

ⓑ 나는 색이 빨간 자전거를 살 것이다.

ⓒ 너는 이름이 Eric인 소년을 아니?

ⓓ 그녀는 영화를 보러 가기 전에, 자신의 일을 끝낼 것이다.

15 (1) '~할 때까지'라는 의미의 접속사 until을 사용하여 문장을 완성한다.

(2) '~한 후에'라는 의미의 접속사 after를 사용하여 문장을 완성한다.

16 ② ⓐ의 접속사 since는 '~한 이후로'라는 의미를 나타내므로 '~이기 때문에'라는 의미의 이유를 나타내는 접속사 because로 바꿔 쓸 수 없다.

|해석| ⓐ 우리가 처음 만났을 때부터 나는 그녀를 좋아했다.

ⓑ 나는 삼촌이 런던에 살고 있는 친구가 있다.

17 stand up: 서 있다 / wake up: (잠에서) 깨다

18 ⓐ 그림 속 혹등고래들은 잠을 자고 있다고 했다.

ⓒ 혹등고래는 완전히 잠들지 않는다고 했다.

|해석| ⓐ 그림에서 혹등고래는 놀고 있다.

ⓑ 혹등고래는 수면 근처에서 잠을 잔다.

ⓒ 혹등고래는 항상 완전히 잠이 든다.

ⓓ 혹등고래는 숨을 쉬기 위해 물 밖으로 나올 필요가 있다.

19 '이 작은 물고기(그것)의 가장 좋아하는 먹이'라는 의미가 되어야 하므로 소유격 대명사를 대신하는 소유격 관계대명사 whose가 알맞다.

20 조개는 대개 모래 아래에 숨어 있어서 '쉽게 발견되지 않는다'는 내용이 되어야 tuskfish가 조개가 나타날 때까지 모래에 입김을 분다는 다음 문장과의 연결이 자연스럽다.

|해석| ① 매우 빨리 헤엄쳐 가 버릴 수 있다

② 스스로 움직일 수 없다

③ 쉽게 발견될 수 없다

④ 모래 속에서 먹이를 얻을 수 있다

⑤ 껍데기를 단단히 닫을 수 없다

21 |해석| tuskfish가 가장 좋아하는 먹이인 조개는 단단히 닫혀 있다. 하지만 tuskfish는 포기하지 않는다. 그것은 조개를 여는 데 바위를 이용한다.

22 But 다음에 '너는 ~해 본 적이 있니?'라는 의미를 나타내는 「Have you ever+과거분사(seen) ~?」가 오며, seen의 원형은 see로 지각동사이므로 「지각동사(seen)+목적어(a fish)+목적격보어(jump)」의 형태가 되도록 배열한다. '~하기 위해서'는 목적을 나타내는 부사적 용법의 to부정사로 쓴다.

23 ⑤는 a flying bird를 가리키고, 나머지는 a giant trevally를 가리킨다.

24 ① giant trevally는 170센티미터에 80킬로그램까지 자랄 수 있다고 했다.

25 ③ 뒤에 so로 연결되면서 '그래서 사람들은 나를 흰고래라고도 부른다'라는 말이 나오므로, 온몸이 '하얗다(white)'고 하는 것이 알맞다.

01 ④　**02** ②　**03** ②　**04** I wonder / I'm curious about
05 (1) I wonder how high it is.　(2) The newspaper says
Mt. Everest is about 8,850m high.　**06** ③　**07** how cold,
the South Pole　**08** ②　**09** ②　**10** (1) go hiking　(2) red
autumn leaves　(3) takes about two hours　**11** ⑤　**12** ③
13 ①　**14** ③, ⑤　**15** ④　**16** (1) 모범답 since he
came back from holiday　(2) 모범답 until the snow melted
(3) 모범답 When spring comes　**17** ④　**18** When they
wake up, they come out of the water for a deep breath and
dive back into the sea.　**19** ③　**20** ⑤　**21** But don't
let its size fool you.　**22** ⑤　**23** ⑤　**24** ④　**25** (1) in
the Arctic Ocean　(2) fish and clams　(3) when it grows up,
its body becomes white

01 ①은 Arctic(북극 (지방)), ②는 smash(때려 부수다, 깨뜨리다), ③은
calculate(계산하다), ⑤는 forecast(예측, 예보)의 영어 뜻풀이다.
④는 discover(발견하다)의 영어 뜻풀이다.

02 up to: ~까지 / go without: ~ 없이 지내다
|해석| • 이 기계는 한 번에 3부까지 복사할 수 있다.
• 나는 일주일 동안 스마트폰 없이 지내는 것이 쉽지 않았다.

03 ② 내 눈물을 '감추기' 위해 얼굴을 돌렸다는 의미가 자연스러우므로
hide(숨기다, 감추다)를 쓰는 것이 알맞다.
|해석| ① John은 자신의 팔로 아기를 꽉 안았다.
② 나는 내 눈물을 발견하기(→ 감추기) 위해 얼굴을 돌렸다.
③ 상자 안에 세 개의 빛나는 금화가 있었다.
④ 화성은 태양으로부터 네 번째 행성이다.
⑤ 할머니를 위한 파티를 여는 데 얼마나 들지 계산해 보자.

04 궁금함을 표현할 때 I wonder ~.나 I'm curious about으로 말할 수
있다.

05 (1) '나는 ~이 궁금해.'는 I wonder ~.를 사용해 표현하며, 뒤에 의문
사절이 이어질 때 「의문사+형용사+주어+동사」의 어순으로 쓴다.
(2) '신문에 따르면 ~.'은 The newspaper says ~.로 표현한다.

06 ③ 남극의 평균 기온이 7월에는 약 섭씨 영하 58도이고, 12월에는 약 섭
씨 영하 26도라고 했으므로, 7월이 12월보다 더 춥다. 따라서 warmer
를 colder로 바꿔 써야 한다.

07 대화에서 미나는 남극이 얼마나 추운지 궁금해했다. wonder 뒤에 이
어지는 의문사절은 「의문사(how)+형용사(cold)+주어(it)+동사(is)」의
어순으로 쓴다.
|해석| 미나는 남극이 얼마나 추운지 궁금했고 Tim이 그녀에게 그 답
을 알려 주었다.

08 ② 지구상에서 가장 추운 곳은 남극이라고 했다.
|해석| ① 텔레비전에 나온 아기 펭귄들은 무엇을 하고 있는가?
② 지구상에서 가장 추운 곳은 어디인가?
③ 남극에는 얼마나 많은 종이 사는가?
④ 남극에서 3월의 평균 기온은 얼마인가?

⑤ 남극에는 왜 눈이 많이 내리지 않는가?

09 일요일에 등산을 가는데 함께 갈지 물었으므로 이에 대한 수락이나 거절
의 말을 해야 한다. 대화의 마지막 말을 통해 일요일에 같이 간다는 것
을 알 수 있으므로 빈칸에는 제안을 수락하는 표현이 들어가야 한다.

10 (1) 두 사람은 일요일에 남산으로 등산을 가기로 했다.
(2) 남산은 지금 빨간 단풍잎으로 덮여 있다.
(3) 가장 짧은 등산 코스는 약 두 시간 정도 걸린다고 했다.
|해석| 그들은 일요일에 남산으로 등산을 갈 것이다. 남산은 현재 빨간
단풍잎으로 덮여 있다. 남산에서 가장 짧은 등산 코스는 약 두 시간 정
도 걸린다.

11 '~할 때'라는 의미의 시간을 나타내는 접속사와 '언제'라는 의미의 의문
사 역할을 하는 것은 when이다.
|해석| • Austin은 금메달을 땄을 때 겨우 17살이었다.
• 너는 네가 언제 소포를 보냈는지 기억할 수 있니?

12 첫 번째 빈칸은 '그 소년의(그의) 자전거'라는 의미로 소유격 대명사 his
를 대신하는 소유격 관계대명사 whose가 알맞다.
두 번째 빈칸은 빈칸 뒤의 절에 주어가 없고 선행사(the thief)가 사람
이므로 주격 관계대명사 who나 that이 알맞다.
|해석| • 자전거를 도난당한 그 소년은 매우 화가 났다.
• 경찰은 어제 자전거를 훔친 도둑을 체포했다.

13 ① who를 '그 친구의 가장 좋아하는 숫자'라는 의미로 소유격 대명사
his(her)를 대신하는 소유격 관계대명사 whose로 고쳐 써야 한다.
|해석| ① 나는 가장 좋아하는 숫자가 1인 친구가 한 명 있다.
② 그녀는 선생님이 말하고 있는 것을 이해할 수 없었다.
③ 그들은 내가 나올 때까지 문 앞에 서 있었다.
④ 지퍼가 고장 난 그 재킷은 나의 것이 아니다.
⑤ 나는 숙제를 다 한 후에 쇼핑을 하러 갈 것이다.

14 ③ '~하는 동안'은 접속사 while로 써야 한다. until은 '~할 때까지'라
는 의미의 접속사이다.
⑤ 관계대명사 뒤의 절에 목적어가 없으므로 소유격 관계대명사
whose를 목적격 관계대명사 who(m)나 that으로 고쳐 쓰거나 생략
할 수 있다.

15 ④ 빈칸 뒤의 절에 주어가 없고 선행사(the letter)가 사물이므로 주격
관계대명사 which나 that이 들어가야 한다.
①, ③, ⑤ 소유격 관계대명사 whose가 알맞다.
② '누구의'라는 뜻의 의문사 whose가 알맞다.
|해석| ① 그들은 눈이 각기 다른 색인 고양이가 있다.
② 너는 누구의 그림이 상을 탔는지 내게 말해 줄 수 있니?
③ 나는 엄마가 은행에서 일하시는 아이를 만났다.
④ 너는 오늘 아침에 온 편지를 봤니?
⑤ 이름이 Melisa인 소녀가 너를 기다리고 있다.

16 자연스러운 의미가 되도록 주어진 접속사와 말을 연결하여 문장을 완성
한다.
|해석| (1) 나는 그가 휴가에서 돌아온 이후로 그를 만나지 못했다.
(2) 나는 눈이 녹을 때까지 집에 머물렀다.
(3) 봄이 오면 나는 많은 나무와 꽃을 심을 것이다.

17 ④ 여기서 Since는 '~이기 때문에'라는 뜻으로 이유를 나타내는 접속

사로 쓰였다.

18 혹등고래는 잠에서 깨면 심호흡을 하러 물 밖으로 나왔다가 바다로 다
시 뛰어든다고 했다.

|해석| 혹등고래는 잠에서 깨면 무엇을 하는가?

19 (A) 뒤의 them은 조개를 가리키므로 tuskfish가 조개를 '열기' 위해
도구를 사용한다는 의미가 알맞다.

(B) 모래 아래에 숨어 있어서 발견하기 쉽지 않은 조개를 찾는 방법을
설명하고 있으므로 조개가 '나타날' 때까지 모래에 입김을 분다는 의미
가 알맞다.

(C) 조개가 단단히 닫혀 있지만 tuskfish는 바위에 내리쳐서 결국 여
는 것으로 보아 '포기하지' 않는다는 의미가 알맞다.

20 ⑤ tuskfish가 조개를 열기 위해 바위를 이용한다는 내용은 있지만
tuskfish의 서식지는 글에 나와 있지 않으므로 알 수 없다.

21 사역동사(let)의 목적격보어로 동사원형을 써야 하므로 to fool을 fool
로 고쳐 써야 한다.

22 ⑤ 글 속의 spot은 '발견하다'라는 뜻의 동사로 쓰였다.

23 ①, ④, ⑤ 물 밖으로 뛰어올라 날고 있는 새를 잡는다고 했다.

② 글에 나와 있지 않으므로 알 수 없다.

③ 빠르다(quick)고 했다.

|해석| ① 그것은 새를 먹지 않는다.

② 그것은 날고 있는 새에게 먹힐 수 있다.

③ 그것은 매우 느리다.

④ 그것은 물 밖으로 뛰어오르기에는 너무 크다.

⑤ 그것은 날고 있는 새를 잡을 수 있다.

24 주어진 문장은 '그것이 사람들이 Beluga 고래를 흰고래라고 부르는 이
유이다.'라는 뜻이므로 'Beluga 고래의 온몸이 하얗다'는 내용 다음에
오는 것이 알맞다.

25 (1) Beluga 고래는 북극해에 산다.

(2) Beluga 고래는 수로 물고기와 소개를 먹는다.

(3) Beluga 고래는 태어날 때는 회색이지만 다 자라면 몸이 흰색이 된
다.

|해석| A: 나는 오늘 beluga 고래에 관해 배웠어.

B: 오, 그것은 북극해에 살아, 맞지?

A: 맞아! 그것은 동그란 머리를 가졌고 주로 물고기와 조개를 먹어.

B: 그렇구나. 그것에 관해 다른 건 뭘 배웠니?

A: 그것은 태어날 때 회색이야. 하지만 자라면 몸이 흰색이 돼!

B: 흥미롭구나!

01 ③ **02** ⑤ **03** (1) up to (2) In the end **04** (1) large it
is (2) says it is about 30m long **05** ② **06** the coldest
place, doesn't snow **07** The average temperature is
about -58℃ in July and -26℃ in December. **08** I wonder
how long camels can go without water **09** ② **10** ③
11 ④ **12** ④ **13** (1) 모범답 my brother drew a picture
(2) 모범답 I have kept a diary (3) 모범답 aunt is a famous
chef **14** ⓐ → while 이유: 「주어+동사 ~」가 있는 절이 왔으므로
전치사 during을 접속사 while로 고쳐야 한다. **15** ② **16** ②
17 모범답 Many plant and animal species are found only
in the rainforests. **18** ③, ④ **19** ② **20** The tuskfish
blows on the sand until a clam appears. **21** ②, ⑤
22 ③ **23** ⓑ → It can calculate the speed and distance
of a flying bird. ⓒ → It can grow up to 170cm and 80kg.
ⓓ → When the bird flies nearby, the giant trevally jumps
out of the water and catches it. **24** ② **25** (1) the ocean
floor, small fish (2) The octopus whose favorite food is
small fish lives on the ocean floor.

01 ③ '두 장소나 두 물건 사이의 공간'은 distance(거리)의 영어 뜻풀이다.

|해석| ① 바다거북은 멸종 위기에 처한 종이다.

② 우리는 자전거를 고치기 위해 도구를 몇 개 사야 한다.

③ 서울과 부산 사이의 거리는 얼마인가?

④ 오늘 아침에 기온이 영하 10도까지 떨어졌다.

⑤ Monica는 경탄과 놀라움으로 불꽃놀이를 봤다.

02 ⑤ 두 문장 모두 '발견하다'라는 뜻의 동사로 쓰였다.

① 완전한 〈형용사〉 / 완료하다, 끝마치다 〈동사〉

② 책 〈명사〉 / 예약하다 〈동사〉

③ 땅, 육지 〈명사〉 / 내려앉다 〈동사〉

④ 바보 〈명사〉 / 속이다 〈동사〉

|해석| ① 그 프로젝트는 완전한 성공이었다.

너는 그 일을 너 혼자 끝마쳤니?

② 내가 지난달에 너에게 빌려준 책을 돌려줄 수 있니?

그녀는 지금 당장 제주도행 표를 예약할 필요가 있다.

③ 그 땅은 매우 건조해서 식물이 그곳에서 살아남을 수 없다.

너는 새가 저쪽 강 위에 내려앉는 것을 보았니?

④ 내 실수를 알아차렸을 때 내가 바보처럼 느껴졌다.

그 남자는 그 사고에 대해 모두를 속이려고 했다.

⑤ 너는 어떻게 멀리서 나를 발견할 수 있었니?

그 글에서 오류를 발견하면, 그것을 연필로 표시해 줘.

03 (1) up to: ~까지 (2) in the end: 마침내, 결국

04 (1) 대왕고래가 가장 큰 동물이라고 했으므로 얼마나 큰지 궁금해하는
것이 자연스럽다.

(2) 책의 정보에 따르면 대왕고래는 길이가 약 30미터이다.

05 ② 평균 기온이 7월에는 약 섭씨 영하 58도이고, 12월에는 약 섭씨 영
하 26도라고 했으므로, 7월이 12월보다 더 춥다는 말이 알맞다.

06 남극은 지구상에서 가장 추운 곳이라고 했으며, 그곳은 매우 춥지만 눈은 많이 내리지 않는다고 했다.

|해석| 남극은 지구상에서 가장 추운 곳이지만, 눈은 많이 내리지 않는다.

07 남극은 평균 기온이 7월에는 약 섭씨 영하 58도이고 12월에는 약 섭씨 영하 26도라고 했다.

|해석| 남극은 얼마나 추운가?

08 인터넷에서 찾은 정보가 낙타들이 물 없이 2주 정도 지낼 수 있다는 내용이므로 빈칸에는 낙타들이 사막에서 물 없이 얼마나 오래 지낼 수 있는지 궁금하다는 내용이 알맞다.

09 ⓐ 두 사람은 낙타에 대해 궁금한 점을 책이 아닌 인터넷에서 찾아본다.
ⓑ 낙타는 사막에서 물 없이 3주가 아닌 2주 정도 지낼 수 있다고 했다.
ⓓ Tony는 언젠가 사막에서 낙타들과 여행을 하고 싶다고 앞으로의 바람을 말했다.

|해석| ⓐ 그들은 그들의 질문에 대한 답을 책에서 찾아본다.
ⓑ 낙타들은 사막에서 물 없이 3주 동안 살 수 있다.
ⓒ 수지는 낙타들이 매우 흥미로운 동물이라고 생각한다.
ⓓ Tony는 현재 사막에서 낙타들과 여행을 하고 있다.

10 첫 번째 빈칸에는 '그 산(그것)의'라는 의미로 소유격 대명사를 대신하는 소유격 관계대명사 whose가 알맞다.
두 번째 빈칸에는 빈칸 뒤의 절에 목적어가 없고 선행사(Most people)가 사람이므로 목적격 관계대명사 who나 whom이 알맞다.
세 번째 빈칸에는 '~하는 것'이라는 의미로 선행사를 포함하는 관계대명사 what이 알맞다.

|해석| • 꼭대기가 눈으로 덮여 있는 산을 봐.
• Emma가 집에 초대한 대부분의 사람들이 나타나지 않았다.
• 내가 쇼핑몰에서 산 것을 너에게 보여 줄게.

11 ④의 whose는 '누구의'라는 의미의 의문사이고, 나머지는 소유격 관계대명사 whose이다.

|해석| ① 날개가 분홍색인 요정에 대해 내게 말해 줘.
② Jack은 취미가 축구를 하는 것인 사촌이 있다.
③ 우리는 매우 넓은 정원이 있는 건축가를 찾았다.
④ 나는 누구의 장갑이 책상 위에 남겨져 있는지 모른다.
⑤ 가방이 흰색인 소녀의 이름은 무엇이니?

12 ④ whose는 The novelist를 선행사로 하는 소유격 관계대명사이다.

|해석| ① 개미는 큰 무리를 지어 사는 곤충이다.
② 그는 여기로 이사 온 후로 저 집에서 산다.
③ 우리는 개를 산책시킨 후에 박물관에 갈 것이다.
④ 이야기가 상상력으로 가득한 그 소설가는 내가 가장 좋아하는 작가이다.
⑤ 옥상에 아름다운 정원이 있는 건물을 봐.

13 (1) while: ~하는 동안에
(2) since: ~한 이후로
(3) 소유격 관계대명사 whose가 이끄는 관계대명사절이 선행사 a friend를 수식하도록 문장을 완성한다.

14 |해석| ⓐ 나는 David가 식물에 물을 주는 동안 바닥을 대걸레로 닦았다.
ⓑ 우리는 그가 도착할 때까지 기다려야 한다.
ⓒ 결정을 내리기 전에 신중하게 생각해라.

ⓓ 너는 성이 Smith인 노인을 아니?

15 ② '사람들의(그들의) 집'이라는 의미로 소유격을 대신하는 관계대명사가 필요하므로 whose로 고쳐 써야 한다.

|해석| • 겨울은 가을 뒤에 오는 계절이다.
• 집들이 태풍에 의해 부서진 많은 사람들이 있다.
• 그림이 미술관에 있는 그 남자는 내 이웃이다.
• 네가 휴가에서 돌아올 때까지 내가 네 고양이들을 돌봐 줄게.
• 나는 열 살 때부터 피아노를 쳐 왔다.

16 ⓐ 주어가 「분수+of+명사」인 경우 동사는 of 뒤의 명사의 수에 일치시키므로 are가 아닌 is가 되어야 한다.
ⓒ that이 아니라 '무엇'이라는 의미의 의문사 what이 쓰여야 한다.

17 '서로 유사한 특징을 가진 동물이나 식물군'은 species((분류상의) 종)의 영어 뜻풀이다.

18 ③ 혹등고래는 잠을 자는 동안 꼬리로 서 있는다고 했다.
④ 혹등고래는 수면 근처에서 잠을 잔다고 했다.

|해석| ① Ray: 지구의 3분의 2는 대양으로 덮여 있다.
② Amy: 대양은 수많은 종의 서식지이다.
③ 태호: 혹등고래는 잠을 자는 동안 머리로(→ 꼬리로) 서 있는다.
④ 지나: 혹등고래는 수면에서 멀리 떨어져서(→ 수면 근처에서) 잠을 잔다.
⑤ Joe: 혹등고래는 잠에서 깨면 숨을 쉬기 위해 물 밖으로 나온다.

19 ② so는 '그래서'라는 뜻으로 so 뒤의 절의 내용이 so 앞의 내용의 결과를 나타내므로 위치를 바꿔 쓰면 내용이 완전히 달라진다.

20 '~할 때까지'를 뜻하는 접속사 until을 사용하고, 주절과 부사절의 동사를 단수형으로 쓰는 것에 유의한다.

21 조개가 얼마 동안 닫혀 있는지와 tuskfish가 먹을 수 있는 조개의 수는 글을 통해 알 수 없다.

22 새가 물고기를 잡기 위해 바다로 날아 내려가는 것을 본 적이 있을 것이라는 첫 문장 다음에는 역접의 접속사(But)로 그 반대의 상황인 물고기가 새를 잡기 위해 물 밖으로 뛰어오르는 것을 본 적이 있는지 묻고(B), giant trevally가 주변에 있을 때 새들은 조심해야 한다는 말(D) 뒤에 그 물고기의 크기를 설명한(A) 후, 그 크기에 속지 말라고(C) 하는 흐름이 자연스럽다.

23 ⓑ 날고 있는 새의 속도와 거리를 계산할 수 있다고 했다.
ⓒ 170센티미터에 80킬로그램까지 자랄 수 있다고 했다.
ⓓ 새가 가까이에 날고 있을 때 물 밖으로 뛰어올라 새를 잡는다고 했다.

|해석| ⓐ giant trevally가 가장 좋아하는 먹이는 무엇인가?
ⓑ giant trevally는 무엇을 계산할 수 있는가?
ⓒ giant trevally는 얼마나 크게 자랄 수 있는가?
ⓓ giant trevally는 어떻게 새를 잡는가?
ⓔ giant trevally는 얼마나 높이 물 밖으로 뛰어오를 수 있는가?

24 ② 팔이 8개라는 설명만 나와 있다.

25 (1) 문어는 바다 바닥에 살고, 가장 좋아하는 먹이는 작은 물고기라고 했다.
(2) 소유격 대명사(Its)를 대신하는 소유격 관계대명사 whose를 사용하여 두 문장을 연결한다.

기출예상문제집
중학 영어 **3-2** 중간고사 이병민

정답 및 해설

영역	브랜드	초1~2	초3~4	초5~6	중1	중2	중3	고1	고2	고3
독해	[중등] 기본서 READING CLEAR				READING CLEAR 1	READING CLEAR 2	READING CLEAR 3			
	[고등] 기본서 Supreme 구문독해 / 유형독해							Supreme 구문독해	Supreme 유형독해	
	[중·고등] 문장독해 공식으로 통하는 문장독해 기본 완성							공통문 기본	공통문 완성	
듣기	[중등] 듣기모의고사 LISTENING CLEAR 중학영어 듣기모의고사				LISTENING CLEAR 1	LISTENING CLEAR 2	LISTENING CLEAR 3			
	[고등] 듣기모의고사 Supreme 수능 영어 듣기 모의고사 기본 실전							Supreme 수능 영어 듣기 모의고사 20회 기본	Supreme 수능 영어 듣기 모의고사 20+5회 실전	
기출	[중등] 기출예상문제집 특급기출 (중간, 기말) 윤정미, 이병민				특급기출 중학영어 2-1	특급기출 중학 영어 3-2				
어휘	[초·중·고등] 영단어, 영숙어 뜯어먹는 시리즈	뜯어먹는 필수 영단어 1	뜯어먹는 필수 영단어 2		뜯어먹는 중학 1200	뜯어먹는 중학 1800	뜯어먹는 중학 1000	뜯어먹는 수능 1등급 1800	뜯어먹는 수능 1등급 1800	뜯어먹는 수능 2등급 1200
	[중·고등] 영단어 보카클리어				보카 클리어	보카 클리어	보카 클리어	보카 클리어 고교필수편	보카 클리어 수능편